HIPPOCRATES IN A RED VEST

HIPPOCRATES IN A RED VEST

The Biography of a Frontier Doctor

By Barron B. Beshoar

AMERICAN WEST PUBLISHING COMPANY

PALO ALTO - CALIFORNIA

To

My grandmother Annie Elizabeth Maupin Beshoar,
who "saved his things,"
and my wife Sally,
who helped put them all together.

Library of Congress Card Number 72-90945
ISBN 0-910118-31-0

Table of Contents

Preface

MOST OF THE MATERIAL for this book is based on the personal files of Dr. Michael Beshoar, including letters to and by him between the years 1865 and 1907, his daybooks and journals; his own newspapers, magazines, and historical publications; papers delivered to medical societies; texts of speeches to gatherings of editors, educators, businessmen, Union Army and Confederate veterans, coal miners, members of old settlers' associations. Masonic chapters, and political conventions; and stories in newspapers and magazines by him and about him.

Other major sources were interviews and correspondence with a number of persons now deceased, including businessman J. C. Jarrett of Colorado Springs; Confederate veteran W. H. "Billy" Jarrett of Little Rock; banker Lantie Martin of Pocahontas, Arkansas, who shed much light on M. Beshoar's Arkansas days; and Coloradans Dr. Ben B. Beshoar, Dr. John Maupin Beshoar, Dr. Benedicta Beshoar Joerger, Mrs. Annie Elizabeth Maupin Beshoar, Mrs. Mary Egan Shanly, Trinidad editor Fred Winsor, Governor Julius C. Gunter, Lieutenant Governor Earl Cooley, Judge A. Watt McHendrie, and Trinidad businessman Leo Gottleib.

I am grateful for generous help and guidance from Mrs. Alys Freeze and her highly skilled staff at the Western History Division of the Denver Public Library, always a western writer's first port of call, and to the staffs of the library of the Colorado State Medical Society and the library of the Colorado Historical Society in Denver, of the Charles Leming Tutt Library at Colorado College in Colorado Springs, the Carnegie Public Library in Trinidad, and to Dr. Gene Gressley, director of the Western History Research Center at the University of Wyoming in Laramie, Wyoming. Arthur Roy Mitchell, regional curator of the Colorado State Historical Society, and Dr. Morris F. Taylor, professor of history at Trinidad Junior College, also were most helpful.

The book never would have been written without my wife, who aided in assembling the materials, indexing, researching, typing, and asking all sorts of what, when, where, why, and how questions that needed answers.

And finally I am most grateful to my editor, Donald E. Bower, for his sharp eye, thoughtful suggestions and criticisms, and encouragement.

Foreword

NO DOUBT most small boys have heard stories about their grandfathers. I started hearing them about mine when I was five. Each aternoon, after my nap, I was allowed to go out in the yard and play between our house and Grandpa's. He had been dead since I was six months old, but he seemed to my young mind to be very much alive. His influence and his things were all about me. There was the old house in which he had lived for so many years, packed with his books, his medical things, and knickknacks picked up in the antebellum South, on the high plains of the Sioux and Cheyenne, in Mexico, and in early-day Colorado. In the dining room there was a large, securely locked, bowfront glass china cabinet with an intriguing bottom shelf mantled with a silk Confederate flag. It covered, I was told, some of Grandpa's choicest memorabilia, and I longed for the day when I would get a peek under it. In the book-lined study there were big Mexican sombreros and Indian pottery and baskets along with life-sized busts of Hippocrates and Aesculapius, and there were closets off the long corridor to the kitchen at the rear filled with dusty saddles and bridles, old boots whose leather had become hard and brittle with the years, a moth-eaten buffalo robe, and other wonders. At this period my grandmother, she of the severely upswept graying hair and the starched white waists with lacy collars, would tell me stories about Grandpa, often with a wild Indian or cowpuncher thrown in—a concession, I'm sure, to my then prime interests in life. Grandma would suck air in around her dentures when the story contained a little blood or a killing, but Grandpa always came out on top.

As I grew older, the stories became more sophisticated. They came not only from Grandma, but from my father, who had begun his practice of medicine in his father's office; from uncles, aunts, and other relatives; and then, as my horizons broadened, from the professional and business men of our little city and state, and from Anglo and Mexican cattle- and sheepmen, from miners, and shawled old Mexican women who always thought of him as *el patrón* as well as *el doctor*. Sometimes I was shocked to have someone give Grandpa a dig and to realize that, during a long lifetime on the frontier, he had made enemies as well as friends. But mostly those who spoke of him did so in admiration: he was the good and senior medical man of southern Colorado and northern New Mexico, the kind old medico who struggled through blizzards to succor a dying man or deliver a baby; he was the courageous editor who fought the big, rapacious coal corporations; he was the Democratic party leader who led the forces of righteousness against the vested interests and their crooked henchmen; he was the judge who saw to it that smart-alecky lawyers didn't overstep the bounds of propriety; he was the educator who urged special schooling for ethnic minorities decades before its modern-day sponsors were born; he was the shrewd business entrepreneur who wheeled and dealt in coal lands, prospected for gold and copper, published newspapers, operated drugstores, a billiard hall, a brickyard, a real estate company, a brewery, a steam laundry, ranches, and other enterprises; he was the mysterious and eccentric figure who wore his hair down to his shoulders, packed a .41 caliber Colt under his red vest and a lock knife in his hip pocket; he was the scholar who could speak several languages and who read Burns, Bryant, Addison, Hazlitt, and Samuel Johnson in leather-bound tomes; he was the man who provided jobs and meal tickets for broken-down men and the man who sometimes ran other men out of town; he was the distinguished civic leader who headed up worthy enterprises, and he was the little old man who ate cheese and drank dark, heavy beer with other old Germans in Richter's Saloon; he was the unhappy father who finally disowned a dissolute son and later kept his boy's bones in a copper box under his desk until he could complete the building of a mausoleum; and he was the man who paused on his way up Fifth Avenue in New York to visit a railroad magnate to wire his wife: "I am glad the cow got through her trouble all right."

There were many sides to Grandpa. He could shoot a man, knock him out with a blow to the head, or stick him with that wicked knife—and having done so, drag him back from death's door with a skill that was admired in his day. He could do major surgery in a tipi or on the open prairie, deliver a moving eulogy at the graveside of a pauper, preside in the courtroom, address a convention, or tell an off-color story that would set town and state rocking with laughter for days. And he was the busy man of affairs who could stop whatever he was doing to talk gravely and politely with a child. He was the man who filled my mother's back screen door with roses every day for a week when he found she was with child.

And finally, after all the stories, I came into possession of his books, papers, diaries, daybooks, notebooks, letter-books, ledgers, journals, writings of various kinds, filing boxes and cases filled with letters, and box after box of newspaper clippings, each dated and each bearing Grandma's penciled scrawl: "About Dr. Beshoar. Save." It was a treasure-trove, providing much of the material used in this book. Since Michael Beshoar was a raconteur with a love for the direct quote, and so was his son, Dr. Ben, part of the material came out of their mouths. Occasionally a direct quotation has been put together to summarize an incident or provide a conclusion, but in all such instances care has been exercised to make the quotation an accurate reflection of the incident or happening.

My evaluation of Michael Beshoar is, naturally enough, partisan, but many others held him in high esteem. Perhaps one of the best summations was written by Honorah DeBusk Smith in a master's thesis (University of Colorado, 1930) titled "Early Life in Trinidad and the Purgatory Valley" in which she noted his skill in surgery and medicine. "He was benevolent and catholic in spirit," she said of him. "He was the sort of doctor needed in a turbulent frontier town. He served Indians, Mexicans and outlaws with the same skill and care he gave the cattle barons of Kansas City or Edinburgh."

Chapter 1
Medic for the Confederacy

IT WAS LATE in the afternoon of Saturday, April 5, 1862, before the infirmary tent was set up in a small clearing a mile and a half east of Shiloh church. The yellow flag of a Confederate surgeon flapped idly above the door, while nearby the ambulances stood waiting, their wheels fat with mud gathered on the miry roads north from Corinth, Mississippi.

General Sherman and his Yankees were camped up ahead between Owl and Licking creeks with their backs to the Tennessee River, careless and unsuspecting and unaware that General Albert Sidney Johnston and seventy-five cocky regiments of the Army of the Mississippi were just about to swoop in on them and run them clear out of Tennessee.

As the twenty-nine-year-old surgeon of Colonel Robert G. Shaver's Seventh Arkansas Regiment, First Brigade, Hardee's Third Corps, made last-minute checks on his infirmary and its supplies, the corps moved into position in the woods around him.

Since receiving his commission on June 20, 1861, Surgeon Michael Beshoar had seen some hard campaigning in Kentucky where the Seventh had helped cover the retreat of General Johnston's Central Army of Kentucky after the fall of Forts Henry and Donelson, and he had little stomach for what he feared lay just ahead. He was, nevertheless, caught up in the excitement that gripped the eager young soldiers who marched by in seemingly endless columns. They were tough and ready, and "Gawd hep them Yankees."

He didn't have any ether, but he had chloroform, morphine, and opium balls, and he had bandages, lint, cotton batts, muslin, plaster, tourniquets, silk ligatures, desiccated soups, gelatin, tea, extra drawers and shirts, and most of the other items prescribed by the medical department in Richmond. He was also carrying the drugs he needed for the morning sick calls, which included the regulars with venereal diseases and malaria.

Some of the regimental surgeons were newly appointed and had been sent to their regiments from someplace else, but Michael Beshoar had been with the Seventh Arkansas since it was mustered in by Colonel Shaver June 16, 1861, at Camp Shaver near Pocahontas, the county seat of Randolph County in the northeast corner of the state, with a complement of 1,250 men. Many of them were friends and patients, including Major James T. Martin, the regiment's third-ranking officer, who was both his partner in the Pocahontas newspaper and his favorite drinking companion.

A wiry, quick-moving man, Michael gave the impression of being somewhat taller than his fully stretched five feet six inches, partly because he was slender. He weighed just under 130 pounds. He wore his black hair neatly trimmed at collar length and a black moustache. His hazel eyes were set deep in a sun-tanned face, and his cheeks were somewhat sunken as a result of bouts with malaria, the chronic ailment of Arkansas and the South. He had small hands and feet, with the former well kept as became a surgeon and a poker player.

Michael Beshoar was not a genuine son of Arkansas or the South although he had won complete acceptance long before the war. Yankee-born, he was the eldest son of Daniel Beshoar, a solid, deeply religious, hard-working Pennsylvania Dutch farmer. Michael was in the Confederate Army for the simple reason that all his friends and neighbors were in the army. He had been a surgeon of the Arkansas Militia since 1858, a coveted position for a young doctor, and when the Arkansas Militia went into the regular Confederate service, its surgeon went with it. Whatever his sentiments about the war, he had a financial stake in Pocahontas and Randolph County. He had a medical practice, a newspaper (the *Advertiser and Herald*), a drugstore (Beshoar & Putnam) that sold such much-wanted items as Dr. M. Beshoar's Unrivaled Cathartic and Anti-Bilious Pills and Dr. M. Beshoar's Tonic and Antiperiodic Pills, and a good farm at Fourche Du Mas, nine miles north of Pocahontas; and he had speculated successfully in land, corn, hogs, and cotton. He had lost the corn and hogs to foragers in the first days of the war, but he still had the rest of his property, including a few bales of cotton hidden around the county. He hoped to save all or most of his assets for the end of the war, which should come quickly. Meanwhile he had to stick with his friends.

In the nine years since he had received his medical degree from the University of Michigan and left his father's home in Dry Valley near Lewistown, Pennsylvania, to locate and buy a medical practice, he had formed strong attachments to the people of Randolph County. Many of them were unschooled, and few fitted a Pennsylvania Dutchman's concepts of industry and thrift, but they were good people. He liked them, was proud to be one of them, and had twice married daughters of Randolph County. His first wife was Winifrit, the lovely daughter of Colonel and Mrs. Mitchell of Fourche Du Mas. She had borne him a son, Mike (Michael, Jr.) before dying of consumption at the age of twenty. Michael was married the second time—some people said much too soon—to nineteen-year-old Jane Hilburn, who had been Winifrit's close friend. During his wife's illness and the bleak days following her death, Jane had given many hours of loving care to young Mike. She was generous and affectionate, and seeing her devotion to his small son made it doubly easy for Michael to love her and ask her to be his wife and Mike's mother. But Jane also died of consumption, four days after Christmas 1856, only six months after their marriage.

After Jane's death Mike was cared for by the J. C. Jarrett family, while Michael threw himself into his practice and his businesses, traveling the county day and night, sometimes on horseback and sometimes in a two-wheel cart, delivering babies, patching up the injured, and dosing the sick. There were fifteen other doctors in the county, but only three were competitive. Some of the fifteen were getting on in years, some gave more time to farming and business than to medicine, and some, never having seen the inside of a medical school, were self-taught practitioners of the art and limited in what they could do. Michael practiced medicine in an intense and personal way. His patients were also friends. They had sent him to the legislature in Little Rock and they had elected him county judge of Randolph County. By the time war came along, he was well on his way to being an important man in northeast Arkansas.

Major Martin visited him twice in the infirmary after dark, telling him what he knew of the plans for attack. Jim was confident but very much on edge, as was Michael. He tried to sleep but tossed in his blankets until he heard the officers rousing their men.

He had cold biscuits, coffee, and a gulp of whiskey and gave last-minute instructions to Assistant Surgeon Headley, the stretcher-bearers, and the ambulance drivers as the troops began to move through the wet woods. He instructed his men to use their morphine, whiskey, tourniquets, and bandages as first aid only; all cases requiring more extensive care were to be brought to the infirmary as quickly as possible.

The sun was shining in a clear blue Tennessee sky and the sound of cannonading was heavy when the first ambulance returned, its horses lathered and blowing. Surgeon Beshoar stood at his table with his surgeon's knives, slender blades nine inches long on four-inch black handles, and his pistol-grip saw, bandages, cotton, and chloroform all ready at hand. The regulations required him to ask, "Do we have your permission to operate?" The first man brought in was a middle-aged soldier from a Tennessee regiment with his right leg shattered below the knee. Some regimental surgeons had announced they would not operate or give care to men from any regiment except their own, but Michael had decided he would care for any man placed in front of him, and that included the enemy. The Tennessean readily gave permission to operate, but screamed and fought while aides gave him chloroform. The second man was more stoical, giving up an arm without much trouble. They came in quick succession, some moaning and tossing, some still as death, and soon the bare boards of the table were soaked with blood despite frequent sloshing with water from a bucket.

During the morning and early afternoon, Michael used chloroform, and when that gave out, he gave each man a stiff drink of whiskey with an eighth to a quarter of a grain of morphine. When the morphine was gone, he used whiskey and opium balls, and when the opium balls were almost gone by late afternoon, he put the few remaining ones aside and used just whiskey. His blood-soaked aides put only arms and legs in front of him. Men with chest and abdominal wounds were simply laid on the ground outside as there wasn't much he could do for them. Most of the abdominals would die. But the arms and legs got attention as fast as he could give it. The minié ball, conical in shape and low in velocity, made a nasty, tearing wound and, when it hit bone, shattered it. Many of the men were half dead from rough handling and from hemorrhaging in the jolting ambulances before they got to the infirmary.

Throughout the day the wounded were brought to his table in an endless stream. As night fell, Michael's eyes were bloodshot and his arms were heavy with fatigue. Ordering lanterns lighted, he worked on while a soft rain tapped on the canvas above his head.

A sharp incision . . . leave enough now for flaps . . . saw . . . tie off the arteries with oiled silk . . . be sure to leave long enough loose ends . . . stitch. The ligatures took too much time, but the technique was the one he had learned from Professor Moses Gunn at the University of Michigan, Professor Gunn and his lone, hard-to-come-by cadaver teaching bright-eyed boys the flap operation devised by William Cheselden in the eighteenth century. It was faster than the traditional circular operation and left a better stump. But it had disadvantages, too; it used up more of the limb and made a bigger wound. With the wounded coming faster and faster as the night wore on, Michael sought a shorter method and soon found one that proved effective. He used it first on a Georgia leg. He plunged the knife as deeply as he could and as close to the bone as possible, transfixing all the soft parts. With a quick twist he turned the instrument and cut through to the outside with a circular sweep of the blade. The arteries were so badly damaged there was no need to tie them.

During the rest of the night and early morning, he did arms below the elbow and legs below the knee in less than five minutes. The deep incision . . . the sweeping cut . . . pull back the soft parts to expose the bone . . . saw swiftly . . . trim the muscle if it is too heavy . . . pull the soft parts down again . . . sew.

When the armies locked again at dawn Monday, he was still at the table. An occasional gulp of whiskey and a biscuit now and then for the surgeon and the same for his aides; whiskey and only whiskey for the patients, but lots of it. He had long since stopped asking for permission to operate. There was no time for regulations, no time for rest, no time for anything except transfix, cut, saw, and sew. . . .

There were several disturbing reports about the progress of the battle Monday morning, but the surgeon paid little attention. The only realities for him were the bloody table, the buckets, the sloshing, the scared white faces, and the screams. Then in early afternoon came an order: retreat. Michael, so sick and numb with fatigue that he stumbled as he walked, directed the loading of wounded until the ambulances were filled. Then he made the rounds of the wounded who must be left behind, doling out whiskey and quinine. To one boy who was crying out in pain, he gave the last of his opium balls.

"Sorry," he mumbled to each man in turn, "but the Yanks will be coming along soon and they will take care of you."

From the door of the infirmary, he could see the narrow road he had come up Saturday jammed with troops. Some of the men were throwing away their canteens and knapsacks, but most were in good order. It was a retreat, not a rout. The Seventh, or what was left of it, was still a regiment under the vigilant eyes and lashing tongue of Major Martin, the surviving line officer. It swung past as the last of the ambulances pulled out.

There was no thought of dismantling the hospital, no time for it, and no way to transport the tent and its equipment if there had been, as everything on wheels was filled with wounded. The surgeon wiped his knives and other instruments and put them away in their rosewood case. What to do with them? They were fine instruments, bought by his father from Wade & Ford in New York as a graduating present when he had finished at Ann Arbor. He couldn't carry them; the box was too bulky and too heavy. He finally wrapped some rags around it and buried it, along with his personal papers and some of his Masonic emblems, at the side of the tent.

Minutes later a soldier brought up a horse, informing him that Major Martin had ordered him to join the regiment immediately. With the help of the soldier, he managed to drag himself up into the saddle, the soldier clambering up behind. The yellow flag above his operating tent still fluttered, but tiredly, as though it too had seen and heard too much.

Slumped heavily in the saddle, Michael knew he was up with the regiment when he heard Major Martin yelling, "Keep together, men. Don't straggle all over. I don't want to see a gun dropped. . . ."

After its hungry march back from Shiloh, twenty-four long miles in rain and sleet and mud, the Seventh set up Camp Hardee in

Corinth. This was a busy time for its surgeon. There were reports to be made out, supplies to be scrambled for whenever the cars brought in any from the south, and the wounded to be tended day and night. Major Martin's report showed the Bloody Seventh's losses in the two days of fighting to be 109 dead, 546 wounded, and 38 missing.

Many regimental surgeons had their wounded jammed into Corinth's Tishomingo Hotel, where they filled every room and covered the floors of the corridors until it was all that attending surgeons and nurses could do to pick their way among them. Michael had distributed his wounded in tents, private homes, and for a few a colonnaded female seminary, believing that those under canvas were more apt to escape the dread miasmas than those on the blood-soaked floors of such places as the Tishomingo.

As there was virtually no asepsis and no sanitation in Corinth, gangrene, dysentery, and typhoid quickly became widespread. Medicines were in such short supply that the surgeons frequently came to blows when meager supplies were distributed. In one such encounter, Michael was rolling in the dust with an Alabama surgeon when a member of General Beauregard's staff, who was riding by, saw the fight and broke it up. Michael turned away promising himself and all within hearing, "If I ever see that son of a bitch again, I will kill him."

Though they were busy with their respective assignments, Major Martin and Surgeon Beshoar found time to do some plotting about their own futures. They decided they should get out of the command as quickly as possible, suspecting, and correctly as it turned out, that it would not be returned to Arkansas but would continue to campaign east of the Mississippi. They also heard that Major General T. C. Hindman, once he was recovered from the wound suffered at Shiloh, would be given a new assignment to raise troops in north Arkansas for defense of that area. The two Pocahontas men were agreed that "Napoleon" Hindman was an impossible, feisty little martinet, but they were willing to serve under him in almost any capacity if they could only be close to home.

Both submitted their resignations and, three weeks after the Battle of Shiloh, were detached from the Army of the Mississippi and returned to the Trans-Mississippi Department. Major Martin was assigned as a colonel of militia forces stationed on the Arkansas-Missouri border under the command of Brigadier General Solon

Borland with headquarters in Pocahontas, and Michael was assigned to the same command as its chief medical officer. They
couldn't have been happier, short of having the war called off
altogether; they would be at home serving under a general who had
their respect. Some professionals were inclined to dismiss Borland
as a political general, but he had had considerable military experience. A medical man by profession, he had served as a major of
cavalry in 1846 in Mexico.

The night before they left for Memphis, Jim Martin and Michael
Beshoar depleted the ample Corinth whiskey and brandy supplies
to the best of their considerable abilities. They were up most of the
night, toasting Beauregard, "Napoleon" Hindman, Borland,
Mississippi, the great State of Arkansas, Jeff Davis, Colonel Shaver,
the marriageable young ladies of Poca and Randolph County, and
Alexander Stephens—the last at the insistence of Michael, who had
long been an admirer of the Confederacy's vice-president for his
opposition to conscription and to suspension of habeas corpus.
They also did a great deal of tipsy reminiscing. A stranger would
have thought they had been gone from Arkansas for years instead
of a few short weeks.

Michael was anxious to get back to Pocahontas to see his young
motherless son and to take care of his practice and his property.
Major Jim wanted to return to his kinfolk, especially his father,
Judge James Martin, Sr., who was getting on in years and was try-
ing to take care of the Martin interests by himself. (Another son,
Joseph Corfman Martin, was serving with Company D of the Fifth
Regiment of Trans-Mississippi Arkansas Infantry operating in the
western portion of the state.)

Jim's father was a well-read, cultured man of considerable means.
He raised cotton and other crops, and he was the largest slave
owner in Randolph County with twenty Negroes on his place at the
time war broke out. The judge—and it was a title he bore rightfully
having served three terms as county judge of Randolph County
(in addition to several terms as postmaster of Pocahontas, the county
seat)—was known as an enlightened slaveholder. He had a reputation for never selling a slave without the slave's consent. Nevertheless, there had been trouble out at the Martin place on the
Fourche last spring, not long after Fort Sumter had been fired on
and a wave of war hysteria had swept over the South.

Slaves belonging to the Martin, Mock, Jarrett, and other families had planned to rebel, kill their masters, and make off with their goods including horses and livestock. When the plot was revealed by a young Negro caught stealing meat from a smokehouse, two of the leaders of the plot, a white man and a Negro, were hanged from a tree on the Martin place.

Practically every white man in the county attended, including Michael. Those who had slaves brought them along even though they were not part of the plot. Michael would have ducked out if he could have done so without raising suspicion about his loyalty. As it was, he scarcely glanced at the two doomed men, looked mostly at the ground or at the strained faces of his neighbors and friends and at their frightened blacks huddling together like so many sheep. He felt sorry for the whites, for the blacks, and for himself.

It took Jim and Michael several days to make their way home. They shipped their horses from Corinth to Memphis on the cars, crossed the river on a ferry, and then rode cross-country to Pocahontas. They avoided the main roads, quickly concealing themselves whenever they saw or heard parties of horsemen who might well be Yankees or, worse yet, murderous bushwhackers.

Once safely back in Pocahontas, Michael checked into the St. Charles Hotel and was happy to get his old room back; facing on the square, it afforded a good view of everything going on in the business district. The proprietress, Nancy Evans, who hugged him when he walked in the door, had always taken good care of him, seeing to it that his clothes were laundered and that he ate his meals regularly.

From the hotel he rode to the J. C. Jarrett home to see his eight-year-old son. Mike was overcome by his father's sudden appearance. Nestled in his lap, he asked question after question about the war and the great battle at Shiloh. Michael, too, was overwhelmed. He would answer questions and then, hugging Mike closer, tell him how glad he was to see him again. He thought Mike looked a bit thin and his clothes were getting ragged; but they were clean, and it was obvious that Mrs. Jarrett had given Mike as good care as her own fourteen-year-old Billy, who also had a lot of questions about the war. Mrs. Jarrett said Billy was plaguing her to join up but that she thought he was too young. Michael said that was true, knowing while he agreed that boys Billy's age and younger were serving in the ranks.

When he was ready to leave, Mike begged to go with him, but the father said that Mike was better off with the Jarretts and that anyway they would see each other every day. He considered the Jarretts almost as family, having enjoyed a close relationship with them, beginning with Michael's purchase of Dr. Jarrett's practice.

On his return to the center of town, he put his horse up in Fisher's Stable and walked across the square. He felt happier than he had at any time since he'd left Poca with the Seventh; his boy was all right and the town seemed about the same. He walked slowly past the courthouse that dominated the square and thought about the courtroom on the first floor where he had presided as county judge. The county offices were upstairs. He remembered that the floors were quartered pine and there was a large fireplace on each floor.

He went on past the courthouse to the drugstore of Beshoar & Putnam on the south side of the square. It had always been a money-maker. He had designed the handsome cards that were sent out when he and his youthful partner, Dr. Isaac Putnam, had opened it: "Our assortment of drugs, chemicals, medicines, paints, oils, dyestuffs &c are all fresh, having been bought under our personal supervision, at low rates, and will be sold very low, for cash only."

Isaac Putnam, or "Put," was waiting for him and greeted him warmly. Their clerk Sherman Lynde was off with his regiment, but Put had kept the store open. His report was about what the senior partner had expected; they still had some stock, but business was poor and the "cash only" requirement had long since gone by the board. Isaac had been trading drugs and merchandise for pork and corn. From the drugstore the two proprietors went to the nearby *Advertiser and Herald*, where they found Jim Martin busy inspecting the place. It was intact, but publication would remain suspended as no newsprint was to be had.

After reporting to General Borland, Jim and Michael performed minimal duties as militia officers. Northeast Arkansas was quiet for the moment, but everyone knew that it wouldn't stay that way very long and that Poca would be a focal point of any new action, as it was a river port, a regular Confederate staging area, and on the direct route of any federal thrust out of southeast Missouri toward Little Rock.

Soon after his return to Pocahontas, the physician moved Mike from the Jarretts' to the home of Mrs. George Hill, who said she'd like to have Mike as company for her little Amy. He had been paying Mrs. Jarrett fifty cents a week for Mike's board and for washing and mending his clothing, but with the move to the Hill home he simply canceled out a debt of $100 owed him for medical service and presented Mrs. Hill with a receipt. He told Put, "Things have come to a fine pass when I find it easier to cancel a hundred-dollar debt than dig up fifty cents cash money every week."

In June, General Hindman, recovered from his Shiloh wounds and promoted to the rank of major general, was back in Little Rock as commander of the Trans-Mississippi Department charged with the responsibility of raising new troops to defend Arkansas and invade Missouri. He commissioned Jim Martin and Michael Beshoar to raise a new mounted command of unlimited size for garrison and patrol duty in northeast Arkansas. Jim was given the command, and Michael was named second in command with the rank of captain.

In the weeks that followed, Major Martin scoured the area for men and Captain Beshoar examined them, each recruit being required to undergo a physical examination and to provide his own horse. The physicals were, to say the least, broad-minded. Michael didn't reject a single man.

After one particularly successful recruiting day, Jim and Michael repaired in late afternoon to Beshoar & Putnam. Both were low on money, but the drugstore had in stock proprietaries that were made up largely of what the physician described as "first-rate drinking alcohol." They sat around and talked and drank "cocktails" off the shelves, about "ten dozen of them" as Martin remembered later. As the evening wore on, they consumed, among others, antiperiodic tonics, diarrhea cordials, and blood tonics. Michael told his friend to forget all about the labels as "they're all good, all about eighty percent alcohol." They drank steadily until after eight o'clock when they decided, for no apparent reason, to ride out to "Bully" Evans' house and pay a social call. When they got there, Evans sized up the situation as trouble and refused to let them in. The two celebrators then conceived the idea of building a fire out of some laths stacked at the side of the house, in the process managing to set fire to the building. This brought the Evans household and the neighbors out in a hurry, shouting and yelling. While buckets of water were being thrown on the fire, Michael and Jim embraced a couple of the more comely young firefighters, whereupon all the firefighters forgot the blaze and threw buckets of water on the two young men. With all the noise and confusion, their horses, which had been tied to a nearby fence, broke away and ran off down the road. Their well-soaked owners staggered after them.

When they finally caught their mounts, the carousers rode back to the drugstore for more "cocktails" and wound up the evening reveling around the public square. Jim had a lantern from the store and an old almanac from which he read aloud while Michael, according to his companion, "quoted scripture, spouted Greek and Latin and for all I know said Mass."

A few days later Major Jim and a couple of new men went on a scout. They rode eight miles up the Black River to Skaggs Ferry, where they turned off and crossed through a bottoms area to the high land of Cherokee Bay. A half mile farther they came to the Current River, turned north up its east bank, and were captured by a Federal patrol. In due time it was learned they had been taken to the military prison on Johnson's Island at Sandusky, Ohio.

The physician sorely missed Jim Martin; he was not only his best friend but the military man of their little combine. However, there was nothing to do but carry on. Continuing the recruiting campaign, Michael mustered a full company late in June and by the first week in July had "a mounted squadron of 220 rank and file." They drilled, somewhat lackadaisically, at Camp Shaver south of town. Since most of the men knew how to ride and shoot before they signed up and many of them had already seen service, they didn't need much training in the opinion of their commanding officer.

Aside from the loss of Major Jim, it was a rather pleasant interlude for Michael. He was the military man in charge, he did some private practice, he saw his boy almost every day, and he managed a little social life. The latter consisted mostly of visiting with Nancy Evans' younger sister Maggie James. He saw the girl regularly at her mother's home in Poca or at the St. Charles, and on occasion they took walks along the river. In prewar times he would have driven a young lady about the country in his gig, but thieves had long since made off with the two-wheeled cart along with everything else except the buildings on his farm out at the Fourche. And anyway it was too risky to wander very far into the countryside.

Maggie was only sixteen and rather plain, but she was an intelligent girl and a good companion despite the difference in their ages. The physician considered her "foremost" among the marriageable young ladies of Poca. He enjoyed her company and spent as much time with her as he could.

In July, with his company itching for action, he joined up with Captain Timothy Reeves, who also had a command in northeast Arkansas, for a raid on Captain William T. Leeper's Twelfth Regiment Cavalry, Missouri State Militia, in Greenville, Missouri.

Michael, who had great faith in the therapeutic efficacy of alcohol, also saw it as a military weapon and was quite proud of a strategy he worked out for the Greenville raid. Poca men, dressed as civilians, were sent ahead to Leeper's camp with a wagonload of whiskey, which they offered for sale. By the time Reeves and Beshoar led their respective commands charging into Leeper's camp at dawn, a good portion of the Federals were in a drunken stupor and in no condition to fight. It was short and sweet as far as Michael was concerned. His losses were negligible and the company's share of the spoils—consisting of wagons, carbines, pistols and pistol holsters, sabers, saddles, bridles, harness, clothing, and food— was welcome.

Early in the fall, worn by weeks of piddling little patrols and skirmishes, Michael was laid low by malaria. Although Isaac Putnam dosed him with quinine while Nancy Evans and Maggie James nursed him, he wasn't able to be up and out until the middle of October. When he felt strong enough to mount a horse, he made short, periodic scouts into the countryside with patrols, but once again northeast Arkansas was fairly quiet, with only an occasional Federal patrol or bushwhacker foray to provide excitement. On one scout he captured a bushwhacker who claimed he was a patriotic southern man. Michael and his men listened stiff-faced, since they all knew his reputation for making a business of preying on hapless people regardless of their loyalties. When the man had had his say, they bound him, hand and foot, and then hanged him.

On returning from another patrol, a few days later, Michael's left leg hurt him as he climbed the stairs to his room in the St. Charles. When he pulled off the boot, his leg was covered with blood. The wound in his calf was apparently not serious, but he was puzzled about how he had got it; he hadn't seen anyone shoot at him nor had he felt anything. He let Put clean and bandage the wound for him but declined his partner's offer to cut the ball out. He wouldn't have left the ball in any other leg, but he wasn't going to let anyone cut into his if he could help it.

A short time later he had more trouble, this time with typhoid. He diagnosed the illness himself: an occasional chill, headache, malaise, constipation, temperature rising by steps. Deciding he ought to have more expert care than Isaac Putnam could provide, he made arrangements for a couple of his men to take him to a colleague and longtime friend in nearby Walnut Ridge. The doctor and his wife took him into their home and nursed him for more than a month. When the doctor reluctantly agreed Michael could leave, arrangements were made to transport him back to Poca on a mattress in the back of a light wagon; he was much too weak to sit a horse or even sit up in a carriage. The doctor's wife thought he should stay until he had his strength back, but he longed for his own room in the St. Charles. As he was preparing to leave, the doctor was called away on an emergency. At the last minute Michael found he was too weak to walk out to the wagon and asked his hostess to call the driver in to assist him. With tears in her eyes, she said, "We don't need a man for this," scooped him up in her arms, and carried him to the wagon. He felt a sense of shame at being carried by a woman, but he also felt very helpless: Michael Beshoar weighed eighty pounds.

Back in his room in Poca he took things easy, nursing what little strength he had and gaining weight with the thick soups and gruels Nancy Evans made for him. After a time he did some easy walking to build up muscles and was soon able to get on a horse, though riding quickly tired him. He decided what he really needed to complete his convalescence was a vacation away from his command, away from Pocahontas and Randolph County. He had two things to do before he could get away: arrange with General Hindman's headquarters for an extended leave, and spend the Christmas holidays with Mike.

With the help of Mrs. Evans and Maggie, the Christmas party— complete with fried chicken, jellies and jams, and other delicacies that came out of hiding for the occasion—was a great success. A number of friends of Beshoar senior and Beshoar junior were on hand to help make the affair a happy one. Whatever else the party accomplished, it did help ease the physician's conscience about his small son. He knew he was neglectful and that he ought to spend more time with the thin-faced, bright, and affectionate boy, but somehow there never seemed to be time for Mike. The physician loved his son, but he had a lot of demands on his time: there was the company and there were private patients whose illnesses needed his attention; then, too, there was Maggie James. Perhaps when things got back to normal, Maggie might become his wife and Mike's mother. Mike needed his father, but he also needed a home and a mother.

Michael left Poca on leave early in January, riding with a small detachment of cavalry that was en route to Little Rock. It didn't pay to travel alone these days, even on main roads in friendly territory. He had a number of friends in the state capital from his legislative days, including a couple of Catholic priests his own age. During his term in the legislature, he had become acquainted with Andrew Byrne, bishop of Little Rock, who had died in the past year. Through the influence of the bishop, the first Roman Catholic clergyman he had known well, he had become a convert to Catholicism, with some unhappy results. His brother Masons in Randolph Lodge No. 71, Free and Accepted Masons, had not been pleased, to put it mildly; and the reaction in Dry Valley, Pennsylvania, had been even worse. His father had made no reply to his letter explaining his defection from the Church of the Brethren. After a lapse of some months he had received occasional brief notes that talked about the family and the farm but made no mention of religion or his conversion. And since the start of the war, there had been only silence from home though he had written his father several times. Cousin Joe Rothrock, who had followed Michael to Pocahontas in 1857 to teach school, learned from his family back in Lewistown that old Daniel Beshoar—stiff-necked German, rigid member of the Brethren, Mason, and Republican—had with great difficulty managed to conjure up excuses for his eldest son's becoming a Roman Catholic and even a Democrat but was completely unable to accept his service in the Confederate Army.

Daniel, himself the son and grandson of Michael Beshoars, spoke good English but was very much a Pennsylvania German. The family, wearied by the constant wars that ravaged the German Palatinate, had come to the New World in answer to the call of an Anabaptist leader named Conrad Weiser, who promised a better life. They had made their way down the Rhine to Rotterdam, thence to Southampton, and finally to Philadelphia in 1742 on the ship the "Red Mary" along with a number of other Palatinates.

In Pennsylvania they had clung tenaciously to old customs and the mother tongue, worked hard, developed good farms, and raised large families. Their sons served in the Continental Army. Daniel, born in 1805, had married a neighbor, Susannah Rothrock, whose people also were farmers, although by the time Michael was a small boy, they had produced several physicians. Susannah died in 1847 when Michael was fourteen, but it was her counseling and urging that sent him into medicine. Daniel, believing that a boy should follow in his father's footsteps, never fully understood his eldest son. When Michael went off to medical school, however, Daniel supported him with encouragement and money but would joke with his friends, "Michael's hands are too soft to do farm work."

After he had enough of visiting in Little Rock and had reported to General Hindman's headquarters there, Michael decided to go on to Hot Springs, sixty-five miles to the south and west. Once again he managed to join a party of horsemen and make the trip without incident. It was the wrong time of year, however; Hot Springs was virtually deserted. Most of the permanent population of two hundred had left for Texas, and not only were most of the hotels closed, but the bathhouses, doctors' offices, stores, and saloons along the single street of the straggling little village also were shuttered. Michael checked into one of the two hotels that were still open and simply loafed for several days since there wasn't much else to do. He tried the mineral waters but couldn't decide whether they benefited him or not. Neither the waters nor the table at the hotel could have held him very long, but there were whiskey and cigars and the companionship of several poker-playing officers and a civilian or two who had also picked this unseasonable time for a vacation. He had never met any of his fellow guests before, but he knew some of them by name, including one civilian, Sam Hilderbrand, who had a sinister reputation as a bushwhacker, killer, and all-around badman. Expensively dressed and apparently well supplied with money, Hilderbrand seemed to be behaving himself, and the physician kept what he had heard to himself. Since Hilderbrand was supposed to be from Randolph County and to have a family in Warm Springs, there was no need to do a lot of talking and get involved in some way that would cause trouble later on home ground. Though he was sure he had not met the man before, Hilderbrand apparently knew Michael.

The tranquillity of the place was broken for the physician at the end of his first week by the theft of his horse, along with two others, from the hotel stable. Michael was terribly upset. The thefts were followed immediately by something much worse. After quarreling with one of the other guests Hilderbrand shot the man to death on the steps of the hotel; then, gun in hand, he walked to the hitching rack, coolly selected a horse, and galloped off. Everyone, including the owner of the horse, simply watched him go. Later they all said they were too stunned to do anything, but Michael suspected that they, too, knew Hilderbrand's identity and reputation and had no desire to tangle with him.

The day after the shooting Michael decided he had had enough of the almost deserted resort. He would take the stage to Little Rock and, once there, figure out how best to get on upstate to Poca. While he was packing his saddlebags, the thought occurred to him that Hilderbrand had left his horse and fine clothes behind. He went to Hilderbrand's room and, finding it unlocked, in minutes was arrayed in a new coat, resplendent vest, new trousers, and shiny boots. The arrangements with the hotel were simple: he paid Hilderbrand's hotel bill, the board for his horse, and a bit extra to the clerk and the hostler and was soon on his way. The clerk bade him goodbye with a shake of his head: "God help you if you run into that man with that rig on and riding his horse."

Hilderbrand's big, well-mannered, chestnut gelding with a deep chest, a slender barrel, and long legs needed no urging. Its fast running walk was an easy gait, and Michael hummed to himself as he rode. Although it was hot and sticky for this time of year, riding was pure pleasure. It was going to be a fine day. He had been on the road about two hours when the canebrake at the side parted and a man with leveled pistol stepped out in front of him. The chestnut snorted and plunged, then stood and quivered under the bite of the bit.

"Get 'em up," the man with the pistol said. "Up, I said. Oh, hello, Doc. I didn't recognize you. Wait 'til I get my horse and I'll go along . . . say, that's my horse! What in hell are you doing with my horse?"

The desperado's eyes narrowed: "And, by God, that's my vest."

Hilderbrand, still holding his gun on the physician, stepped closer. "And my coat and my pants, and, well I'll be damned, my boots. Well, I'll be damned to hell!"

Michael felt his skin crawl and the roots of his hair tingle. This ruffian was a cold-blooded murderer. Sweat started down the physician's face; he knew he was a dead man, but there wasn't anything he could do about it. Suddenly Hilderbrand started to laugh.

"By God, that's the funniest looking outfit I ever saw," he said. "You keep the duds, Doc. Now that I've seen 'em on you I don't want 'em. But I'll take my horse. Where's yours?"

His aching arms down at his sides once again, Michael weakly explained about the thefts and how he had paid Hilderbrand's bills. The bushwhacker said shortly, "Well, I think I saw your horse yesterday. We'll go get it."

After they had swapped horses, Michael ending up with the one stolen from the hotel hitching rack, they followed the road about an hour, before turning off and riding along a trail to a small cabin at the edge of a draw. The two men lounging in front of the cabin made no move to stand as Hilderbrand and the physician rode up.

"Get up, you sons of bitches," Hilderbrand snarled, pulling out his pistol. "You got the doc's horse from Hot Springs. Get it."

He told one of the men to stand fast while the other brought the horse. The older of the pair trotted off to the draw and returned leading three horses. "I don't know which is his'n," he said surlily.

Michael told him he'd take the bay with the one white foot. He dismounted, changed the saddle to his own horse, and remounted. The two horse thieves stood side by side, looking at Hilderbrand.

"Any fool ought to know better than to steal a doc's horse," Hilderbrand said, "'specially one that's a good and true friend to Sam Hilderbrand." With that he shot the older man in the face. The younger, his face ashen, stood perfectly still. Hilderbrand took aim, and then lowering his gun, allowed as how the man had best turn around and beat it.

For three days Hilderbrand and his unwilling "good and true friend" rode leisurely northward. The physician was sure Hilderbrand would kill him any minute. Twice they hid while small cavalry detachments went by, Hilderbrand explaining that he was a southern man and a true one but that he stayed out of the way of all soldiers when he was traveling.

Whenever Hilderbrand took the lead on a narrow road or trail or as they were fording a stream, Michael would wonder if he could shoot him in the back. He was sure he couldn't best him in a face-to-face encounter, but neither could he bring himself to shoot when the desperado had his back to him. He debated then, and for years afterward, whether his failure to kill the outlaw was rooted in morality or fear. He never was able to resolve the question.

They were well north of Little Rock, riding in heavy timber splashed with bright sunshine, when they ran head on into a young Yankee lieutenant, riding alone. Before the officer could recover from his surprise, Hilderbrand had him covered with his pistol.

"I'm Sam Hilderbrand," the desperado said. "I suppose you've heard of me?"

"Can't say that I have," the young officer replied coolly.

"Well, you have now," Hilderbrand snarled. "Do you know what I do with Yankees?"

"I have an idea," the officer replied.

Hilderbrand untied the rope on his saddle, tossed the loop to the Yankee: "Just slip it over your head and fit it real good around your neck."

"Sure, anything to oblige."

The physician watched in disbelief. Did the Yankee think this madman was joking? Hilderbrand tossed some cord to the physician. "Tie his hands behind his back, Doc, then throw this end over that limb yonder."

Starting to protest, Michael found himself looking into the muzzle of Hilderbrand's pistol.

When Hilderbrand and Michael rode on, the maniac was laughing to himself. He said he would like to see the faces of the Yankees when they came along and found the body. "I hate to lose that rope, but that's the way I want them to find him."

At dusk Hilderbrand pulled up his horse and stared at the physician. Michael shivered, certain he was finally going to have to draw his gun. But Hilderbrand said, thoughtfully, "Doc, you're just too damned chicken-hearted for me, so I'm going to cut off here. You just mosey on to Poca." With a careless flip of his hand, the bushwacker was gone.

Beshoar walked his horse for a hundred yards or so; his tongue was dry in his mouth and he felt cold all over. Then he put the horse into a gallop. After a couple of miles, he turned off into the brush and hid until morning.

Chapter 2

A Change from Gray to Blue

CAPTAIN BESHOAR'S COMMAND was transferred in February to Lieutenant Colonel Robert Shaver's Infantry, a new regiment named for the commander of the Bloody Seventh. Within a few days, tired of being a line officer and anxious to get back to medicine, Michael resigned his captaincy. But he was not to return to civilian life. Orders came from Little Rock assigning him as surgeon of Colonel Lee Crandall's cavalry regiment.

For several weeks he galloped about northeast Arkansas and southeast Missouri treating cavalrymen for malaria, typhoid, diarrhea, dysentery, pneumonia, drunkenness, and injuries incurred when their horses threw, kicked, bit, or fell on them. He also treated some of them for syphilis and gonorrhea. There wasn't a lot of venereal disease, but it showed up more often in the horse outfits than in the infantry because the cavalrymen, more mobile than foot soldiers, got around more and picked up more things than pigs, chickens, corn, and watches. Since they ate better than infantrymen and suffered less from fatigue and exposure, they were generally a healthier lot, even though their gunshot wounds were just as ugly and just as deadly as those suffered by other troops.

During the spring and summer of 1863, Michael got a chance for more private practice than at any time since he had first entered the Confederate service. There was a strong demand for medicines and drugstore products of all kinds. With mortar and pestle, pill tile, spatula, and graduate, he prepared most of what he sold: pills, ointments, elixirs, emulsions, liniments, cosmetics, hair dyes, and anti-baldness preparations. Beshoar & Putnam sold more hair dye to captains, majors, and colonels than to the store's women customers. In addition to his compounding, he bought whatever drugs he could from doctors who were retiring from practice or leaving the area. He made careful entries in his daybook of drugs purchased, prepared, and dispensed; of patients attended and their treatment; and of formulas obtained from one source or another, often with special headings and comments. "A good cosmetic," he wrote on one page: "take a small piece of gum benzoin and boil it in spirits of wine till it becomes a rich tincture. Fifteen drops in a glass of water will look like milk & emit an agreeable perfume. Wash with it. If left on the face it will render the skin clear and vibrant. A good remedy for spots, freckles, pimples and eruptions if they have not been of long standing."

Patients were entered by name in his daybook with some exceptions: slaves were listed simply as "Plott's Negro" or "Jarrett's Negro," and in cases where he didn't know the white person's name at the time of the entry, he simply wrote down a description, such as "the large woman at Elliott."

There were some nonmedical entries in his daybook at this time that would have caused a fine uproar in Randolph County had they fallen into the hands of the Confederate authorities or the more fervent southern civilians. Union sympathizers, knowing his attitudes about the war, frequently confided in him, and he, in turn, kept lists of them in his daybook. In Columbia township alone he listed the names of fourteen Union men, noting after one name that the man had "repented" after the departure of Federals who had occupied the township briefly.

He also wrote in his little book details about such things as his cotton speculations, a practice frowned on by the Confederate authorities, who burned any cotton they could find to keep it out of the hands of the Federals. Michael had a patient and cotton man named Jeff Houghton do his buying for him "at not exceeding ten cents per pound in the lint." He handled it through Rayney's gin as the people there could be depended upon to remain silent.

While there was not a great deal of military activity in Arkansas at this time, there was some, and as the summer wore on, more and more of his close friends were killed, wounded, or captured. Major Jim, still in the military prison in Ohio, was apparently all right, but more catastrophes came to the Martins. On July 4, Joseph C. Martin, Jim's twenty-five-year-old brother who was then a major in Rogan's Regiment of Arkansas Infantry, was mortally wounded in the Battle of Helena and died four days later in Phillips County.

His father, the judge, died the same day.

Other families in the county were suffering in a similar fashion, with sons and the fathers of young families dying in battle and the older generation dying from too much grief and too little food. Some families, after a visit from Union foragers who carted off everything edible, found themselves at the point of starvation.

During the second week of August 1863, Michael received orders from Little Rock transferring him from Crandall's cavalry to a new command being set up by the flamboyant General M. Jeff Thompson, who reveled in the nickname the "Swamp Fox." He arrived in Pocahontas Friday, August 21, making as grand an entry as he could, with his horses and those of his aides clattering across the square to the St. Charles Hotel, which the general had selected for his headquarters.

After meeting the general and his staff, including the new adjutant Captain Ruben Kay, Michael had to dash off to deliver a baby at a farm north of town. Problems with his horse made it an especially arduous trip. When he returned to the St. Charles shortly after 2 P.M., the day had grown hot and sultry and he was weary. There were few people about. The Swamp Fox and Captain Kay, both in their shirt sleeves, were at work in an improvised office with maps spread out on a table. The general had announced he would soon bring new troops into northeast Arkansas and that he would then move against the Federals in Missouri. Michael assumed that he was planning his campaign, but as for himself his business now was medicine, not military strategy, and besides he was almost out on his feet from fatigue. He made his way up to his room on the second floor, pulled off his boots and uniform, and sprawled out on the bed in his underwear.

When he was awakened by the sound of horses and shouted commands, he was lying in a pool of water, his underwear and the bed both soaked. He reached for his watch sleepily. It was ten minutes to four. He jumped out of bed and went to the window to discover that the public square was jammed with milling cavalry. General Thompson had certainly gotten troops into Poca in a hurry. Still befuddled by his nap, he was pulling on his pants when a Federal officer, pistol in hand, pushed open the door and said, "Sir, you are my prisoner."

He was allowed to finish dressing and then escorted downstairs to the "office" where General Thompson sat grinning, apparently

enjoying all of the excitement. Federal officers he had known in
Missouri before the war were coming in to shake hands with him,
and soldiers were poking their heads in at the window to get a
look at the prize catch. The general introduced his brand-new
and unused medical director to the officer in charge, Captain H. C.
Gentry, Second Missouri State Cavalry. Michael managed a weak
grin, confessing to the captain that when he had looked out his
upstairs window he had thought the dust-covered blue uniforms
were gray and that "you were our men." Thompson laughed up-
roariously at this. "They're not ours, but you might say we are
theirs," he said.

Captain Gentry, son of the president of the Hannibal and St.
Joseph Railroad, treated his prisoners courteously, telling them
they had the freedom of the St. Charles but they must not attempt
to leave it. He said his superior, Colonel R. R. Woodson, Third
Missouri State Militia Cavalry, and commander of the 600-man expedition, would be along shortly.

It was dark when Lieutenant John Miller of Crandall's regiment
rode into town, dismounted in front of the hotel, and handed his
reins to a soldier. At the door his way was barred by a sentry who
said, "You can't come in here unless you are an officer."

"I'm Lieutenant Miller," the new arrival said testily. "I am here
to make a report."

The sentry stepped aside and Miller strode confidently into General Thompson's office. Saluting smartly, he observed Captain
Gentry and another Union officer who were sitting passing the time
with Thompson. "General, I see you have caught some Yanks,"
he said.

"Yes, I have caught a great many of them."

"How did you catch them?"

"By their catching me," the general replied with a chuckle.

Captain Gentry rose from his chair, put his hand on Miller's
shoulder, and said, "Sir, you are my prisoner." He demanded
Miller's arms and papers, the latter of which caused quite a stir
when Colonel Woodson arrived and had a look at them. They consisted of a report from Crandall on the number of men, horses, and
guns he had and would be bringing into Pocahontas immediately.
Colonel Crandall, like General Thompson, had a marked tendency
toward spread-eagle reporting, but the Yankees, having no way of
knowing that, took it literally. There were worried frowns and

hurried conferences behind closed doors. The original Federal target had been Batesville, some forty miles farther south, where a number of prominent Confederate officers, including General Jo Shelby, were recuperating from wounds; but with an unexpected prize safely in hand, the Federals were beginning to see promotions and headlines if they got the Swamp Fox safely back to Missouri. The conferences concluded, Colonel Woodson announced he would take his troops and prisoners to Missouri, and would leave at midnight.

Michael was allowed to go to his room and get such possessions as he could carry on his person. He stuffed what money he had in different pockets and in his boots, and pinned some to his underwear. He tied his watch under his arm with a piece of cord that ran around his shoulder and was pinned to his underwear to keep it from slipping. He put his daybook and a pencil in his pocket.

The Yanks smashed up a number of stores, including Beshoar & Putnam, after removing their stocks. There wasn't much, but whatever there was they took. They set fire to a number of business places, including the *Advertiser and Herald.* Shortly before midnight, with much blowing of bugles and shouting of commands, General Thompson, his staff, and about fifty Randolph County men, some of whom had been picked up by the Federals on their way into Pocahontas to prevent their riding ahead with an alarm, were lined up in front of the St. Charles. The physician had hoped he could send a note to Mrs. Hill and Mike, but there was no opportunity. Thompson was put on a horse, and so were a number of other officers including Surgeon Beshoar. As soon as they were mounted, the girths were removed from their saddles so they couldn't make a break for liberty. Some of the men were put in wagons, while the remainder were told they would have to walk. At exactly midnight the bugles sounded again, the officers waved forward with their right arms and cried "ho," and the column moved out.

During the next few days Michael was faithful, if brief, about making entries in his daybook:

[August] 23rd

Reached Dr. Fishers some 15 miles north of Pocahontas about an hour after daylight—had some breakfast (crackers and saw fat bacon). Today I rode in a wagon, my horse having been taken from me at Dr. Fishers. Reached Doniphan about sunset. Supped on green corn and pilot bread. We were quartered in an old storehouse that night which was alive with fleas.

24th
A nice breakfast furnished General Thompson, Col. Simington, Lt. M. Russell and I by Mrs. Waugh who also sent me one of her husband's shirts—mine having become very dirty. I rode on horseback today. Reached a farm house four miles south of Reaves station that night where we bivouacked over night.

25th
Rode nearly half the day in a wagon and was forced to walk the ballance [sic]. Bivouacked at Patterson tonight.

26th
Rode in a wagon all day today. Reached Pilot Knob and lodged in the Guard House.

27th
Nothing occurred except we were searched and our money was taken from us.

28th
Had a hearing before the District Provost Marshal.

29th
Was examined by Provost Marshal. Nothing transpired.

30th
Nothing but quiet prison life.

31st
Nothing of note.

Sept. 1st
Was re-examined by General Fisk.

Sept. 2nd
Nothing worth noting.

Sept. 3rd
Was released on parole from 9 A.M. till 9 A.M. tomorrow by General Fisk.

Sept. 4th

Reported at 9 A.M. and again paroled till 9 A.M. tomorrow
by General Fisk.

His treatment at the hands of Clinton B. Fisk, brigadier general
commanding the District of Southeast Missouri with headquarters
in Pilot Knob, was most courteous. The general was interested in
his Pennsylvania background, that he was a graduate of the University of Michigan, that he was a doctor and not a fighting man,
and that he was a Master Mason. The general ordered his money
returned to him, a consideration Michael appreciated even though
it was taken away again a short time later by three hard-faced ruffians of the First Missouri who said he could either give them the
money and keep quiet about it or they would shoot him and claim
he tried to escape. They didn't get his watch. It was still hidden
under his arm.

With the capture of the Swamp Fox, the Federals were confident
all the little foxes had taken flight from north Arkansas. The Union
commanders pushed hard and took Little Rock September 10, forcing the Confederates to move their government to Washington
County. It began to look as though Arkansas might not be in the war
much longer. Michael expected to be sent north, possibly to Johnson's Island, but when Jeff Thompson and his aides were put on the
cars in Ironton and sent to St. Louis, Beshoar remained behind in
Pilot Knob. However, his lot was not too difficult as he was soon
put to work as a physician through the good offices of Union medical officers and fellow Masons on the headquarters staff. It was good
to be working rather than simply sitting in the guardhouse or hanging in suspension on temporary parole in Ironton. But he felt very
lost and alone. He sent letters off to his father and to Mrs. Hill in
Poca. No word came from old Daniel Beshoar, but Mrs. Hill replied that Mike was all right and he must not worry.

On October 5, in response to a written petition signed by two
medical colleagues, Drs. Drake and Youngblood, he was released
on a bond of $1,000 with two Masons, Judge Carter and Hiram
Long, as his securities. The bond required that he remain in the
vicinity of Ironton and that he not go south of Pilot Knob and
Ironton. He was later sent into St. Louis where, on October 20,

he took the oath of allegiance before the provost marshall:

I, Michael Beshoar of Randolph County, State of Arkansas, do hereby solemnly swear that I will bear true allegiance to the United States and support and sustain the National Sovereignty paramount to that of all State, County or Confederate powers; that I disclaim and denounce all faith and fellowship with the so-called Confederate Armies, and pledge my honor, my property and my life to the sacred performance of this my solemn Oath of Allegiance to the Government of the United States of America.

M. Beshoar.

Transcribed and sworn to before me   Age 33 years
this 20th day of October, 1863 at   Height 5 ft. 8 in. [sic]
St. Louis, Mo.   Color eyes Hazel
  J. P. Lodge   Color hair Black
   Lieut. & Ajt. Pro. Mar. Gen.
Witness: Laren M. Johnson of St. Louis, Clerk.

Written by hand on the printed form were the words: "To remain in the State of Missouri, North of Pilot Knob, during the war."

With the approval of Lieutenant T. H. Macklind, provost marshal in Pilot Knob, he rented a two-room shack in Ironton and set himself up in the practice of medicine; and with the help of a former Pocahontas businessman, R. A. Oakes of Stewart, Oakes & Matthews, general commission merchants with offices at No. 25 Pine Street in St. Louis, he bought enough drugs and supplies to get started again. Oakes recommended that he move into St. Louis as soon as he could. The merchant was certain the Union would soon win the war and that there was no future for either of them in Pocahontas or Arkansas.

Throughout the fall of 1863, the physician worked diligently to make a little money and establish himself with the people of the community. He made some progress, but the going was hard as there was a great deal of feeling against southerners and his having taken an oath of allegiance didn't seem to count for much. One of the problems was that many people who took the oath ignored it afterward, maintaining that it was meaningless. As proof of his own good intentions, he transferred his membership from Randolph County Lodge No. 71 to Ironton's Star of the West, Lodge No. 133, A.F. & A.M. This seemed to help some. Of utmost importance to him, the fraternity furnished by the Masons provided entree to men and places that would have been barred to him otherwise, and gave him a bond with Union men who were active in the order, a bond that transcended North and South.

As soon as he had a little money ahead, he wrote Mrs. Hill and asked for Mike. She arranged for a southern man who was en route to St. Louis on business to bring the boy, pitifully thin and thread-bare, to Ironton. The physician shopped for some clothing for Mike and fixed him a bunk alongside his own in the back room of the office. The first three or four days were great fun for father and son, but though Mike was well-behaved and anxious to please, it quickly became apparent that he couldn't keep a nine-year-old boy on an all-day, all-night basis. With the help of a patient, he managed to place Mike as a boarding student, five days a week, in Arcadia Academy in nearby Arcadia. Mike got schooling, board and room, and considerable bullying because his father was a Johnny Reb on parole. The boy spent Saturdays and Sundays with him in Ironton, with tearful sessions each Sunday afternoon when he took Mike back to the academy, the boy pleading that if he couldn't stay with his father he wanted to go back to Poca and his friends. The best the physician could do was promise that they would have a home again someday.

His own schedule was a seven-days-a-week backbreaker. He opened his office as early as 7 A.M., keeping it open until nine and sometimes ten o'clock at night. He closed it for a couple of hours each morning and again in the afternoon to make calls in Ironton, Pilot Knob, and Arcadia and at farms in the district. On the whole he was treated fairly well, though occasional threats kept him constantly on the alert.

The terms of his parole forbade his having arms, but he acquired a pistol through a fellow Mason. It gave him a sense of security. When anyone came to his office and banged on the door at night, he kept the gun in his hand until he had ascertained the identity of the caller and the nature of his business. He would not open his door or go on a night call unless the people who came for him were either known to him or could satisfy him they were bonafide callers.

Thus it was that he had his gun in hand when he answered a banging on his door one cold midnight in November. The caller, identifying himself as Charles Hogue, said he had a southern family at his house with a sick girl who needed a doctor. Knowing Hogue as a reliable man with southern connections, the physician readily agreed to accompany him to his house just south of Ironton. The family staying with Hogue were a Mr. and Mrs. John Maupin from Westport, near Kansas City, and their daughters—and they had had a lot of trouble. Their farm had been visited several times by Kansas militia raiding over into Missouri; the Jayhawkers had driven off their stock, carted off their furniture and other possessions, and added insult to injury by hanging Maupin by his thumbs while they loaded their wagons. After the last depredation his three boys, John, Tom, and James, had gone to join their neighbors Jim and Cole Younger and Frank and Jesse James, who were serving the Confederacy under William Quantrill's black flag. Maupin held on for a time after the boys left, but finally deciding he had had enough, he loaded his wife and daughters into a wagon and headed east for the old family home in Nicholasville, Kentucky. He had been forced to stop at Hogue's and seek help when his youngest, Rachael, had become ill.

The girl had typhoid, and during the next three weeks the physician made frequent calls. He became well acquainted with the Maupins, including daughter Annie Elizabeth, a proud, shy girl of fifteen. The Maupins were bitter about the war and their treatment at the hands of the Jayhawkers, and they were worried about their boys. When Rachael was well enough to travel again, Michael was sorry to see them go. They were the kind of people he had cherished as friends in Pocahontas, and they had become, in the comparatively short time they were at Hogue's, more than just patients. But when their wagon disappeared down the road in the general direction of Cape Girardeau, where they hoped to cross the river, Michael expected never to see them again.

During the remainder of the year, he put away as much money as he could, although it was almost as scarce a commodity as it had been in Pocahontas. Some of his patients couldn't pay anything and some could offer him only pork, corn, and other produce. But he still managed to pay Arcadia Academy for Mike and put a little bit aside for the time when he could get out of Ironton. In January he made a partial break; keeping his Ironton office, he moved Mike

to the Christian Brothers' Academy in St. Louis (some 70 miles
north of Ironton). A bit later, in the spring of 1864, after the provost
marshal at Pilot Knob said there was a good possibility of his being
released from his bond in the near future, he asked Oakes to look
around for an office space for him in St. Louis. When the word got
around that he might soon leave, there were new hostility and new
threats. Typical was an unsigned letter that came to him in the mail.
Dated March 28, 1864, it read:

> Doctor Beshoar
> Dr. Sir
>   It pains me very much to inform you your life is in danger
> and would advise you as a friend to wind up your business and
> leave at your earliest opportunity. Do not fail!! As you will
> regret it.
>   It was my luck as a friend of yours to overhear a chat today of
> two citizens in regard to your being in the Rebel army and they
> were in hopes you would not leave for two or three weeks yet
> so that they could carry out their plans. Do not fail to leave on
> your peril as there is something up. So look out. Will be back in
> a week or two and will come to see you. In the meantime look
> out.
>
> Farewell.
> Friend
>
> P.S.
>   Would sign my name but am afraid the postmaster would get
> hold of it someway. Your
>
> Friend

The letters didn't bother him very much as he had become accustomed to threats and to being on guard, but the red tape of
getting released from his bond and having his citizenship restored
in accordance with President Lincoln's amnesty proclamation was
worrisome and time-consuming. He had to secure letters of recommendation and he had to get them from his new Masonic and Union
Army friends in Missouri. Letters from Pocahontas would be of
no value, and in any event there was considerable hard feeling in
Randolph County as a result of his having taken the oath of allegiance. He'd even had some threatening letters from Pocahontas,
mostly warning him to not come back as traitors were not wanted

in Randolph County. Isaac Putnam wrote that he suspected the letters were written by some of the people "who owe you money."

But on May 23, 1864, after a number of recommendations had been written, even one by old foe Captain Leeper, who described his Greenville opponent as "the victim of circumstances as the citizen of a seceded state," Colonel I. P. Sanderson, provost marshal general of the Department of the Missouri in St. Louis, issued "Special Order No. 135. Extract: Michael Beshoar of Randolph County, Arkansas, is hereby released from the obligation of the bond heretofore given by him." The physician then sent a letter to the provost marshal June 6:

> I learn that I have been released from the bond heretofore given by me. The application for release was made in order that I might take the benefit of the President's amnesty proclamation. I called on the District Provost Marshal at Pilot Knob to take the amnesty oath. He said he could not administer it to me as the order releasing me from my bond said nothing about the oath. Will you do me the kindness to inform me whether I can be permitted to take the oath, or whether it is necessary to reinstate me in all the rights of a citizen. If I can be allowed to, I wish to take a position in the army in the Medical Department.
>
> Very Respectfully etc.,
> M. Beshoar

Six days later he received a letter from the provost marshal in St. Louis: "The Provost Marshal General directs that you go before Lt. T. H. Macklind, provost Pilot Knob, Mo., & take & subscribe to the Oath of Amnesty prescribed in the President's proclamation. On presentation of this letter Lt. Macklind will administer the oath."

Lieutenant Macklind had him stand in front of his desk at Pilot Knob, right hand upraised, and repeat after him:

> I, Michael Beshoar of the County of Randolph, State of Arkansas, do solemnly swear, in the presence of Almighty God, that I will henceforth faithfully support, protect, and defend the Constitution of the United States, and the Union of the States thereunder; and that I will, in like manner abide by and

faithfully support all acts of Congress passed during the existing rebellion with reference to slaves, so long and so far as not repealed, modified, or held void by Congress, or by decision of the Supreme Court; and that I will, in like manner, abide by and faithfully support all proclamations of the President made during the existing rebellion with reference to slaves, so long and so far as not modified or declared void by decision of the Supreme Court: so help me God.

Michael Beshoar couldn't see that the oath accomplished anything that hadn't been accomplished by the Oath of Allegiance with one important exception: he was again a United States citizen.

Oakes found him a suitable upstairs office at the southeast corner of Third and Pine streets. The building had an entrance at No. 44 Pine Street, one door below Third, and a second at No. 35 Third Street, two doors below Pine. He made haste to set himself up in practice, as the city was full of physicians of one kind or another and competition was sure to be heavy. He had cards printed with the words "Late Army Surgeon" under his name—no need to specify what army on a professional card. He usually added the word "accoucheur" on professional cards, but he dropped it this time on the assumption that not too many babies would be born to the kind of women who had been drawn into St. Louis by the big army payroll. Instead of accoucheur he had the printer put on the cards: "Special attention to private diseases, viz.: Gonorrhea, Syphilis, Gleet, Stricture, Spermatorrhea, Seminal Weakness, Impotency &C. Office Hours—from 7 to 9 A.M., and from 3 to 5 and 7 to 9 P.M."

It had been eleven years since a twenty-year-old physician, with a brand-new medical diploma from the University of Michigan, a case of new and untried surgical instruments, and $400 in his pockets (a parting gift from his father), had stepped off a boat in St. Louis and walked the streets of the river town looking for a likely place to locate. An old doctor on the riverfront had told him that a Dr. Jarrett in Pocahontas, Arkansas, was well up in years and wanted to sell his practice. Young Michael Beshoar had spent $200 of his little hoard in St. Louis stores for a beaver hat and clothes suitable for a professional man before he had set out to find Randolph County and Dr. Jarrett. Now that he was back, he again bought new clothes: a silk hat, a dark coat, striped pants, and a brightly colored vest with pearl buttons. Oakes and some of his other friends particularly admired his vest, which was reversible, red on one side and blue on the other.

His new practice started off very well although he didn't like his specialty and would much rather have been in general practice. But what he needed most was money, and the best way for a physician to get it in sinful St. Louis was was the way he was getting it. He slept in his office, lived as frugally as he could, and soon had a small stake once again. He followed up the cards with pamphlets printed on pale blue paper. Addressed to "Gentlemen:" and promising secrecy in all cases, it advised: "I am a graduate of one of the most respectable medical colleges in America and have been for eighteen months a regular army surgeon. No court can compel me to reveal anything communicated to me professionally. My rooms are private and can be entered and left without being observed."

He wrote a series of such circulars, issuing them as Special Circular No. 2, Special Circular No. 3, and so forth. By the time he got to Special Circular No. 5, he was making perfectly outrageous statements; for example:

My mode for treating syphilis, or Pox, in its various forms and stages, has met the hearty approbation of some of the most eminent medical men in America and is, in fact, the same principle as that now practiced in Venereal Hospitals in Paris, and recently introduced in some of the hospitals of Philadelphia and New York.

In the treatment of the effects of Onanism or Self Abuse, the views which I have adopted are acknowledged by all scientific physicians, to whom they have been explained, to be the only successful treatment. Some of the symptoms produced by ONANISM, or solitary practice, are pimples, blotches, nervousness, general weakness, constipation, dyspepsia, dejection of spirit, despondency, fear of imaginary evils, dislike of female society, timidity in the society of females, &c, and if allowed to run on, chorea, epilepsy, insanity, mania, consumption, &c. are not infrequent results.

His next effort was to make a deal with a newspaperman to pay one dollar each time his name appeared in the reporter's news-paper. Many readers must have been confused by such items as, "Fire destroyed a small shed on the Klein property which is just one and one-half miles from Dr. M. Beshoar's office at No. 44 Pine Street." But the results were gratifying. A steady stream of men who had sampled the commercial pleasures of the town went to No. 44 Pine Street, paying him stiff fees for his services.

His success excited envy and then attack from some of the quacks who catered to the military. He answered them with a circular:

The medical profession has long had to regret seeing private diseases fall into the hands of miserable quacks, the effects of whose treatment is often worse than the original disease. It has become apparent that this species of quackery could not be put down except through some of the regular profession who evinced a peculiar tact in the treatment of this class of disease to devote themselves specially to their treatment. In St. Louis this duty has fallen on me. If you know of any cases of the kind in your neighborhood, please hand them this circular and caution them against boasting quacks whose own circulars and advertisements condemn them as humbugs.

Now that the war was over as far as he was concerned and he was once more a citizen in private practice, he again tried to open communication with his father in Pennsylvania. When his letters brought no response and were not returned, he wrote D. E. Robeson, secretary of the Masonic lodge in Lewistown, and asked him to intercede with Daniel Beshoar. The request got a reply.

I received your letter several days ago and have delayed answering thinking that I could get to see your father and get some information from him, but have not been successful. I had several conversations with him about six months ago and never at any time did he give the least intimation of disowning you, although he regretted and was very much pained with the course you saw proper to pursue in the troubles that afflict our country. He even tried to give or think you perhaps have some excuse for that course. Should I see him soon and get any additional information I will write you again.

With more money in his pockets with each passing week and his practice growing, the physician eventually took in a partner, Dr. A. W. Leffingwell, a former Union Army surgeon. The two men got along well, and Leffingwell made it possible for him to have a little freedom from the office, which he took full advantage of by enrolling for a six-months course of lectures in St. Louis Medical College. Confident he could carry a heavy load, he signed up for physiology under Dr. John T. Hodgen, anatomy under Dr. C. R. Gregory, chemistry and pharmacy under Dr. A. Litton, principles of medicine with Dr. M. L. Linton, and principles of surgery under the dean of the school, Dr. Charles A. Pope. After a week he added two more: surgical anatomy under Dr. Charles R. Stevens and materia medica and therapeutics under Dr. Frank W. White. By the time he was well into the courses, he began to sicken of his office at No. 44 Pine Street and its clientele. The money was good, but he couldn't help feeling that he was in some way affiliated with prostitution.

The problem was how to get out of it. Should he go back to Pennsylvania; should he hold on in St. Louis until the war ended and then try to go back to Arkansas; should he simply stay in St. Louis or perhaps go on west? He finally decided that the Union Army might be the answer on at least two counts: it would get him out of his venereal specialty, and it would clean up his war record in later years if he were to have had some service on the northern side. And it would look better to his posterity and make the way easier for them.

He asked Leffingwell whether he would buy him out if there was a spot open in the army, and his partner said he would jump at the chance. With that Michael went to see Dr. Madison Mills, medical director of the Department of the Missouri. Admitting frankly his reasons for wanting to return to army service, he said he was willing to serve almost any place but hoped to finish his course of lectures at the medical school. Dr. Mills was encouraging; he said there was a current need for surgeons, that the examination could be taken at once, and that Dr. Beshoar could be assigned in St. Louis. Before he left Dr. Mills's office, he was in for a surprise. His rosewood case of instruments and his other possessions buried near the hospital tent at Shiloh were brought out and returned to him. It was explained that the freshly turned bit of earth had been noted and dug up and that his possessions had simply been held on the theory that "a man with a name as odd as yours would eventually turn up."

The examination before a U.S. Board of Medical Examiners was comparatively easy, and Michael soon found himself employed as an acting assistant surgeon, United States Army. His June 27, 1864, contract provided that he would at all times perform the duties of an army medical officer, "agreeable to army regulations," and that he would furnish and keep in good order and accessible complete sets of amputating, trephining, and pocket instruments. In exchange for this "the said Surg. Mad. Mills, Medical Director, promises and agrees on behalf of the United States, to pay or cause to be paid, to the said Dr. Michael Beshoar, the sum of one-hundred dollars for each and every month he shall continue to perform the services above stated, and one-hundred thirteen 83/100 dollars per month and transportation in kind, when performing service in the field, which shall be his full compensation and in lieu of all allowances and emoluments whatever." It was good pay considering that the medical regulations of the army provided that surgeons with ten years of service in that grade should be paid $80 per month and that the surgeon general was paid the munificent sum of $2,740 per year.

His first assignment put him in charge of a ward for white refugee women and children at Benton Barracks. Subsequently he was given the lying-in wards and still later did ward duty and post-mortems in the St. Louis Post and Jefferson Barracks hospitals.

In the course of duty in the various hospitals and attending classes at the medical college, he made a number of friends, including three fellow surgeons, Hiram H. Latham, James E. Folsom, and A. Rubillard, and two fellow students, E. C. Gehrung of Denver and Harrison A. Lemen of Illinois. One other friend, although Michael didn't think of him as such at the time, was a tall, good-looking young Sioux half-breed who used the English name John Smith as a matter of convenience in classes. He was shy, had no background for medical school, and was most grateful for the help Michael gave him with his studies.

Since the students at the college and the medical officers spent much of their spare time talking about what they would do and where they would practice after the war ended, Gehrung, who had practiced in Colorado, was the star of many of the sessions. A good storyteller, he painted glowing pictures of towering, snow-capped peaks, broad mesas, and endless plains where a man could see for a hundred miles or more. Colorado Territory, he said, was rich in gold and silver and would offer opportunities for alert young men who wanted to get ahead in a business way. But most of all he praised the climate, assuring his fellow students that it was free from malaria and the swamp fevers, and that it was good for consumptives. The clear, dry air, he said, was better than any medicine.

Gehrung's stories, coupled with discouraging word from Pocahontas, started Michael thinking seriously about a possible army assignment in the West. Arkansas was prostrate as 1865 opened. Isaac Putnam and other friends had tried to collect some of the accounts due him, but with little success. When Put pressed for payment, former patients insisted either that they had paid Beshoar or that the physician owed them a comparative amount for some service or other.

"What shall I do?" Put wrote. "They always stall me in the same way, apparently believing you will never return. At the same time I can't advise you to come back to Arkansas as conditions are too chaotic and we have no way of knowing if they will improve again." The physician didn't have much better luck when he tried to collect delinquent accounts in Ironton through John Edwards, a lawyer.

In addition to worrying about his professional future, Michael had personal problems in St. Louis. Mike, Jr., unhappy with the Christian Brothers, constantly begged to be taken out of the school. Every meeting was a tearful one for the boy and a depressing experience for the father, so much so that the physician didn't see as much of Mike as he knew he should. The matter of time and attention for Mike was further complicated when the physician became deeply involved with Mollie Allen, the daughter of an army officer. What hours he could spare from his duties as acting assistant surgeon were spent with her. There was considerable good-natured joking around the hospital about who would be invited to the wedding and when and where it would take place. Michael liked Mollie and they had good times together, but he couldn't bring himself to the point of a proposal even though it soon became apparent that Mollie was looking forward to marriage at an early date. But he was too restless, too uncertain.

Finally, in the early spring, he made a decision: he would get out of St. Louis, take an army assignment in Arkansas or the West. Almost immediately possibilities in both Arkansas and Missouri presented themselves. While these were simmering, he and Surgeon Latham went to J. W. Barnes, assistant adjutant general of the Department of the Missouri, who said he needed surgeons on the plains and would either of them be interested in Fort Kearny in Nebraska Territory? Both said they would. Barnes, it turned out, had only one place open at Kearny and, after quizzing them on their backgrounds, gave it to Michael on the basis of his past service as a Confederate surgeon. Fort Kearny, the assistant adjutant general said, would soon be garrisoned by Confederate soldiers who had taken the oath of amnesty and agreed to serve on the plains against Indians. He said something else should show up shortly for Latham.

When the orders came through, Michael was named post surgeon at Fort Kearny and medical purveyor of the territories, in which latter capacity he would have the responsibility of dispensing drugs and medical supplies to military posts on the frontier west of Fort Kearny and to pilgrims passing through the fort on their way up the Oregon Trail.

Getting off was hectic business. There were toasts to be drunk, letters to be written, and tearful sessions with Mike. He promised the boy he would send for him when he could find a location for private practice and make a home for him. Although Michael prided himself on being a gentleman, he didn't measure up to that self-estimate on his departure from St. Louis—as he went off without telling Mollie he was leaving.

Chapter 3
Aftermath at Fort Kearny

THE YEAR 1865, soon to be known as the "Bloody Year on the Plains," was fairly quiet when Surgeon Beshoar took over the Fort Kearny Hospital, March 26, replacing Surgeon William McClelland of the First Nebraska Volunteer Cavalry (who moved to Post Cottonwood, a hundred miles up the Oregon Trail). Since McClelland had just finished caring for several smallpox cases, Michael's first task was to clean up the hospital and to burn bedding, clothing, and other items.

Located in the southwest corner of the one-and-one-third-mile-square post and about two hundred yards from the small, four-acre parade ground, the hospital was a one-story frame structure with three ward rooms capable of accommodating twenty patients. There was a small, 10 by 12 feet, dispensary, and a small storeroom and laundry. Adjacent to the hospital and just behind the officers' quarters, the surgeon had his own small, scantily furnished house. Both the hospital and the house were well painted, well lighted, and snugly insulated and heated against the cold winds that whistled down the Platte and howled across the treeless plains stretching endlessly north from the river.

As a supply depot Kearny had large stocks of drug and medical supplies, a delight to a former Confederate who had often had little to work with, but Michael found the bountiful supplies a mixed blessing; he was caught up from the first day in a constant round of "counting pots and pans," inventories, reports, boards of inquiry, and other bureaucratic requirements. Thefts from the supplies were almost routine, and each loss called for an inquiry. But after a few weeks Michael found he liked the big post better than he had expected. After one go at it, he passed up the buffalo hunts that were a regular sport for the post's officers, but there were other things to do: dances, concerts by the military bands, visits with the people who came in with the big wagon trains, and a stream of distinguished visitors. An occasional clash between a patrol and a band of Indians added excitement and zest.

And there was nearby Dobytown* and, if one wasn't too particular, Dirty Woman's Ranch and its "girls." Dobytown was squalid, tough, and mean, consisting mostly of saloons, dance houses, gambling parlors, and boarding ranches; and the denizens of the one-story sod buildings were as motley a collection of saloonkeepers, gamblers, robbers, confidence men, thieves, murderers, and prostitutes as ever assembled in any frontier town.

There were also some legitimate residents, such as Leigh Richmond Freeman who had bought the *Fort Kearny Herald* from Seth Mobley of the Seventh Iowa Cavalry and converted it into the *Frontier Index*. Freeman was also the telegrapher at the fort and as such was accepted by the military, though he and his brother, F. K. Freeman, were much disliked by Moses Sydenham, the post sutler, who had founded the *Herald*. Sydenham told all who would listen that Leigh had been a telegraph operator for the Confederates and that both brothers were Democrats of "the strongest secessionist kind." Michael found them charming. They were kindred spirits, southerners of a sort, Democrats, newspapermen, good drinkers, and more alert and knowledgeable than most of the other people around the fort.

In April, Michael was thrown into an uproar when the grapevine reported there would be a general shakeup of officers, including surgeons, and that he might be sent out to one of the small, off-the-beaten-track posts. He immediately wrote everyone he knew who might help him avoid such a catastrophe and soon had assurances that he would neither be transferred nor have to go on any lengthy expeditions.

Through the remainder of the spring and on into the summer, he was busy with his routines and with taking care of members of the Third U.S. Volunteers, the former Confederates, who now staffed the post and were jokingly referred to up and down the trail as the "Whitewashed Yanks" or the "Galvanized Yanks." He had six of them in his hospital at one time after a fourteen-man detachment

*Its official name was Kearney City. The name Kearney was spelled "ey" to distinguish it from Ft. Kearny.

was attacked by Indians May 18 at a point two miles east of Elm Creek Stage Station while en route from Fort Leavenworth to Fort Kearny. The men, sent out of Leavenworth without weapons, were defenseless when set upon by the war party. Two of the soldiers were killed and six were wounded, including twenty-year-old John W. Twyman, a sandy-haired, six-foot farmer from Hodgenville, Kentucky. He was knocked down by a saber wielded by one Indian and then scalped by a second, who gave him another whack with a saber before leaving him, half-conscious and bleeding.

It was a curious affair. The Indians wore buckskin leggings, had short, roached hair, carried bows and arrows and sabers, and took pains to identify themselves as Sioux and Cheyenne, even offering the wounded men arrows as proof. At the fort it was generally believed they were Pawnees and probably U.S. Army scouts stationed at either Fort Kearny or Post Cottonwood.

Twyman excited much attention in the post hospital. The curious who crowded into the ward scarcely glanced at the men who had been wounded by arrows, but everyone wanted a look at the man who had been "scalped alive." Surgeon Beshoar's treatment had a twofold purpose: to promote healing as rapidly as possible and to take the sags out of Private Twyman's big freckled face. With the assistance of his steward, he had cleaned the wound, pulled the edges of the remaining scalp as far up on the cranium as possible, and stitched them to the fibrous aponeuroses with silk ligatures. He covered the wound with lard and applied a light dressing, so there really wasn't much for the visitors to see. In his report Michael wrote that the soldier received "a scalp wound on the 18th of May, 1865, near Elm Creek station, Nebraska Territory, when attacked by hostile Indians. Weapon: a scalping knife. About three and a half by five inches of scalp removed. Also two saber wounds received on the same occasion, one fracturing the occipital bone near its upper angle and the other fracturing the mastoid portion of the temporal bone. He will not, in my opinion, be able to do duty as a soldier within the space of six months."

With a company of Pawnees and another of Omahas stationed at the fort, and their families, relatives, and hanger-on friends camped along the river, Michael found himself caring for Indians as well as whites. Mostly he handled the big emergency cases as the Indians preferred their own remedies for ordinary illnesses. However, in the course of some general practice among them, he picked up considerable information on their herbs.

Many of the plants were familiar to him, but there were some new ones, such as osha root. His U.S. Dispensatory mentioned it as a little-known Mexican umbellifera containing oshaic acid. When he learned it was used widely by the plains Indians, he did some experimenting with it and found its active properties readily extracted by alcohol but not by acetic acid. His Indian patients insisted on applying osha to their wounds and used it freely for many other purposes. Of it Michael wrote:

> The natives use it by chewing the root and swallowing the saliva and of course considerable of the fiber. They use it for anything that may ail the stomach, bowels or kidneys. I have found it one of the most pleasant and efficacious stomach tonics I have ever prescribed or taken into my own stomach. It has some value as a stimulating expectorant.
>
> But it is used, not only as a remedial agent, per se, but also by hunters under the belief that by chewing the root and having it on the person, deer and bear will not scent them and they can therefor [sic] get in better gunshot range of their game. It is also the prevailing belief that having it on the person is a sure protection against vicious beasts, witches and evil spirits. It is said deer and bear are fond of it—the deer consuming the herb and the bear digging up and eating the root.
>
> As it grows in great profusion in the rich aluvium [sic] along streams throughout the region, I believe that in the not very distant future, osha will take its proper place in our materia medica.

In addition to treating wounded Indians, he had to make out reports on them for Washington. When dead scouts were brought in lashed to their ponies, he had to examine the bodies, ascertain what had happened, and fill out forms for War Department records in Washington. He found the Indian funerals "somewhat pompous affairs." When the bodies of Ste-tuc-ta-la-rick, Te-kitilia-hu-ras (Man that Gives the War Cry Before Striking the Enemy) and Taw-kaw (Gray Fox) were brought in, he made the usual reports but subsequently wrote: "Large graves were prepared and the bodies deposited therein, with a buffalo robe, a bow and a quiver of arrows, flint and steel, punk and jerked meat placed on each body.

Then each man's pony was made to stand on the edge of the grave with Indians supporting him from the distal side. The pony was then shot and caused to fall into the grave, which was then filled with earth. One of the scouts told me the dead man was thus provided with his pony which would enter on a new life with the brave in the happy hunting ground and the implements of the hunt which he used in life would be useful to him in the next and he would enter on a happy career in the beyond."

He also had opportunities to study at close range some of the dietary habits and obstetrical practices of the Indians. Often he had tongue in cheek when he wrote about them, but sometimes he admired their efficacy. As with any other army surgeon of his day, whether the bowels were open or closed was paramount:

> The Indians would live exclusively on meat for a month at a time and enjoy the best of health as cattle diseases were unknown among the buffalo. Much of the meat was jerked for use after the herds had passed. Then attacks of acute constipation became common, there being few articles of diet with which to sufficiently dilute the dried meat.
>
> However, the Indians kept themselves supplied part of the time with artichokes which were found in many places in the river bottom.
>
> One of the favorite medicines was wild squash, a drastic purgative—the more drastic purgatives being decidedly in favor. But in the absence of purgative herbs, abdominal massage was practiced in a crude manner but generally with the effect of free purgation.
>
> Their favorite part of an animal was the marrow gut. At one time when we had had no meat except venison for an extended time a bunch of steers was brought out from the Missouri River and I was so beef hungry that I arranged for a piece out of the first steer killed.
>
> While I was waiting for it on the prairie outside the fort, several hundred Indians were also hungrily waiting. The

beeves were butchered on the ground to be dressed on their
own hide and when the entrails of the first beef were rolled
out on the ground there was a scramble for them. The foremost
Indian grabbed the marrow gut and ran away with the end of it,
eating it the while, simply stripping back the dung with his
finger and thumb, yet not so clean but that as he ate the dung
ran from both angles of his mouth.

The next most powerful Indian would tear off a section from
the first and take the next, till the entire entrails were taken
and eaten the same as the first section. Dung was not
especially objectionable as long as they got the gut, and
the tape worms were doomed.

In the late spring Michael accompanied Captain Belden and a
company of Pawnees and Omahas south to the Republican River.
When they left the fort, each man had government rations of hard-
tack and bacon for more than a week. But at the end of two days,
the Indians had eaten all of their rations and were hungry. Wrote
Michael:

The captain and I were obliged to sleep on our haversacks to
prevent them from stealing what we had left to eat.

Riding along in the hot sun if a lizard was scared up all the
Indians who saw it would scramble for it and the victor, when
he grasped it with some dry grass, would at once begin to eat
it without the formality of first butchering it.

When we reached the river there were plenty of grasshopper
fattened turkeys and the starved Indians had a feast—not
waiting to cook the fowl until their appetites had been partially
satiated.

On our return they lashed turkeys, feathers and all, to their
ponies which made fair meat for about 24 hours, but they ate
them for a week—highly flavored after two days, but they
seemed to be relished, yet we hadn't a colic or other ailment
during the expedition.

During this period he met a number of Indian midwives, whom
he found to be densely ignorant "though a few are ingenious in
their ways." He was called to one Pawnee tipi near the river where
he found an Indian midwife attending a case of shoulder presen-

AFTERMATH AT FORT KEARNY 57

tation. She had successfully turned the fetus and converted it to a breach position by his arrival, "but I never met another such."

He described the usual Indian method for delivering a woman as follows: The usual position of the several parties engaged is as follows:

1st. The patient on a skin on the floor with a strong cord of rawhide, hair or hemp with a large knot on the lower end of it extending from the top of the tipi or ceiling to a point she can reach while kneeling erectly. This she grasps and swings her weight upon during labor pains. In the intervals she sits on her heels.

2nd. The midwife kneeling in front who, during pains, passes her hands over the patient's buttocks and shakes the pelvis, her finger ends pressing the sacrum and, between pains, she too sits on her heels or on one hip and smokes her cigarette.

3rd. A strong man, usually a neighbor, who during pains kneels behind the patient—her back resting against his chest—while he spreads his hands over and presses downward on the womb toward the child's proper point of exit. He occupies his time between pains as does the midwife.

During the first stages the woman often makes a circuit of the tipi or room—so timing her movements as to reach her station in time for the next pain.

During the entire labor all the neighbors who are at peace with the family, the family heads with their children from the suckling to the blooming maiden and the dashing lad, crowd in, loading the atmosphere with smoke *puncha* (bad tobacco) carbon dioxide, sulphured hydrogen and mutually congenial bacilli.

In time (due or otherwise) the baby makes its advent. Then the hurrah begins. The cord is tied in two places, about two inches apart, with a deerskin, a piece of buckskin or rawhide, the upper one being quite long and also tied around the woman's thigh, and divided between the two ties.

If the midwife has good teeth, the cord is cut by biting it off, otherwise it is divided by a knife, sharp flint rock, or any cutting instrument which may be handy. The end of a piece of porous wood or corncob, having been providentially lighted, is used to sear the baby's end of the cord.

A long band about two inches wide passing several times around the baby's hips completes the umbilical dressing. The baby is then wrapped closely from the top of its head to its feet—its arms straight down at its sides—to keep it warm and to prevent it from scratching itself and from sucking its thumbs. It looks like a miniature Egyptian mummy.

The man at the rear still occupies his position pressing the womb downward. The string fastened about the woman's thigh to prevent the womb from sucking it in out of reach is maintained till after the afterbirth has been discharged and secured at which time the thigh string is cut or untied and the afterbirth goes into the fire. If there are any firearms available they are rapidly discharged in front of the door to promote the discharge of the placenta.

The afterbirth having been discharged, the woman is bandaged with a strip about five to eight yards long, which is passed about the hips, the folds passing alternately over and just above the hips, one pressing the womb downward and the other backward, and a bowl of *atole* (hot gruel made from parched blue corn) is administered, and her head is bandaged till she looks somewhat like a brunette Sister of the Sacred Heart, and all doors and windows (if there are any) are closed tightly and all the blankets and robes are spread upon her to prevent the baneful influences of *el aire* (the air) from striking her.

After three days she usually performs some (if not all) of her household duties and after forty days takes a bath.

Throughout the summer of 1865, pilgrim wagons lumbered through Kearney City in an almost solid line, as many as four hundred a day, moving slowly west. There was a lot of other traffic, including the regular stages with their drivers yelling for the right-of-way over the heavy wagons and then galloping their horses the last quarter of a mile into the station as required by company regulations. Along with other officers Michael managed to meet many of the stages to gossip with passengers and occasionally spot an important congressman or other public figure. He also left the fort several times, mostly traveling up the trail with cavalry detachments to Plum Creek, Smith's Ranch, and on up as far as Post Cottonwood. At no time was he in any real danger on the road, but he did have one close call off trail. He and two soldiers, traveling in a light ambulance, were on the prairie hunting for a couple of cavalrymen standing guard over a trooper who had been thrown by his horse and painfully injured. As they drove north of the river, they saw about thirty Indians, all painted, coming at them. There was no time to make a run for it and no place to run anyway. They pulled up, jumped out of the ambulance and stretched out on the ground. The two soldiers looked nervously to their carbines; Michael had only a pistol. The Indians came on fast, broke into two parties, and came at them from two angles. The escorts raised their guns to fire but lowered them as the lead Indian threw up his arm and called out loudly to his companions. As the warriors reined in, the man who had signaled trotted his pony toward the three men on the ground, right hand upraised. When he reached them he slid from his pony, saying, "My God, Doc Beshoar, what are you doing out here?" As Michael recalled it later: "It just didn't seem possible. I thought I had lost my mind when this painted savage spoke my name. But it was John Smith, the young man who had attended lectures with us in St. Louis. We talked briefly and he asked about others who had attended the course and then told me to take my men and go. When he and his band rode off it was the last time I ever saw him."

Two weeks later he made another trip out of Fort Kearny and off the trail, this time with a small detachment of cavalrymen. A civilian, said to be a part-time hunter, guide, and trapper, who had a small cabin a day's ride from Kearny by horseback, had been caught unaware and wounded by either Cheyenne or Sioux. A patrol had reported he was in serious condition. When Michael and his escort, one of whom was Private Polk Nesbit, reached the cabin, it was already dark. By the light of a lantern, the surgeon made a quick examination. The arrow had lodged in the left arm, just beneath the shoulder; the man was suffering intense pain, had a high fever, and was delirious. Michael sniffed the rotting flesh and told the soldiers the gangrenous arm would have to come off. He instructed them to take the door off the miserable cabin and lay it on the ground. He tried to talk to the wounded man about the amputation, but the trapper was not rational enough to make any decision about surgery. Permission wasn't important anyway. The arm had to come off at once.

He was given a copious amount of whiskey and morphine and was placed on the door. While Private Nesbit held a lantern, Michael laid out his small instrument kit and got a saw from his saddlebags. At a nod some of the soldiers held on to the man's legs while others held his good arm and head. As Michael went to work, a big full moon rose majestically above the prairie adding some light to that cast by the lantern. It was only a matter of minutes before he knew he would have to perform a disarticulation of the humerus from its socket. It had been a big arrowhead, strongly driven, and it had done a lot of damage. And the wound had gone too long without attention. The surgeon worked carefully to find and ligate the big blood vessels. He took part of the scapula when he found infection in that area. Mercifully the man was unconscious throughout the operation.

When the work was done, the patient, still on the door, was carried into the cabin and covered with blankets. While the escort bivouacked outside, Michael sat beside the blanketed figure throughout the night. Whenever the man moaned or stirred restlessly, Michael gave him whiskey from his flask and then took a drink himself. Soon after dawn he had one of the soldiers watch beside the man while he slept for an hour and then he resumed his vigil throughout the day. Late in the afternoon an ill-kempt, sad-faced man of middle age arrived on a bony horse that was as nondescript looking as its rider. He said he was a friend and had come to help. Michael, positive his patient didn't have a chance, told the new arrival he and his escort would have to leave for Kearny by morning but that he would provide him with detailed instructions on how to care for his friend. He also said that as soon as the amputee was strong enough, he should be brought to Kearny for an examination.

As they rode away just after sunrise the next morning, the physician told Polk Nesbit and the others in the escort that it was a miracle the man had lived through another night but that he would be dead within a matter of hours, as he couldn't possibly survive such drastic surgery under such conditions. Four weeks later the trapper-hunter presented himself at the Fort Kearny Hospital for the promised examination. He had lost a great deal of weight, he was very weak, and his color was bad, but he was alive, much to the surprise of his surgeon.

By the fall of 1865 when the caravans began to dwindle and the Indian hostiles went off to hunt the buffalo as they migrated southward in great, slow-moving black masses, Michael found himself frustrated and restless. He was sick of counting pots and pans, sick of bureaucracy, and ready to get out of the army. With the thought that he might go back to Pennsylvania, he wrote Masonic secretary E. D. Robeson in Lewistown to ask about his father. The reply, dated October 18, 1865, said in part:

Your letter of Sept. 1 came duly to hand and in answer I can say that your father is still alive but this summer the family all moved to Indiana. . . . I think from several conversations I had with your father that if you would write to him you would get an answer.

Several letters went off to the new address in Monticello, but Daniel, whether he never received them or was still unforgiving, gave no answer.

Michael next decided he would simply settle down in Dobytown. He bought a small building, purchased a supply of drugs in St. Louis, had cards printed that promised to keep "constantly on hand everything usually kept in Eastern drugstores"—all with the approval of his commanding officer. His stock was in place and the store open for business when Surgeon Latham arrived from St. Louis on a temporary assignment as an assistant in the post hospital. The pair had a celebration that started in the hospital and moved to the officers' club, then to Dobytown, back to the hospital, and finally to the surgeon's residence where they slept it off. In December, with Latham still on duty, Michael was ordered to take over a hospital at Fire Steel Creek in Iowa. He had to do some fast politicking to circumvent the order and hang on to Kearny until his time expired in March. When the dust settled, Latham was ordered to Fort Sedgwick in Colorado Territory, and Surgeon Beshoar was left holding the fort, as it were, at Kearny.

Michael was sorry to see Latham leave but promised to think seriously about Colorado Territory and the possibility of joining him in business ventures there as well as in the practice of medicine. The ebullient Latham, whose mind raced day and night with all kinds of money-making schemes, was positive that the new El Dorado abounded in business opportunities as well as "fine locations" for medical men of their worth and was so excited he could hardly wait to get started. Since Latham was going to Fort Sedgwick by horseback in company with some cavalry, Michael managed to unload on him an extra horse he had picked up in payment for medical services. He got $150 for it by convincing Latham he would be able to make a profit on it when he got to Fort Sedgwick.

While Latham was eager to move on west, Michael was determined to stick it out at Dobytown for awhile longer, though the prognosis for Fort Kearny and neighboring Dobytown worsened with each passing month. Indian operations were moving farther west and southwest, and when the railroad came in from Omaha by the fall of 1866, the Oregon Trail would be finished. Soon after Latham left, Michael wrote the medical director in St. Louis asking if he could be released from his contract before March, which would be the end of a full year. After some shilly-shallying, the director sent him a letter releasing him as of February 11. He wasn't actually released from the fort until April, owing to mixups in assignments and bureaucratic confusion that would have left the post hospital without a surgeon part of the time if he had not been available. During the spring of 1866, he cleaned up most of the "pot and pan" business, appeared before several boards of survey made up of officers of the First Nebraska Volunteer Cavalry, the Seventh Iowa Cavalry, and the Third U.S. Volunteers. In several instances he brought in witnesses to testify to the disposition of property; in others he had affidavits from men who had been transferred away from Kearny or had been mustered out. He also made sworn statements before Probate Judge John C. Lindell of Kearney County in Dobytown and submitted them to the boards of survey. Acting assistant surgeons were similarly occupied at other forts in the West.

However, it was not until August 10, 1866, that Michael received his final clearance from the Property Division of the Surgeon General's office in Washington. Long before that he had had a final inventory session with his successor, Surgeon S. M. Horton.

Soon after he became a "late army surgeon" and a full-time resident of Dobytown—once again resplendent in a reversible vest, red on one side and blue on the other—Michael Beshoar found himself one of the leading citizens of Kearney City. His practice and drugstore prospered, he gave the Freemans a helping hand with their *Index* whenever the editorial spirit moved him, and he was elected mayor of Kearney City by an almost unanimous vote. He boarded with a Mrs. Moreland and slept, as he had in Ironton, in the back of his office. That is, he did when he slept. Dobytown roared most of the night, and he not only had to be on hand when some roisterer got himself shot, cut, or beaten, but he had socializing of his own that needed tending. His pastimes were mostly drinking and gambling, if viewed on a quantitative basis, but as an unencumbered young professional man, with all the medical mystique women find so attractive, he didn't lack for female companionship, even in a community where there were dozens of men for every woman. Mostly he dated the Buckeye Girl, as she was known at the fort and to gallant officers up and down the trail. There were some others too, but since he considered himself a gentleman, he never said anything about a woman friend in any of his correspondence. However, a dishonest steward by the name of Louis Kallander, whom he had bounced for theft, wrote him early in 1866:

> When you receive these lines I am on my way to New York. I only send this letter to tell you that you acted shamefully on me. When you accused me of theft you did not even get me a chance of defending me. Whoever has told you any story about me is to blame for it not you. You did not think of me knowing *every one of your secrets* and that your welfare can be destroyed by me at any moment. Only think of such affairs as Mrs. Russell, Mary Dees and The Buckeye Girl. But enough of this. It is my only warning to you. Only speaking about me will be your certain destruction. Mind, I am well informed from Kearney about everything concerning you and have ample means of fulfilling my word.
>
> Louis Kallander
> This name has been only assumed during the U.S. Service and has made room now for my real name which you will never learn.

As was his custom, Michael folded the letter, wrote "Louis Kallander Letter" on the back of it, and carefully filed it away.

Through the late spring and summer of 1866, Dobytown got a strong play from the wagon trains and the traffic west. Money flowed freely. Because of Indian troubles to the west, the military insisted that pilgrims travel in trains of not less than a hundred wagons as a matter of protection. Small groups were held up until the one-hundred requirement was met, and the delays meant money in the waiting pockets of Dobytown. Michael got his share. Income was so good, in fact, that he managed to pay off most of his indebtedness to the Christian Brothers' Academy for Mike's board, room, and tuition, have some new clothes made up for himself by St. Louis tailors, and add to his drug stock. A letter from Mike dated April 16, 1866, had indicated all was going well with his eleven-year-old son:

> Dear Father
> I received your letter on the 7th inst. April and was very glad to hear from you being in good health at present and hoping this letter will find you the same. I received three of the most necessary Sacraments namely Baptism, Confirmation, Euchrast on Sunday last. I felt very happy on that day, much happier than any day of my life. Theire were 21 boys besides myself received Euchrast and Confirmation on that same day. We will have a nice picknic and I am very pleased with this school. Please send me some money for the nice picknic. Baptism for a name I took Augustine so my names are Michael A. Beshoar.
>   This letter is from your son
>   M. A. Beshoar
> Send some money for the picknic please. ANS. THIS.

Subsequent letters from Mike, not so happy in tone, were crowded with expressions of affection and pleas to be allowed "to come home." Mike began to complain of difficulties with other students and with his teachers, and there were letters from teachers explaining unpleasant happenings in the classrooms and dormitory when Mike defied authority.

At Eastertime a more encouraging letter came in which Mike enclosed a bit of palm and asked him to "please keep it always for it is blessed by a priest and also send me some money. Tell me if you have gotten out of the service."

In addition to thanking Mike for the letter and the bit of blessed palm, Michael sent ninety dollars to the school with a request that

Brother Edwards put it into a pocket-money fund for Mike and that it be doled out to the lad on a weekly basis. The letters made him uneasy, but he couldn't see any way he could have Mike with him. Dobytown was not a suitable place for a young boy. In a few days Mike's letters took a happier turn. He wrote twice a week with bits of news about the teachers, his fellow students, and their ball and marble games. Best of all, to his father's mind, he wrote in one letter "I am happy to say that I am very well and I think I am succeeding in my studies." Reports from the school bore him out insofar as his studies were concerned but said that his conduct left something to be desired.

While Mike's letters came with every post, the father's replies were often interrupted for extended periods, as they were at this time by a smallpox epidemic that swept everything else out of his mind and kept him on the go day and night. Whatever his personal problems and obligations, he was first and last a physician.

Scarcely was the epidemic over than Dobytown experienced its biggest show of the year. The former Fort Kearny commander, Colonel Henry B. Carrington, received orders to set up a new Mountain District that would take charge of Fort Reno and two other posts on the Bozeman Trail in the Powder River country north and west of Fort Laramie, where the Sioux and Cheyenne were congregating in strength. Jim Bridger and his assistant Henry Williams, who had spent several weeks around the fort and in Dobytown, including some loafing time in the drugstore, were to lead Colonel Carrington and his forces into the new area.

The exodus of what was immediately dubbed Carrington's "Overland Circus" took place from the fort Saturday, May 19. It was a clear, sunny spring day. Led by Bridger, wearing his old store-boughten clothes and soft, slouchy felt hat with the low crown, looking for all the world like an old broken-down Arkansas or Missouri farmer, and Williams, looking no more like a scout than his chief, the army marched out of the fort and through Dobytown to the broad road west.

It was a great sight, and the mayor of Dobytown (Kearney City) and the residents with whom he stood to watch the parade, as representative a group of businessmen, gamblers, saloonkeepers, hangers-on, and prostitutes as one could find anywhere in the West, applauded as the troops went by. Michael felt a tingling sensation and wished he were going too. To the martial music of the Eighteenth Regiment's band, a thousand dismounted men of the Second and Third battalions (all in heavy, new blue uniforms that were much too warm after only a few minutes of marching) were first in line, followed by 226 mule-drawn wagons, most of them driven by civilian teamsters. Then came a thousand head of beef cattle, herded by civilians, followed by a long line of ambulances filled with women and children, with chicken coops and milch cows tied on behind. The cavalry brought up the rear.

Surgeon Horton, with contract surgeons Mathews, McCleary, and Buelon, had ambulances and drivers, with their saddle mounts tied behind. Horton gave the mayor of Dobytown a cheery wave and told him he'd better come along.

The circus-like atmosphere gave no hint of the fate that awaited many of the men before the year was out. To them and to the mayor and his constituents standing along what passed for a main street, it was simply a big brave military show.

It was June and Dobytown was hot and dusty when Michael discovered why the letters he had sent to his father in Indiana the previous fall were never answered. Isaac Putnam wrote from Arkansas that a Pocahontas man on a business trip north had heard a report that "Dr. Beshoar's father is dead." Put said he couldn't verify or disprove the report but thought he should pass it along. Michael again turned to Masonic secretary Robeson and got back an indifferent letter saying:

> Your letter to hand and I am unable to give you any direct information of your father except that there is no doubt of his death. I heard it shortly after it occurred and that must have been six to twelve months ago. The time slipped my memory entirely nor do I know to whom I could refer you for information. He had been to Monticello for some time and his business was pretty much closed up here.

Late in the summer a letter arrived from Latham who was happily ensconced in the post hospital at Fort Sedgwick in Colorado Territory. He wrote that he was hoping to open a drugstore in Julesburg, as a new town was being rapidly built to replace the one burned by hostiles in 1864.

How is His Honor, the Mayor? How is Trade? Are you doing the right thing by all those girls? I sold your little horse for $205. I could have had him raffled at $250, but did not care to have my name connected with a gambling operation. The raffle is on the square, but sounds bad. My other horse is all right, has the name of being the best horse in the garrison. I ride all over the country. Am in the saddle every day. Went out south 15 miles and saw clouds of antelope. There are the finest openings in the world here for ranches.

We are building a town here and I am in for a building and a drugstore. This is the country to make money in.

Michael's correspondence during the fall months came from old friends in Pocahontas, from St. Louis, and all up and down the Oregon Trail, as well as from more than a dozen home states of men who had been mustered out of the Galvanized Yanks. A good deal of it came from patients and much of it from women, including a substantial number of prostitutes who wanted medicine for their occupational ailments, and from frightened, overworked women in stage stations and the so-called "ranches," or stopping places along the trail, who pleaded in illiterate scrawls for an abortifacient when they found themselves pregnant.

One poor creature, in a scarcely legible hand, wrote from Elm Creek Station "pleas send the medison and you shall be payed emediatly. rite the directions on a peace of paper how it shud be taken, but fix it so no one can get information from it but me. I am gren as I can be and I know that it is wrong but I cant bare the thought of being burdened with this child for I cant make a living for myself any other way. dont let no one know what this medison is for. you will not lose nothing if you will set me free."

There is no indication in his papers as to whether he set her free or not. But the physicians on the frontier often had to make decisions and do things that didn't jibe with all the niceties of civilization back in the cities—or with the neatly printed and framed codes of ethics on the walls of medical offices.

Like any other druggist of his time or later, Michael sold a great many things besides drugs. There were sundries of all kinds, including gambling equipment. He not only sold them in his Dobytown store but he solicited business at other forts and from people in the West whom he had met at Fort Kearny or in Dobytown.

When he received a large supply of playing cards, he sent off a number of letters, offering them for sale "at reasonable prices." One went to Jim Bridger's assistant, Henry Williams, whom he had last seen at the forefront of Colonel Carrington's "Overland Circus" trek into the Powder River country in May. It drew a reply from Fort C. F. Smith, dated October 12, 1866:

> Dr. M. Beshoar, Dear Sir.
>   Your note of Aug. 17 has just come to hand. I have been to Virginia City with Jim Bridger and have supplied myself with all the cards and a kenough set. At present I have all I can use. Since I have seen you I have received from Groufere 9 dos. of different kind of cards, but I shall want some more this winter if I stay in this country and shall be happy to order some from you. I am on my way to Fort Phil Kearney the headquarters of the district where I shall probably stay. The Indians have been raising hell this summer. They have killed 94 men on this route that I have seen or helped to bury and they are getting braver every day. They now larriat them instead of shooting them and take them into the bluffs and torture them to death. I hope the government will attend to those Ducks this winter. Drop me a line when you can and I will keep you posted. And send me some of your waist newspapers. I must conclude yours truly Sir.
>
>   Henry Williams

Busy merchant Beshoar bundled up back issues of his regular St. Louis paper, the *Westliche Post*, wondering idly whether Scout Williams or any of his friends could read German, and sent them off.

The Union Pacific Railroad and Major General W. T. Sherman, both impressive by any standard, arrived at Fort Kearny during the third week of August. The railroad didn't reach the fort proper and would not as it was building along the north side of the river, but on August 21 it was only five miles away and everyone knew the whistles on its little work engines were tooting the end of the fort and the Oregon Trail.

Michael, along with other residents of Dobytown and officers and men from the fort, rode across the river to watch the crews lay track in the hot August sun. And the railroad crews in turn brought new business to Dobytown, as well as more crooks, more gamblers, more prostitutes, more saloons.

General Sherman was snorting and whistling like a locomotive when he arrived at the post for an inspection on the first leg of a trip that eventually took him up the trail to Fort Sedgwick, thence to Denver, and on to Fort Garland and Fort Lyon in the southern part of Colorado Territory. Upon his return to Washington in September, he reported the roads free of danger and whites traveling unarmed but anxious to promote Indian scares so they could sell supplies, fodder, and beef to the army. And finally: "God only knows when, and I do not see how, we can make a decent excuse for an Indian war."

It was the middle of November when Michael decided to quit Dobytown and go west. The cold winds were bringing the first winter snows out of the northland and a few tardy ducks and geese were hurrying south along the Nebraska flyway when he made up his mind. A great many Dobytown residents were planning to follow the railroad, which was already west of Plum Station. The iron road across the river spelled the end for Dobytown as well as for the fort. Besides, letters from Surgeon Latham at Fort Sedgwick and an occasional note from Dr. Gehrung in Denver had persuaded him that his future might well lie in Colorado. And a move was fairly simple. As to family, he had only Mike, who would have to stay in the St. Louis boarding school for some time yet regardless of where his father located.

Michael had both liabilities and assets as he prepared for his move. He had a few debts, which aggregated less than two thousand dollars. On the plus side he had money due from patients, a drugstore to sell, and some intangibles that were even more valuable: a University of Michigan medical degree and thirteen busy years of experience as a private practitioner, army surgeon, editor, legislator, judge, farmer, cotton speculator, businessman, and mayor of the toughest town on the Oregon Trail.

The preparations for the move were on the feverish side, because once he was fully committed, he wanted to be off, not waiting for spring or summer, the normal seasons of travel up the trail. He sold his Dobytown lots, with the exception of the one on which the drugstore stood, for $500; he bought two large wagons and eight heavy mules; he had his drug stock and other merchandise carefully packed in boxes. Recruiting wagoners was not difficult as there were always restless men ready to go anywhere for a bit of money. He signed on drivers for passage, food, and fifty cents a day cash money. Each man would have his own arms. And since the military insisted travelers band together in organized trains as protection against Indian attack, he worked out arrangements with eight men who had their own outfits and wanted to go to Colorado Territory. Two of them would carry some of his goods. Ten wagons was much too small a train under army regulations (a hundred were normally required during the summer), but since things were quiet along the trail and Michael was the former post surgeon, he was given written permission to travel from Fort Kearny. He was warned he would have to get passes at Post Cottonwood and again at Fort Sedgwick.

His chief concerns in traveling four hundred miles across the plains to Denver in December were the low temperatures, blizzards, and blowing snow. He didn't worry about Indians; they stayed in out of the cold during the dark winter months when their unshod ponies were thin and weak from lack of forage.

In addition to buying equipment, packing his merchandise, and selling his lots, Michael had a great many other things to do. He resigned as mayor and gave a power-of-attorney to a fellow townsman and Mason named John Siddell, who agreed to sell the store building and collect the physician's delinquent accounts on a commission basis. There were letters to get off to Mike, to Poca, to St. Louis, and to Latham and Gehrung. There were goodbyes to say out at the fort, in Dobytown, to the Buckeye Girl.

His little wagon train left Kearney City shortly after dawn December 6, 1866. It was dark and cold, and a bitter wind swept across the squalid little community. Michael, wearing a buffalo coat and cap, had elected to ride his horse out of Dobytown. It seemed only proper for the conductor of a train to be in the saddle and not huddled up on a wagon seat. A handful of well-wishers was on hand to bid them goodbye as he waved his arm for the wagons to move out. The whips of the drivers cracked, and the mules dug in to get their burdens moving. The cold, dark morning and the tiny train were a far cry from Colonel Carrington's circus of the previous summer, with its brave boys in blue, its band, its officers' ladies waving gay goodbyes. Michael Beshoar's little train moved slowly past the hovels of Dobytown and headed west along the broad road that led to Colorado.

Chapter 4

Trinidad and the Race War

THE TRIP FROM FORT KEARNY to Fort Sedgwick in Colorado Territory should have been an easy one. While it was Michael's first venture on the plains in the role of train conductor, he had had experience with army trains and had observed literally hundreds of pilgrim trains at Kearny and Dobytown. Also he had had a lot of presumably expert advice from trail-wise friends in Dobytown; he had planned the trip carefully; he had good teams and good wagons and had provided adequate supplies of shelled corn for the animals and provisions for his wagoners, most of whom had made the four-hundred-mile crossing to the mountains one or more times. December was a good time to travel, not only because the Indians stayed close to their villages during the winter months, when their ponies were poor, but because the month was usually fairly open on the high plains. Ordinarily the big winter storms held off until mid-January or even February. There was another safeguard in that there were twenty stage stations between Kearny and Sedgwick, separated by an average of ten miles. Between two of them, Fremont's Springs Station and O'Fallon's Bluff Station, the distance was only two miles, while the greatest spans between any two, that from Plum Creek to Willow Island and from Elkhorn to Alkali, were each only fifteen miles. At each station there was a ranche* or store and high-walled corrals. Some had bastions for defense and all could provide meals of sorts and supplies for the trail.

In his first seventy miles on the trail, conductor Beshoar had the usual emergencies: a lost mule shoe, a lame mule, a broken wheel,

---

*"Ranche," in the vernacular of the day, signified not a ranch in terms of cattle raising, but a place where stock could be supplied with provender, a defense could be made against attack, and a store provided supplies for travelers.

a fight between two drivers. By Christmas Day the little train was at Diamond Springs Station, only thirty miles out of Fort Sedgwick, and fighting snow. Before it got to Fort Sedgwick, an eastbound stage, plowing through four inches of new snow, stopped long enough to impart the news that the garrison at Fort Phil Kearny had been wiped out by Red Cloud's warriors. The stage driver said a telegraph report from Horseshoe Station in Wyoming said two hundred troopers had died. Michael was stunned. It seemed only yesterday that Carrington's Circus had marched so proudly through Dobytown on its way to the new Mountain District and Surgeon Horton had waved and called that he had better come along. The news of the Fetterman massacre was the sole topic of conversation for the remainder of the trip to Fort Sedgwick, but there was no real uneasiness among the drivers as they were more than two hundred miles south of the battle site.

When they reached Fort Sedgwick December 28, Michael had his drivers pull on to the Big Flats near the river where there was joint stem grass for the stock and plenty of room for a camp. Once the mules were put out to graze and the camp was set, he rode up to the fort.

Fort Sedgwick, established in May 1865 by Colonel C. H. Mc-Nally, Third U.S. Volunteers, to protect the overland route to California, stood on a flat piece of ground on a rise a quarter of a mile from the south bank of the river, opposite the mouth of Lodgepole Creek. It commanded a good view of the valley, which was at this point about three miles wide. The ford was five hundred yards below the fort, and a short distance below it were the ruins of Julesburg No. 1, destroyed by a thousand Cheyennes and Arapahoes January 7, 1865. A new and noisier Julesburg had been built three miles downstream, again on the south bank.

At the fort he turned his trail passes in to the post adjutant, shook hands with several officers, and asked where he would find Surgeon Latham. One of the officers said he had seen Latham going to the hospital and offered to escort the visitor. When they walked in on Latham in his dispensary, he let out a whoop.

"Have you heard the terrible news about Fetterman?" was Michael's first question. Surgeon Latham said he hadn't yet heard anything about Horton but presumed he was safe as there had been no reports to indicate that the lost troopers had been accompanied by a surgeon on their dash out of the fort. And the latest reports said that the casualty list was more like a hundred rather than the two hundred originally reported. Latham locked the dispensary and led his visitor to his quarters, a comfortable room, 24 by 25 feet, across a corridor from the ward room. "This is a light period," Latham said. "I've got one man with a leg broken by a horse kick and another with a catarrhal affection, but otherwise the ward is empty."

Of adobe construction, the hospital was two hundred yards to the rear of the parade ground and toward the bluffs that rose a half-mile to the east behind the fort. It consisted of one L-shaped building, 28 feet front by 100 feet deep, with Latham's quarters in the wing. In addition to his quarters and the 25-by-25-foot ward, there were the dispensary, a steward's room, a kitchen, a dining room, and a storeroom—all with ceilings 10 feet 6 inches high. The ward had ten beds, providing each patient with 656 cubic feet of air space. There was no bath or washroom, and no water closet connected with the hospital. And there was no surgery.

"We've got good dry air here so we've had no lung troubles," Latham said. "And we've got a good bakery, good water wells, plenty of buffalo and antelope meat so we're pretty well off. And our mail is regular."

There had been some scurvy at the fort from time to time as a result of a lack of fresh vegetables, but army surgeons had soon found a regular source of Vitamin C in the prickly pear cactus. Details gathered the pears on the prairie and pickled them for use as needed.

During the next five days, while waiting for an improvement in the weather and for his stock to get rested, Michael bunked in the surgeon's quarters with Latham. They had a lot to talk about. Bits and pieces of news about the Fort Phil Kearny fight kept coming in on the wire and dominating their conversations, but they also had gossip and news to exchange about Jefferson Barracks, Benton Barracks, Kearny, and Dobytown. The tall and graceful Latham was Michael's equal as a raconteur, and each had a fund of new stories and anecdotes to pass along.

Michael also talked with Latham's hospital steward, Mortier Gale, who would be up for discharge soon and hoped to find a job in the West. "If I don't get those drugs away from you and you finally open a drugstore some place you could do no better than hire Gale as a clerk," Latham said. "He is a good man when sober."

While at the fort Michael did considerable drinking with the officers during long poker sessions. Actually most of the officers were away with the Thirtieth Infantry, but, as Michael laughingly told Latham, "Apparently all the card sharps were left behind in case some innocent happened along."

Riding with Latham over to Julesburg No. 2, he told his enthusiastic guide that the place looked like a junior-grade Dobytown; but Latham, who was already doing a private practice in the budding community, said it would grow when the railroad built in during the coming year. Latham suggested that, with all of those nice drugs in his wagons, Michael might like to set up a drugstore in Julesburg and that they could work out a mutually satisfactory partnership.

But Michael couldn't see Julesburg as anything except another railroad town—a quick boom and then a swift decline after the construction crews moved on west. It would be Dobytown all over again. Besides, he was determined to go on to Denver and then perhaps on to the mines; he had been doing some reading about mining, and it sounded as though there might be some money to be made in that line. It was true, as Latham said, that he had no fixed plan and no fixed goal, but he was confident that a medical man with a stock of drugs would get along all right.

By January 2 the conductor and his drivers were anxious to get on the road again. The snow clouds had cleared out of the area, and the sun was warming it up to a comfortable 40 degrees or so each midday. From the adjutant's office he secured the last pass he would need:

Headquarters, Fort Sedgwick, C.T.
Jan. 2, 1867

Special Order No. 1.
Extract
Mr. M. Beshor, having been appointed conductor of a train whose organization is complete, is hereby permitted to pass this post with train loaded
with drugs
going West
Conductor Beshor will be held strictly responsible for the conduct of the men under his charge, and a failure on their

part to obey all legal orders will be reported to the nearest
Military Commander.

By order of:

Capt. James P. McNeil

Walter Halleck

2nd. Lieut. 18th U.S. Infantry

Post. adjt.

The next morning shortly after sunrise, conductor Beshoar and
his train, augmented by four additional wagons bound for Denver,
started out along the south bank of the Platte on the last two hundred miles of the journey. For the first four or five miles, Latham
rode with him, keeping up a running fire of comment about the
country and its great potentialities. When he turned back, he ex-
acted a promise that Michael would write him as soon as he had
decided on a location.

"You may want to set up in Denver," he said in taking his leave.
"It is growing fast and undoubtedly has a great future. I will probably go to Denver myself in the very near future. In any event I
will see you wherever you do settle."

Denver City, with a population just short of four thousand, was the
largest and most important community in Colorado Territory in
January 1867, enjoying a preeminence it would retain through the
years. It was this same year that it was designated the permanent
capital of the territory. Its leadership, business and professional,
was sharp and aggressive. As the most forward-looking city in the
territory, it was the immediate goal of most of the new people
moving into the mountain West. Many would go on to the mining
areas, but many would stay to build the city. Located at the con-
fluence of the South Platte River and Cherry Creek, where gold had
first been discovered in 1859, the city was out on the plains but had
a superb backdrop of snowcapped peaks a few miles to the west.

Denver boasted good public corrals where trains could put up,
but Michael decided he could save money by setting up a camp on
Cherry Creek, just south and east of the city, while he prospected
the town and decided on his next move. He paid off his drivers,
rehired one as a camp tender and guard, and set forth to hunt up a
couple of former Kearny soldiers and a northeast Arkansas man who

were supposed to be in Denver, but mostly he wanted to see his former St. Louis classmate, Dr. Eugene Gehrung. They had exchanged letters since their St. Louis days, and Michael was carrying Gehrung's card, clipped from the *Rocky Mountain News:* "Dr. Eugene C. Gehrung, physician and surgeon. He may be consulted in the French, English and German languages. Office and residence on Larimer Street, next door to the *News'* office." As it turned out, the *News* had moved three months earlier from the Murdock Building to a spanking new two-and-a-half-story building of its own a short distance away on Larimer, just off G. Street, and the Murdock Building had been taken over by Count Henri Murat, Horace Greeley's whilom barber, who had converted the onetime editorial sanctum into a saloon and poolroom.

Although Michael received a warm welcome from Gehrung he got a cold reception elsewhere in Denver. The town was deep in an anti-southerner campaign led by William N. Byers, editor of the *Rocky Mountain News.* The word was out in Denver: "No Confederates, no Copperheads wanted here." Michael was under no illusion that his service time in St. Louis and Fort Kearny had given him the status of a Union veteran, but he had thought it would spare him some of the opprobrium being heaped on former Confederates. Later he was to understand that the hostility he encountered in Denver was simply an early manifestation of the political tactics that would be pursued by the Republican party and the Grand Army of the Republic on their march to power in the years following the war.

However, in the midst of all the hostility, he turned up several interesting items: the town of Pueblo, south of the divide and on the Arkansas River only 130 miles from Denver, was beginning to show promise; there were said to be quite a few southerners in Pueblo, and the names of the two leading businessmen, John A. Thatcher and Mahlon D. Thatcher, who were engaged in general merchandising, were familiar.

"I went to school with them in Pennsylvania," he told Eugene. "We were classmates at Tuscarora Academy in Academia, just out of Lewistown. I remember them very well."

Inquiries at the shop of G. W. Kassler & Co., dealers in "fine tobaccos, seegars [sic], books, stationery, newspapers, periodicals, &c." disclosed that, while there was one doctor in Pueblo, a Dr. P. R. Thombs, there was no drugstore and no newspaper.

"In fact, there isn't a drugstore of any kind between here and Santa Fe," Kassler told him. "If you should start one, we would be happy to serve you and on terms that would be satisfactory to you."

A growing town, southerners, old Pennsylvania schoolmates, one doctor, no drugstore, and no newspaper—and all on the banks of the good old Arkansas River—sounded just right to Michael at this particular moment. When he told Eugene he had decided on Pueblo, his friend said he hoped the decision wasn't based solely on the hostility he had encountered, as that would undoubtedly be a passing thing. But, he admitted, the arguments for Pueblo were impressive.

With a new set of wagoners, Michael broke his Cherry Creek Camp and headed for the southern part of the territory.

By the end of his first day in Pueblo, Michael was almost physically ill. Having discharged his wagoners, put wagons and stock up in a corral, and engaged a man to watch over them, he treated himself to the luxury of a room in the Planter's Hotel. He took a walk around the adobe village, but there wasn't much to see; the wretched little community had fewer than four hundred residents, although there were said to be another four hundred scattered around the county, which was, insofar as he could see, mostly barren, treeless prairie. There were some magnificent mountains off to the west and south, but there was nothing magnificent about Pueblo. It was bounded on the east by the Fontaine qui Bouille, little more than a dry creek bed, and on the south by the Arkansas River, which bore little resemblance to the Arkansas River of fond memory.

By the end of his second day, he began to feel better. Arrayed in his best suit, a red vest, and his top hat, he had called on the Thatchers to renew boyhood friendships. If they were surprised by all the finery, they didn't show it. They not only welcomed him to Pueblo but found him a suitable building for his drugstore on Santa Fe Avenue, arranged a place where he could keep his goods until the store was ready, and said they would tend to the matter of disposing of his wagons and mules—all at the regular Thatcher commission for such services.

He shed his finery for work clothing when it came to the business of putting his new store together. As in times past he set up his medical office in the drugstore along with a bunk for himself. He put in the shelving himself, bought some used showcases from the Thatchers, and ordered letterheads and cards from the Denver Daily Printing Company, since there was not so much as a job shop in Pueblo. This time he devised a combination letterhead; on one side it listed, "Dr. M. Beshoar, Physician and Surgeon," and on the other, "M. Beshoar, Dealer in Drugs, Chemicals, Toilet Articles, Fine Liquors, Stationery, &c." promised prospective customers "a full assortment of tobaccos, cigars, pipes, and smokers' articles. Also, flavoring extracts, popular games, fresh garden seeds, fishing tackle, sporting goods of every description, and everything generally sold in a Drug and Variety Store." There was nothing like it between Denver and Santa Fe, a distance of four hundred miles—if drugstore meant a place where drugs and other kinds of merchandise, including notions, were sold. A man named Jack Allen had opened a "drugstore" in Pueblo two years earlier, but the name was a misnomer; the place was nothing more than a "Taos Lightning" factory designed to provide the natives with an unbelievably potent whiskey when the regular supplies of this most important of all products failed to get through from the Missouri River. However, there were people in Pueblo who believed a double shot of Allen's special product would cure any ailment. It was said to be made of alcohol, chili, yucca and cactus thorns, old boots, rusty bayonets, and Arkansas River water.

As was Michael's practice, he made a neat entry in his daybook when he was ready for business: "Commenced business at Pueblo, Colorado, Feb. 11, 1867, with mdse $4,900.25. Bills receivable $445.03; cash, $20; owing, $280.00."

After the first few days, Pueblo looked much better to him. The hard physical labor involved in getting his drugstore and office together had raised his spirits, but the big boost came when he discovered that Pueblo boasted a number of educated men. He had known the Thatchers would be gentlemen, but he had not expected to find so many others who could qualify: men such as Wilbur Fisk Stone and George A. Hinsdale, two very able young lawyers destined to play leading roles in the development of the territory and later the state. In his sudden and unexpected enthusiasm for the town, he fired off letters on every stage—to Fort Sedgwick, Dobytown, Fort Kearny, Jefferson Barracks, Benton Barracks; to Major Martin who was again living in Pocahontas, and to Mike in St. Louis. He offered Fort Sedgwick Hospital steward Gale a job in the drugstore and told F. K. Freeman to forget about Nebraska Territory and hurry to Pueblo with a printing press and start a newspaper.

Dr. Latham was one of the first to reply:

> So you are located in the Valley of the Arkansas? I think that is as well as you could do. I am flourishing as usual. My oxen are doing finely. I think I will invest in a small stock of drugs and open a shop at the termination of the railroad. We had a big robbery here a few days ago. The sutler was robbed of $8,000. The 30th Infantry are home and will stay for two months. Business is quite brisk. I know your climate is the best in the world. I think I will try to work south. I hope you may prosper and make your pile. Write often and I will do the same.
>
> Truly,
> H. Latham

In a separate letter from Sedgwick, Gale wrote that he had his discharge in hand and was on his way to Pueblo. John Siddell wrote from Dobytown that he was still trying to sell the drugstore building there and collect accounts, and Mike wrote that he wanted to drop Latin, that a boy had been stabbed by another boy in a corridor between classes, that he was homesick, and that he needed money.

One of the newsiest letters came from F. K. Freeman in Omaha:

> Council Chamber
> Omaha, Nebraska
> Feb. 7, 1867
>
> Dear Doc:
> Your most acceptable letter of Jan. 23rd reached me a day or two since. You must have had a tough time on the road, but I am certainly glad to know you have found a favorable location & that your prospects are so promising. I am tied down here in this confounded abolition radical legislature which will adjourn about the 20th of this month. Soon after which it is conjectured the state legislature will convene, as it is said Congress will drag us in over old Andrew's veto. If, however, the colored amendments do not meet a majority approval a convention of the Territory will be called upon its rejection to frame a new state constitution. I may be kept here for two or three months. I would like very much to join you, but it will

be impossible to do so now. I might arrange to start out in April or May if the Fifth District will release me. There is precious little pleasure in being here with a Legislature that stands two to our one. All we can do is throw brickbats at them.

I received a note from Mrs. Moreland today saying that you desired to know whether I could come out at once with the press &c or not. Also that another party contemplated establishing a paper in Pueblo. If they commence before May they will be ahead of me.

Omaha is not doing a great deal of business. Kearny is dead. Dibble, the A.A.Q.M. has been arrested and is on trial as a defaulter for tons of hay and cords of wood. He has resigned upon the strength of it.

Leigh's prospects in Montana are brightening. He is in the trading and sawmill business and expects to do a handsome business next summer.

How far is Pueblo from Denver and in what direction? You did not tell me how your trip affected your health. I would like to have your opinion of Pueblo as a town of permanence. How far will the U.P.R.R. run from you? Are there any rich mines in your neighborhood? Any Indians, Spaniards or Chinamen near at hand? Any pretty girls with pewter in their pockets? Have you disposed of your teams?

Dr., write immediately and give me all the details. Hoping you are well and flourishing, —I remain, your friend.

F. K. Freeman.

With the one Freeman brother in Montana and F. K. languishing in the territorial legislature in Omaha and their *Frontier Index* shut down while work was suspended for the winter at the railhead in Nebraska, there seemed little chance that either of them could be lured into southern Colorado. By June the Freemans would be in Julesburg publishing the *Index* and would move from there into Wyoming, staying just ahead of the work crews until the work was finished. Michael soon decided that he would either have to entice one of the Denver publishers into the little community on the Arkansas or start a newspaper of his own.

The first few weeks in Pueblo were busy ones, but as soon as

Mortier Gale arrived and familiarized himself with the drugstore, Michael set forth on horseback for a look at his new territory. He rode south, crossed the muddy St. Charles River, and made straight for Hicklin's Greenhorn Ranch on the Huerfano River, where he would make his first stop. Zan Hicklin's place, a few hundred yards from the "orphan" tor that gave the river its name and served as a landmark for travelers, had a spectacular setting. Off to the west were the Greenhorn, or the Cuerno Verde as many called the big mountain, and the snow-capped peaks of the Sangre de Cristo Range, while to the south were the bald mountain that marked La Veta Pass, the peaks of the Culebra Range, and the Spanish Peaks or Wah-hah-toyas. On the southern horizon was Fisher's Peak in the Raton Range, the landmark above the little Mexican village of Trinidad.

The proprietor of Hicklin's Greenhorn Ranch was as spectacular in many ways as the setting. A big, powerfully built man with thick brown stubble on his chin and pale blue eyes set deep in a face creased from much laughing with and at his fellow man, Alexander "Zan" Hicklin had a good, strategically located ranch, raised sheep, and played host to travelers up and down the road between Pueblo and Santa Fe. He was illiterate but a shrewd businessman in many ways. His wife, Estafina, was a daughter of Charles Bent, first territorial governor of New Mexico and brother of William Bent, founder of Bent's Fort. The Hicklin table was a notable one, and most of those who had sampled its regular fare of Mexican beans, chili, stewed apples, savoury steaks and roasts, and hot biscuits and tortillas, all topped off with *sopapillas* served with wild honey, were anxious to do so again. But not all. Zan was a great practical joker whose greatest joy was scaring the wits out of tenderfeet. One of his favorite stunts was to drop the word casually during dinner or supper that the antelope or buffalo meat on the big platters was really young Ute or Arapahoe or Cheyenne, and another was to stand with a confederate or two outside of a guest's door in the black of the night and whisper loudly, "Shall we go in and cut his throat now or wait a bit?"—this to the accompaniment of much scraping of boots on the rough floor. Nothing tickled Zan more than when the frightened guest fled through the window with his clothes.

There was another side to Zan. He had been a southern sympathizer during the war and had aided the rebel cause whenever he got an opportunity. He still referred to himself laughingly as "Old

Secesh." When Michael Beshoar arrived, "Old Secesh" was nursing a deep cut in his left leg from an accident in his corral. After the timely visitor had taken care of the wound, Zan pronounced him the official Greenhorn Ranch physician hence forward and said he was to make the ranch his headquarters as often as he wished.

From Zan's place the physician made a leisurely and pleasant ride to Trinidad, a cluster of adobes on the Purgatoire River with majestic Fisher's Peak as a backdrop on the south. Crossing the river, he rode slowly up Bridge Street, took a turn along the main street, and then reserved a room at William Walker's hotel on the south side of Main. Within an hour after his arrival, he had acquired several patients, who quickly spread the word that a real, live doctor was in town, bringing still more to ask for his professional assistance. In the course of his first twenty-four hours, he took care of a couple of dozen men and met most of the little town's leading citizens: Postmaster William Bransford, Don Felipe Baca, merchant Jesus Maria Garcia, Henry Barraclough, and a number of others both American and Mexican. They were unanimous in declaring that Trinidad urgently needed a doctor and a drugstore and would welcome Michael Beshoar. As for his having been a Confederate, that was all to the good as most of them had also been in the Confederate Army. Upon scouting the area near the town, he found numerous indications of coal, which excited him. Before he returned to Pueblo, he made two major decisions: he would open a drugstore in Trinidad and he would learn Spanish as quickly as possible. He spoke German fluently and had a solid background in Latin and French, but he would need Spanish in the Southwest for the sort of close and intimate relationship a doctor must have with his patients.

The new Trinidad venture, a combined drugstore and medical office was opened in the express office on Main Street on August 16, 1867, under the firm name of "Beshoar & Lynde" with his former drug clerk in Pocahontas in charge. While Sherman Lynde was not a medical doctor, he was an experienced drug clerk and in a medical emergency could be expected to lend a hand. In his daybook Michael noted that the new enterprise began with merchandise valued at $1,140.38 and that the store offered "drugs and medicines, fine liquors, vinegar, toilet articles, tobacco, cigars, smokers articles, sporting articles, stationery and confectionery."

Shortly before opening the Trinidad store, he had the good fortune to sell his old drugstore building in Dobytown. When John Siddell wrote that the building was sold but that he had not had much luck collecting delinquent medical accounts, the physician told him to extract his commission from what he had on hand, to pay any pending Beshoar obligations, and to send the balance to Pueblo. He knew he'd never get a dime on the old medical accounts at this late date. His letter to Siddell must have gone astray, as he next heard from him from Julesburg:

Dear Doc

If you are alive or dead for God's sake let me know as this is the third time I have written you, but still no answer. It may be on account of the wandering life we lead your letters have miscarried. We moved from Kearney to Platte City, stayed there a month and shoved out for this point from whence we expect to be routed ere the next moon. When I came here a month ago Julesburg was no bigger than a portable bean box. Now it contains some 3 or 4 hundred houses, mostly saloons and restaurants well seasoned with gamblers, whores and whore houses. I verily believe that all those wretched cusses who are happily destined to line the road to Hell when that awful day arrives are collected here. You are losing greenbacks by your absence from this delectable hell. In a few weeks clap will be a specialty thick enough to dig off with a shovel. You could not scare up an uglier set of old whores, no, not even in Mexico. Business in lively. Freeman is here printing his Index. I paid him the amount of your indebtedness, so soon as I hear from you I will remit. Hoping you are well and doing well, I am yours &c.

John Siddell

During the fall of 1867, with Gale handling the day-to-day work in Pueblo and Lynde caring for the Trinidad store, Michael traveled back and forth between the two towns, mostly by stage. While he still had reservations about Pueblo and Trinidad, he felt better about his choices every time he got a letter from Arkansas or from one of his former colleagues in St. Louis or Nebraska Territory. Medical college friend Dr. James Folsom wrote that St. Louis was crowded with more than eight hundred doctors and so-called doctors and that the biggest mystery in the river city was how they all managed to make enough to stay alive. He had been to the Christian Brothers' Academy to see Mike, Jr., and had had the boy into town for a visit to the Mercantile Library Hall and other points of interest. "He says he doesn't get much yaller legged chicken, that the fare is common and the discipline strict, but I don't think you can do any better," Folsom said in his letter. "The city is quite healthy though there is some cholera—25 cases last week and 20 deaths, mostly among children under five."

Also during the fall of 1867 Michael decided to move his official residence to Trinidad and to run as a Democratic candidate for the territorial legislature against an incumbent Mexican representative, Tomas Suasso, a miller, to represent Huerfano and Las Animas counties in the Twelfth Representative District. He would rather have run for the territorial council of the Eighth Council District, which included Huerfano, Las Animas, Pueblo, El Paso, and Fremont counties, but his new friend, Pueblo lawyer George A. Hinsdale, wanted that nomination. In the election Michael received 181 votes in Las Animas County to Suasso's 125. Subsequently the official count boosted his majority to 69 votes. Incumbent Suasso claimed he had a majority of 70 votes in neighboring Huerfano County and hence had been reelected by one vote. The *Rocky Mountain News* exulted: "One majority for us: good as a thousand," and later that the Democrats in Trinidad had a jubilee on the basis of the results there consisting of "four grand bonfires with poor whiskey and eggnog. They have rather doleful looking faces tonight on account of the defeat of Dr. Beshoar."

In the resulting contest the Republican majority in the House, deciding that one vote looked just as good to it as it had to the *News* and that it was a true vote, seated Suasso. Hinsdale also had a contest but managed to win a council seat by ousting incumbent B. B. Field.

In selecting Trinidad as his residence, Michael rented a one-room adobe house for sleeping quarters but made no effort to cook for himself as he had the good fortune to join a bachelors' mess conducted by Mrs. Bransford in her comfortable jacal on the northwest corner of Bridge and Main streets. The other boarders were James M. Stoner, county treasurer and former postmaster; Judge Spruce M. Baird, a onetime associate of Sam Houston who was dabbling in the budding land-grant business and bringing sheep and cattle into the territory from New Mexico and Texas; and Tom

Leightensdorfer, who with his brother Eugene had done his first freighting with the Bents as early as 1829 and had been associated with them, at their fort and along the Santa Fe Trail, in one way or another for many years. Leightensdorfer was the son of Gerrasio Probasco Santuario, an Italian soldier of fortune, who had broken jail in Milan, made his way to Switzerland, where he changed his name to John Eugene Leightensdorfer, and then emigrated to the United States and Missouri. And finally there was husband Billy Bransford, who had started as a green young hand working as a freighter for the Bents and later as a supervisor at their fort on the Arkansas in the forties. Billy had always been a so-called free hand who worked for the Bents only intermittently and was free to come and go as he pleased.

It was an interesting group that gathered around the table each day, representing as they did some of the earliest pioneers of the region, but none was more interesting than Mrs. Bransford herself. Red, as she was known, was a handsome woman of forty, a sister of Red Cloud, chief of the Ogalala Sioux who had masterminded the Fetterman ambush and was continuing his efforts to close the Bozeman Trail into Wyoming. Red and an identical twin, according to one story, were married to Marcellin St. Vrain at Fort St. Vrain in 1840 when the girls were only thirteen. Subsequently the sister committed suicide because she thought Marcellin was partial to Red. In the nine years Red lived with Marcellin, she bore him a daughter and two sons, one of whom served in the Confederate Army and died in a Union prison camp.

Between the time he married Red and her sister and the time he returned to Missouri in 1848, Marcellin "married" still another Indian woman, a six-foot-tall Pawnee, who bore him two sons. He abandoned her, and she was last seen with her two children in the vicinity of Pueblo trying to scratch out a living. But Red fared better because Marcellin's brother, Cerañ St. Vrain, cared for her and her children in Mora, New Mexico where he had a store and a gristmill. The diminutive, blackhaired Marcellin was said to have assured Red he would return for her someday, but he did what so many white mountain men and traders did once they abandoned their Indian wives and returned east: on June 26, 1849, he married Elizabeth Jane Murphey in Missouri. Making a quick trip to New Mexico in 1851, he picked up his two sons and took them back to Missouri. After that Red watched for him and her boys for a long time, sitting on top of a small hill staring toward the east. She finally married Billy Bransford and bore him seven children during a long and happy marriage.

Christmas Day 1867 in Trinidad, C.T., was sunny, mild, and alcoholic. It started out quietly and traditionally, with Franciscan Padre Peter John Munnecom, a sturdy and handsome Hollander with curly brown hair and an eye for business and dollars, singing the second, or dawn, Mass of the liturgy in his bare, dirt-floored adobe church. The congregation of swarthy Mexicans and a half-dozen Americans included Michael Beshoar, who, though a convert to Catholicism, would have been more at home attending a simple Dunkard meeting with stolid German farmers in his native Pennsylvania or even a Bible-thumping Baptist service in the Ozarks. After the Mass, the worshipers drifted over to Jesus Maria Barela's corral to watch the cock fights and place a bet or two, after which they made their way to the saloons on Main and Bridge streets for the kind of dedicated drinking and gambling that not only were proper on a festive holiday, but were, in fact, the only amusements available aside from an occasional horse race. Michael, Padre Munnecom, and three or four other congenial persons were settled down at a card table in one of the saloons for some serious drinking and five-card draw when the trouble started. There are several versions of how it began and of the sorry series of events that followed, some of them written by men who were contemptuous of Mexicans, considering them in the same class with Indians, and some by men who came to Colorado long after the incident. The physician, a witness and a participant, had his own version, one that was to bring down on his head the wrath of a number of the Americans of the town.

The trouble began on Main Street when a drunken American, obviously looking for trouble, offered to wrestle any one of a crowd of Mexicans who were standing around talking near the intersection of Main and C streets. A stout young Mexican named Pablo Martinez accepted the challenge, promptly flipped the American on his back, and pinned him. When Martinez let the American up, there were angry words, the American charging that Martinez threw him before he was ready to wrestle. "Put up your hands and fight, you Greaser," the American yelled drunkenly. More angry words were passed, but no blows were struck. Frank Blue, a stage driver, gambler, and regular patient of Michael's, was drinking in a saloon close by. When he heard the commotion, he ran out of the saloon brandishing a Colt navy revolver, but before he reached the American and Martinez, he was struck by a stone. With that Blue fired directly at Martinez. Now there were enraged yells on all sides, stones were thrown at Blue, and several revolvers were discharged. Americans who ran to the scene also picked up rocks and began hurling them at Mexicans, who returned them with will.

When the physician, hastily summoned from his card game, arrived, he found Pablo Martinez dead, "having received two gun shot wounds, one in the neck and one in the right hypochondrium. Charles Lafera, an American, was seriously wounded and a number of other Americans and Mexicans were slightly wounded, principally by stone throws."

The crowd went after Blue, who took refuge in a nearby adobe house on the south side of Main Street. The furious Mexicans tore the roof off, but Blue escaped by kicking out the back of a fireplace to get into a second room. The crowd was attempting to break into it when Deputy Sheriff Juan Cristobal Tafoya and Jesus Maria Barela appeared and, with drawn guns, succeeded in quieting and dispersing the belligerents.

Blue had not fired the only shots. Some other Americans had taken shots at whatever Mexicans were within range, and no doubt some of the Mexicans had fired revolvers too. But the American firing was joyous and unrestrained according to Charles Christy, who rushed into the fray [to give his all in the cause of bad racial relationships.] His unabashed account of the affair is pretty typical of the attitudes of a majority of the Americans who joined the fight.

". . . I was celebrating Christmas Day at Trinidad, Colorado by getting gloriously drunk, and I was feeling just ripe for a row, which up to that hour had been the only thing lacking to round out my day to my perfect enjoyment. But all things come to him who waits and that Christmas Day was destined to bring me all the joy I wanted.

"I was in one of the side rooms of a dance hall when a row suddenly broke loose among some Greasers and whites in the street, and yells, oaths and shots rang out all at once. The sound was music to my ears and I rushed out to enjoy it. A free-for-all fight was in full swing and I was just drunk enough to mix in without stopping to think who was in the right or wrong; it was enough for me to see that the Greasers and Gringoes were hard at work slugging one another.

"Putting my back against an adobe wall, I began blazing away with my six shooters at every Mexican in sight. My first shot went wild and the Greaser I aimed at took advantage of the moment to hit me in the jaw with a rock. I fixed him though; my next shot took him in the mouth and tumbled him in the gutter. My third shot rolled another off the flat roof of a shanty across the street, where he was aiming to get the drop on me, and he fell to the ground dead. With every crack of my six shooters I let out a yell that beat a Comanche war whoop. But suddenly a bullet hit me a glancing clip on the side of the head and I went down and out for the rest of the fight."

The dance hall from which Christy had emerged so bravely was turned into a hospital, and Michael began the task of patching up the wounded, Mexican and American.

An hour or so later, Sheriff Juan Gutierrez, armed with a writ from Justice of the Peace Barela, put Frank Blue under arrest, charged with the murder of Pablo Martinez, and lodged him in a vacant adobe building that served as a makeshift jail. Because there was so much racial feeling, Sheriff Gutierrez deputized a special guard, which varied from four to twelve men, half Americans and half Mexicans, to stay in the room with the shackled Blue and keep watch over him.

At an examination held before Justice Barela beginning on December 26, a large number of witnesses were heard, both for the defense and the prosecution. Michael Beshoar gave testimony regarding the gunshot wounds. Crowds gathered outside the hearing room while Deputy Sheriff Juan Tafoya and several other deputies, armed with rifles, kept an eye on them. The examination continued steadily until the evening of the thirty-first, when it was recessed until January 2.

Feelings in the community ran high when, on the night of December 30, someone (it was assumed that it was a Mexican, but it could just as well have been an American seeking to stir up more trouble) fired a shot through the window of Blue's jail room. Early the next morning several Americans complained to Deputy Sheriff Tafoya that "someone" designed the assassination of Blue and that he must be better protected. The deputy sheriff said that if they would tell him who fired the shot, or whom they had reasons to suspect, he would arrest him; and that he too would try to find the guilty party and "promised that he would place a guard outside the house, which evidences of good disposition on the part of the deputy sheriff were satisfactory to the majority of the American population."

But this was all just so much talk, as neither the Americans who were satisfied with these precautions nor the sheriff knew what was in store for their community. After Blue's arrest, one of his pals, a gambler named John Dunn, had slipped out of Trinidad and gone to Cimarron, New Mexico, where he solicited the assistance of a small detachment of troops, claiming that Mexicans were just about to murder all of the Americans in Trinidad. But the officer in charge said he could not take any action without direct orders from Fort Union. Dunn next fell in with a party of men headed for the Moreno Mines, and representing himself as the sheriff of Las Animas County, Colorado, called upon them to help rescue the Trinidad Americans. They agreed.

In his report of the affair, Michael wrote:

> On the night of 31st Dec. ten Americans, names unknown to deponent, said to be miners, arrived in Trinidad and took lodging in P. B. Sherman's Hotel. During the same night or early the next morning John Dunn, who had left Trinidad the night of the 28th or 29th and gone to Red River, arrived on the coach. The miners and he expressed it as their business to release Blue. At about 7 or 8 o'clock in the morning, Dunn called the miners into line in front of P. B. Sherman's Hotel and called for additional volunteers to rescue Blue. Three or four joined him at that time. He then marched them to the place where Blue was confined and told Deputy Sheriff Juan Tafoya, who was in charge of the guard, that he was relieved from duty as sheriff. Tafoya, being overpowered, surrendered and the prisoner was released. As soon as Blue was released he was given arms by Dunn's party who were well armed and the party then commenced firing at any Mexican in sight. With regard to who fired the first gun deponent's information is somewhat conflicting. The Mexicans charge that an American commonly known to them as Little Keno and one of the Dunn party fired the first gun. Of the Americans present about half corroborate the Mexican charge and the other half claim that a

Mexican fired first.

Dunn's party, having killed and stampeded all Mexicans on the main business street proceeded to P. B. Sherman's Hotel and the new house of Wise & Swatzkoff directly opposite and placed a picket over Davis & Barraclough's store. Tafoya immediately commenced raising a posse to retake the prisoner and to arrest Dunn and his party and in three hours had some 200 men which was increased during the day to 300 men.

While all this was going on, a number of Americans rushed to Sherman's Hotel and aided the Dunn men in fortifying it. Holes were punched in the walls to permit firing at anyone approaching, and arms and food were assembled from nearby business establishments. The motives of the Americans who went into the hotel with Dunn varied widely: some feared the Mexicans were so aroused over the Blue killing they would massacre all Americans, some simply disliked Mexicans so much they welcomed a confrontation regardless of the merits of the case, and some obviously were helping their "white brothers."

At the outset the physician took a public stand: he would not join the besieged Americans in the hotel and he would not actively assist the Mexicans in their efforts to dislodge the Americans and capture them. As the only physician within ninety miles, he would keep a neutral stance; he would treat the wounded of both sides. The Americans in the hotel growled that "any white man worthy of the name" would be in the hotel helping them fight off the Mexican demons outside. The Americans who remained on the outside took the position they were supporting law and order in the persons of the duly elected authorities in charge of the posse, though admittedly there were Mexicans wild with anger and ready to kill the Americans in the hotel if they could get their hands on them.

Putting guards at each end of town, the sheriff stopped all coaches and escorted them around the town. None was allowed to go along Main Street to the regular stage station. Michael's report said:

"The sheriff divided his men into several parties and placed them at several posts about town, the largest in Jesus Maria Barela's corral, about 100 yards from Dunn's men, the others so as to cut off escape by any direction, and to cut off all access to water and to prevent anyone from showing himself outside of the houses. The stores were nearly all in the possession of Dunn's party and from them they supplied themselves with whatever arms, ammunitions and provisions they required, forcibly if the merchants did not supply them freely. During the day, Mr. Gray, who is one of the county commissioners, went to the sheriff under a flag of truce to enquire what terms would be offered Dunn's party. The reply was that if Blue, Dunn and two others who were named were given up the rest would not be molested. Dunn's party sent back an answer that the four mentioned would leave the place not to return if the sheriff would require four certain Mexicans [Roules, Lame Frank, Liestes Martinez and one other] to leave the place and not return."

The sheriff rejected the proposals. Tension rose sharply in both camps when two hundred Utes rode into Trinidad and offered to get the Americans out of their improvised fort. The sheriff rejected the offer and warned the Indians that if they interfered in any way he would attack them with his force. The warriors then went to a near-by hill just south of the village, made fires to warm themselves, and watched the show from the best vantage point in the area.

Throughout New Year's Day, Michael took care of wounded and held himself available to go to the hotel or to any of the posts set up by the sheriff. He was irritated that Sherman Lynde, who should have been helping him, was in the hotel giving his support to Dunn and Blue. At the close of the first day, the Mexicans had two dead and seventeen wounded while the Americans in the hotel had three with minor wounds.

During the night of January 1, while Mexican sentries peered into the frigid blackness and the Ute campfires blinked on the hillside, Blue, Dunn, Gus Rande, and J. Flathead took four Spencer carbines from their sleeping comrades-in-arms, loaded themselves with most of the ammunition in the hotel, and slipped out and through the Mexican guards. They managed to steal three horses and make their getaway. When their absence was discovered, some of the Americans wanted to surrender then and there, but, after heated arguments it was determined to wait until morning.

After daylight there were more angry arguments in the hotel. Some of the hotheads, who were sure that one American was worth any number of Mexicans, wanted to continue to fight, but the plight of the group was now desperate and most of them had sense enough to realize it. They had had no water for many hours and no prospects of getting any. They had lost four rifles and most of their ammunition. More importantly, morale was extremely low.

Commissioner Gray and E. F. Mitchell again went to the sheriff to discuss possible terms, but the sheriff had had enough. He sent them back with word that, if the Americans did not capitulate by sundown, he would take the hotel and adjacent business houses by direct assault or by burning them out.

With Gray still serving as intermediary, a plan was then worked out whereby each side would name three commissioners to draw up the terms of surrender. The Mexicans named Lorenzo A. Abeyta, Juan H. Gutierrez, Jr., and Juan Tafoya, all leading citizens, while the Americans picked hotelman Philo B. Sherman, D. L. Taylor, and Captain O. M. Smith. The six men, meeting in a closed room, haggled for more than an hour and a half before they agreed that fifteen men whom the Mexicans considered "ring leaders," now that Blue and Dunn were gone, were to be jailed and charged. The remainder would be held for their own safety until the next morning, January 3, when they would be permitted to keep their arms and go about their business after first taking an oath to support the civil authorities in the future. The group in the hotel agreed, and the battle was over. Some of the Americans who surrendered were noncombatants. They had simply been trapped and had been unable to get away.

At a citizens' meeting, resolutions were adopted calling for the intervention of troops on the grounds that only a third party could restore peace and order in the town. A total of thirty-four signed, about half of them Mexicans. One of the Americans who signed, Michael Beshoar, made a short speech, telling the group that he agreed troops were indicated but that he felt the sheriff's officers had handled themselves well under severe provocation by "roughs." He referred to the affair as a riot caused by "bad booze and bad blood," whereas some of the jailed Americans, of whom A. W. Archibald was an example, called it a war and referred to themselves as "prisoners of war."

The Americans in the hotel had also managed to send messengers, even before their surrender, to Forts Lyon and Reynolds asking for aid; hence petitions for troops came from both sides. A further call reached the world outside of Trinidad through the stories of a *Rocky Mountain News* correspondent, covering the affair from the safety and comfort of Pueblo. His lurid dispatches contained such passages as, "The Mexican forces on the outside are being augmented by the hour. It is presumed by this time that they number at least five hundred. If such is the case the little band of whites must be in a critical situation with the five hundred worse than savage demons outside burning with all that insatiable spirit of revenge known to their nature which can only be gratified and their treacherous natural and avengeful spirit appeased by the shedding of blood and the slaughter of all those their crazy imagination leads them to believe has given the slightest provocation. I am informed messengers have been dispatched to Forts Union and Reynolds for military assistance. A general uprising is anticipated; large bodies of Mexicans from Taos and other Mexican towns (and) if the ball keeps rolling it may be interesting—Colorado against New Mexico—grand opportunity for chivalrous characters to display their military ability in a war with poor Mexicans. I sympathize with them, think the government should send out commissioners to make a treaty and select a reservation. They should be liberally furnished with extract of corn and chile and placed on a pleasant reservation in Walrussia where they can enjoy bear hunting unmolested by poor uncivilized whites."

The Denver correspondent reported there were "seven Mexicans dead and more that ought to be . . . we are expecting a messenger every hour from the seat of war. We wait with breathless expectation for news to expel the horrors of our overwrought imagination."

The day before this appalling report appeared in the capital city, the "Trinidad War" ended with the arrival of Brevet Brigadier General William H. Penrose and Captain Matthew Berry with three companies of mounted infantry and C Company of the Seventh Cavalry after a fantastic march: 130 miles in thirty hours in temperatures ranging as low as 26 degrees below zero. The troops left Fort Lyon at sundown Friday, January 3 and arrived in Trinidad at 8 A.M. Sunday, January 5 with half the original complement of men and horses. Four hours later Lieutenant Henry H. Abell came in from Fort Reynolds at the head of Company L of the Seventh Cavalry after a spectacular ride of 126 miles in the severe cold. Soon afterward Mexican and American volunteers set out in wagons to rescue men who had dropped out of the forced marches.

General Penrose immediately put the town under martial law with Captain Berry, a rough-and-ready redhead, as provost marshal. The citizens were summoned to Alires Hall, where Judge S. M. Baird introduced General Penrose and Captain Berry. The two officers spoke briefly, managing to please everyone—so much so they received cheer after cheer. They said peace would be maintained in the community and the fifteen men in jail would remain there until the due processes of law could be carried out.

At a meeting later that night, prominent Mexicans and Americans decided they ought to put the sheriff's side of the case, the law-enforcement side, before the governor as quickly as possible. They had not yet seen a Denver newspaper, but they were pretty sure the *Rocky Mountain News* would carry hostile and distorted dispatches. As the only man present with journalistic experience, Michael assured the group that not only would the first reports in the newspapers be unfavorable but that Archibald and others hostile to the Mexicans would take their stories to the Denver newspapers as soon as they got out of jail. Before the meeting ended Michael roughed out a written report, and it was agreed he would go to Pueblo, give U.S. Marshal Holloway an oral report, and then go on to Denver and present the written report to Acting Governor Frank Hall "on behalf of the civil officers and citizens of Las Animas County." Before he left on the coach the next morning, the physician amputated a wounded Mexican's leg and had an unpleasant session with drug clerk Sherman Lynde over his part in the riot. He asked Lynde and Lieutenant Abell to contact Assistant Surgeon Fitzgerald at the army camp and ask him to look after the wounded.

In the capital he gave an interview to the *Tribune*, presented the report to the governor, and then hurried back to Trinidad by the next coach. The *Tribune* story of the interview, which was similar to the report he gave the governor, brought an angry response from Americans who had been in the hotel and from some who had not. They met and adopted a series of resolutions: "1st, 2nd and 3rd Resolutions—compliments to Penrose, Abel and Berry; 4th, that the statements in the *Colorado Tribune* of the 9th inst. purporting to have been given by Dr. M. Beshoar of Trinidad are a gross misapprehension of facts and a libel on the law abiding citizens of the town; 5th, that the sheriff and others tried to engage the Indians to indiscriminantly massacre Americans; 6th, praying for troops; 7th, to publish the above in the principal newspapers." The signatures of thirty-one Americans, including lawyer A. W. Archibald and Sherman Lynde, were affixed to the resolutions.

There were some other aftermaths to the riot: Sheriff Gutierrez resigned, as did Justice Barela, and the complaints against the fifteen Americans jailed after the hotel siege were withdrawn, officially because of "lack of evidence" but also because the county was broke—didn't have money to feed or prosecute them—and by common consent felt it was better to let the whole business die as quickly as possible. A few days after the Americans were discharged, Acting Governor Hall paid a visit and promised that troops would remain as long as necessary. This made everyone happy, as troops meant business in a little western town with no other markets available.

There was one last round to be fired: From Fort Lyon, Assistant Surgeon J. A. Fitzgerald sent Michael a bill for thirty dollars for his medical services. Since he knew he wouldn't ever receive a dime from the patients, Michael blew off to Captain Berry, who reported his reaction to Fitzgerald no doubt with some embellishment. In a nasty letter, the army surgeon said he could have made "some interesting fees" had he known that Beshoar didn't intend to pay him and that he would be in Trinidad soon "when you can find me if you have an apology to make." Michael sent back a sizzler, devoting two pages to the subject of reciprocity among physicians, and concluding by saying Fitzgerald could "have any satisfaction that could be expected among gentlemen." Fitzgerald hastily replied that "harmony is preferable to me than misunderstandings of this nature."

The Trinidad War was closed.

Michael Beshoar, thin from malaria during the Civil War.

Buffalo clothing was none too heavy for winter in a Nebraska fort.

Trinidad's main street in 1867.

Family group in 1882: Michael and Annie with daughters Bonaventura and baby Benedicta, and Annie's parents, Mr. and Mrs. John Maupin.

"Red" Bransford, sister of Red Cloud, aunt of Crazy Horse, and Michael Beshoar's first landlady in Trinidad.

Michael in 1863—age thirty.

Winifrit Terry, Michael's first wife.

M. BESHOAR,
Pueblo, Colorado,
DESTRIBUIDOR en DRUGAS,
Medicinas, Liquores finos, Colores,
Escobetias, Pedrerias, Libros y Estacionares,
Aparejos de pescar, Municiones, Efector de reca-
mara y Nociones en Generalemente.
DENVER DAILY, PRINT.

Drs. BESHOAR & GREEN,
PRACTICING
PHYSICIANS, SURGEONS,
AND ACCOUCHEURS,
TRINIDAD, COLORADO.

This prescription may be prepared by any competent druggist.

The druggist must write the directions distinctly. No fancy hand nor flourishes are tolerable, and the letters of one line must in no instance encroach on any of another, neither above nor below.

When the directions are in any other than the English language, every letter, capital and lower case, and punctu-ation and accent mark, must be accurately copied.

The name of the patient and date of the prescription must in no instance be omitted.

In no case will the druggist repeat the filling of a pre-scription without the written order of the writer. The di-rections must be written with ink, pencil writing cannot be permitted.

Omission to observe any of the above requirements will be sufficient to characterize the druggist as incompetent and unsafe.
M. BESHOAR, M. D.
H. L. GREEN, M. D.

The card above (1867) advertised the first drugstore between Denver and Santa Fe. The one at right (1862) is on the back of a prescription form.

Trinidad in the late 1800s, Fishers Peak in the background. The business district was built on the south side of the Purgatoire River.

This magnificent rococo Victorian house on Main Street, built in the 1880s by cattleman Frank Bloom, is now a state-owned museum.

The Southern Hotel on Commercial Street was a fine hostelry in the late 1800s. In the background is Simpson's Rest.

Chapter 5
Launching the "Chieftain"

WITH THE RACE WAR a closed incident, except for the continued presence of seventy-five troopers in a camp on a hill two blocks south of Main Street and some antagonisms that would take a while to heal, Michael resumed his practice in Trinidad and Pueblo, traveling back and forth between the two towns. His mind was feverish with money-making schemes. He prospected a hogback on the Apishapa River a few miles north of Trinidad and scouted the piñon-clad hills north and west of town looking for signs of gold, but he was well south and east of the Colorado mineral belts. He found frequent outcroppings of coal and made notes on them, but there was no industry and hence no market for it within hundreds of miles. In addition to prospecting he opened a second business in Trinidad, the Eldorado, in competition with the Exchange Billiard Saloon. Both places had bars, but his Eldorado boasted the only Phelan billiard tables (the best brand name of the day) in southern Colorado, brought all the way across the plains from St. Louis. The physician also startled the citizens of Trinidad by shipping in the town's first buggy. It was assembled by a blacksmith with much encouragement and gratuitous advice from a throng of experts, including Michael's bachelors' mess companion Judge Baird, a man of florid countenance and bleary eye, who explained the construction and fine points of the contraption and swore that it marked the dawn of a more civilized era in southern Colorado. The blacksmith had no trouble until he got to the tires. He couldn't make them stay on, but the difficulty was solved by Judge Baird's suggestion that they be tied on with strips of rawhide. The judge's ingenuity earned him the first ride, which honor he acknowledged by making a short christening speech and pouring a little bourbon on the buggy before climbing up beside the physician. The judge, who sometimes

wore red flannel underwear over his outer clothing, to the amaze-
ment of strangers and the amusement of his intimates, was a regular
in periodic all-night poker games with Michael, Billy Bransford,
and Father Munnecom. They played for blood and stayed at it until
just after dawn, when a devout Mexican layman tolled the church
bell to summon the faithful and the celebrant to Mass. The padre,
to the delight of his fellow players and anyone else within hearing,
always said the same thing when he threw his cards down: "There
goes that damned bell again."

Michael enjoyed a social life that extended beyond his bloodthirsty poker games. During sojourns in Pueblo he frequently escorted "respectable women" to Masonic affairs, often danced the
night through to "The Arkansas Traveler," "Five Miles From
Town," "The Devil's Dream," and "Soapsuds Over the Fence,"
while the pots and pans and skillets hanging from the ceiling of
Thatcher's store, immediately beneath Rice's Hall, danced and
jangled despite the two-by-fours that were put in to prop the ceiling
whenever a dance or gala ball was held.

The business operations and his practice, spread out as they
were over such a large area, should have been enough to keep a
man busy, but Michael Beshoar was about ready for new enterprises, particularly the newspaper business. There was no newspaper nearer than Denver, and he felt strongly that Pueblo and the
rest of southern Colorado must have a voice if they were to move
ahead. Of course there were problems: in this miserable winter of
1867–68, times were hard, money was difficult to come by, the
weather was extremely bad, and Indian bands that normally sus-
pend operations during the winter months had been forced out of
their lodges by hunger. They had raised such hob along the trails
that the military had held up traffic between Fort Larned, Kansas,
and Fort Lyon, Colorado. Those who had to travel did so at their
own peril and mostly at night; the mail coaches were being escorted
by soldiers. Certainly it was an unpromising atmosphere for a new
business of any kind.

There had been a newspaper, the *Times*, in nearby Canon City,
but after a brief period of starvation, it had closed up shop in the
winter of 1862–63 and moved north into South Park near the
mining town of Fairplay. The only other newspapers were also in
the northern part of the territory—papers such as Byers' *Rocky
Mountain News*, Woodbury's *Tribune*, Fred Stanton's *Gazette*, all

in Denver, and the *Colorado Transcript* in Golden City. But the vast and empty area bounded by Denver and Santa Fe and Council Grove and Salt Lake City was without a newspaper.

"Looking at it purely as an opening, it seems to be a big thing," the physician jokingly told friends in Pueblo, Canon City, and Trinidad as he began a campaign to raise $3,000 in advance subscriptions and advertising. At the outset he intended making the newspaper a Democratic organ, but soon after beginning his canvass he decided he would publish a nonpartisan paper—as the Democrats talked a good game but were tight when it came to money. In Fremont County, Thomas Macon of Canon City, a Democratic party leader, started out with enthusiasm to raise $500 for the venture, but finally wrote the physician:

> I have seen almost every man in the county and have succeeded in getting but three who would agree to sign the subscription paper & they would only agree to five dollars. I never was more deceived in my life. I had hoped and been led to believe from conversations with different men that I could get from three to four hundred dollars, but when I called on them to show their faith by their works they showed the white feather most ingloriously. They all say they will take the paper and some say they will take two copies and I believe they will, but they are afraid to pay anything until they see the paper.

It was the same story every place: lots of encouragement but little in the way of hard cash. But Michael was convinced that he was an agent of progress and that he would play an important role "in the development of one of the greatest empires in the world on its way to destined greatness" if he started a newspaper. A newspaper would provide the southern half of the territory and the northern part of New Mexico with a political voice; also, by making known the potential of the area, it would lure settlers; and finally it would act as a civilizing influence to insure law and order. He also admitted to a certain amount of bitterness toward the Denver establishment and its newspapers for the manner in which they played politics and ignored the southern part of the territory.

If he couldn't raise enough money to launch his newspaper and carry it during its early months, then he would do as he had done before: start it on credit and nurture it with what he could make practicing medicine and carrying on a drug business.

He named his new enterprise the *Colorado Chieftain*, ordered a Washington hand press and other printing equipment, including a stock of paper, through Stebbins & Porter of Denver and secured a site on East Fourth Street between Santa Fe and Summit. He got part of the site by filing on it with the United States Land Office in Denver at a cost of $3.75, a filing made possible when Probate Judge Mark Bradford entered Pueblo as a townsite in the land office. He bought an adjacent lot and a shell of a house from Philander Craig, who, in a burst of civic pride at the thought of Pueblo having a newspaper, remitted seventy-five dollars of his asking price as his advance subscription.

Since there were no printers in the southern part of the territory, Michael went to Denver to find one. He stayed away from the *News* and the *Gazette*, but editor Woodbury of the *Tribune*—with whom he had corresponded as to the possibility of Woodbury's investing in a newspaper in Pueblo—suggested that a good man might be found on the *Colorado Transcript* in Golden City. In Golden, Michael told *Transcript* editor and proprietor Captain George West that he was looking for "a good compositor and a good job printer, and one who can write locals if necessary."

Captain West said he had a man subbing in his office who was a gentleman in the full sense and possessed all the required qualifications, but who was, "on his last legs with consumption."

The physician asked whether the man was temperate and, assured that he was, said he'd like to meet him as he'd rather have a dying but temperate printer than a vigorous drunken one. Taken to the back shop, the physician was presented to Sam McBride. He liked him on sight and, after outlining what he proposed to do in Pueblo and showing McBride a duplicate of his order for press and material, offered him the job as foreman and job printer. He would be allowed to pay his personal expenses out of current receipts and receive as salary half of the net profits for a period of three years. Any losses would be the responsibility of Michael Beshoar and would be paid by him. In addition, McBride would be listed in the masthead as coproprietor of the *Chieftain*.

Sam's eyes glistened. "It's a layout," he said. "But I'm so far gone with consumption I probably won't live six months. And in those six months I probably couldn't be of much service."

"Take off your shirt," the physician said.

While the others watched, McBride was given an examination.

"You don't have consumption," Beshoar said. "You have a severe and chronic bronchitis, tracheitis and laryngitis. You come to Pueblo with me and I'll make a stout and healthy man out of you before the end of the three years."

"I'll take it," McBride said.

Since Sam was poor as a "lame coyote," in the words of his new associate, the physician gave him money for coach fare, told him to get on down to Pueblo, and do what he could around the building until the press and other equipment arrived.

In hiring McBride, factors other than Captain West's recommendation entered into Michael's thinking: he and Sam seemed to hit it off well, and the printer was a fellow Mason and, it turned out, a brother of Justice of the Peace Pat McBride of Trinidad. The clincher was that Sam, unlike his brother, was indeed a temperate man, a rare and highly desirable quality in a printer for a town where there were no subs on call.

Michael took the stage from Golden to Central City, spent a couple of days looking over mining properties, and then staged it back to Denver, where he found his paper and press had arrived. He was short a thousand dollars of what he needed to pay for the shipments and send them on their way to Pueblo via freighter Pat Dolan and his mules. Everyone at Stebbins & Porter looked grave for a few minutes, but the matter was settled when Henry M. Porter sat down, wrote out a personal check for the needed $1,000, and handed it over, saying, "Pay me back when you can."

Since Denver was a small town and everyone knew what everyone else was doing, the arrival of the press, type cases, and other material was a matter of common knowledge. The *Rocky Mountain News* announced April 14, 1868: "The publication of a paper at Pueblo seems to be a certainty. Dr. Beshoar has associated with him Mr. S. H. McBride, an experienced and practical printer, and the material has been in town for several days, will be sent on to its destination this week. The paper is to be called the *Colorado Chieftain*, will be independent in politics and issued weekly. It will be devoted to the great material interests of the Arkansas Valley and for this purpose has our most cordial wishes for success."

Before a jubilant Michael caught a stage south, political leaders Charles Thomas and Hog Johnson called on him and suggested he forget Pueblo and establish a Democratic newspaper in Denver.

"Not a chance," he told them. "I'm about to fill the biggest journalistic hole anyone ever saw with a good, nonpartisan newspaper."

When the Washington hand press and a small job press had been installed, Michael told his new partner they should plan on getting out their first issue in late June but that he hoped they could start taking in printing jobs immediately as they needed every cent they could get. Sam McBride agreed. They made the first stone out of pine boards. The editorial desk was a large box in which glass had been shipped; they nailed legs onto the crate and set it up in the front room of the two-room building. A light barrel was sawed halfway through the middle. The unsawed upper half made the back, and the perfect lower half, filled with straw and covered with gunny sack, completed the editor's chair. Sleeping bunks, three tiers high, were built into the front room to permit use of the editorial and business office as a dormitory at night.

"I'll take the top one because it is warmest in the summer," the physician told Sam, who coughed before he replied: "And in the wintertime too."

But Michael knew he could not practice medicine in two towns ninety miles apart, make long calls off the beaten paths when emergencies arose, solicit subscriptions and printing over the vast territory, and still do all the writing for his *Chieftain*. His solution was to set up a scholarly volunteer editorial board to carry the writing burden. Several of the best-educated and most distinguished citizens of the community agreed to serve, providing the *Chieftain* with an editorial staff far superior to the crude, barely literate editors who held forth in the average frontier newspaper shop. The board consisted of:

(1) Wilbur Fisk Stone, a native of Litchfield, Connecticut, graduate of the University of Indiana School of Law, former tutor in its classical department, and former editor of the *Evansville* (Indiana) *Daily Enquirer*. He was practicing law in Pueblo in 1868 and was to become one of the promoters of the Rio Grande Railroad and a member of the Federal Court of Private Claims. He was well-versed in Spanish and was an historian and writer of considerable ability.

(2) George A. Hinsdale, a fine writer and lawyer who, after service in the territorial council, was to become lieutenant governor of Colorado.

(3) Moses Hallett, sometimes known as "Moses the Meek."

Hallett had been named chief justice of the territorial supreme court in 1866 and had been assigned to the Southern District. A shy, industrious man with tenacious opinions, Hallett was to remain chief justice until statehood in 1876 and then serve on the federal district bench until his retirement in 1908.

(4) Henry C. Thatcher, a member of the banking-business family.

(5) The Rev. F. S. Winslow, rector of St. Peter's (Episcopal) Church.

(6) Dr. H. C. Miller, surgeon at Fort Reynolds.

With two exceptions, all were in agreement that the *Chieftain* should be nonpartisan and nonpolitical, should at all times play hard to get with the politicians on the ground that politicians take their partisans for granted and devote their energies and money to wooing the indifferent and hostile. Hinsdale, an intense partisan, thought a newspaper ought to support a political party, and McBride thought it would be good business for the *Chieftain* to be Democratic and an offset to Byers and his *Rocky Mountain News*, deep in Republican and Union Army politics.

In the first week in April, while busy with his canvassing and other preparations for the newspaper, the physician had an unexpected patient. He was working in the *Chieftain* office when a message came from his medical office to the effect that General Kit Carson, en route by coach to his home at Boggsville eighty-five miles east of Pueblo, was ill and wanted to see him. The physician reached his office only a minute or two before Carson, who had been having something to eat at the Planter's. The general, a man of sixty with light brown hair tinged with gray, was the same size as Michael—five feet six inches—and strongly built. He looked tired and drawn, and explained that he had contracted a severe cold in Washington and that the doctors there, in New York, and Boston, had not been able to help him. Under questioning, he revealed that, in addition to the cough, he had been suffering from chest and neck pains for some time and that he had frequent attacks when "I can hardly breathe."

After his examination Michael knew he couldn't help Kit Carson either. The scout's heart action was rapid and he had an aneurism of the carotid artery—a bulge in the weakened wall of the artery— big enough to be seen. It might break any time. It could be a matter of minutes, hours, days, or weeks, but death was imminent. He advised the general to stay over for a couple of days' bed rest before going on to Boggsville, but Carson said that was impossible; his wife was expecting and he had to get home as soon as possible. Michael gave him syrup of wild cherry with opium to quiet his cough and tincture of veratrum to regulate his heart action, advised him to see Surgeon Tilton at Fort Lyon as soon as he got home. "What do I owe you, Doctor?" the general asked and fished three silver dollars out of a pocketbook to pay the fee. As he was leaving, the physician added some horehound drops and a plug of tobacco to his offering of remedies. The general, with a glance at the street outside, where a small crowd had collected to see the famous frontiersman, gave the medical man a friendly half salute and a "muchas gracias, compadre" as he left.

The next day Michael left by horseback for Trinidad to tend to patients and business, putting up overnight at Zan Hicklin's. As he rode up, he was surprised to see two bodies hanging from a cottonwood tree about 150 yards from the house. Hicklin, quite proud of the two figures swaying gently in the wind, told the physician he planned to cut them down and dispose of them in the morning.

"Chicken thieves," he snorted. "Damned chicken thieves. I'm a justice of the peace now, Doc, so I gave them a fair trial and then hanged them."

The next morning while everyone was at breakfast, a messenger rode in from Pueblo, took his place at the table, and ate swiftly. When he had finished, he said most politely that the U.S. Marshal had sent him down, that he understood Hicklin had some chicken thieves and was going to hang them.

"The marshal says you can't do that," the messenger said. "He told me to tell you to send them up to Pueblo for trial."

Hicklin brought his fist down on the table with a bang and yelled: "The hell I can't. You go take a look out yonder."

Although Michael had told Sam McBride they would probably not get their first issue on the press until late June, they finally set the third week in May as the time for their bow to the area. As they neared the target date, M. C. Reed, a local genius who practiced dentistry, paperhanging, photography, and sign-painting when he wasn't drinking, made them a sign "Chieftain Printing Office." He painted it on canvas tacked to a board, which was then put up with one end nailed to the *Chieftain* building and the other to a post set up six feet in front of the entrance. It made the building look like a newspaper office. Sam printed up letterheads, ornate affairs that listed M. Beshoar and Sam McBride as proprietors and offered "Every Variety, Plain and Fancy Printing, executed at the lowest prices!" The price of the newspaper was set at five dollars a year, three dollars for six months, and twenty-five cents per copy.

Michael went back to Trinidad to try to collect some of his accounts and raise more subscriptions. He had not been gone more than four days when he received a letter from Sam:

Pueblo, C.T.
May 4, 1868

Dr. M. Beshoar:

Dear Sir: Have been busy painting the sashdoors, etc. of the office, and if I can get enough glass tomorrow I will put it in. Then the building will be ready for use. I am expecting the arrival of the material. There are 4,292 pounds and it was shipped at 1 3/4¢ per pound, which will amount to $75.11. The money and orders came in good time; but for them I do not know how I could have met the freight bill. If I succeed in collecting all the orders you sent we can, with the cash subscriptions we will be able to collect on issuing the first number, get the concern running in pretty good shape. I had engaged Charley French in Denver as a printer, but he has decided not to come and will send Leonard. The latter is dissipated and not near as good a printer as French, but we can arrange this matter when you come over. You must come over as soon as you can. We can issue the first number by the 21st if the material arrives within four or five days. Thursday suits best as publication day, on account of the mails. Write me by return mail.

Yours respectfully,
Sam McBride

The *Rocky Mountain News*, which took an intense interest in its prospective rival, reported on May 15, 1868: "The *Colorado Chieftain* is expected to be out the twenty-first. We hear that Dr. Beshoar, one of the proprietors, is a staunch Democrat; that Mr. McBride, the other proprietor, leans that way though he is not strongly partisan...."

The *Chieftain* starts out as a neutral, whether 'armed' or not doesn't say; how long it will remain so is another thing. Probably one or the other side will soon buy it and run it altogether in their interest as to politics."

The May 21 target date came and went without a newspaper as a result of one foul-up after another, but eleven days later half the population turned out, including the distinguished contributing editors, to see the first issue, dated June 1, 1868, roll off the press at the rate of 200 per hour.

It was a pretty handsome job. Unlike other newspapers in the territory, it carried no advertising on its front page. The heads were small, one-line, ten-point cap affairs, but the important thing was that the seven-column front page of the four-page fledgling was filled with well-written stories. At the top of the page in the first column appeared a "salutatory" under the heading "Our Newspaper":

We publish today the first number of the *Colorado Chieftain*, and without any studied or lengthy "salutatory" we send it forth to meet its just deserts at the hands of the public, and take its chances for "life, liberty and the pursuit of happiness."

We make no windy promises of what we shall do either to increase or retard the earth's motion, but natural ambition and self interest will prompt us to make the *Chieftain* the most acceptable paper possible for the people, limited in our exertions only by their liberality and our finances. We think, however, that we may without ostentation congratulate Southern Colorado upon the issue of our paper—the first in this part of the territory and that it may be taken not only as a sign of growth in population and business in the Arkansas Valley, but as another of the harbingers of the onward march of civilization westward.

Hoping to merit the good wishes and material aid of all who appreciate value and importance of a home paper as a medium of news and business advertising, we make the venture, confidently trusting that Southern Colorado will support at least one newspaper published in her business centre.

A lead story, written by Wilbur Fisk Stone and occupying the third column, reported "Death of Kit Carson."

"The melancholy intelligence reaches us that Kit Carson is no

2

more. He died at his residence on the Las Animas on the 24th inst. of disease of the heart," Stone wrote. He gave a brief biography of Carson and then eulogized him in a manner that gave faithful expression to how the people of the West felt about him:

He stood pre-eminent among the pathfinders and founders of Empire in the West, and his long career is unsullied by the record of a littleness or meanness. He was nature's model of a gentleman. Kindly of heart, tolerant to all men, good in virtues of disposition rather than great in qualities of mind, he has passed away—dying as through his long life he had lived—in peace and charity with all men, leaving behind him a name and memory to be cherished by his countrymen so long as modesty, valor, unobtrusive worth, charity and true chivalry survive among men.

The issue contained other important news. It recorded the arrival a few days earlier of the telegraph line, built from Denver by the Denver and Santa Fe Telegraph Company: "The old familiar sight of the long line of poles stretching away through the valley, over the hill and across broad mesas till lost sight in the dim distance, recalls the memories of other days and yet seen here for the first time, where a short time since Indians and trappers camped in the sage brush and bartered their beaver skins, seems marvelous and dreamlike. We seem to be near the old folks at home with these pine poles and bits of wire. An office has been opened here in the drugstore which, as it also contains the post office, is the most suitable place in town. The first communication received over the wire to Denver was obtained at 4:30 on Saturday, and on Sunday we received the first through news dispatches, which will be found in another place. All hail to the telegraph, say we, and so say all."

The issue was heavy with news of Colorado and the Southwest. Said that harbinger of civilization, the newly born *Chieftain*, in reporting that two army deserters, Charles Watson and Frank Hudson, had stolen four horses and been pursued by a posse for fifty miles before being caught downriver from Fort Lyon: "We might, by giving romantic details, make a sensational story for Eastern newspapers, as to the fate of these two scalawags, but we choose simply to say that without any loss of time, or expensive preparations, they were hanged to the limb of a noble old cottonwood until they were dead. Such is the retributive end meted out to this class of border ruffians."

And in line with the editor-in-chief's belief that a newspaper had civic responsibilities, the first issue of the *Chieftain* said sharply: "We note that a good many hogs are running at large in our streets in violation of the statutes. Their presence in the streets is a nuisance which ought to be abated. Why is the law not enforced?" And like any other newspaper, before or since, it didn't fail to carry a buttery bit on the doings of the town's most prosperous merchant, who might be expected to be a good advertiser: "M. D. Thatcher received nineteen heavy wagon loads of freight on Friday last. He now has a splendid stock of goods."

When the last of the first issue was off the press, Michael broke out bottles. Everyone felt pretty good about the paper; they felt even better after they had properly toasted the new baby. Several went out in front and stood under the new sign while Stephen S. Smith took their picture. It was a glorious day and Michael was elated. The noise of the press had sounded as good to him as that first cry of a newborn babe.

Volume 1, Number 1, of the *Colorado Chieftain* was an unmistakable success. The *Rocky Mountain News*, in a lead editorial in its June 5 edition said, "We are constrained to compliment the enterprising proprietors on its handsome appearance and the quality of its matter, original and selected. It fills a long felt want in Southern Colorado and we predict for it success."

The *Tribune* in Denver took note as did the *Gazette*, and numerous citizens either wrote complimentary letters or called at the *Chieftain* office in person to express their approval. In the weeks that followed, the *Chieftain* went along about as expected. The board of editors wrote, the doctor practiced medicine and solicited subscriptions and printing to support the enterprise, Sam worried, and Leonard got drunk. Typical of the McBride letters was one he wrote to Trinidad:

Pueblo, C.T. July 3, 1868

Dr. M. Beshoar:

Dear Sir:

We are getting along pretty well in the office, but I am dunned on every occasion for money. Last night I paid the tender for the plasterers the sum of $9.00 and everybody you owe wants something. When you write me again tell me what understanding you had with the plasterers. I thought the thirty dollars covered the whole bill, but they say not.

The people here are getting quite patriotic this morning. The Stars and Stripes are floating over The Pueblo House and preparations are being made for a picnic tomorrow evening at the grove across the river on which occasion the Hon. C. L. Hall will deliver an oration in response to the call of numerous citizens. Big time is expected. It is thought it will be a grand affair. I do not expect to attend, owing chiefly to my low state of finances.

Before the letter reached Trinidad, Michael had a costly go-around with Indians. As he himself told the story:

"In June, 1868, the Ute Indians had a battle with Arapahoes on the Canadian River some 70 miles south of Trinidad, and secured several Arapahoe scalps, but the son of war chief Curicanti fell into the hands of the Arapahoes with a wound that shattered one shoulder joint. They beat him severely, took his scalp and departed, believing him dead.

"Next day Curicanti with his warriors returned and found the young chief still alive. They daubed his head over with balsam of fir mixed with powdered herbs. With willow bark they wove a sheet of willow twigs and bound up the arm and shoulder with buckskin and over that the willow matting tied on with buckskin strings.

"They then lashed the small ends of two long poles to the sides of a pony and made a drag with a bed or mat near the distal end and in this manner conveyed the wounded man to Trinidad, making their camp on a small plateau west of the town."

When a half-dozen Utes arrived at his office and asked him to go with them to the Ute camp to attend the wounded man, Michael packed a bag with instruments and chloroform, rounded up an assistant, and went with the Indians. When he got to the camp, he worked out an agreement with the father before he would so much as examine his son.

"I had a distinct agreement with Chief Curicanti that I would do my very best to cure his son, but that if I should fail it would not be my fault. This was important to me because if a doctor undertook to cure a sick or wounded Indian and failed, the tribe considered it the right thing to kill the doctor.

"I at once amputated the shoulder and was fortunate in securing the efficient assistance of Mr. Joseph Davis who had seen considerable service as a hospital steward in the Army of the Potomac, and administered to the scalp wound as best I could.

"Well, on the Fourth of July, the Trinidad peoples' patriotism was all aglow—each celebrating the day according to his own capacity for enjoyment—and the Indians joined in with a scalp dance, having a detail of squaws carrying the stretched Arapahoe scalps on poles much as white people carry banners. Only the children and most of the squaws were in camp.

"Some time after the battle on the Canadian the Arapahoes learned by some means that the young chief had come to life and had been taken to Trinidad. They were at the time at war with the whites. The head war chief of the Arapahoes called for volunteers to penetrate the white settlements and kill the young chief and as many more Utes as they might encounter. Twelve braves responded to do the hazardous work.

"On the Dry Cimarron they captured a Mexican from Trinidad and required of him on penalty of his life to guide them safely to the Ute camp, and he did it well.

"While the bucks were jollifying in the business section the twelve braves rode around the town and directly to the Ute camp. At the first whoop the squaws with their children jumped into the river and kept themselves concealed under a washout in the river bank, maintaining themselves by holding to protruding tree roots. The Arapahoes had no time to hunt for squaws.

"The only buck they caught in camp was the young chief whom they killed sure enough. They partially destroyed the camp, took the entire pony herd, including my fee pony, and hastily departed.

"I had a patient by the name of Lucero, about three miles east of Trinidad, and when some of his family saw the Indians on their rapid retreat they called out "Los Arapahos!" The sick man, who had not been out of bed for two weeks, arose and ran to the little 8 by 10 window, and when he saw the Indians he fell back dead.

"I found myself loser two patients and a pony."

In addition to practicing medicine and soliciting business for the *Chieftain*, Michael also served the paper as a correspondent and did some writing from the field, signing his reports "By Editor, Chieftain." He also wrote features and mailed them to McBride in bulky envelopes.

Sam McBride's letters, which came in multiples on every coach when the editor was in Trinidad, give an intimate picture of a pioneer western newspaper fighting for survival:

July 11, 1868

Dear Sir:

I have nothing of importance to write you this evening except Leonard is on a general drunk and I am almost sick from the effects of hard work. I do not suppose Leonard will work any more for a week as it usually takes him that long to get off a spree. It will be very hard on Crooks and myself to get the paper out on time.

Yours respectfully,
Sam McBride

Pueblo, Colorado Ter. July 14, 1868

Dear Doctor:

We are getting along pretty well with the exception that money is played out. I had expected to hear from you by the last two coaches. Please send me some money. It is impossible to run the office without it and it don't come in here fast enough to do much good. What time do you expect to be back?

Yours, etc.
Sam McBride

Pueblo, Aug. 21, 1868

Dear Doctor:

. . . .I have had to work almost day and night to get the paper out and barely succeed. Leonard has been on a big drunk and I had to almost kill myself on that account. But I have discharged him now and tomorrow I expect to have another printer from Denver, one who does not get drunk. Doc, I want you to collect some money and send over by Monday's coach to pay Leonard. There is about eighty ($80) dollars due him and I haven't a dollar to pay him. The subscribed loans and work on the office has taken up nearly all the first quarter's advertising so times are very hard with me. Send over money enough to pay Leonard as I want to get rid of him as soon as possible. I

mean I want to get him out of town. I am afraid to leave the
office unless Crooks or someone else is in it for fear he will do
some mischief. . . . By the way, Captain Gillette has been picking up government horses and he found a U.S. on your pony.
He told me to tell you of it when you came back and if you
did not have the proper paper he would have to claim him as
U.S. property. Don't fail to send me the money.

> Yours etc.
> Sam McBride

Money or no money, the *Chieftain* was informative and fun to
read. It ran serious, if somewhat bloodthirsty and one-sided, articles
on the Indian problem and carried stories on Negro riots in the
South, science, medicine, and other topics. The editor-in-chief
wrote a summary of an *Atlantic Monthly* article that he found interesting and personally relevant: it contended that "too many surgeons" during the late war in their haste amputated for trifling
wounds and took too much of limb. The *Chieftain* ran many articles
on the area, its geography, peoples, and potentialities. Michael
wrote a number of these, digging into the life of the Pueblo Indians,
their customs, and ways. Often the paper ran short items that caused
merriment throughout the territory; for example, "It will be seen by
reference to our election returns that Hon. Wilbur F. Stone defeated
Dick Wootton for district attorney by a majority of 1,249 although
Dick is one of the oldest practitioners at the bar in the territory."
A substantial number of *Chieftain* readers had either seen the aging
mountain man and proprietor of the Raton Pass tollgate at work on
a bottle in a saloon or knew of his prowess in this line. And the
Chieftain had opinions, even while reporting the news: "A valuable
horse was stolen from Hon. J. W. Henry Wednesday night. The thief
broke open the stable and made a successful flight with the stolen
property. Such crimes are becoming so frequent that a little judicious hanging will have to be resorted to."

The fun wasn't limited to the local scene by any means. In a comment on the growing scandals of the national administration, the
Chieftain said: "Grant called on Mr. Commissioner Rollins a few
days since to inquire who are the thieves who are plundering the
government. It is said the answer will make a closely printed volume somewhat larger than Webster's Unabridged Dictionary."

During a ten-day stay in Pueblo, Michael sold his drugstore. Gale had gone off on a spree and disappeared; two clerks in succession had proven unsatisfactory, and it was plain he wasn't going to be in Pueblo enough to keep an eye on the business. He kept his medical office, as he needed a base of operations other than the *Chieftain* office. While getting rid of the drugstore, he bought a nonoperating brewery, which he proceeded to advertise in the *Chieftain*: "Pueblo Brewery, Pueblo, Colorado. M. Beshoar & Company. Capable of producing Lager Beer and Cream Ale." It may have been capable, but it produced little of either and practically no revenue. He finally released his license to Henry Goldstein, a newcomer looking for business opportunities, and leased the brewery for "$50 a month, payable in advance."

Relations between the physician and Lynde had been strained since the race war, and to complicate matters, Michael was beginning to suspect that something was wrong with the accounts; but he continued to push the Trinidad store with large display ads in each issue of the *Chieftain*: "Beshoar & Lynde, Trinidad, Colorado. Drugs and Medicines, Fine Liquors, Vinegar, Toilet Articles, Tobacco, Cigars, Smokers Articles, Stationery, Confectionery, Nuts and Notions Generally."

The store seemed to do a good business, but it wasn't returning as much as he thought it should. At the same time Lynde was becoming more and more of a figure in the gambling houses. One night after the store was closed and locked, Michael went in, spent an hour looking over the books, and put them away with the idea of taking a second look the next night. But, unknown to him at the time, Lynde had seen him in the store poring over ledgers, and when Michael returned the second night, all the records had disappeared. There was an angry session the next morning with Lynde accusing his partner of making off with the books. Michael told him that their partnership was dissolved, that he was taking full possession of the store, and that an accounting would be made as soon as the records could be produced. Later in the day he got Judge McBride to issue an order to Lynde to produce the books. When that was not productive, Michael had circulars printed and put a notice in the *Chieftain* saying: "Notice: Whereas a number of my notes, account books and other evidences of debt have been embezzled and stolen and are at this time fraudulently concealed beyond my reach so that I have failed by process of law to recover them, therefore, all persons are hereby warned against purchasing or in any manner contracting for any notes, books, accounts or other evidences of debt against any person or persons whomsoever, due or to become due the undersigned or purporting to be due Beshoar and Lynde." He followed it within a week by a second notice in the *Chieftain* stating that the business partnership of Beshoar & Lynde had been dissolved and that he would not be responsible for any debts contracted by Lynde. The clerk retaliated by taking the notice, reversing the names, and placing it as a paid ad in the *Rocky Mountain News* in Denver. Michael didn't get his books back, but Lynde was out. He hung around town for another two months, got himself into serious trouble when he tried to kill his attorney, and finally left the territory.

Michael turned management of the Eldorado Billiard Hall over to Ed Dupont, assuming the active management of the drugstore himself. He hired a general clerk to relieve him and take care of the store in his absence but decided he would prefer not to take in another partner.

He thought he had everything on an even keel once more, but late in September he began to fret about the extremely partisan stories Hinsdale was writing for the *Chieftain*. Sam McBride, who favored a political newspaper, would print anything Hinsdale handed him. After two particularly partisan stories, Michael wrote Sam an angry letter:

I conclude he is somewhat insane on political subjects and incapable of anything unless it was editing a newspaper of the class of the *LaCrosse Democrat* or the *Denver News* and as our associate to tell you the truth I am afraid of him, afraid he will do us more harm than good unless you control him and reject his spleen articles. His so-called quotation from the *News* that Holister is "either a fool or a knave" is in very bad taste in a high toned newspaper such as we propose to publish. His references to recent cases of ague and his conclusion that they are due to the fact that Southern Colorado is Democratic looks like a labored attempt to drift us into line as an ordinary political party newspaper. The article about the governor on the first would have become Brick Pomeroy or the *Vindicator* very well, but I think it an exotic in the *Chieftain*. I hope while I am interested in the *Chieftain* it will maintain its first independence of party.

Sam managed to put a checkrein on Hinsdale, but the *Chieftain* continued to be a worry to its editor-in-chief, as it was a constant drain on his resources throughout the fall and early winter of 1868–69. Everyone wanted money. He doled his dollars out to those who dunned him the hardest. He had drug suppliers to pay, paper houses, clerks, printers, rent on the Jacob Beard house in Trinidad he was using as a combined residence and office, rent on his office in Pueblo, and livery charges in both Pueblo and Trinidad, as he now kept a saddle horse in each town and did all of his traveling between the two towns by coach.

The Christian Brothers were becoming impatient about sums owed them for Mike's room, board, and tuition. Michael managed to send them $333, receiving a prompt acknowledgement from the president, Brother Edward, along with a note saying the Christian Brothers had their problems too and would like the balance due of $606,95 at the earliest possible moment.

The letters from the brothers and from Mike distressed him. Mike had had a quarrel with Brother Adrian; Mike had threatened to run away; Mike had played hookey for four days and had been out "some place in St. Louis"; Mike had been defiant. Mike complained bitterly about the "Black Egyptians," accused the brothers of stupidity, brutality, and insulting "you, mother and myself by the names they call me."

That the physician, hard pressed by the demands of the *Chieftain*, his practice, and other interests, neglected Mike there can be little doubt. He received letter after letter filled with tearful pleas "to come home":

St. Louis, Aug. 28, 1868

Dear Father:

I take this opportunity to write you a few lines in which I shall ask you the reason why you never write to me. Do you not like me or my letters? Is it the fault of the mail or is it your fault? If you want to treat your only son in that kind of style I wish you would let me know. If you do not like me let me know that also. If the Brothers have said anything about me it is all true. I will tell you the whole tale when you send for me. I want to come home. Please answer this as soon as received.

Your Son,
M. A. Beshoar

In a letter dated September 10, Brother Edward wrote that Mike was giving the school a great deal of trouble, and warned that "if he does not do better I will request you to call him home."

The situation in St. Louis had obviously become intolerable, and something would have to be done at once. For the life of him, Michael couldn't think what he would do with a fourteen-year-old in a tough, frontier town, but perhaps Brother Edward had the answer: put him to work. He was big and strong enough to do hard work. Within a couple of days after Brother Edward's letter reached him, the physician wrote Mike a long, serious letter saying he could plan on leaving the Christian Brothers, but asking whether he would like to go to a university or come to Colorado and work:

Mike immediately opted for work:

"I will take home over university for where is there a more lovely place than home," wrote a boy who had never known such a thing as a home of his own. "Just to be with your parents is the best of all. All I wish is to be with you once again. When I come home I want you to put me to work and I want it to be hard work. I prefer to work in the printing office as there I can learn a trade and as much other things as I could learn at school. The state is going to give a fair here next month at Benton Barracks. Please send me plenty of money for the occasion and a note so I can stay out in town with Dr. Folsom for two or three days."

Late in December, Sam McBride said he had enough. He had worked long and hard; and while he had had a place to sleep and enough food and his health had improved, even as the physician had promised, the lack of profits had kept him from receiving any salary. Michael agreed that the best thing they could do at this moment was to dissolve their arrangement. Sam wrote in the January 7, 1869, *Chieftain* that his health would not permit continued confinement in the office, and Michael wrote in the same issue: "We part from our late associate with feelings of deep regret and deplore the necessity which forces him into retiring from the business." The *Rocky Mountain News* sniffed that the *Chieftain* had been a good-looking paper due to the efforts of McBride.

Against the possibility that Sam might fold up or take off, the physician had long had an understanding with the printers' union in Denver that it would find and send a good, temperate man if he ever had need for a foreman.

Years later, in a banquet address, he told fellow editors about what happened when Sam departed:

I telegraphed by the Denver and Santa Fe telegraph line to the printers' union for a good, all-around man. He came promptly on Jones' jerky line, which arrived in early morning and carried Joe Chaffee and A. C. Hunt as well as my new printer, who was no less a personage than R. M. Stevenson.

After a hurried breakfast at the Hiney Hotel, Stevenson hastened to his new field of occupation. We never locked the door of that office dormitory. There was no occasion for locking. When he entered, he stared at the assorted revolvers and carbines hanging on the bunks and walls. I was just beginning to pantaloon myself, which is an athletic exercise in an upper bunk. Whether he saw me or not I don't know to this day, but he passed right through to the main room, which served all the purposes of the press, composing, job printing, and carpentry departments. In the center of this big room was a large wood stove of the box pattern with extemporized seats on either side. The stove was red hot and the devil had gone to the next building to cook the *Chieftain* people's breakfast.

Well, when I had finished my toilet, which was mostly putting on a pair of jeans pants and two government boots, one No. 6 square toed and a No. 7 round toed (washing and combing being an after consideration), I walked into the big room and took the seat opposite the stranger and began to contemplate the object before me. He was a stately gentleman of superior personal appearance—muchly of the royal English type.

Presently he gave me a somewhat contemptuous glance and inquired when the editor would be in. I told him the editor was in right then. He said he wanted to see him as soon as he came in. I said, 'Now suppose you take a good square look at me.' He said 'No, I want to see the editor.' It took me some time to convince him that I was the man he was looking for. He at once pulled off his coat, rolled up his sleeves, and went to work.

Stevenson was all that McBride was not. He could write, he was a
good printer, and he had a good business head on him. Within a few
weeks the *Chieftain* was healthier than it had ever been. It was, to
Michael's delight, making money; not much, but a little.

Fearful that Stevenson might leave or get shot or suffer some
other calamity, the physician decided he would sell the newspaper
while it was in the black and get out of Pueblo completely. He liked
Trinidad better and he had a hunch that someday coal would make
Trinidad an important city.

Stevenson had talent, charm, and ambition, but no money and no
way of acquiring any. Sam McBride, who had small talent and no
money, had spent most of his adult years in a print shop and had a
feeling for the business. He had been working in a political job and
thought he'd like to be back in the newspaper business if he could
raise some capital. The physician thought Sam's prospects poor,
but the former *Chieftain* printer managed to raise sufficient cash for
the required down payment and was willing to sign notes, one to
fall due every three months until the balance was paid. Michael
insisted he secure a satisfactory co-signer. On March 10, 1869, the
deal was consummated. Michael Beshoar bade his baby and Pueblo
goodbye with a "valedictory" on the front page:

Two years ago it occurred to me that the growing business
and population of Pueblo and the surrounding country demanded a newspaper organ. I never lost sight of the project to
establish here a newspaper until it was accomplished. After
the press and material had been purchased I associated myself
with Mr. Sam McBride in the conduct of the *Colorado Chieftain*. From that time to the present the Colorado public knows
the history of the enterprise. In taking leave of the *Chieftain* I
cannot withhold my congratulations to the people of Southern
Colorado upon having an organ fixed upon a permanent basis
from a business point of view and shall watch its future with
intense interest. Other affairs claim so much of my attention
that I am compelled to sell the establishment in order to do
justice to them. The knowledge that I leave the paper in worthy
and competent hands reconciles me to a parting with that public with which I have had such pleasant relations. With the
kindest feelings toward the conductors of contemporaneous
papers with whom I have been associated, I take leave of the

Chieftain. If I have committed errors in my intercourse with any of them, they have been of the head and not of the heart.

Commending the *Chieftain* to the continued favor of the public, I close with a fond farewell to its friends and patrons.

M. Beshoar

And just to make sure that no one thought his good wishes extended to editor Byers of the *Rocky Mountain News*, he took one final pot shot:

The editor of the *Rocky Mountain News* extols himself as the master of his business. Not quite yet, although he displays much promise. The Good Being, who created in men the sense of contempt, undoubtedly created objects upon which it might be legitimately exercised. To be one of these objects is doubtless the business of the editor in question, and by elevating himself a few degrees he may yet rise to the level of his business.

As might be expected, Sam McBride didn't last long; there wasn't anyone he could write to for money. He sold the *Chieftain* in June 1870 to Captain John J. Lambert, quartermaster at Fort Reynolds. The captain's brother, Nicholas N. Lambert, was entrusted with the conduct of the paper until the captain got out of the army in 1872. He converted it to a daily in May of that year.

Sam, active in Masonic and civic affairs, went into the insurance business with W. J. Woodworth and, under the firm name of Sam McBride & Co., sold insurance for seven national and international insurance companies "representing" so he claimed, $40,000,000 solid insurance assets." He held a number of jobs and political offices and made one more effort in the newspaper business with an eight-page monthly devoted exclusively to advertising. But Sam McBride's *Advertiser*, born in May 1872, died quietly and unnoticed in August 1873. Sticking with political offices until 1876, Sam was easily one of the most popular men in Pueblo. In that year as treasurer of the Pueblo school district, he had custody of $14,000 the district had voted for a new school building. Sam went east and took the money with him. Everyone was loath to believe what seemed probable. It was kept quiet for several weeks, but finally the story broke in the *Chieftain* under the heading "Have You Seen Sam?" No one had, and no one ever did again.

Chapter 6
Survival in a Frontier Town

DR. MICHAEL BESHOAR was sitting in the bar of the United States Hotel in Trinidad with Jacob Beard and a couple of other cronies drinking bourbon and watching a bunch of tenderfeet who had crowded into the place for refreshment. They were part of a big Santa Fe–bound train that had come in at midafternoon, much to the joy of the businessmen along Main and Commercial streets, to whom a train of such size meant substantial sales of all sorts of merchandise: clothing, ammunition, flour, beans, salt pork, canned goods, dried foods, feed for oxen and horses, parts for wagons, harness, and other supplies.

The physician, as was the case with everyone else in town, found diversion and entertainment watching pilgrims and visiting with them. And he, too, found them an important source of income. Tonight he would keep the City Drug Store open and he would stay close, ready to serve the men and women of the train as customers or patients. During the early hours whole families would come in from the camp at the edge of town to make purchases. Later, with the saloons and gambling places roaring and the board walks crowded, some of the visitors, and some of the locals too, were bound to get bruised or even shot. Trinidad's physician stood ready to help them with their illnesses, their contusions, and their wounds, and to lighten the burden of greenbacks they would have to carry over Raton Pass when they resumed their journey westward on the Santa Fe Trail.

He and Beard were idly speculating about the possible past and almost certain future of one obnoxious pilgrim, whose voice constantly rose above the hubbub in the bar, when suddenly a hush fell as a towering figure strode in. Although he had fifty-three hard years behind him, Richens Lacy Wootton was still a magnificent man: six feet four inches tall, 260 pounds, size 11 1/2 boots. He still wore buckskins and was still every inch the popular conception of a trapper and a mountain man.

Beard motioned to the newcomer to join them, but at that moment one of the tenderfeet said in a loud whisper: "That's Uncle Dick Wootton, the famous frontiersman!"

Uncle Dick's powerful muscles might have softened a bit over the years, but he still had perfect hearing. He stiffened, glared at his friends at the table, and shouldered his way up to the bar.

"Gimme a drink," he snarled in a most un-Wootton-like voice. The startled bartender, who had known Uncle Dick for a long time, hastily poured him a glass of whiskey.

Picking it up, Wootton glared once again at the group at the table and then at the tenderfeet before he tossed it off. Then, to everyone's astonishment, he stuck the whiskey glass in his mouth and began to chew. "Gimme another," he growled.

Michael whispered an exclamation to Beard, jumped to his feet, and rushed out of the hotel. He hurried west along Main Street, turned right at Commercial, and almost ran to his office on the east side of the street, a couple of doors below Main. Quickly he got out his forceps, needles, and suture material. Then he sat and watched the front door. In a few minutes he heard a peculiar scratching as if an animal were clawing at the back door. When it continued, he went to the door, unlocked it, and threw it open. There, down on his knees, with blood streaming from his mouth and tears from his eyes, was Uncle Dick Wootton.

"Oh, my gawd, help me," Wootton moaned. "Help me, Doc, I'm dyin'."

The physician assisted the suffering man into his office and in the next hour managed to pick countless little pieces of glass out of his cheeks, tongue, and gums. He had to sew several deep cuts.

"Well, I hope we got all of them," he said finally. "Now, Uncle Dick, the last thing you are going to want to do for awhile is eat with that mouth, but you may have swallowed some of that glass so I want you to go some place and stuff that big belly of yours with flour tortillas or biscuits if you can find any. Incidentally, how did such a thing ever happen, Uncle Dick?"

Wootton gave him a sharp look before he answered: "It was an accident, Doc, and I don't want to talk about it."

A few days later, on a horseback trip to visit another patient, the physician stopped in at Uncle Dick's place on Raton Pass to see how he was getting along and saw still another side of the justly noted pioneer. Uncle Dick was working on the tollgate, but he looked gaunt and mean. He talked through stiffly held lips, moving his tongue as little as possible. While Michael was examining his mouth, four wagons came up, en route to New Mexico. Uncle Dick collected toll from three of them, but the fourth driver, surrounded on his high seat by his wife and four bright-eyed, towheaded youngsters, said he didn't have any money, and he said it in a surly tone. It was the wrong day to be surly with the usually good-natured Richens Lacy Wootton. "Where you from?" he asked through tight lips. When the man said "Kansas," Uncle Dick climbed up on the wheel, reached into the back of the wagon, and came up with a hundred-pound sack of flour. Handling it as though it were a sack of feathers, he jumped down on the road, held the sack straight out with one arm, drew his hunting knife, and slit it. Doing an Indian dance as he shook the flour out over the road, he bawled, "All right, yuh damned Jayhawker, go on through."

Fifteen-year-old Mike Beshoar left the college of the Christian Brothers February 10, 1869, making the long journey to Colorado by train and stage by himself. There were younger boys than he doing a man's work and sometimes fighting Indians on the plains, but Mike had been under the tight rein of the brothers since he was ten years old, and knew virtually nothing of the world outside of the college grounds at Eighth and Cerre streets and the school's farm ten miles out of the city, "close by" the Kansas Pacific Railroad. However, the boy was well supplied with admonitions, notes of instructions, "to whom it may concern" letters, tickets, a purse with meal and ready money, and extra money pinned to his underwear. He went directly to Pueblo, where he was met by his father. Tired, dirty, and tearful, he rushed into his father's arms in a reunion remindful of one they had had years earlier when Michael had come back to Pocahontas after Shiloh.

The physician could not hide his deep emotion, and returned his son's embrace. Mike was a good two inches taller than his father, but he was pale and thin. Colorado sunshine and fresh air would soon fix him up.

They spent a day around Pueblo visiting with Michael's friends and acquaintances, and seeing the *Chieftain* office and the old drug-store. Mike had received the newspaper regularly and obviously had read it, as he had a surprising amount of knowledge about the town and its people. Never one to forget business, Michael also filed on some federal land during the day. But one day was enough, and after a good night's rest, they took the coach to Trinidad.

Mike had brought with him a final bill from the college. Shortly after they got to Trinidad, the mail brought a sharply worded note from Brother Edward in his neat, precise, almost feminine hand-writing: "I received your last letter telling me you could not get any money just now. I assure you we need it very much now. As you are aware our institution is not endowed so we need every cent as soon as possible."

Within a week or so after young Mike's arrival, they were settled into a routine that the father knew could not last. He had the boy bunking in the back of the drugstore, but meals were a problem. Red was no longer taking boarders, and for some time the physician had been buying his meals in so-called restaurants and in saloons, living the typical bachelor life in a raw, almost womanless fron-tier town. He had accounts at most of the places, finding it politic to spread his business around, but Mike presented a special prob-lem. The father finally settled on John Kinnear's place for Mike to take his meals. John was a deputy U.S. marshal and kept better order than many of the other places; he provided an edible meal for seventy-five cents, a drink for fifty cents, and a dance with one of the girls for twenty-five cents.

Kinnear's was hardly the place for a fifteen-year-old boy, but it seemed the best place for the moment, while Michael did his card-playing, drinking, and gambling elsewhere. If he had stayed in Pueblo, it would have been easier to handle Mike, perhaps, as it had a better class of people and more "refinements."

The problem of what to do with his son reached a crisis one eve-ning when Michael walked into Kinnear's in time to see one of the girls running her fingers through Mike's hair while the boy was eat-ing supper. The next day he sent Mike off to manage his ranch in Stonewall, thirty miles to the west in the Culebra Range, offering to give him the ranch for his own if he could make a go of it. Filled with enthusiasm, Mike said it was just what he had always wanted. He worked with a furious energy—planted wheat, barley, and oats; built fence, raised pigs, and generally did a man's work. He bombarded his father with letters asking for advice on crops, irrigation, animal husbandry, and other problems, and also received considerable help from the neighboring ranchers. But Michael wanted something more for his boy. After the first crop was in, he raised the question of more education, suggesting that either law or medicine would offer more of a future than ranching. Mike said he didn't want either, that he was satisfied. Finally the father suggested a career as an army or navy officer. Mike didn't show any enthusiasm but agreed, after several long talks, that he would go to Annapolis if an appointment could be obtained.

Michael wasted no time going after an Annapolis appointment, and it didn't take him long to find out how such an honor was secured. Engaging Henry Thatcher, the Pueblo lawyer, to handle the matter, he soon learned: "About five-sixths of the consideration is to go to a third party not named in our conversations, and is to be contingent upon your son actually securing the place; the other sixth is to be contingent upon the examination. But as beyond all question your son will pass the examination, there is little contingency about it. All negotiations are to be made through me, so that you need write to no other party. The appointment of your son is a foregone conclusion if the above terms meet with your acquiescence. I will at once ascertain in what your boy will be specially examined when he applies for admission and communicate with you. If you send your son to school the latter part of January there will be due a little over $1,300 at that time."

With the heavy outlay for an appointment just ahead of him, Michael cast about for more money. Collections from his practice were slow, the drug business had dropped off sharply, and Sam Mc-Bride was behind on his *Chieftain* payments. The physician asked lawyer Thatcher to put pressure on McBride; hired a lawyer in Ironton, Missouri to try once more on delinquent accounts in that area; and sought the aid of Isaac Putnam, who had been his proxy representative in Arkansas since the war, and Pocahontas lawyer Rufe Black in settling up his Arkansas estate and collecting some of the debts owed him since the war. In his replies lawyer Black used quotation marks around the word estate, indicating it was practically nonexistent since all of his land had been seized and sold for nonpayment of taxes. And many of the people who owed Michael for medical services, drugs, notions, cotton, or whatever, had been killed in the war or had left Randolph County and their whereabouts were unknown. Worse yet, as soon as Putnam and Black began to stir in his behalf and it became known Dr. Beshoar was practicing in Colorado Territory, a number of people came forward with claims against him. Mrs. Hill filed a claim with Black for board and room money she said was due her for taking care of young Mike while his father was a prisoner. The physician immediately filed a counterclaim for medical services to the Hill family. Mrs. Nancy Steward wanted $80 for the mare she had let him borrow the day he was captured by the Federals and which he had had in his possession less than an hour. He refused the claim on the ground he had never had title to the animal and that it had been taken from her by the Federals, not Michael Beshoar.

Finding it hard to believe he had lost everything in Arkansas, he wrote Colonel James Martin and asked him what he thought of his returning to Pocahontas, not only to collect his estate and the accounts due him but to remain and practice medicine. Jim urged him to return:

Old friend, why don't you come back here where you are so well known, where you stand first in your profession, and where all admire you. Politics is a dead cock here or at least it stands in abeyance. There are only a few Radicals in the county, say 60 to 80, and about 600 registered conservatives, and though the Radicals now hold office the first election we get we'll put them out and put good men in office. We are biding our time and we have pretty much our own way in the county. Taxes are no higher than before the war and as to the Negro he doesn't push us as there are none here of any consequence. The county is building rapidly and in two years will be better than ever. There were 5,000 hogs slaughtered here this year for which there was in cash eight cents paid. Crops were good last year and large breadths of cotton and tobacco will be planted this year. There are ten buildings going up in town, including a large hotel, larger than the St. Charles, on the lot adjoining the one where old Mrs. James' house is. There is a Catholic Church, a priest, and five Sisters of Charity will come here to live.

I wish you would come here and enter the arena as a merchant. A man with capital could buy low here and sell at a profit of 33 per cent. If you will come all of my talents are at

your disposal. Doc, if you were here now how much of the
good things of life you could get deponent doth not say, but all
the James family are here and single. I am married to a good
woman and am virtuous. You are virtuous. Therefor Brick
Pomeroy would naturally say 'virtuously muchly all.' I will
send you the *Express* of which I am editor. You will see in it
about the Catholics. I think I will join them; nothing to prevent
it but Masonry and secret order and I think they may get
over that.

In one of his letters about "the estate," lawyer Black devoted
more space to informing bachelor Beshoar about the available girls
and the marriage situation in Randolph County than about business.
He had himself married Jennie Criddle upon his return from the
war. "There are many young ladies who have come on the carpet
since you left us," he said; "in fact most all of those you knew as
'little girls' are now in the market waiting for bidders, and your old
friend Maggie James is still single. As to the government, unless our
friends in the North stretch out their hands to us we are destined to
be ruled by the Negro. But I must say I think the Negroes are
clothed with more honor and dignity than the Radicals in the
County."
These and other letters from Pocahontas filled Michael with
nostalgia and homesickness. He walked the board walks of Main
and Commercial streets and stared at the flat-roofed adobes and
longed for Arkansas; he ate tortillas and frijoles, and hungered for
good old razorback-type pork and black-eyed peas. He thought of
Maggie James and all those girls "on the market," compared them
in his mind with those "on the market" in Trinidad, and wished he
were in Arkansas.
It was at this dark moment that he got a break: Isaac Putnam wrote
that he needed a change and was coming to Trinidad. Michael was
delighted. He had been as close to Put as he had to Jim Martin,
although Put lacked Jim's capacity for fun and joyous living. They
had been perfect partners because they got along and worked well
together. He found his friend a place to stay and put him in charge
of the drugstore. In addition Put practiced a little medicine. There
would soon be other doctors in Trinidad, but for the moment they
had the town to themselves. It was a happy time for Michael, having
with him an old and close friend—a man he could trust implicitly

and a man who shared old friendships in Arkansas and memories about "the good old days" in Poca. But it was too good to last. In a few months Put became so homesick he was almost physically ill. When Michael saw him off, he almost wept as the coach swung out on Main Street with the driver yelling ". . . eeee yahh!" and cracking his long whip above the backs of his mules.

Michael almost "went home" to northeast Arkansas that week, but it was not to be. He was too committed, at least for awhile. His practice was growing, and collections were beginning to pick up again; the drugstore was doing better. To the ranch at Stonewall, he had added two more to the east of Trinidad, along with considerable acreage in Las Animas, Huerfano, and Pueblo counties on which he had filed claims in the U.S. Patent Office in Pueblo. Besides he had the responsibility of two elective offices: president of Trinidad School Board District No. 1 and assessor of the Las Animas County.

Serving on the school board with him were Isaac Levy, a merchant, and George Semmes Simpson, who was an interesting man by any standard. A native of St. Louis, the fifty-one-year-old Simpson was a son of a distinguished St. Louis physician, Dr. Robert Simpson. His sister had married General Andrew Jackson Smith; a cousin, Raphael Semmes, had commanded the Confederate raider "Alabama," and another cousin, Mary, had married George Champlain Sibley, the explorer who had laid out the road between western Missouri and Santa Fe. Trinidad's George had trapped with Old Bill Williams, finally settled down in southern Colorado, and married Juanita Suaso.

Simpson shunned heavy work, describing himself as "a desultory sort of man." He was well read and sometimes quoted by others, as when he observed that if the Piute "had been a little more human or a little less brute, Darwin would have rejoiced and proclaimed him the missing link."

Michael not only liked the Simpsons and was liked by them in return, but he was fascinated by George's medical history. Years before he settled in Colorado, George was traveling down the Mississippi on a boat during a cholera epidemic. When he contracted the disease, he called the captain, gave him a bag of gold, and begged him not to bury him on some sandbar, as was being done with other victims of the disease, but to pack his body in ice and deliver it to his father in St. Louis for proper burial. Recognizing Simpson's father's name, and recognizing the gold, the captain carried out the instructions when George died, duly packing the body in ice. Some two or three days later when George began to twitch in his bed of ice, he was hastily unpacked and found to be a well man.

The business of getting Mike into Annapolis proceeded slowly. There was no problem about his age, as cadets as young as fourteen were being accepted. But Thatcher wrote that there might be a delay of as much as six months because the congressman had found he didn't have an appointment for Colorado Territory. A Colorado cadet in the Academy who had been scheduled for dismissal was hanging on through the intercession of political friends, but the good congressman said he would look around for a vacancy from one of the other territories. If one wasn't found, the President would be asked to make Mike one of his ten appointments-at-large. Thatcher supplied literature from the academy, pressed McBride to pay up, and sent specifics on what Mike would be examined in when the appointment did come through. When Mike expressed doubts that he could pass the examination, his father brought him in from Stonewall and got him a good tutor in the person of Mrs. Rice, wife of the Methodist minister and head of the Rice Institute.

Mike could be the most lovable of boys and the most contrite when he had done something wrong. He could also be sullen and uncooperative. He covered both extremes much of the time he was under Mrs. Rice's tutelage. He would work hard for two or three days and then refuse to study or cooperate in any way. But as the time for the appointment drew near, the physician's hopes were high. He had no doubt that the life of a cadet and its promise of adventure and a career would appeal to Mike once he got into it. When Thatcher wrote that the appointment would be made in a few days, Mike received the news sullenly, telling his father he expected it would be "pretty much like the Christian Brothers' school." A day later Mike disappeared, along with his horse and tack. A search revealed no trace; it was a big, open country, and he might have gone in any direction. Michael was frantic, but, short of having the Las Animas County sheriff send out wanted circulars as was done for criminals, there was no avenue of search available. There were no agencies for tracing people and there was no family to whom Mike might have gone. The physician felt certain Mike would not head for St. Louis or Arkansas, but, if he did, his father was sure to be informed. Other possibilities were that Mike might head for the mines in the northern part of the territory or look for ranch work in southern Colorado, New Mexico, the Nation, or Texas. For two long months Michael fretted and worried, and then his mind was eased somewhat by a letter postmarked Sipes Springs, Texas, in which Mike said he was working as a cowboy, that he was doing well, loved the country, "and am loved by the people here."

Since there wasn't much he could do about it, the father had to content himself with writing Mike a letter telling him that he would always be welcome when he was ready to come back, and to take care of himself. A second letter went off to lawyer Thatcher, canceling the Annapolis project. He decided he'd best be philosophical: perhaps a bit of cowboying would do Mike a lot of good.

Michael had given some thought to starting a newspaper in Trinidad, but before he reached a decision, the *Trinidad Enterprise* began publication, October 1, 1870, with J. P. Smith as publisher and editor. Smith was a printer, not an editor or writer, and his newspaper—a five-column sheet printed in both English and Spanish—showed it. Smith didn't survive long; after one issue which so irritated a group of citizens they announced they intended to shoot him on sight, he made a hurried departure. George W. Chilcott, a northern Colorado Republican with political ambitions, bought the *Enterprise* and sent E. G. Stroud, a massive, six-foot-four-inches-tall man, to run it. Stroud used an old table for a desk; he fastened two clothespins to it and hung two revolvers on them, announcing he was in town to stay.

Michael, who had more newspaper experience than anyone within a couple of hundred miles, thought the *Enterprise* show was great fun. Since Stroud, too, was a printer type, the physician predicted his early "d or d" (which he said meant departure or demise). Fortunately for Stroud it was the former and came after he deeply offended Jim Lord, the local stage jehu, by criticizing drunken stage drivers in general and Jim Lord in particular. Lord was away on a trip at the time, and Stroud didn't expect any trouble. The rest of the town, knowing Lord as one who was not to be trifled with and as one who had killed a man in Cheyenne for insinuating he was a liar, awaited his return with considerable anticipation.

When Lord read the story, he rushed to the *Enterprise* office, and put a .44 under Stroud's long, aristocratic nose, and told him to get his hands in the air. Stroud obeyed.

"Why did you write that lie?" Lord demanded.

"I. . . I. . . didn't," Stroud stammered.

"You lie," Lord said, "and you know it."

"Let me off and I'll take it back in the next issue," Stroud pleaded.

Lord let him go and awaited the next issue. But Stroud knew he was a ruined man in Trinidad. He wrote a terrible roast on Lord under the heading, "How We Apologize," informed the printer where to put it on the front page, and gave him careful instructions on when the paper should be run off the press. With that he put his hat on and was last seen walking north on the trail to Pueblo.

Once again there were demands that Michael Beshoar do something about a suitable newspaper for Trinidad, but he laughed them off. The *Enterprise* achieved a somewhat sounder basis when A. W. Archibald became the editor and proprietor, and hired the former owner, J. P. Smith, as a printer. He and the physician didn't hit it off very well; at times they were friendly and the next minute they were at each other's throats. Archibald hired an assistant editor, John C. Fitnam, an Episcopal clergyman, and the two of them played Republican politics, occasionally getting poked and having their lives threatened. They did some threatening in return. After one particularly steamy go-around with Archibald, the physician got a tip that Archibald and "a friend" were going to kill him that very night. Michael had been sleeping in the back room of the drugstore, and everyone in town knew it. He rigged his bed up with rolls of blankets and a buffalo hide and slipped out in the darkness. He bunked with a friend, returning early the next morning to find a back window broken and his bed riddled with buckshot. He had no proof as to who did it.

But there was no doubt who did the shooting on December 3, 1872, when Archibald was blasted by both loads from a double-barreled shotgun in the hands of J. P. Smith, who shot Archibald from a distance of about fifteen feet. Archibald survived, but suffered some crippling of the right arm. The shooting supposedly resulted from a dispute over wages, but darker speculations were passing around. Smith was tried before Judge Hallet and ever afterward carried the sobriquet "Shotgun" Smith.

Through all this excitement Michael tried to keep his distance. He had decided he would not get into the newspaper business again. With new physicians coming into Trinidad, he meant to devote himself to his practice and any good business deals that came along. He told his friends that he didn't consider a newspaper in Trinidad a good business deal by any stretch of the imagination. The arrival of medical competition caused him to have a schedule of fees printed. Suspecting his new colleagues might not have medical degrees, he prefaced his "Fee Bill" with the statement:

I beg leave to mention that before entering upon the practice I obtained a thorough medical and surgical education, and graduated with honor at one of the best medical colleges in the United States; that I have also the experience of an extensive and successful practice of over sixteen years; that I keep myself constantly supplied with an assortment of pure drugs, and all the instruments and appliances necessary in any emergency: that, having no other business, I can always give the patients the attention they require, and that my charges are moderate as seen by the following:

Fee Bill

Office Practice:

Prescriptions in ordinary acute cases..........................$3 to $5
      "   " chronic and venereal cases........... 5 " 25
Minor surgical operations .... 5 " 25
Tooth extracting... 2
Blood letting or cupping 2.50

Town Practice:

One visit per day, including medicine $4
Two " " " " " 6
Three " " " " " 8

Country Practice:

Visits, $2 for first and $1 for each successive mile, medicine extra.

Miscellaneous:

Visits at night or in inclement weather, double the above rates.

Detention with patient by request of the family or necessity of the case, $1 per hour after the first hour.

Ordinary obstetrical cases, $15; tedious or difficult, $25 to $75.

More important surgical operations, $25 to $100; capital, $100 to $200.

The above rates are at least one-third lower than those adopted by the Colorado Medical Association—the rates charged by nearly all the physicians in the Territory.

Respectfully, &c
M. Beshoar, M.D.
Physician, Surgeon, Accoucheur

New doctors in town included the Menger brothers, Charles and Oscar, Jules Le Carpentier, and J. F. Lines. Michael still had the only drugstore, but the town was growing. New buildings were going up and new businesses were coming in. Traffic through the town, to and from Raton Pass, was heavy; as many as a thousand oxen at a time had been counted, standing or resting in their traces along the two sides of Commercial Street in the short three-tenths of a mile from its intersection with Main Street to the bridge across the Purgatoire. There was an air of excitement on Main and Commercial streets day and night. Anything could happen. And at noon the excitement mounted when the daily coaches from Kit Carson, Pueblo, and Santa Fe all came in at once and unloaded their passengers for dinner at the Overland House while the teams were changed. There were horse teams and mule teams, with the latter often hitched five to a coach, two mules at the wheel and three in the lead.

But there was more to the growth than just business. The Sisters of Charity had arrived and had a school going, as did Elial J. Rice, the erudite Methodist minister and health seeker whose wife had tutored Mike before he decamped for Texas. The Reverend Mr. Rice had been on the faculty of Kansas State University and then president of Baker University in Baldwin, Kansas, where his wife held the French and Latin chairs, before they moved to southern Colorado. When he had first arrived in Trinidad, he had rented a room in the United States Hotel and preached what was said to be the first Protestant sermon ever delivered in the town.

He later noted that there were "only thirteen native American families" in Trinidad. To incoming Americans the term "native Americans" meant English-speaking persons of Anglo-Saxon, Protestant background to the exclusion of Spanish-speaking natives and "pestiferous Red fiends." The Reverend Mr. Rice not only started his Rice Institute and made it a going school but planned a Methodist University for Trinidad.

The development of education and the expansion of religion didn't do much to change Trinidad's view of itself or the image it presented to the territory and the West as a whole. It was known widely as a tough town, a gathering place for roughs of all kinds, including cattle rustlers and horse thieves. With wealth in the form of fifty thousand cattle, eighty thousand sheep, and a thousand horses roaming the open range of Las Animas County, and other thousands in other counties of southern Colorado and northern New Mexico, the temptations for theft on a large, organized scale were great. And Trinidad, on the border of the two territories, was a natural place for gang headquarters.

But the hospitality of the citizens was becoming strained as their businesses improved from sources other than crooks and murderers. In his capacity as physician and surgeon, Michael found the roughs a nuisance. When they were shot or otherwise injured, they were both dangerous to handle and poor pay. After one term as assessor and one as coroner, the physician was now serving as county clerk, but he had to show up at every coroner's hearing as the expert witness. The demise of Nibbs was a case in point. Nibbs—alias Charles J. Reed, alias Lewis A. Berry, alias St. Clair, alias Williams—was only twenty-five years old, but he had earned a bad reputation in Maine, Michigan, Georgia, Florida, Missouri, and no doubt in other states under other names. He was known to be an army deserter, a claim jumper, a bounty hunter, and a murderer. When he swaggered down Commercial Street or along Main, the better citizens avoided him if possible.

On a bright spring morning, the word went around that there was a very interesting object hanging on a tree about three-quarters of a mile northwest of town. A goodly number of citizens nodded their heads knowingly. The night before, after Nibbs had been arrested that day for horse-stealing, he had been taken away from the sheriff's officers between ten and eleven o'clock by a group of masked men armed with rifles, shotguns, and pistols; so it figured something would be hanging someplace nearby.

The roughs thought they knew who it was, and there was considerable excitement among them. Neither the sheriff nor the coroner went out for a look during the morning. Shortly after 10 A.M. three citizens went to the tree, stood around awhile, and came back to town to say it was Nibbs all right.

Coroner Charles J. Riffenburg caught Dr. Beshoar on Commercial Street about 10:30 A.M. and asked him whether he'd go out and examine "a corpse I hear is hanging to a tree northwest of town a bit." Michael said resignedly that he would and asked how soon he wanted the examination made. Riffenburg, grinning, told him if he had other business to go ahead and do it, that sometime after dinner would be plenty of time. Michael agreed. When a community had a desperado hanging from a limb, it paid to let the the corpse swing for awhile; if you cut it down too quickly, you were apt to lose some of the good expected from a hanging.

After a milk punch with hotelkeeper Sherman and dinner, Michael went out to examine the body, getting there, foresightedly, just as Riffenburg arrived with his jury: Sherman, Joseph Davis, Frank G. Bloom, A. J. McLain, John Hough, and Lee Keizel—all members of the town's establishment. They stood for a few minutes and looked with satisfaction at Nibbs swinging gently to and fro. He had on greenish pants, a dark flannel shirt, a gray vest, and a velvet coat. His hands were neatly tied behind his back, and there was a look of anguish on his face. His long brown hair hung down over his shoulders.

"It would make a nice scalp," Michael said after the body was cut down and he began his examination. Riffenburg swore in his jury, and in five minutes or so the expert witness was ready for them. He described the body, explaining that Nibbs had been pulled up and died by strangulation. The condition of the tree limb, showing severely rubbed places, and the fact that the neck was not broken were the bases for this statement, though there were people who said most everyone in attendance at this required legal procedure knew doggone well just how Nibbs had been hanged. When Michael had concluded his testimony, the jury took about two minutes to find that Nibbs had come to his death at the hands of persons unknown. With that the expert witness and the coroner and his jury went back to Sherman's for a drink, leaving the body to be cared for by friends if any.

Chapter 7
Vigilantes and a New Bride

BIG NICK WARDAMOUNT, one of Michael's regular patients, had the note with him when he brought his coach in from Willow Spring, New Mexico Territory, in time for his passengers to get their supper at the Overland House. Big Nick was tired and hungry, having driven since morning all the way from Red River, but he started out immediately to find the physician, a not too difficult task as at least a half-dozen persons along Main Street reported the good doctor was playing cribbage with lawyer George Boyles in E. B. Sopris' saloon at C and Main streets.

"Sayre busted a leg and wants you over at Willow Spring as soon as you can make it," Big Nick said, handing over the short, terse note. "He got throwed and his leg is hurting a lot, Doc, and you know how Sayre is." As a matter of fact, Michael knew Smith Sayre only by name and by his reputation as the cranky, irritable, and short-tempered landlord of the Willow Spring stage station. He had seen Sayre a couple of times while going through Willow Spring on trips to and from Red River, but he had neither met him nor had him for a patient.

"I'll get over there first thing in the morning," he told Big Nick as the husky driver went off to get his own supper. Since he could always look in on other patients if he was mobile, Michael decided he would go by horseback rather than by coach, leaving Trinidad at dawn.

It was a beautiful, sunny day. He followed the Raton Pass road, the old Santa Fe Trail up Raton Creek. Indians, mountain men, pilgrims, freighters, soldiers, the stage lines, cattlemen and their herds, and all other manner of travelers had been going up and down this pass for many years. After the first ten miles, he left the scrubby cedar and piñon and moved into tall pine and oak brush.

It was cool and refreshing for late August. Another three miles brought him to Wootton's tollgate. After a brief visit with Uncle Dick, he hurried on, his horse climbing steadily until they reached the summit, 6,869 feet above sea level and fifteen and a half miles from Trinidad. Behind him, off to the north, were the Spanish Peaks, their summits thrust high into the bright blue sky, while to the west were the serrated peaks of the Culebra Range, which separated Las Animas County from the great San Luis Valley. And straight ahead, stretched out below him for many miles to the south, were rolling, treeless range lands interspersed with blue and purple mountains. From this point on to Willow Spring, a distance of ten miles, he was in New Mexico Territory, moving steadily downhill to the stage station and one of the most pleasant surprises of his life.

The "surprise," togged out in a pair of men's pants and men's shoes for a short hike with the Sayre children, had stepped into her brother-in-law's parlor to ask how he was feeling when the physician rode up and tied his horse. Panicked at the thought of being seen in such an outfit, her first thought was to run, but there was no way out except through the doorway the physician was now approaching, medical saddlebags thrown over his left arm. Sayre, stretched out on a sofa, was startled to see her crawl under the table that stood in the center of the room, covered with a heavy, red, floor-length cloth.

Michael had just started his examination when he caught sight of a man's shoe protruding from under the tablecloth. It didn't seem likely that anything could be wrong in broad daylight in the parlor of a respectable stage-keeper who was incapacitated with a fractured leg, but he had been on the frontier too long to take any chances. He fished his gun out from under his vest and said quietly, "I don't know what this is about, Sayre, but you can tell that man to come out from the table."

The stage-keeper, who was in considerable pain, groaned: "Annie, come out from under there! What on earth is the matter with you?"

When Annie Elizabeth emerged, her face aflame, the physician stared at her in astonishment—a pretty young woman hiding under a table! At that moment Mrs. Sayre, who had been busy with the children when Michael arrived, came hurrying into the room, and after greeting her the physician turned back to the business at hand. As he set Sayre's leg, he kept wondering who the girl was and why she had been under the table. Later, when Sayre had been made as comfortable as possible, the doctor got embarrassed explanations from Mrs. Sayre and Annie Elizabeth as they gave him dinner.

"Annie recognized you when you rode up and didn't want you to see her in men's ciothing," Mrs. Sayre said. "You were the doctor who took care of one of my other sisters years ago when the family was on its way to Kentucky. It was during the war."

With a rush it all came back to him. Ironton . . . John Maupin, the man from Westport fleeing from Missouri to Kentucky with his wife and daughters . . . one of the girls had typhoid . . . and this young woman . . . of course, now he remembered the girl—Annie Elizabeth.

In the intervening years she had grown into a most attractive young woman, still small and slender with lively brown eyes and a wealth of dark hair. Her erect carriage gave her an air of dignity as she moved quickly from stove to table serving him.

Mrs. Sayre told him that still another sister, Susan, was the wife of W. T. Burns, a stock-grower in Las Animas County.

It was explained that Annie Elizabeth had come out from Kentucky to tutor the Sayre children. Mrs. Sayre, who did most of the talking, said their parents were living in Nicholasville, Kentucky, that one brother, Tom, had been "murdered by the Yankees" while serving with Quantrill, while two other brothers, John and James, who had also served with the guerrilla band, were living in the Nation where John had recently married a Chickasaw girl. She gabbled on and on, while Annie said little, her embarrassment continuing until the doctor said his goodbyes and started back to Trinidad.

In the weeks that followed, Michael made several trips by coach and horseback to Willow Spring to see his patient. Each time, after solemnly examining Sayre's leg, he visited with Miss Annie. As she overcame her shyness, he found her delightful. Although she had had little formal education as a result of the war, she was well read and was an interested and appreciative listener to the tales he told of the war and his life on the frontier.

With each visit Michael became more interested in the gentle young woman; he was even making calls to look at Sayre's scrawny appendage when Sayre was back in the saddle again. Finally the stage-keeper asked irritably whether he was being charged for all the trips to Willow Spring or were they just social calls.

Without so much as a smile, the physician handed him one of his fee schedules: two dollars for the first mile and one dollar for each additional mile—a total of twenty-six dollars per visit. When Sayre finally calmed down enough for him to get in another word, Michael explained with a grin that he would compromise the bill provided of course that Sayre had no objection to his continuing to call to see Miss Annie. Sayre said he reckoned that would be all right.

With the courtship an established fact, Miss Annie made it a bit easier for her suitor by moving from the Sayre home to the Burns home, a few miles down the river from Trinidad, to help Susan with her young children. Now that he was able to see her more frequently, Michael drove her on picnics; he told her about the two wives he had lost in Arkansas and about Mike, Jr., who was off cowboying in Texas; and he talked about the future and what he hoped to do in medicine, business, and politics. What he didn't tell her was that he was tired of the life he was leading: tired of poor food, tired of dance hall girls, tired of the kind of women who throw themselves at a doctor, tired of saloons, tired of a lonely cot in the back of a drugstore.

He took her to several dances, feeling both pleased and alarmed when she was surrounded by admirers and would-be suitors. Well-bred young women were rare in the territory, and he soon realized that there was no time to be lost if he was to have her for his wife.

Like any other suitor for a lady's hand, he had to show off a bit in the process of putting his best foot forward. He acquired a new buggy and bought Buck from Joel Roe, proprietor of the Pueblo Livery, Feed & Sale Stable. The new turnout had the citizens of Trinidad agog as he and Annie flashed by behind the fast, high-stepping stallion. When owners of ordinary horses and miscellaneous broncos and Indian ponies asked about Buck, his new owner was prepared to whip out the horse's papers: bred by the famous Kentucky breeder, Thomas Benton Cory of Montgomery County, sired by the thoroughbred Messenger of Maine, "a descendant of the imported Messenger." Buck's dam had been sired by the imported Coburg and her dam by the Kentucky Whip. Buck had been a trotter on the Kentucky turf. The doctor meant for the Kentucky horse to impress Miss Annie, but whether it did or not he was much impressed by his Kentucky girl.

He proposed in mid-October and they were married a month later before the Reverend Father P. J. Munnecom. Since Annie was a Presbyterian and the wedding could not be performed in the Catholic church, the ceremony took place Wednesday evening, November 13, 1872, in the United States Hotel. Annie Elizabeth was a lovely bride in her white organdy gown, made with a tight-fitting bodice, a long, full skirt trimmed with handmade lace, and a bustle. An overskirt formed the train. Her tulle veil was clasped with a coronet of artificial orange blossoms. There were no fresh flowers in November, so she carried a small bouquet of artificial roses made for her by the handsome and talented Doña Juanita, wife of old mountain man George Simpson. The bridegroom wore formal dress ordered out of St. Louis, all alterations by Jesus Carrion, who had never seen such a garment before.

Young Jerome Abbott, a comparative newcomer and deputy in County Clerk Beshoar's office, was the best man, and Susan Burns (who had early won the town's admiration by strapping a .44 around her waist and walking twelve miles into Trinidad, carrying one baby and herding the others, after Indians had come skulking around while her husband was away) was matron of honor.

There were four hundred guests from southern Colorado and northern New Mexico, 400 Anglos and Spanish-Americans. Old mountain man Uncle Dick Wootton, all dressed up for the occasion, was there with his wife. So were Billy Bransford, Felipe Baca, Don Jesus Maria Garcia, and Don Casimero Barela. Cattle kings, doctors, lawyers, public officials, merchants, butchers, saddlers, carpenters, cabinetmakers, blacksmiths, printers, editors, Protestant ministers, pool hall proprietors, saloonkeepers, gamblers, and sheepherders were packed into the hotel to witness the wedding and attend the reception and supper that followed.

The physician had sent only one invitation to Pennsylvania, to a cousin, Dr. D. B. Amick, one to Texas, to Mike, Jr., and three to Pocahontas to Colonel James Martin, Colonel Thomas S. Symington, and Dr. Isaac E. Putnam. None of those listed under "Distance" was able to make the long and arduous trip to Colorado Territory.

The *Enterprise* summed up the wedding in its Friday issue and gave the happy bridegroom a bit of advice:

> To give a full description of the splendid supper and magnificent entertainment would carry us beyond our limited space. But if there be one thing more than another in a com-

munity which in the eyes of a stranger gives evident marks of thrift, energy and prosperity, frequent marriages can by no means be counted among the least. The awful mysteries and serious ceremonies connected with the celebration of the marriage vow have not been scenes of ordinary occurrence in the Land of Las Animas, partly owing to our meagre supply of women, and partly to indifference or want of courage among men. But of late, marriage services together with midnight dances have been frequent occurrences to gladden, enliven and quicken the hearts of our rising populace. And it now remains for you, Dr., to go forth with the eyes of mankind critically gazing upon you, with the same mental vigor and and earnest resolves which we are compelled to believe has actuated you to take the one thing needful—a wife.

The weeks following his marriage were busy ones for Michael. He settled Annie in a rented three-room adobe house on Convent Street, bought such furniture as was available in Trinidad, and promised "good furniture from Denver or St. Louis" as soon as they could buy or build a house of their own. He hired a Mexican girl for $1.25 a week and meals, to help Annie with the housework, cooking, and washing—and then brought her a couple of gifts that complicated her household: two round little bear cubs. Their mother had been encountered by Mrs. Bransford and a couple of Bransford's ranch workers as they were on the way to Trinidad from the Bransford place, fifteen miles east of town in the Ratons, with an ox-drawn wagon loaded with goat, sheep, and cow pelts. The two men chased the bear up a canyon and past the cabin of a Colonel Snyder. When his dogs started to howl, the colonel ran out, rifle in hand, and killed the terrified animal. The two cubs were found minutes later and were brought into town and presented to Dr. Beshoar, compliments of Colonel Snyder.

The cuddly little balls of fur were fun at first; Annie named them John and Lucy, and kept them chained to a small woodshed directly behind the house. But she had second thoughts when they began to grow in size and appetite, and suggested that one cub would be enough. Michael gave the male away and moved Lucy with her chain to an open space between the rear of his drugstore and the arroyo that ran through the main part of town. Some days later a delegation of gamblers called on him at the store. Their spokesman said there had been some discussion about the fighting qualities of a bulldog owned by one of them and they would like to match the bulldog with his cub, "and of course we'll cover any bets you might want to make on your cub, Doctor." The physician was horrified. He eyed with distaste the dog they had brought with them. It had eyes as bloodshot as those of the man holding its chain, an underslung jaw with jutting lower canines that curved wickedly, and a short breath, made noisier by a runny nose. Michael told the delegation he wouldn't think of allowing such a match and would they please go back to their faro tables and take their panting, bowlegged brute with them.

But the gamblers were not to be put off so easily. They all knew him well, knew he had well-developed gambling instincts; he patronized their establishments with some regularity and was not averse to high stakes. Furthermore, most of them were his patients. However, he kept saying no until one of them proposed that a chain be kept on the dog and that it be pulled off and the fight ended the moment a judge said the dog or the bear was getting the best of it. Bets would be paid off on that basis, and it would not be necessary for either animal to suffer any real damage. They smirked when he agreed; it was apparent most of them thought the dog would make short work of the bear. He told them the match would have to be late that afternoon as he had work scheduled for most of the day.

That evening, shortly before dark, a large crowd gathered in back of the drugstore. Michael had a man holding his little cub on a chain near the edge of the arroyo. The snarling dog, also on a chain, was held near the back door of the building. After Judge Baird, his silk hat gleaming, had announced the ground rules and all wagers were covered, including the fifty dollars the physician placed on his cub, the signal was given, and the dog handler, holding to the chain, rushed forward with the bulldog. Lucy was sitting on her haunches, a little round bundle of dark fur. Michael's heart sank as the slavering dog launched itself. As the dog reached the cub, she came to life, slapped out with her right paw, caught the dog on the side of its head, knocking it over into the arroyo and jerking the chain out of its handler's hands. The gamblers whooped and yelled at this unexpected turn, and everyone ran to the edge of the arroyo and started whistling and calling for the dog. When there was no response, several men crawled down to search; but though they looked up and down the arroyo for a couple of hundred yards in either direction, there was no sign of the animal. After the bets had been paid off and the crowd had left, with much argument, laughter, and raillery, the physician examined Lucy carefully and couldn't find a mark on her. A day later, as a wagon train moved slowly west along Main Street, a cry went up from one of the spectators. The fighting bulldog, looking much the worse for wear, was slinking along under the wagons, dragging his chain.

But though rough and ready Trinidad had to have its rustic fun, there were serious things going on, too. There was a lot of railroad excitement in the air. The Santa Fe reached as far west as Granada in eastern Colorado by 1873, and though it had to hold up there because of financial difficulties, it was sure to come on west again. Some thought it would go up the Arkansas Valley to Pueblo; some thought it would ignore Pueblo and follow the Purgatoire River to Trinidad, and some thought it would do both. And General William J. Palmer's Denver & Rio Grande Railway, the first north-south railroad in the Rocky Mountain area, was putting down rails and moving steadily south from Denver, its goals El Paso and Mexico City. But first it wanted to tap the rich Colorado mining areas and divert the lucrative Santa Fe Trail trade from St. Louis north to Denver. While the Union Pacific and Kansas Pacific railroads were battling for supremacy in the northern part of the territory, Palmer made it into Pueblo late in 1872. It was as though a wizard had walked into the little town and waved a wand. The adobe buildings started coming down, and brick and stone structures went up. The population doubled and then tripled. Soon the railroad would start south again, and Trinidadians could hardly wait. They didn't much care whether it was the Rio Grande or the Santa Fe; they just wanted a railroad and the prosperity that would accompany it. A railroad would mean development of the rich coal lands of Las Animas County.

Lest there be any doubt in the minds of any railroad company that Trinidad was awaiting it with open arms, the citizenry met and organized the Las Animas Railway & Telegraph Company, capitalization: $1,000,000, and objective: to build a railroad from Trinidad down the Purgatoire River to La Junta. Thomas Stevenson was elected president; Michael Beshoar, vice president; Frank G. Bloom, treasurer; and Joseph Davis, secretary. Elected directors were Beshoar, Davis, Bloom, and Henry A. Barraclough. Once the corporation was set, the county commissioners ordered an election "to test the willingness of the voters" to approve a bond issue of $250,000 to back up the corporation, and Beshoar and Davis were dispatched eastward to tell the Santa Fe people what the alert citizens of Trinidad had accomplished. Alarmed by the Trinidad action, Pueblo did the same thing a short time later. Led by such citizens as Mahlon and Henry Thatcher, the citizens organized the Pueblo & Salt Lake Railroad, and the county voted to support the corporation with a subscription for $350,000 worth of the company's stock. Purpose: to build a railroad from Pueblo to the western terminus of the Santa Fe.

Michael acquired several tracts of land along the river east of Trinidad at this time on the theory their value would appreciate substantially when a railroad came up the Purgatoire. Also, he bought into the sheep business in a small way, acquiring two bands of about six hundred ewes each and hiring Mexican herders to pasture them on the free range east and southeast of Trinidad.

In the spring of 1873, Trinidad experienced a senseless killing that shocked its top citizens into action. There had been rumbles previously when a Trinidad sheriff had been murdered, with many citizens complaining that something ought to be done to stop such things. All through the West people were saying, "Watch out for Trinidad; it's an easy town to get killed in." The newest killing resulted from a disagreement that started on Main Street when Ed Clark, who wasn't very well liked, met Barney O'Neal, an esteemed citizen, to discuss a town lot a block or so south and west of the United States Hotel. O'Neal said he owned the lot; Clark said it belonged to him. After arguing for a few minutes, they walked up the hill to take a look at the property. A short time later three shots were heard. Sheriff George W. Thompson rushed to the scene, found O'Neal prostrate, and arrested Clark. When Michael got there, O'Neal was dead, examination showing that he had not only been shot but had been beaten over the head, probably with a revolver. Michael was terribly upset; O'Neal was an old friend, and had been one of the guests at his wedding.

Sheriff Thompson took Clark before a magistrate for a preliminary hearing, but a crowd of angry citizens appeared and took Clark away from him. They marched him to a nearby empty building, asked him a number of questions about what had happened, and then voted to hang him forthwith. They took him to the intersection of Main and Commercial streets and announced that Clark would be hanged at once. With the crowd swelling rapidly, the chant began: "To the cottonwood tree . . . to the cottonwood tree." They marched down Commercial Street, and as they passed a little adobe house, a woman standing in the doorway called out in a high-pitched voice:

"Goodbye, Ed. Goodbye."

"Shut up, you whore," Clark screamed back at her.

One of the good citizens leading him poked Clark in the ribs with his pistol and said in a commanding voice, "Shut up yourself. As long as we're treating you like a gentleman, try to act like one."

Clark was marched to the river and to a large cottonwood on the near bank that had served for a similar purpose on previous occasions. "String him up," several yelled. Clark revealed just before going to his Maker that, as was the case with so many Trinidad citizens, he had been using an alias. He said his real name was Arthur Bell. But whatever it was, he was soon swaying from a limb.

That night, May 20, 1873, fifteen of the town's leaders gathered in the combination law office and residence of E. J. Hubbard on Main Street between Commercial and A streets. To a man they felt that the killing of O'Neal was an outrage, and to a man they felt Clark got what he deserved. But they also believed it was time someone put a stop to lawless mobs. Before the meeting ended they had agreed to set up an organization, require an oath of its members, and a unanimous vote to admit any new members. They elected Hubbard chairman and Jerome Abbott secretary. The minutes were plain spoken:

Pursuant to a request, a number of citizens met at the office of E. J. Hubbard for the purpose of having a consultation and to deliberate upon the most effectual means of enforcing law and order in the town of Trinidad and the County of Las Animas, to protect the lives and property of all law-abiding citizens, and insure peace and tranquillity throughout the entire community. On motion, E. J. Hubbard was elected chairman and Jerome G. Abbott secretary of the meeting. The chairman then stated the object of the meeting and was followed by

Messrs. P. A. McBride, H. G. Pearson and A. W. Archibald, all of whom spoke at length, arguing and urging the necessity of devising some means by which all shall be made to obey and respect the laws of the country. The flagrant transgressions and total disregard of law as exhibited in several instances of late seemed to impress upon the minds of all the necessity of an organization which should take matters into its own hands, punishing criminals according to their just deserts.

On motion a committee of five was appointed by the chair, consisting of Messrs. P. A. McBride, E. F. Mitchell, H. G. Pearson, A. W. Archibald, and J. R. Winters, to draw up a constitution and by-laws to govern the actions and proceedings of the organization. On motion of Mr. Mitchell, E. J. Hubbard was added to the above committee. Mr. A. W. Archibald then offered the following resolution which was unanimously adopted:

"Resolved, that we who have met here tonight do pledge ourselves individually and collectively to use our greatest efforts to enforce law and order in our midst; to protect the lives, rights and property of our citizens; and secure peace and quiet throughout the entire community."

At the second meeting Archibald, Pearson, and Michael Beshoar were named to draw up an oath and a form of organization. They did so before the meeting adjourned, and the oath was taken by the fifteen men present—Hubbard, Pearson, Bernard, Cordova, Hammond, Barraclough, Mitchell, Dupont, McBride, Bond, Booth, Bright, Winters, Archibald, and Beshoar.

The word "vigilantes" does not appear in their minutes, and few of the fifteen members had any thought of doing any night-riding, but they were prepared to do that, too, if it was necessary to keep the peace in Trinidad. They resolved at their third meeting:

First: To aid the civil authorities in the enforcement of the law against criminals.
Second: In cases where flagrant outrages against law and order or where great crimes shall hereafter be committed and the civil authorities shall appear for any reason unable to perform their duties or where for any reason it appears that the

ends of justice will be evaded and thereby the guilty will escape, *to take such measures* as will in the opinion of the members of this organization effectually ensure the punishment of the guilty.

They decided they would limit their "interference" to crimes of murder, assault with intent to commit murder, burglary, robbery, rape, arson, and larceny. And they decided they would not hide behind darkness or neckerchiefs. In its comment on the hanging of Clark, alias Bell, the *Pueblo Chieftain* had noted that "the voice of the people was for hanging and this just sentence was executed with commendable promptness" and that this "was not masquerading or night business. All was done by good citizens without disguise of any kind and in broad and open daylight. Whatever consequences may follow the citizens of Trinidad are prepared to meet like determined men who have performed a deliberate act."

To keep their organization "in the daylight where it can be seen by the good and the bad alike," they set up a Committee of Safety whose membership would be public and whose duties would be to hear the complaints of citizens and refer them to the general body, which would remain anonymous and make decisions on what action should be taken on the complaint if any. Named to the committee: Messrs. Hubbard, Beshoar, Cordova, Barraclough, and McBride.

Although the general membership was supposed to be secret, it consisted, as did the five-man Committee of Safety, of the business and professional men of the community, most of whom had a background of Freemasonry. Everyone knew who they were and what they were going to do. Within hours after the third meeting, a chill wind was blowing along Main Street and down Commercial Street, so chill in fact that a number of roughs saddled up and left town.

Law and the preciseness of legal terminology appealed to Michael almost as much as medicine and journalism. It was his pleasure to write resolutions, draft bylaws for any type of organization, prepare formal documents of all kinds. He and Archibald had done the actual writing of the Committee of Safety bylaws, and he was probably the author of the *Chieftain* comment on the Clark hanging. Contracts and memoranda of agreement were Michael's special delight. One of the most novel he prepared at this time stemmed directly from a confinement case. He was called to the home of a poor Mexican family in a one-room hut of adobe and stone about three miles above town. The house had a flat dirt roof with a growth of weeds, four walls, and a dirt floor. It was explained that the woman had given birth to a stillborn baby, unattended, a week earlier and had been ill since. The physician quickly determined that she had puerperal fever and was near death. He did what he could, but the woman died shortly before midnight. On the only other bed in the hut, two little boys, nine and eleven, slept as the husband and father wept. He said he had nothing, no relatives, and did not know what he would do with the two little boys. Under questioning he said he did have a sister and, though she had several children of her own to feed, she might be able to take one of his. The physician said, "I'll take the older one. You come to my office in town after you have buried your wife and we will talk about it."

The result was another "present" for Annie, one she found more acceptable than the cubs, and another document:

This indenture, made and entered into this 28th day of August A.D. 1873 by and between José Susteno Pina, a minor of the age of eleven years on the fourth day of September last, of his own free will and accord, by and with the consent of Macedonia Pina, his father, of the County of Las Animas and Territory of Colorado of the one part and Michael Beshoar of the Town of Trinidad, County of Las Animas and Territory of Colorado of the other part, witnesseth:

That the said José Susteno Pina hath placed and bound himself apprentice to the said Michael Beshoar to learn to speak the English language and to become accustomed to American manners, customs and labor and to dwell with the said Michael Beshoar, continue with and serve him for the term of seven years from the date hereof until the said José Susteno Pina shall have attained the age of nineteen years to wit: until the 4th day of September A.D. 1880, and the said José Susteno Pina on his part agrees that during the said term he will well and faithfully serve the said Michael Beshoar and keep his secrets and obey his lawful commands; that he will do no injury or damage to his said master, to his goods, estate or otherwise, nor willingly suffer any to be done by others, and

whether prevented or not shall forthwith give notice thereof
to his said master; that he will not inordinately embezzle or
waste the goods of his said master nor lend them without his
consent to any person or persons whomsoever; that he will not
play at cards, dice or any other unlawful game; that he will
not contract matrimony during said term or haunt or frequent
groceries, tippling houses, places of gaming, brothels or the
residences or places of meeting of lewd women; that he will
not at any time of day or night depart or absent himself from
the service of his said master without his leave; that he will in
all things as a good and faithful apprentice demean and behave himself to his said master during said term.

And the said Michael Beshoar on his part agrees in consideration of one dollar to him paid, the receipt whereof is hereby
acknowledged, to teach and instruct the said José Susteno Pina
in the art of speaking the English language, and in American
manners, customs and labor so far as he may learn the same
by dwelling with the said Michael Beshoar and with his family
as such apprentice.

And the said Michael Beshoar further agrees to send the said
José Susteno Pina to a good English school one half of each
and every year—vacations and recesses and time of sickness
of said José Susteno Pino only excepted—and to furnish him
with such necessary school books and stationery as may be
directed by the teacher of said school.

And the said Michael Beshoar further agrees that he will
find and allow unto the said José Susteno Pina meat, drink,
washing, lodging and apparel, both linen and woolen, and all
things necessary in sickness and in health, meet and convenient for such apprentice during the term aforesaid.

And the said Michael Beshoar further agrees that he will
cause to be taught to the said José Susteno Pina the catechism
of the Roman Catholic religion and faith, and will afford him
at such time or times as may be directed by the parish priest
of the Roman Catholic Church the necessary means and opportunity of approaching the sacraments of said church and
also of attending Mass once on each Sunday and Holy day of
obligation in said Church.

And the said Michael Beshoar further agrees that at the
expiration of said term of service he will give to the said José

Susteno Pina twenty-five dollars in current money, a horse, saddle and bridle of the value of one hundred dollars, and two new suits of clothes suitable to his condition in life.

The killing of O'Neal over a town lot had caused a great deal of public uproar, but land disputes threatened killings on a large scale as the year progressed and land speculation increased throughout the area. For Michael it became an even more exciting and profitable game than it had been in Arkansas during his first years in that state. Large acreages could be had by merely filing on them in the U.S. Patent Office in Pueblo. Still other large and desirable tracts could be purchased for modest sums from people who had filed claims but were afraid of cloudy titles. Michael was as land hungry as he had been when he thought he was building a fortune in Arkansas before the war. He secured a block of 160 acres within the limits of Trinidad as well as extensive acreages in the county, including additional farm and ranch lands east of Trinidad and potential coal tracts in the piñon-covered hills to the west of town and in the Gray Creek area, five miles south and east of Trinidad.

Sound titles were difficult to come by, partly because of carelessness and lack of surveys, but mostly because of early Spanish land grants, which stood as potential threats. Men stood guard day and night over newly acquired properties. Charges and countercharges filled the newspapers, and the territorial legislature was petitioned for an investigation of land-grabbing. Along with many other Trinidad citizens, Michael joined in the cry for an investigation, leading the Las Animas County delegation in the territorial legislature to take a stand in behalf of righteousness and honesty. But the three-man delegation was soon discouraged as Representative Mariano Larragoite explained in a letter to constituent Beshoar:

Dear Friend:
   A few days ago I recive a leter of your which I did not answer immeditely but weytt more, so I can give some news. The House is composed by a majority of ignorants Republicans members who do only what the Denver ring want them to do. The council was organized Democratic but soon the Democrats sell out to the ring if you read the papers you

will see that they sell out the confirmations and still they
are at the market.

According to this order of business you can see that we the
members of the minority on the House are in bad fix. Perhaps
the Republicans will devided and then we may get something
to say about things but I don't think they will.

Writte me and let me know what is in regard to that steel
of land that the land grabbers trayed to make in our county.

Post me in all so I can memorialized to Congress.

Before the 1874 session ended, the physician tried to get the
legislature to offer inducements to the railroads to build into Trinidad; but the legislature, as it had been since its organization, was
in the hands of the Republican representatives of the northern part
of the territory, who were not interested in Trinidad. Convinced
he could get no action in Denver, Michael set out to sell his town
in another way. He wrote a series of frankly booster articles for the
Enterprise. When they appeared, marked copies were sent to territorial officials, railroad executives, members of boards of trade, and
colonization agencies in the East. In each article he pictured Trinidad as the very center of the finest scenery to be found in the
United States and as the service community of an area rich in
natural resources: "The Town of Trinidad, with the country surrounding it, so recently reclaimed from the untutored savage, is
situated on the right bank of the Las Animas or Purgatoire River,
in the midst of the finest agricultural and grazing region of Colorado
and New Mexico, and is surrounded by numerous veins of the finest
stone coal in the West and unsurpassed by any in the East. Trinidad
is adapted by nature to become a large town." And he didn't over-
look the health angle which he believed would soon become of
major importance to Colorado.

"To the health seeker," he wrote, "Trinidad offers a pure and
balmy air, exhilarating to the spirits, and imparting strength and
vigor to all who breathe it. The malarial diseases and epidemics so
common in the states are unknown." In one article he stressed that
Trinidad had not been "galvanized into a spasmodic existence by
crafty speculators or some monied monopoly," was free from law-
lessness, and could prove its claims to respectability by the presence of four religious denominations and "a considerable number
of American ladies." The reference to crafty speculators and monied

monopoly was a shot at General Palmer of the Rio Grande railroad, who was exhibiting as much interest in the promotion and sale of town lots, to the detriment of established communities along the line, as he was in actual railroad-building.

Michael's demands for an investigation of land-grabbing, his promotional efforts to bring new settlers to southern Colorado, and his own filings on land seem contradictions. Within a little more than a year, when he would be in the public eye throughout the territory, he would hear himself described as a land-grabber and worse by political opponents.

During this same period he got himself into an anomalous medical situation. He received an ad eundem degree from Miami Medical College of Cincinnati on presentation of a paper (advocating that coroners should be medical men, not laymen and not lawyers) and the payment of the usual fee. There was nothing wrong with this, as it was accepted practice for graduates of recognized and reputable medical schools to receive ad eundem degrees from other medical schools, and certainly this one had been a long time in the making. His first discussions with Miami had occurred in 1865 while he was at Benton Barracks in Missouri. But where he would get himself into hot water was in accepting a second ad eundem degree, this one from Dr. John Buchanan's American University in Philadelphia. The eastern medical establishment was gunning for the institution on the grounds that it was a diploma mill.

Whether he was bemused by the circumstance of the degree being offered by either an institution in his native Pennsylvania or by a fellow Mason is not clear. He was two thousand miles distant in a day of poor communication and may not have been aware of Buchanan's reputation, but whatever the background, he did submit a thesis on consumption and did receive an ad eundem degree. Some months later when Buchanan listed him in the University catalogue as "emeritus professor of medicine," he wrote Buchanan that the designation was unexpected, unsolicited, and that he had not known of it in advance. If he subsequently demanded a correction, there is no record of it in his surviving papers. At any rate, he seems not to have fully recognized the potential danger to his professional standing in having his name associated with Buchanan in any way. But he was to hear a lot more about it in due course.

His feelings of resentment toward the northern part of the state—

toward the Denver & Rio Grande Western Railroad and its land policies, the Republican organization of the north, and the general Denver attitude of looking on Pueblo and, even more, Trinidad as "those Mexican towns to the south of us"—led him into another medical venture at this time. When the territorial medical society was organized in Denver in 1871, a number of his close friends, including former St. Louis classmates Drs. Harrison Lemen and Gehrung, were charter members, but there were no physicians from southern Colorado on the rolls; they all lived and practiced in either Denver or one of the adjacent gold camps, which were booming. It was undoubtedly an oversight on the part of the territorial society, but whatever the reason, it pained Michael and he saw in it more of the familiar back-of-the-hand treatment from the north. His answer was to organize and incorporate the Rocky Mountain Medical Association for doctors in southern Colorado and northern New Mexico. The association was launched with seven members: Michael Beshoar, Thomas E. Owen, and Edward H. Weir (Michael's medical partner) of Trinidad; John Russell and Benjamin Dennie of Las Animas; Pembroke R. Thombs of Pueblo; and Robert H. Longwell of Cimarron, New Mexico. Beshoar was elected president, Owen secretary and Russell treasurer for the ensuing year.

At this first meeting the new association considered bylaws, adopted a mortar and pestle surrounded by the words "Rocky Mountain Medical Association" as its emblem, decided on the type of certificates of membership and ordered 200 printed, and elected Michael Beshoar as its delegate to the 1874 American Medical Association meeting in Detroit.

When the new president of the new medical association left on the stage for the Santa Fe railhead at Granada, Annie Elizabeth and José Susteno were on hand at the Overland House to see him off. He had thought of taking Annie with him, but the panic of 1873–74 had made money tight. He had in his pocket a letter from the Santa Fe, authorizing its agent in Granada to sell him a half-fare round-trip ticket to Detroit as a delegate to the AMA meeting. In one hand he had his traveling bag; in the other, a cage with an eagle in it, a present for the officers of the AMA. By the time he reached Kansas City, the bedraggled bird had become such a bother that he shipped it from there to Chicago to Dr. Edmund Andrews, who had been one of his professors at the University of Michigan School of Medicine. There is no record of what Dr. Andrews said or did when he received it.

On his arrival at the Biddle House in Detroit, the delegate from Trinidad, C.T., found that by some feat of magic or other Annie had gotten two letters there ahead of him. It was their first separation of any duration, and he was so overwhelmed by her thoughtfulness that he forgot to call her Miss Annie or Mrs. Beshoar in his return letter:

> My own Darling:
> You cannot imagine my delight at seeing letters from you today. Truly while you are not absent from my mind for a moment you have not forgotten or neglected me. I was so pleased that my face flushed, and I almost shed tears of joy. How good it is to feel that one is loved truly and devotedly by the object nearest the heart.

He wrote her each day and, in his last letter before leaving Detroit, reported on the first of a series of shopping trips he would make over the next three decades:

> Again I am delighted by the receipt of a letter from you. You cannot imagine how pleased I am to hear from the great . . . the sole object that is dear to me. I thank the gods that I shall be with you within a week. Time seems longer to me than ever before in my life. I shall take my bed in the cars tonight and shall go to my dear home as fast as steam can take me to Granada and the S. O. M. & Express line can transport me. I did not attend the meeting this forenoon as I had to canvass the city to find dove-colored gloves. I got the best I could find, two pairs, and a good supply of fine French perfume— "New Mown Hay." This cannot reach you more than one coach in advance of me. I am gratified to think that I have accomplished all I expected when I left home, but hereafter when I go away on such a trip I will have my dear little wife with me. Then I will be content, now I am not.

He was pretty pleased with himself. His Rocky Mountain Medical Association had been granted recognition by the AMA—which was something the territorial society could put in its collective pipe and smoke—and he himself had been made a "permanent member" of the national organization. There weren't any other AMA members, permanent or otherwise, in southern Colorado insofar as he knew.

What he didn't know was that Dr. Thomas Owen was simmering because Michael had gone to the Detroit meeting rather than himself. Michael was fully aware of the intense jealousy that existed among physicians everywhere, and he knew that in Trinidad much of it was directed against himself as the senior medical man, but all had seemed amicable enough at the first meeting of the new association, and there was no outward indication of how Dr. Owen felt about the trip even after Michael returned. Within two days the delegate mailed to the members of the association a report on the AMA meeting and a short time later called a meeting, at which time the proposed bylaws were adopted and sent to the printers. Dr. Owen seemed to be cooperative and even enthusiastic about the Rocky Mountain Association and its prospec

No matter what the rest of the territory might say about Trinidad and its all too frequent assaults, mayhems, and murders, its gambling halls and their cold-eyed dealers waiting behind stacks of gold coins, its noisy dance halls and painted girls, the residents of the town had a gift that often stood them in good stead: they had a sense of humor and they could laugh at themselves. They enjoyed light banter and indulged in it frequently though it sometimes led to trouble, especially when the liquor had flowed too freely. Above all they liked a funny story, particularly if it was local and involved people they knew. They liked, for example, the story about Jabez Fisher, an unfortunate little man who had suffered a spinal injury in the upsetting of a coach, and walked about the streets of Trinidad holding a pillow to his back. He was small, weak, and crippled, but scrappy and always looking for a fight. One fine day he challenged Michael's brother-in-law, cattleman W. T. Burns, to a duel over some fancied injury. Burns declined on the grounds that Fisher would present too small a target to shoot at, hence the challenge was invalid. Another typical yarn concerned another cattleman, George Thompson, the irrepressible Zan Hicklin, and A. G. Thornhill, sometimes Las Animas County deputy sheriff and sometimes Trinidad liveryman. Having gone to Taos on business, they got into a poker game with an overdressed English dude. Shortly before midnight when he was $600 ahead, Zan Hicklin wanted out, but since custom dictated that the winner could not break up a game or pull out, he had to continue playing. Zan was chewing a huge wad of tobacco. When he was $750 ahead he started spitting on the Englishman's shiny boots. When there was no reaction to this, he finally broke up the game by shooting a brown stream onto the Englishman's stiff white shirt. The Englishman challenged Zan to a duel. Hicklin, with the choice of time, place, and weapons, chose the coming dawn, the public plaza, and bows and arrows. When dawn came, Thompson, Thornhill, and Zan were reeling around the square looking for the challenger, but he failed to show.

Michael was a popular figure along the streets and in the saloons and gambling halls as he had a wealth of such stories, not only the local variety but Arkansas-Ozarks yarns that were cut from much the same pattern. He was reducing his drinking and gambling, as behooved a happily married man, but he still frequented his old haunts as they were the places in Trinidad where one met friends, business associates, and potential political supporters. Besides that, a substantial percentage of the customers and the men and women who cared for their needs were his patients as well as his friends.

During July, while listening to a saloon argument about how difficult it was to get from Trinidad to the San Luis Valley on the other side of the Culebra Range to the west, he conceived the idea of building a direct route. As matters stood in 1874 (and 1973), the only way one could get from the Purgatoire River Valley to the San Luis Valley was by circuitous routes southward via Taos or northward via La Veta Pass. Michael, with his current medical partner, Dr. Edward H. Weir, and a William Marr, incorporated the Trinidad & San Juan Short-Route Waggon [sic] Road to build a short route. It was a serious effort. The capital stock of the company was fixed at 150 shares at $100 per share. San Juan was essential in the title, the incorporators said, because in due time they might want to continue the road on from the San Luis Valley to the great San Juan Mountain district of extreme southwestern Colorado.

While he was busy promoting his "waggon" road, Mike, Jr., arrived back in town. If the father had seen his son walking along a street or in one of the business houses or saloons, he would not have recognized him. Towering above his father, he stood five feet eleven and weighed a lean, muscled 175 pounds. His long black hair was in sharp contrast to his bright blue eyes and fiery red moustache. He was, he told his father, a former Texas cowpuncher who had come home to meet Annie Elizabeth and "become a dutiful son." Annie was not pleased with this unexpected intrusion into her new home life. She didn't like Mike's appearance or his manner, and she felt sure that his arrival meant trouble for her husband, who had told her some of his problems with Mike. While Michael had been careful in what he said, Annie suspected Mike had given his father many heartaches.

For his part the physician provided Mike, who was flat broke, with a room and meal and stable money "until we can talk about your future and what you are to do next." But Mike had been in town only a few hours before it was apparent what he was going to do next: two-fisted drinking and roistering with the town's fancies.

Father and son had several talks when Mike was sober enough to emerge from the saloon and dance palaces, but there wasn't any real communication between them. The father spoke from his Pennsylvania Dutch background with its strong concepts of filial duty and the work ethic, while Mike's outlook was shaped by his years as a war orphan, boarding-school student, and cowboy. The physician kept offering to send Mike to college, but all the word college meant to Mike was more Christian Brothers' Academy. After one bitter session about his conduct, Mike disappeared from Trinidad once again. As was the case the first time he left, Michael resigned himself to hoping it would all work out somehow.

In a matter of months, Mike wrote from Sipes, Texas, that he had been working and doing well and that he planned to "come home" again. He must have been surprised at the reply he got, for he wrote back to his father:

> In your letter you say that if I have not changed and become temperate and moral my return home would be regretted by me & cause you many heartaches &c &c. I am coming home again and I intend to behave myself in a becoming manner & by doing so I think I never will regret my return nor cause you any heartaches. If I should cause you any it be but little trouble for me to leave again.

His next letters were from Elgin, Kansas, where he was working on a farm and the next batch came from Stephenville in Erath County, Texas. The father provided money periodically and in due time, after Mike said he hoped someday to own his own farm in northwest Texas, again offered a medical education, to which Mike replied:

> Your most kind and affectionate letter of the 6th inst. received. I have no words to express my sincere and heartfelt thanks for the favors you have bestowed upon me. I acknowledge all you say in regards to the many disadvantages of a farmer's life, but yet I have several objections to the medical profession:
> 1st. I do not think the medical profession would suit me. I do not like it, and it is one of the hardest lives a man could encounter.
> 2nd. It would take some time and a large amount of money to complete my education. That amount invested in something else would by all probability yield me a much nicer income than the medical profession would and I could study and get a good common education that would take me through the world respectfully, doing honor to your name and stamping myself with an irreproachable character.
> I would rather live in N.W. Texas than any place I know of in this world, because I know how to love and I am loved. I have the goodwill of everyone here. Father, I have turned a new page since I saw you. I hope by the grace of God to carry my resolution faithfully to the end. It is true that I cannot expect anything from your hands, but I do not want you to get angry at my many askings. This country is settling fast, very fast and land will in a few years demand a good price. I will close by saying that if you will help me a little I will repay your kindness by strict attention to work and leading an exemplary life that will be an honor to you in your declining years.
> I can and will, if necessary, produce recommendations of my life for the past two years by good citizens & Masons.
> Hoping to hear from you soon, I am, dear Sir
> Your loving son,
> M. Beshoar

At age forty-one Michael didn't think he was in his declining years or about to go into them, but after a few more exchanges of letters and many emotional assurances from Mike, he bought his son 160 acres of good bottomland near Stephenville, Texas. "All I can do now is hope for the best," he told Annie. The purchase of the land, a long trip by Annie, and the 1875 depression, an economic disaster that virtually stripped Trinidad of money, left the physician hard pressed. Annie took the stage to Granada, caught the Santa Fe, and went to the Nation to visit her brothers, John and James. Brother John, a former Quantrill guerrilla with a notable record with blazing Colt navy pistols, was running a general merchandise store at Colbert's Station on the Red River, opposite Denison, Texas. From there she went on to Frankfort, for a two-month-long visit with her parents.

During Annie's absence he wrote her almost daily, filling his letters with detailed accounts of his movements, his practice, jokes, what was happening among the doctors of the town, how the animals were behaving, and of course the woman gossip. When some Utes came into town and sold him a mountain lion cub, he wrote Annie an enthusiastic letter about it, and then a sad one: "The kitten grew rapidly and was quite lively. He would bend up his back and spit and show fight at any animal he saw, even my horse when he came up to the door. All was well until an awful thing happened. I was here in the office alone. José had gone to the planing mill after shavings to make a water cooler. He had gone out the back way and left the door open. The lion was in my office and I was writing at my desk. Unobserved by me the lion went out into the back. Lucy saw her and rushed up to play. To play with such a brute the lion would not. He bowed his back, swelled his tail and spit and then sank his claws into Lucy's nose. She reached for the lion with one paw, caught him by the head, picked him up and then swiped at him with the other paw, tearing him in two. The poor thing expired immediately."

And he wrote Annie that the depression was causing an exodus of doctors. Dr. Weir and his new bride were going to Illinois, Oscar Menger had moved up to Stonewall, Dr. Le Carpentier had moved to Denver, Benjamin Blake to Arizona, and Dr. Cushing was exploring the San Juans with a view to moving to that area.

"The faculty is now reduced to Drs. Small, Owen, Charles Menger and myself and Dr. Owen says he is disgusted and thinks he will not try to practice any more."

Soon after Annie returned, he decided he would seek the office of probate judge being vacated by the alcoholic Pat McBride, who intended to run for the territorial council. Michael not only liked the law but he wanted to test his strength in the county. He won the nomination easily enough, and though McBride had been having his troubles as judge, he too got his heart's desire in the form of the nomination for the territorial post.

At the outset the physician received an accolade from the *Pueblo Chieftain*, which expressed the opinion that "he will certainly be the best posted in the duties of that office of anyone who has been judge of that court since Las Animas County was a county. Though not admitted to the bar, he has a better knowledge of law than many who have the parchment."

His Republican opponent was his sometime patient and often antagonist, lawyer A. W. Archibald. During the campaign they went at it hot and heavy, each issuing circulars expressing doubt about the ability and honesty of the other while proclaiming his own in the florid style of the day. While Michael had the handicap of being a physician rather than a lawyer, Archibald had more serious handicaps in Las Animas County; he had a strong vein of religious prejudice, and his antipathy to Mexicans had come out strongly in the race war of 1868. The *Pueblo Chieftain* predicted that Beshoar would win by 400 votes, also noting that Pat McBride had been reported to be dead but was in fact alive, though desperately ill in his room at the Overland House in Trinidad. Everyone in southern Colorado knew that "desperately ill" meant "dead drunk."

The physician campaigned vigorously as the word was out that, while the Republicans did not hope to win many offices in Las Animas County, they intended, with the party throughout the territory lending support and aid, to defeat Beshoar and McBride whatever it took to accomplish that end.

In the general election only James R. Brooking, Democratic candidate for the controversial office of superintendent of schools, topped Beshoar, who beat Archibald easily by a majority of 498, which was equivalent to a third of the votes cast, while McBride barely squeaked through with a margin of 98 votes.

At the first session of court in October, lawyer J. M. John, who thought the post should have gone to a lawyer, sought to test the mettle of the new judge. When he was fined five dollars for contempt, he tossed the money to the bailiff and stalked out of the courtroom, slamming the door behind him. Three minutes later he was paying another five dollar fine for slamming the door of the probate court and thereby disturbing its proceedings. A day or two later there was a second probe, this one by lawyer J. C. Packer, who was promptly fined fifty dollars for contempt. When he refused to pay, Judge Beshoar sent him to jail. After six hours of meditation, Packer paid up, and from there on the sailing was smooth enough, so much so that the *Pueblo Chieftain* remarked in its issue of October 12, 1875:

"Probate court has been in session (in Trinidad) this past week and the members of the bar are generally gratified at the improvement in the court and the methods of procedure. Attorneys who heretofore did not desire to practice before this court, are now satisfied to do so as they believe justice will be administered with dignity and impartiality."

Chapter 8
Politics and Perfidy

CHANGE WAS THE ORDER of the day in Trinidad and Colorado Territory as the year 1875 waned. For the discerning eye there was no surer sign of what was happening than the occasional visit of a band of Utes. They would wander into town, somewhat apprehensively, not to take scalps or steal horses, but to do a little crow-hopping dance on the streets and pass their big, high-crowned black hats in the hope of getting a few coins for food and whiskey. Newcomers thought the Indians were colorful, but most of the oldtimers ignored them or went out of their way to express their contempt by spitting into the dirt and turning their backs on the "dirty beggars." Michael Beshoar was usually good for a small touch and even a little free medical care on the few occasions when his assistance was sought. He recognized that the Ute visitors and their new status in life were an important sign of change. There were other signs, too, of which Padre Munnecom was an example. After years of tippling, playing poker, transacting business deals, and fattening his pocketbook, Padre Munnecom was replaced by two dedicated Jesuits, the Rev. Carlos M. Pinto, who had been stationed in Pueblo for three years, and the Rev. Alexander Leone, who came across the mountains from a post in the San Luis Valley.

Padre Munnecom was to stick around for another two or three years working, not as a priest but as a businessman, before returning to his native Weert in Limburg; but his ouster by the Bishop of Denver was an important milestone. He had been a controversial figure throughout his Trinidad pastorate, but while many of the complaints against him were undoubtedly justified, he was also a maligned man. After his removal (which was later to be referred to by religious historians as a resignation), he spent part of his time hanging around Michael's office and drugstore, doing some carpentry work and other odd jobs for him. They were good friends, compadres as it were, and the physician didn't want to see him hurt even though he knew that a changing Trinidad and a changing parish needed better spiritual leadership. The Protestants and anti-Catholics of Trinidad had long whispered that Munnecom had killed a fellow priest in Taos before coming to Trinidad and that he had been sentenced by the Pope himself to spend the rest of his life within fifty miles of Taos as punishment. After he left Trinidad, the same people said the padre had taken with him Sister Marcella, a Sister of Charity assigned to the parish school, and that they had fled to St. Louis and were never heard of again. However, he corresponded with a number of Trinidad residents for many years after his return to Europe.

There was some substance to the murder story, but Padre Munnecom's calumniators had it twisted. He and Stephen Avel, who had been ordained a priest in Clermont, France, in 1844, were members of a band of missionaries brought into the American Southwest in 1854 by Archbishop Lamy to replace a decadent priesthood. Fathers Avel and Munnecom were stationed in Mora, the mountain community in north central New Mexico that provided most of the first Spanish-speaking settlers of Trinidad and Las Animas County. In the parish was a kept woman who called for a priest when she became dangerously ill. Padre Munnecom responded but refused to give her the sacraments unless she would send away her paramour, a man named Noel. She agreed, was reconciled to the Church, and died repentant. A short time later Father Avel took an early Mass for Padre Munnecom, who was out on a sick call. The sacramental wine had been poisoned, and Father Avel died soon after drinking it, with Noel present during his death agonies.

Noel accused Munnecom of poisoning the wine, claiming he was jealous that Father Avel was his superior. For two years Father Munnecom lived under a cloud while he was charged and tried for murder. After he was acquitted and restored to his priestly office, the story that he was responsible for the murder lived on, partly through the efforts of the Freemasons.

And there were other changes: The Rio Grande Railroad was laying rails south of Pueblo and advertising that it had trains leaving Denver daily at 8 A.M. to connect with both the Barlow & Sanderson coaches, which left Pueblo each day for Trinidad, Cimarron,

Fort Union, Las Vegas, and Santa Fe, and the Pueblo & Del Norte
Stage Line Company's "mud wagons" to the new mining districts
in the San Juan Valley; there was talk of statehood and a great deal
of lodge activity. The Knights of Pythias had their new Rocky
Mountain Lodge No. 3 very much in business, and such Trinidad
veterans as Henry Barraclough, Michael Beshoar, and Philo B.
Sherman joined with some other business and professional men in
founding Las Animas Lodge No. 28, A.F. & A.M. in the Year of
Masonry 5875.

Although Michael had published a fee schedule of his own, he
felt the changing times (and one local physician's repeated under-
cutting of his colleagues' prices) required some sort of agreement
among Trinidad's doctors to put the practice of medicine on a
sounder and better-paying basis. He called the town's three other
doctors to a meeting to set up "articles of agreement between
Charles Menger, Oscar Menger, T. E. Owen and Michael Beshoar
whereby they do mutually agree, each with the others, or any or
either of them that in consideration & for the purpose of mutual
benefit and protection, they & each one of them will do & perform
the things hereinafter contained, as follows, to wit: 1st: That each
& every one of them will keep a list, to be known and designated
as 'The Black List of the Physicians of Trinidad' which list shall
contain and consist of the names of persons who through dishonesty or neglect, refuse or fail to pay & discharge their indebtedness to any or either of the parties hereto." It was agreed they would
furnish one another lists of such delinquents with their addresses,
that they would not accept cases on a "no cure, no pay" basis, that
they would not accept payment for their professional services in
anything other than money, and that if one of them failed to live
up to the agreement he would pay each of his colleagues $1,000.
Among other items in the pact, it was agreed that: "It is a serious
error in a medical practitioner to give his services free of charge
to ministers of the Gospel. They have no more just claim upon physicians for their services than the mechanic for his work, the merchant for his goods, the baker for his bread or the landlord for the
use of his house. . . ."

The blacklist worked, more or less, for four or five months and
then gradually fell into disuse; the signers were much too secretive
about their practices and too suspicious of their colleagues to exchange lists of deadbeats or anything else on a regular basis. But

the general resolutions about charging had, as Michael intended they should, a good effect on how patients were charged. Some of the items, such as no annual fee for medical care, were being incorporated into codes of ethics by medical societies in various parts of the country.

For most purposes of discipline and order in the profession, his Rocky Mountain Medical Association, complete with a code of ethics very similar to that of the American Medical Association, was serving well. The association was showing a healthy growth. New members were coming in from all over southern Colorado and New Mexico. At a meeting in Pueblo, the association voted to change its name by adding the words "and New Mexico Territorial Society." It also instituted machinery for district societies and elected Dr. R. H. Longwell of New Mexico president. The outgoing president, founder Michael Beshoar, was elected secretary.

Several papers were read at the meeting and it was announced that the AMA had granted the organization two delegates for future AMA conventions. In self-recognition of its growing importance as a professional body, the association set up sections on surgery and anatomy, obstetrics and diseases of women and children, materia medica and physiology, medical jurisprudence, chemistry, and similar subjects. When the Pueblo meeting ended, the participants were aglow about the organization's progress and prospects.

Early in 1875, President Grant appointed John L. Routt, second Assistant Postmaster General, as governor of Colorado Territory. A Kentuckian by birth, who had caught Grant's attention at Vicksburg while serving in the Ninety-fourth Illinois, Routt was sent to Colorado to heal up breaches in the Republican Party and bring warring factions together, a task he carried out with considerable success. On the heels of his appointment, Congress passed an enabling act to pave the way for the territory's admission to the Union. Most of the southern Colorado Democrats were opposed to statehood. Their public reason: they didn't believe Colorado had sufficient population to warrant statehood; privately they feared Republican control and more domination by the northern part of the state.

A constitutional convention, to which the Republicans had elected twenty-four of the thirty-nine delegates in an election on October 25, assembled in Denver late in December 1875. It met for eighty-six days, wrangling about such controversial matters as woman suffrage, tax aid to church schools, taxing of church property, and railroad regulation.

While it was deliberating, Michael was joining with other citizens in getting the town of Trinidad incorporated. The Board of County Commissioners appointed Abner Rowland, Jesus Maria Garcia, Michael Beshoar, Samuel Jaffa, and Isaac Levy as the first Board of Trustees.

Between his practice and his private business (which now included the drugstore, town lots, ranches, cattle, sheep, and more than three thousand acres of farm and potential coal lands) plus his lodge work and his public duties as town trustee, probate judge, and an official of the school board, Michael was a busy man; but he had his eye on bigger things. When statehood seemed assured, he decided he would try for the office of governor or for the United States Senate. He had several major handicaps, which he recognized at the outset: he was a Confederate veteran, a resident of the less populous south, and a "Mexican" county at that, and he was not widely known in the more heavily populated north, particularly in the humming metal-mining areas. But these weaknesses were strengths in some ways. The Democrats would have to give the nomination for at least one major office to southern Colorado, from which their strongest support would come, and they would have to give recognition to the Spanish-speaking element. Miguel Beshoar had little doubt he would have Mexican support for any office he might seek.

During the early spring he made some preliminary soundings throughout the territory, receiving guarded but on the whole encouraging responses. He wrote letters to county leaders, physicians, friends, business acquaintances, and fellow Masons, dropped in at newspaper offices, and had close friends and associates send letters to the various newspapers in the territory saying Michael Beshoar was being discussed for governor or the U.S. Senate. He heard rumors that Pat McBride, who had become enamoured with and by some of the people in the Democratic organization during his service in the territorial council in Denver, also had aspirations and was putting himself forward as the popular man with southern Colorado voters in general and Spanish-speaking people in particular. Since Michael had been treating McBride for alcoholism for a long time and knew the gentleman's strengths and weaknesses well, he was not inclined to take McBride's maneuvering too seriously—a mistake that was to provide him with many a headache during the months ahead.

On April 6 politics and everything else were suspended for the day in Trinidad while everyone went in buggies, carriages, and wagons, on foot, and on horseback, to El Moro, a new town four miles to the east, to see the Denver & Rio Grande Western Railroad put down the last rails into the town and bring in a little narrow-gauge engine with a string of cars loaded with lumber, household goods, machinery, and other freight. There were both excitement and resentment. The railroad's Colonel D. C. Dodge had ordered a new town built, and he had had his superintendent of construction A. C. Hunt, the former territorial governor, send J. R. DeReimer, assistant general engineer, to lay it out. DeReimer had bought up all the land in the vicinity and had named the town El Moro because the battlements of nearby Raton Peak reminded him of those of Moro Castle in Havana. The Trinidadians had sneered at first, but now they were deeply concerned. Homes, store buildings, shops, saloons and warehouses were going up; big outfits such as Otero, Sellers & Company from New Mexico were on hand to do business as was the big commission house of Walsen and Levy. The *Enterprise and Chronicle* had moved from Trinidad to El Moro and had become the voice of the railroad, leaving Urbano Chacon's *Pioneer* the only newspaper in Trinidad. Some said Trinidad would wither and die. Michael was not among the prophets of doom; he contended the railroad terminus was in El Moro because its immediate objectives were Solomon Young's coal mine on nearby Gray Creek and the sale of town lots, which was a big money gimmick with the Rio Grande wherever it went. The wool business could be had just as easily in El Moro as in Trinidad or any other spot in the area as the wool people had to haul their product to the railroad in any event.

But he had seen enough frontier development and knew enough about the country to know that the Rio Grande Railroad had to come on to Trinidad eventually and that it or some other railroad would go on southwest of Trinidad into New Mexico and on to Arizona and California. Some of the people talked about going to El Moro some night and burning the place, but wiser counsel prevailed.

Colonel Dodge thought it would be a fine idea to move the county seat from Trinidad to El Moro, and a crisis was precipitated when armed railroad men appeared in Trinidad in substantial numbers along with reports that they intended to seize the courthouse, appropriate the county records, and move them to El Moro. Volunteers joined sheriff's officers in guarding the courthouse, and the Committee of Safety, which was still in existence, called on loyal Trinidadians to keep their arms and horses in readiness in case any attempt was made to seize the county and forcibly move it.

By midsummer El Moro had more than a hundred buildings, a post office, a baseball team, and other evidences of an established community, but Trinidad was still on the map and still growing. Furthermore, Trinidad merchants, most of whom didn't like the Rio Grande and felt it discriminated against them, asked both the Santa Fe and the Kansas Pacific railroads to send all freight from La Junta to Trinidad by mule and bull teams rather than to Pueblo by rail and thence south from Pueblo on the Rio Grande to El Moro— a maneuver that hurt the Rio Grande seriously as it thereby lost thousands of dollars in freight charges.

When the proposed state constitution, a wordy but workable document on the whole, was submitted to the people for a vote July 1, Michael took little part in the election. He was still opposed to statehood, but in view of his intention to seek high office when it came, he refrained from getting involved in the election on the constitution. It was adopted by a light vote, 15,443 to 4,062, with most of the opposition coming from the southern counties, from people who didn't like the domineering northern part of the state, and from Roman Catholics, who didn't like the provision that no state funds could go to parochial schools. The canvass of the vote was completed July 24, and on August 1, 1876, President Grant issued a proclamation stating that the admission of Colorado "into the Union is now complete." Issuance of the proclamation set the political wheels spinning at top speed.

Michael, in a quick trip to Denver, again set forth his claims to the nomination for governor and stated his aspirations to serve in either that office or in the U.S. Senate. He didn't get much encouragement. In a meeting in a Denver hotel, several party leaders told the aspirant from Trinidad they did not think it would be possible, in view of the political climate and the way the population was distributed in the new state, to put over a former Confederate and resident of the "terra incognita" south of Pueblo as the party's candidate for governor. Again, there might be a way. Bela Hughes, a former Union Army general, stage-line and railroad executive, and presently practicing law, might run for governor, but what he really wanted was a seat in the U.S. Senate. If he was elected governor and then resigned, the lieutenant governor would become governor and could name Hughes to the Senate. A ticket headed by a former Union general who was a business leader in the northern part of the state teamed with a former Confederate from southern Colorado who had the support of southerners and the Spanish-speaking voters would have possibilities.

Any Democratic ticket was sure to have a rough go of it as the Republicans would nominate Routt, who, along with the rest of their ticket, would have the backing of the national administration, business, veterans of the Union Army, the populous north, and the press.

It was all pretty logical, and when the Democrats shook hands at the conclusion of the Denver meeting, Michael had a new target in his political sights: the office of lieutenant governor. Shortly after his return to Trinidad, a newspaper report said: "In political matters, Dr. Beshoar's candidacy for the lieutenant governorship seems to meet with cordial and favorable response in every quarter of the Democratic fold. He is beyond question the choice of Las Animas County and in the convention will get her earnest support for the nomination as long as he has a prospect for success."

With the Democratic convention scheduled for August 29 in Manitou, a medicinal springs and health spa midway between Denver and Pueblo, and the election set for October 3, Michael got his campaign for delegates underway immediately. A letter was prepared and a number of Democrats in Trinidad and elsewhere in the county sent them out over the state:

> Dr. Beshoar is a candidate for the office of Lieutenant Governor and will go into the State Convention with the entire delegation of this and several other counties unequivocally pledged to his support.
>
> It seems to be generally believed that his name will materially strengthen the ticket in Southern Colorado and that he can carry this and neighboring Huerfano County by 1200 to 1500 majority. He ran more than 400 votes ahead of his ticket in this county for Probate Judge last year.

I think our county will ask no other state nomination and that we will be entitled to that one as a matter of justice. I hope you will find it agreeable to procure the instruction of the delegation from your county for our candidate for lieutenant governor.

In addition to the letters, Michael made a trip north to visit Denver and the mining camps in the mountains to the west of the city. He heard that Pat McBride also was out looking for delegates and that he had made some slurring remarks about Dr. Beshoar, but again the physician didn't take it too seriously. After all, he had an agreement with the state officers of the party, and leaders in Denver, Pueblo, Trinidad, and presumably elsewhere in the state knew of it and approved of it. He didn't see how he could miss winning the nomination, but political experience and prudence dictated that he conduct a campaign and obtain as many pledges and instructed delegations as possible.

The *Rocky Mountain News*, no friend of his and no friend of any Democrat, didn't give him a line in its preconvention political stories, but it repeatedly praised Pat McBride, much to the amusement of Trinidadians who knew their former judge as garrulous, irresponsible, and drunken. As a businessman Pat was in a class with his brother, the missing Sam McBride; he had made some money in land and sheep but had frittered it away, seldom paying a bill if he could help it.

Candidate Beshoar and Uncle Dick Wootton set out for the Manitou convention August 27 via the narrow gauge from El Moro to Pueblo, where they visited with lawyer M. B. Gerry, a former Confederate officer, and other members of the Pueblo delegation. In Manitou they had rooms at the handsome 150-room Beebee House, which boasted "three evening hops each week during the summer season." Casimiro Barela and one or two other Las Animas delegates would follow them shortly. If they didn't make it, for any reason, it wouldn't matter as Michael Beshoar had their notarized proxies in his pocket.

During the late morning and afternoon of August 29, they "politicked" with incoming delegates around the Manitou House and other hotels. Uncle Dick was not only a good Democrat and a good handshaker, but he was a fine showpiece and drawing card. People sought him out to shake his big paw, relate some anecdote of the past, and meet his companion, the dark-complexioned, black-haired, quiet-spoken little physician and judge from Trinidad who hoped to be the nominee for lieutenant governor. Pat McBride, loud and boisterous, arrived during the afternoon with several members of the Denver delegation. He ensconced himself in a bar and announced he was the big man with the Spanish voters in southern Colorado, that he was a bosom friend of General Hughes, and that he was a candidate for lieutenant governor. Michael and Uncle Dick found this worrisome, wondering whether it was just McBride's usual drunken talk or there was something afoot they didn't know about.

The convention was called to order at 8 P.M. in the dining room of the Manitou House with the Hon. W. G. Miller, chairman of the Democratic State Central Committee, in the chair. He told the delegates that he saw before him Republicans who had joined up to help fight the corruption stalking the land, and "I see men who are scarred from wounds received under the national banner, as well as former Confederates, all combining to stay the corruption and work together for the good of the country." When he had finished, Pueblo's Colonel Gerry was elected temporary chairman. After more oratory and the appointment of a credentials committee, the convention was recessed until the next day.

The next morning, while the convention was selecting its permanent chairman and candidates were busy maneuvering for delegates, the *Rocky Mountain News* arrived with a story to the effect that a glance at Democratic politics, while waiting for the verdict of the convention might be a "harmless and perhaps not unprofitable amusement." The *News* said there were indications that Las Animas County, through Pat McBride, was going to stand in "with the Denver pool," and that "it is said that McBride is not very much in favor of Beshoar's nomination for lieutenant governor, but he is not unwilling that the nomination should be forced on himself. If he can deliver the Las Animas vote there will be nothing in the way of his receiving the nomination, but Beshoar will have to be placated and will probably require the short term nomination for Congress." Michael knew that McBride had made some friends in Denver while serving in the council, but since he had all of the Las Animas votes in his pocket, the *News* story didn't seem to be anything more than idle speculation.

Late in the afternoon, after the convention had taken an informal ballot that showed Hughes an easy winner and a recess had been taken until 7:30 P.M., a bombshell in the form of an anonymous circular was dropped on the delegates. It charged that Michael Beshoar had:

(1) Stolen 1,000 sheep in Las Animas County.

(2) Forged deeds to 5,000 acres of land in Las Animas County.

(3) Forged and mutilated the records of the probate court of Las Animas County.

(4) Purchased Mexican proxies to the convention at $200 per proxy.

The charges electrified the delegates. Michael, at first bewildered, presently said in a flat, cold voice that he was going to see McBride, and several others talked him out of it, impressing upon him that any physical violence would do him irreparable harm at this point. Besides, they said, there was a chance that McBride was not responsible for the smear, that someone else was attempting to beat him out of the nomination. However, a check among the delegates quickly confirmed that McBride was understood to be both the source of the charges and the man who would provide substantiating evidence at the proper moment. Again Michael wanted to hunt up McBride and again was talked out of it. Once they had his assurance he would not do anything rash, his supporters circulated among the delegates, saying the charges were malicious slanders and that McBride was an habitual drunkard and a frustrated and bitter man.

R. M. "Doc" Stevenson, on hand to cover the convention for the *Chieftain*, assured candidate Beshoar that he had canvassed the delegates and that "everything is going to be all right."

When they re-convened in the big dining room at 7:30 P.M., the delegates quickly nominated Bela Hughes by acclamation, and then proceeded to the business of nominating a lieutenant governor. Under the rules of the convention, an informal ballot would precede the formal and nominating ballot. When a delegate from Clear Creek jumped to his feet and nominated Casimiro Barela of Trinidad, Michael knew he was in for trouble. Barela immediately withdrew, after which T. C. Bigney of Huerfano County placed Michael's name in nomination. That should have ended it, but Arapahoe County's C. S. Thomas, one of the powerhouses of the party in the northern part of the state, nominated a popular southern Colorado sheepman, Joseph Kenyon of Canon City. The first ballot gave Beshoar 46, Kenyon 27, McBride 13, Martin 3, Hough 1, Adair Wilson 5, and Barela 1.

On the motion of delegate Glassman of Arapahoe County, the convention agreed to move immediately to a formal ballot, whereupon McBride announced he hoped all of those who had voted for him would cast their ballots for Kenyon. When the roll was called, the vote was Beshoar 42, Kenyon 51, McBride 3, Wilson 2, and Ellis 1. For a few minutes it appeared that all was lost. McBride was slapping people on the back and shouting, but in the midst of all the tumult someone discovered that the convention had cast 99 votes, or one more than the legal number. The chairman then threw out the ballot and ruled that a second would be taken.

Colonel Gerry, yelling, "Mr. Chairman, Mr. Chairman . . . ," finally got the floor and reported that he had talked with Joe Kenyon shortly before he had left for the East on business and had been told by Kenyon he was not a candidate for any office. Delegate Thomas, in response to a question from the chair, said he didn't know whether Kenyon would accept the nomination or not and that he had nominated Kenyon "at the request of an outsider."

During a brief recess McBride tried to talk to Las Animas County delegates about support for himself and, failing in that, tried to start a movement for Charles Unfug of Walsenburg. When the convention went back into session, Las Animas County delegate Harris obtained the floor. Saying he had only contempt for the lobby that was trying so desperately to defeat Beshoar, he asked the chair to call on Casimiro Barela for a statement on how the Spanish-Americans of southern Colorado felt about the matter.

In his halting English, Barela said, "It is hard for me to say in English the sentiments of myself and my people in the counties of Las Animas, Conejos, Costilla, and Huerfano. I will, however, give our reasons for bringing out Dr. Beshoar as lieutenant governor. Dr. Beshoar carried the county of Las Animas one year ago . . . we want the candidate from our county and we think we are entitled to it. . . . I am here to do my best for Beshoar. Mr. Kenyon will give no strength to the ticket. We do not want anything but the lieutenant governorship and my people will be satisfied with that." Boulder County then announced it was shifting its support to Beshoar, and on the next and final ballot the vote was Beshoar 85 and Kenyon

12. One delegate refused to vote.

As McBride, his face flushed, stalked out of the dining room, Michael thanked the delegates. "I will make speeches during the campaign at places and times where they will do the most good," he said.

The next day, as the delegates were on their way to their respective homes, one Denver newspaper said of Bela Hughes:

> If elected he will never serve as governor beyond a few days. The people may vote the Democratic ticket, but in doing so they do not vote for Hughes but for Michael Beshoar who occupies the second place on the ticket at the present time. The success of the Democratic ticket means the immediate election of Gen. Hughes to the United States Senate. This is the certain alternative of Republican success, and it is an event which persons who know Beshoar cannot contemplate with much satisfaction. His only qualification for the office is his residence for some years in the strongest Mexican and Democratic County in the state. He talks Mexican and has long been their closest associate. He is nominated because he claims ability to control many Mexican votes and because he demanded the office. The question for the people of northern Colorado to decide is whether they want John L. Routt or Michael Beshoar for their governor. Hughes is out of the question for he goes to the Senate if his party wins. It is Routt or Beshoar.

The days immediately following the convention were bitter ones for the physician, for his friends, and for the Democratic party in Las Animas County. Charges and countercharges were made. The Republican newspapers, which made up most of the state press, kept the McBride accusations alive, though the Denver newspapers, with the exception of the *Rocky Mountain News*, were cautious in their treatment, making only oblique references to the charges of sheep-stealing. One, in a report datelined September 8 from Trinidad, said that the Democrats, whom it called "the great unwashed" (which in northern Colorado terminology meant Spanish-speaking persons), had held a rally in El Moro and that when Dr. Beshoar spoke he seemed disconcerted "by the bleating of a flock of sheep with which some Mexicans were threshing their wheat across the way, and after a few labored remarks sat down, doubtless cussing those sheep and Pat McBride."

The *Enterprise and Chronicle* in El Moro, as a mouthpiece of the Rio Grande Railroad and hence of the Republicans in the northern part of the state, was the most ferocious of them all, printing the charges over and over. McBride himself came up against the gun at a heated party dinner in the United States Hotel in Trinidad. A letter that McBride had written after an involved sheep deal some four years earlier was exhibited and read: "Any insinuation to the effect that the doctor had any criminal connection with any purchase, transfer, moving or concealing of sheep is malicious and without foundation in fact." All present were given a look at the signature, including McBride, who acknowledged it was his signature and that the letter was true. He told the group that he had nothing against Dr. Beshoar and knew nothing against him. The *Pioneer* reported: "He only felt the delegates from this county to the state convention had treated him badly. But though he felt he had a right to complain and though he did not regard Dr. Beshoar as his personal friend, yet that should not affect his democracy and in October he would vote the whole Democratic ticket."

The dinner meeting marked the end of McBride, but it was not the end of his charges insofar as the Republican press and Michael Beshoar were concerned. Throughout the September campaign the opposition newspapers made repeated references to them. The *Enterprise and Chronicle*, in its issue of September 20, 1876, said:

> If Dr. Beshoar is an innocent man he has been fearfully traduced. The allegations concerning a little transaction in sheep did not come from a Republican source, the "alligator" was a Democrat and one "dyed in the wool." If McBride knows nothing against Beshoar as he now sees fit to state, then Beshoar is one of the worst abused men in the state and fit to be an angel without any purgatorial probation, and the Republican papers are the most unmitigated liars that ever went unhung. McBride has made a refutation of the charges in a speech in Trinidad. Either McBride made these charges or some very respectable gentlemen who were present at the Manitou convention lied like horse thieves.

Michael paused long enough in his campaigning to assemble with the McBride letter several other papers: a note dated April 8, 1872, in which L. E. Booth promised to repay a loan of $700 to M. Beshoar along with interest at the rate of 1 percent per month; a copy of a bill of sale for 600 ewes, which had been made out to M. Beshoar by L. E. Booth and then posted as security for the loan with E. B. Sopris, Trinidad businessman; the original copy of an agreement between Messrs. Wilbers and Pritchard and L. E. Booth, dated December 1, 1871, whereby the sheep were placed in Booth's custody for a period of seven months; and an affidavit in Spanish, sworn to before Justice of the Peace W. R. Walker by Jesus Gurule to the effect that he had personal knowledge of the acquisition of the sheep by M. Beshoar from L. E. Booth and that he "and my son and a burro of mine were employed by Michael Beshoar as shepherd of a group of sheep purchased by Michael Beshoar from L. E. Booth." Gurule said he had cared for the sheep on Frijoles and San Francisco creeks east of Trinidad and had had them up in the Ratons on the Colorado–New Mexico line for a time before he received an order from M. Beshoar to deliver the sheep to Noah Camblin and Pat McBride. "I always understood that the deal was legal and that Michael Beshoar acted honestly in the transaction, that L. E. Booth had no right to sell the sheep, and that Booth alone was to blame."

With his papers assembled, the physician filed a $10,000 derogation of character suit against the *Enterprise and Chronicle* and proprietor J. M. Rice, and then went off to campaign with Thomas M. Patterson of Denver, the Democratic candidate for Congress. After a rally in Trinidad, they made a trip by buggy to Walsenburg, to La Veta, and over La Veta Pass into the San Luis Valley. In Del Norte they split up, with Patterson going on to the San Juan mining district and Michael staying in the valley to campaign among the Spanish-Americans in the home bailiwick of the Republican candidate for lieutenant governor, Major Lafayette Head of Conejos, a veteran of the Mexican war, former Indian agent and U.S. marshal, and widely known sheepman. Michael made four to five speeches in Spanish each day, drawing an almost hysterical response from a *Denver Tribune* correspondent, who, though he didn't sign his name to his stories, used the personal pronoun freely. One of his dispatches had most of the state chuckling and undoubtedly created Beshoar votes:

One of these blossom-nosed suckers says we now have a man that will put a head on the Negro lover's candidate and his name is Dr. M. Beshoar of Las Animas County; he tried his best licks to put a head on that county commissioner named Martinez of his own county in the following manner: This M.D. would-be lieutenant governor, in one of those memorial election days that occur once a year in Las Animas County, made a drive into one of the Mexican settlements adjacent to Trinidad; after his arrival he took out of his buggy a good supply of that old standby to which the average Democrat is so partial—"old bourbon," and was overjoyed with his success in capturing a few votes. His team, with more respect for themselves than their owner, made their way through the plaza and overturned the vehicle to which they were attached, and of course out went the liquor that was left in the cart. A few inquisitive Indians happened that way and gobbled up the contents of a number of jugs; the consequence was they soon became noisy and made things lively in that particular neighborhood.

This gentleman of pills, having had some misunderstanding with Mr. Martinez, because as I have been informed, he opposed some illicit transactions of this doctor, or some illegal issues of county warrants that was to be made in favor of that renowned ring that has existed to the disgust of all good citizens in Las Animas County for years, makes his way to the United States Grand Jury which was in session in Pueblo, or to the United States attorney who was attending to the business of government in Pueblo two years ago, and made accusations that on the election day above mentioned this man Martinez was selling whiskey to the Indians contrary to the laws of the United States. This man was arrested, dragged to Pueblo, compelled to employ a lawyer and throw himself under the gaze of his friends who at that time held him as a violator of the laws of the land.

While Hughes was subjected to steady attack during the campaign, the more scurrilous and vicious editorial assaults were reserved for Michael Beshoar. They played heavily on northern Colorado sentiments against ex-Confederates and Mexicans, and the supposed cleavage in the party as a result of McBride's behavior in the Manitou convention. The *Rocky Mountain News* sought to widen division in the party with such reports as:

> It remains to be seen whether the southern Democratic vote can be captured with such chaff as General Hughes threw on his flying visit in that direction. He went as far as the railroad would carry him, but didn't appreciate the southern people enough to make sacrifices of his personal comfort for the sake of seeing them at their homes. He met Dr. Beshoar, his associate on the ticket, but rather turned up his aristocratic nose at the doctor, and 'shook him' as soon as possible. And Patterson, if reports be true, wasn't much more gracious. He didn't approve the cut of Beshoar's clothes, nor the style of his last year's hat, nor the appearance of his hands, which are neither so white nor soft as the Honorable Tommy's. But it is altogether likely that Beshoar was touched by the condescension of these two great men and will work for them to the extent of his ability, notwithstanding the fact that they are doing nothing for him but mischief.

Election Day, Tuesday, October 3, was cloudless and serene. The physician had José drive him to his polling place early. A few Mexicans idled about in front. Their white teeth showed as they greeted him, "Buenos días, Señor Gobernador"; they doffed their hats and bowed to him, the bow they kept for a patrón. Their use of the title governor pleased him immensely. He shook hands with them, calling each by name—all of them were his patients.

After he had voted, he made some house calls, saw a number of patients in his office, and then shortly before noon went out to visit along Main and Commercial streets. Everywhere there were friendly hails and assurances. Even his Republican friends stopped to wish him well and hint slyly that they were breaking over. He knew most of them were voting the straight Republican ticket, but some would vote for him and it gave him a warm glow.

Early in the afternoon he forgathered with Democratic party people in a one-room adobe headquarters to read telegrams from state headquarters in Denver and special news dispatches. Laying aside his silk hat and his red vest, Michael sat in comfort as he read the telegrams aloud, first in English and then in Spanish. As the reports came in from Denver, it became apparent that the Republicans in the capital were getting information faster than the Democrats or the newspapers and that, strangely enough, they were getting wires sent in by Democratic county organizations to Democratic state headquarters before the Democrats got them.

"Something is seriously wrong," Jerome Abbott said. "We've sent in three reports now, and the Republicans got them first. I wonder what is going on up there in Denver?"

The physician studied for awhile, chewing a pencil into splinters. Abbott was right; there was no doubt of it. A report from Las Animas County on the congressional fight between Democrat Patterson and Republican Belford had been in the hands of the Republicans a good hour before the Democratic committee got it.

"I've got it," he finally told the crowded room. "I know how we can settle this. But we will wait until tomorrow."

Returns were slow everywhere. In county after county they had to be sent into county seats by horseback or wagon. Some precincts wouldn't be reported for several days. When he went to bed election night, after many a drink with friends and supporters, Michael was hopeful. Annie just knew he had been elected, that no one could possibly beat him, but he thought he had maybe a fifty-fifty chance of winning. Wherever enough votes were in to give any kind of indication, it appeared the two parties were of about equal strength with the Republicans having a slight edge in the early returns.

Wednesday he again made house calls and saw patients in his office before going to the Democratic headquarters to read the telegraphic reports.

"We are going to fix the Republicans and some stinking telegraph operator," he told his associates after he had run through the dispatches. "We'll trap them this time."

He wrote out a telegram and passed it around. "All of you are witnesses," he said. "I want you to read this dispatch and I now state that it is sent to Denver for no other purpose than to expose the perfidy of the telegraph people and our opponents."

Hon. Hugh Butler, Democratic State Central Committee
Denver, Colorado
Please inform me by return wire what number the majority
must be from Las Animas County to carry the state. Yours,
                                                    M. Beshoar

Within an hour the Republican State Central Committee in Denver was charging that a monstrous plot to steal the election was being hatched in Trinidad. The Denver newspapers carried the Republican blast along with acid comments about Michael Beshoar and the crooks and thieves in Las Animas County and among "the great unwashed."

The physician followed his wire with a letter to Hugh Butler:

> You perhaps thought strange a telegram in which I inquired how many majority we must have in this county to elect the state ticket. If you considered it a joke you were right, but it was a joke with an object—a bait at which the sucker bit and was caught.
>
> We had a strong suspicion that the manager of the Western Union Telegraph Company in Denver, as the willing tool of the Denver Republican ring, was violating the secrets of his office in the interest of his master. I thought that in his zeal he would bite at a hook covered with such bait. The dispatch was submitted to the inspection of a half dozen friends, who all thought it would work as designed.
>
> We now see by the Denver papers that it did work like a charm, and we suspect that the dispatch was made out in duplicate and delivered to the Republican State Headquarters simultaneously with the one delivered to you.
>
> Respectfully,
>
> M. Beshoar

And Chairman Butler thought so too:

> I was glad to get your explanation because for awhile I was annoyed and puzzled. As you suspected the enemy had a copy about as soon as I rec'd the original and perhaps before. Chaffee said it was heard passing over the wires at Colorado Springs by some friend of Jackson and that they got it in that way, but that is too thin.
>
> Yrs.
>
> Hugh Butler.

But cute wires or no cute wires, it soon became apparent that the Democratic state ticket had gone down in defeat without electing a single Democrat. The Republicans had made a clean sweep.

Routt, with 14,154 votes to 13,316 for Bela Hughes, had won by a margin of 838 votes; Lafayette Head had 14,191 to Beshoar's 13,093 or a margin of 1,098. However, Michael's proposed majority of "1,000 to 1,500 votes in southern Colorado" had been delivered; in the four southeastern Colorado counties of Las Animas, Pueblo, Huerfano, and Bent, he had garnered 3,075 votes to Head's 1,834— a margin of 1,241. He had run neck and neck with Head in Head's home territory in southwestern Colorado but had been over- whelmed in the north.

One of the first letters to reach Michael after the election came from the congressional candidate Tom Patterson:

> The fight is over and we are both laid out. No blame can be attached to the South for this sad state of affairs, the fault lies with the North, and we bear the blame. Your brilliant canvass more than justified the claims made in your behalf by your friends at the Manitou convention. Were the nominations to be made over again in the light of the late election your nomination would be made without a dissenting voice being raised. What can we say of north of the Divide? As Democrats we feel chagrined and yet we know that we were overpowered by the use of money, and the influence of every railroad, bank and other corporation in the state. We are not discouraged, but we will pick our flints and try again."

Major J. M. Rice, editor and proprietor of the *Enterprise and Chronicle* went east immediately after the election, and his staff said he wouldn't be back for many weeks. But whenever he came back, Michael Beshoar would be waiting to press his suit against him and his newspaper for defamation of character. The physician had his affidavits, written statements, character witnesses, and lawyers all ready to go. He thought he might sue the Denver newspapers, too, but held off as he didn't want to get in too deeply. After Rice and the *Enterprise and Chronicle* were cared for would be time enough. In mid-November the *Rocky Mountain News* ran a piece from one of its correspondents that was reprinted in the *Enterprise and Chronicle:*

The doctor claims that about $10,000 would be sufficient

patch for the rent in his character, but as the ruling price for "character" of a democratic order in the county ranges from a drink of whiskey to a sack of XXX flour many of our fellow citizens think the doctor's figures a little too high, else they were sadly swindled at the last election. It would be better for the doctor to heal the wound in his reputation with some of his own medicine than to try to compel Major Rice to perform that unpleasant operation. The latter, who is a crippled Union soldier, says he will make the doctor's character look worse than Caesar's mantle. I predict that the doctor will be the most sheepish man in the county when the case is closed.

Rice, on his way home, reached Denver the last of November, and the *Rocky Mountain News,* right on the job, told its readers that it would be remembered that Major Rice ran the newspaper in Trinidad which remarked during the campaign that somebody had said the Democratic candidate for lieutenant governor had stolen 1,200 sheep, but the report was a mistake "the number being only 835 or thereabouts."

By March 1877 the suit was ready to go to trial before District Judge John W. Henry in Trinidad. Michael was in court with his lawyers, George Boyles, John W. Waldron, and J. E. Martin. Rice appeared with his counsel, A. W. Archibald and R. F. Dunton of Trinidad and Michael's former *Chieftain* writer, Wilbur F. Stone. Rice's lawyers asked for and immediately got a change of venue to Douglas County in the northern part of the state. In its next issue the *Enterprise and Chronicle* hailed the change of venue with big headlines:

THE GRAND LEGAL TOURNAMENT!
THE CARNIVAL SHOW OF OUR CENTENNIAL YEAR

TRINIDAD AS USUAL THE HEAD CENTRE

THE BLINDFOLD GODDESS OBLIGED TO BORROW
A PAIR OF LATEST HAY SCALES TO WEIGH IT

BESHOAR VS. ENTERPRISE AND CHRONICLE

$10,000 DAMAGES!!

The paper said that "the Goliath, as it were, of Las Animas County democracy, pills, character and things had matters pretty well arranged for a trial in this democratic county. Important witnesses were believed to have been 'conciliated' by little jobs and things until they 'couldn't rest' in any other way than on top of the cover which by some means had been placed over the Well at the bottom of which Truth is supposed to lie perdu.

"Some of our democratic friends believed that our opposing Goliath carried a ready made jury in either pocket and some even thought that our honorable district court could be taken on that giant palm and 'by pressure' be squeezed, be desiccated as it were, entirely dry of justice."

The *Enterprise and Chronicle* had a merry time, telling its readers that after Wilbur Stone moved for a change of venue and the judge granted it, Dr. Beshoar could not articulate the word damages "but contented himself with repeating about once for every dollar claimed, the first syllable of the word, interspersed with other elegant exclamatory phrases . . . his character don't seem to be in sight. About as perceptible as the distant $10,000."

It was a good show, and the newspaper and its proprietor seemed pretty confident. In view of the fact that Major Rice and his lawyers undoubtedly knew what Michael would present in court, his own lawyers felt that the opposition would try to get the source and the only source of all the charges into court and have him repudiate his letter exonerating Beshoar in the sheep transaction. Michael didn't believe they could pull it off as Pat McBride had stood up at the dinner in the United States Hotel after the letter was read and affirmed it. But his lawyers worried.

In any event, the court in Douglas County would not be in session until December and a lot of things could and no doubt would happen before then. Annie was with child, expecting her baby to arrive about the middle of July, and his practice was booming, not only in Trinidad and the county but through the mails. Men and women in towns and small communities and on isolated ranches in several western states sent him their symptoms by mail, requesting medicine and directions by return mail.

If he thought they should come to Trinidad for a visit, he tried to induce them to do so, but if that was not possible, he would make a diagnosis and send them medicine. An example was Mr. Clay Allison, the tall, handsome, polite, and exceedingly dangerous pistoleer who rode in now and then from northern New Mexico for treatment and a contra-indicated but sportive time in Trinidad's ample facilities. But mostly Allison wrote a description of his symptoms of the moment, and since he had only one health problem, diagnosis was easy and accurate; Michael kept the noted gunman supplied, by coaches running south from Trinidad, with *herba del buey* and full directions.

He also received substantial mail from physicians scattered around the West who sought his advice and counsel on medical problems encountered in their isolated practices. Sometimes their queries forewarned him of things to come, as in May 1877 when Dr. L. A. Cooper wrote from Red River, New Mexico: "The small pox is slowly wending its way up from Santa Fe. I shall begin vaccinating soon and would you be kind enough to send me a good vaccine crust. Please let me know what to do about the proper charge for vaccinating and will you let me know what you think of the cream of tartar treatment or can you suggest anything else that will be of service in the treatment of the disease. I hope to avail myself of your greater experience (shall I say—And age?). Thanks for past kindnesses."

The black smallpox may have been slow wending its way from Santa Fe to Red River, but it didn't take long to hit Las Animas County. By the tenth of June it was epidemic. The odd thing was that it was pretty much confined to Indians and to Mexican children between the ages of four and thirteen; few Mexican adults contracted the disease and practically no Anglos. Virtually all of the remaining Indians in the county, regardless of age, were stricken and died.

Michael dropped everything to cope with the epidemic. He and Father Pinto, traveling by buggy, went to the most remote parts of the county, visiting isolated ranches and tiny little adobe hamlets. The physician used scabs to vaccinate on a mass basis with Father Pinto serving as his assistant. When medical arguments failed to persuade a family to permit the children to be vaccinated, Father Pinto provided the voice and authority of the church to get the necessary cooperation. When he wasn't helping the physician, Father Pinto kept busy with baptisms, funerals, long overdue marriages, and other clerical functions.

Within a few days the two men were near physical exhaustion. They got little sleep, drove long hours over poor roads or none at all, and worked hard wherever they found people, all the while living on a diet of goat meat, frijoles, and tortillas. Before they were finished, they had covered virtually all of Colorado's biggest county: 4,798 square miles of mountains, mesas, and prairies varying in altitude from 5,300 to 14,000 feet, and in length and width from 11 to 55 miles.

The Denver newspapers were hysterical about the epidemic, with the *Tribune* reporting six thousand dead in the Trinidad area. The Trinidad merchants took an opposite tack. They disparaged the seriousness of the epidemic, insisting there wasn't anything to it and that reports of the disease were started by merchants in competing cities in Colorado and New Mexico to take business away from Trinidad. Actually about a thousand persons contracted the disease, and 400 of them died.

By mid-July the epidemic had about run its course. The country around Trinidad dried up under the hot sun, and the roads and streets became rivers of dust. Grasshoppers ate the crops, and everyone complained about hard times. For his part, Michael stuck close to home waiting for the new arrival. And Annie was right on the dot, presenting him with a fine baby girl July 13. Or perhaps he presented her with the baby as he delivered the child himself, not trusting such an important family event to an outsider.

He had decided in advance that any children he and Annie might have should have the initials B.B.B., and to this end had bought *The Book of Names* to supply himself with names beginning with *B*. After poring over it for a day or two, he picked Beatrice Bonaventura. Annie was stunned, but if those were the names the doctor wanted. . . . The new baby got the two names formally November 12, 1877, when she was baptized by Father Pinto. That evening most of Trinidad turned out to a supper in Ward & Tamme's Hall, followed by dancing to music provided by Pascal Gerardi's band. It was a fine affair, and everyone congratulated the proud parents, but tongues clucked too: Beatrice Bonaventura; it was almost too much. "But then," as one lady put it to one of Annie's friends, "Dr. Beshoar is a bit eccentric."

July and November were important months to Michael in still another way. When Pat McBride was found dead of alcoholism in a Denver hotel in July, the *Enterprise and Chronicle*'s position in the slander case became hopeless, and by November, Major Rice and his lawyers were ready to get out as best they could be-

fore the December term of court in Douglas County. When they
sent word they would like to settle out of court, Michael was amen-
able. The newspaper paid him a flat sum of money, paid all legal
fees, and printed a story retracting everything it had said about him
during the campaign. Most of the state newspapers took note of the
settlement; some, such as the *Denver Times*, in a simple story:
"A mutual agreement having been effected between J. M. Rice
of the *Enterprise and Chronicle*, and Dr. M. Beshoar, the latter
has withdrawn his suit for slander resulting from the vigor of the
political campaign in 1876." The *Daily Democrat* in Denver put the
cap on the episode with:

> During the excitement of last Fall's campaign, The Trinidad
> Enterprise and Chronicle, edited by Major Rice, published
> unfounded charges against Hon. M. Beshoar, the democratic
> candidate for lieutenant governor. The people of Southern
> Colorado and of the entire state for that matter expressed their
> opinion of this political slander at the polls by giving Judge
> Beshoar the full party vote. And now, after preliminary mea-
> sures in the courts, Major Rice takes everything back. Further
> comment not needed.

Soon after the settlement his card reappeared in the *Enterprise
and Chronicle* along with a special note written by Major Rice:

> In another column appears the 'ad' of Dr. M. Beshoar. He
> is the pioneer physician of Southern Colorado. He is a graduate
> of several of the most reputable medical colleges in America
> and has been actively engaged in the practice of medicine for
> 25 years, the last twelve in the Rocky Mountain country which
> has familiarized him with the climatic influences and the
> phases of diseases peculiar to this country.

Great fellow, Michael Beshoar, but not for long.

Chapter 9

Bloodshed in the Barroom

AFTER SEVENTEEN LONG YEARS of living in hotel rooms, tents, barracks, surgeon's quarters, back rooms of drugstores and medical offices, and, more recently, rented houses that were little more than cottages, Michael Beshoar became a homeowner once more. Unlike his former house, a two-story white frame on his farm at Fourche Du Mas, north of Pocahontas, the new one was a two-story adobe with thick walls, located on Trinidad's East Main Street within easy walking distance of the center of town. He bought the lots from the estate of the late Don Felipe Baca, designed the house himself, and supervised its building by Mexican workmen. It wasn't much to look at, but then Michael didn't have much taste where houses were concerned nor much interest in them. He built the house only because he had Annie and Bonnie, and would probably have more children. He still thought of Colorado as a place to make money, and once his fortune was made he intended to return East to live. So the Trinidad house didn't matter too much so long as it was reasonably comfortable and secure for his family.

The new house had a front library, parlor, back parlor, dining room, and kitchen on the ground floor. A narrow staircase led from the library up to the second floor with its three bedrooms and large storage closet. Behind the house he built three adobe rooms for servants'quarters, each with a single door opening onto the yard, and behind them a large frame barn and a good-sized corral for his horses, and a cow. He put an American type, gabled, shingle roof on his house, but the servants' quarters had flat adobe roofs in the Mexican style. He put in good privies and arranged to buy water for household uses from the town water wagon, which would deliver it regularly each week to the kitchen door. He had an adobe wall five feet high built across the front of his property to screen out dust from the street and to keep out cattle and horses, which were often driven along Main Street in large numbers. When it was finished, his new house and outbuildings looked almost exactly like those to be found on dozens of ranches in southern Colorado and northern New Mexico, neither better nor worse.

Also at this time he took on a partner in the person of Dr. W. G. Scott of Wyandott, Kansas, who was recommended by a close friend and fellow Mason, George B. Wood, president of the Kansas City and Wyandott Railway Co. The understanding was that Scott would relieve him of most of the night calls and much of the office routine, thus freeing him to give more attention to land developments and to his coal acreages, which he believed were enormously rich, and more time for other activities. Shortly after Dr. Scott's arrival, Michael was elected grand chancellor of the Knights of Pythias in the Rocky Mountain area; soon he was doing more traveling putting on degree work and attending K. of P. functions.

The traveling was often tiring and difficult. In a letter written to Annie from the depot in Black Hawk, a bustling mining community in the mountains west of Denver, he pictured some of the tedium and problems of his K. of P. work:

Dear Annie:

I reached Georgetown Monday, saw some Knights and made the forming of a new lodge a sure thing, saw a foot race on which about $500 a side was pending, and saw the firemen practice with hose, hook and ladder. At nearly dark I started in a buggy with Dr. Weiser and another gentleman for Silver Plume and Brownsville over a fearful road, precipices 1000 feet and perfectly perpendicular. I could appreciate, but not enjoy the sublimity of the scenery. We returned to Georgetown at 10 o'clock yesterday morning.

During the day I shook hands with a large number of people and saw one of the new acoustic telephones; I bought one to use from our house to the office. After supper I went to the K. of P. Lodge and conferred the third rank on two persons and then attended a public function at which were present about three hundred ladies and gentlemen. I retired at midnight and got up at 4:30 this morning, took the 5:30 train for Golden and sure enough the passenger car, while backing at one of the worst places, jumped the track. The car was full, 25 to 30

passengers. There was great fright and the car was smashed
up. But fortunately everyone escaped without serious injury
though most of the passengers were frightened nearly to death.
We all walked down here to Black Hawk and the agent
promises he will have another train for us in two hours.
Nothing to do but wait so I concluded to drop you a line.
I will go to Cheyenne this afternoon, return to Denver
tomorrow and catch the first train home.

Yours Truly,

B

The Pythian work, plus missions for his Rocky Mountain Medical Association and the Colorado State Medical Society, in which
he had taken out a membership, along with his work as county
judge and his practice kept him on the go day and night all summer
even though Dr. Scott had taken over part of the practice. But he
was not so busy as to be unaware that Dr. Thomas E. Owen, the six-
foot-four North Carolinian who had served in the Mexican War
under Zachary Taylor and in the Confederate Army, was busy
hatching a political plot, perhaps kindled by the professional jealousy that resulted when Michael—not Owen—was selected to
attend the Detroit AMA meeting some years earlier. Owen had
served as president of the Trinidad Board of Trustees in 1876 and
1877, and was building ambition on ambition as he prospered in
the cattle business. There had been an intimation of his intentions
early in the year when a Denver newspaper reported that the
"Missouri outfit" was planning a Democratic newspaper in Trinidad, to be financed largely by Dr. Owen and with attorney S. S.
Wallace as the "heavy editor and political expounder." Wrote the
correspondent of the Denver paper:

Dr. Beshoar, Jesus Maria Garcia and all the other old liners,
men who have so often led the Democracy to victory in this
county are ignored by this ring of reformers. I have it on the
best authority that the first move will be to assault the official
position of Judge Henry of this judicial district and prepare
the way for his impeachment by the next Legislature. Mr.
Wallace is big with this idea and hopes to get himself elected
to the bench. Judge Beshoar also will catch it from the first
jump. . . .

The promised newspaper didn't materialize, but Michael observed with interest that the Republican-oriented *Enterprise and Chronicle* became friendly to Democrat Owen and his coterie. He had a strong suspicion that any money intended for a new newspaper had found its way to the *Enterprise and Chronicle* but he kept his peace as there was always the possibility the Denver story had been made up out of thin air to cause trouble in the Democratic ranks. Garcia thought it was more than that, and so did Michael when attorney Wallace started writing letters in July to Arkansas, Pennsylvania, and Ann Arbor asking questions about Michael's education, medical background, character, and so forth. Some of the people queried were fellow Masons or former close associates, who promptly sent copies of the correspondence to Michael. It was obvious that an assault was imminent.

By fall the word was around that Dr. Owen would run on the Democratic ticket for county commissioner with the expectation that that office would consolidate his political position in the kingdom of Las Animas and provide a stepping-stone to state office. There were rumors that he intended to run S. S. Wallace for county judge against the incumbent Beshoar and, once in, Wallace would be groomed for the office of district judge to replace Judge Henry.

When the Democrats held their nominating convention in Lynch Hall in September, Michael was on hand, seeking return to the county court and determined to keep Owen from being nominated for the county commission. When nominations were opened for commissioner, he jumped to his feet and nominated Sam Doss, who was fully as important a stockman as Owen. There were no other nominations for commissioner. And Michael was again nominated for county judge without opposition. By the time the convention ended, all seemed harmonious, but that night Doss showed up at the Beshoar house to say he couldn't possibly make a campaign or serve as commissioner as his business required every minute of his time. He was sorry, but he would have to withdraw.

The day after Doss's visit, the *Enterprise and Chronicle* announced that the Democratic Central Committee had met and selected Dr. Owen to fill the vacancy. Michael and Jesus Maria Garcia were furious. They called a number of Democrats to a meeting and, after a long and often heated discussion, decided that they would let the Owen nomination stand even though they believed it illegal and that they would oppose him and beat him with an independent candidate. They chose José Andrés Salazar for their candidate, and Michael sent a devastating letter to the *Pioneer*:

I am a Democrat, as you know, and as such have always been willing to sacrifice my own choice for the choice of the party whenever expressed by the party. But there is a certain individual pretending to run on the Democratic county ticket who has neither been nominated by a convention, nor by a majority of the Central Committee, as a candidate for county commissioner. After Sam Doss, the regular nominee, had withdrawn, a job was put up by which Dr. T. E. Owen was nominated by less than half the Central Committee, who were called together by himself, in his own office, late at night, when and where the door was locked and the windows securely curtained while the plot was effected to foist him upon the ticket. Objectionable as he is for the position to which he aspires, if he had been nominated by a majority of the Central Committee, which is the smallest number which could nominate in the name of the party, I might feel obliged not to oppose his election, but as he was not, there is now no nominee of the party, and as his opponent, Mr. José A. Salazar, is not running on a party ticket, it seems to me that the choice as to which I shall support is a mere question as to the fitness of the two candidates.

Mr. Salazar is an old resident, long and well known in the county. Dr. Owen is comparatively a newcomer, and during the time he has been here his associations have been almost exclusively with such newcomers as happen to be congenial to his nature, principally designing adventurers who entertain a strong prejudice against all old settlers, Mexican or American, and deem themselves superiorly capable of governing the county as soon as they arrive here. Dr. Owen is himself a political adventurer. As a stepping stone to the county commission he has twice run for trustee of the town of Trinidad, and demagogue like, in each instance he appealed to all Democrats and Republicans, and especially to all Missourians and Texans, claiming to Missourians to be a Missourian, to Texans to be a Texan, to Democrats to be a Democrat, and to Republicans to be opposed to Las Animas County Democracy. By wearing these different masks in

approaching different persons he succeeded in having himself
elected in each instance—the first time by quite a large
majority—the last time, when he was better known, by the
skin of his teeth.

As to his honesty I do not wish to say anything. We know
that Salazar is honest, and we do not know whether Owen
is or not. Some of his transactions while president of the board
of trustees leave it an open question which I do not propose
to decide. It is sometimes difficult to judge justly between
dishonesty and ignorance. If he is honest I regard him as
incapable; if capable I regard him as dishonest. He has very
little interest in the honest and able administration of our
county affairs. He lives in the county, it is true, and owns
just enough property to maintain a comfortable residence in
Trinidad, while he keeps his stock on the Panhandle in Texas,
where he escapes paying taxes on them. He uses Trinidad as
a refuge from Indian raids and Las Animas County as a field
to aspire for county office. . . .

The death thrust was in the final paragraph, which said that Dr.
Owen owned some stock in the First National Bank "which he can
draw out any time and put in the Panhandle if he thinks it more
profitable, unless he can get it exempted from taxation by getting
on the county commission."

Dr. Owen made no public reply to the letter until after he had
gone down to defeat in the election by a vote of 872 to 710. In
reporting the result, the *Enterprise and Chronicle* said, "This is
where Beshoar's work shows." When the Owen reply came in the
same paper, it took the form of an attack upon the professional status
of Michael Beshoar. It accused him of being ignorant of medicine;
of having no evidences of graduation from a medical school; and of
attempting to cover his lack of qualifications by asserting he had lost
his diplomas during the war "when said diploma was really a
license to peddle quack medicines in Northeastern Arkansas." He
accused Michael of forming the Rocky Mountain Medical Association for no other purpose than to get himself admitted into the
American Medical Association and to appoint himself as a delegate
to the national body's Detroit convention.

"He wrote his own credentials and signed my name to them as
secretary and hurried off to Detroit," Dr. Owen said. "I suppose he

told them many things about the great RMMA, whose jurisdiction extended from the Divide in Colorado to the southern line of New Mexico, and whose annual meetings were attended by hundreds of physicians almost as well skilled in the healing art as himself. But unfortunately for the RMMA after his return the doctor wrote up the proceedings of an imaginary meeting in Pueblo and had them published in the *Pioneer*. By some means, the secretary of the American Medical Association received a copy of the paper, and also intimations of the mystical character of the RMMA. He wrote me a letter marked private requesting me to give him the exact status of the association. I complied with his request. The doctor never has attended a convention of the association since; the reason may be easily imagined. Having retired from the practice of medicine I feel perfectly indifferent concerning the opinion of Dr. Beshoar's friends about my right to the title of M.D. Unlike the doctor, I exhibit no bogus evidences of graduation to deceive ignorant friends."

The allusion to "Dr. Beshoar's friends" was a reference to street gossip that Owen, who was trying to prove that Michael didn't have a medical degree, had none of his own. The Owen letter caused "Many of Dr. Beshoar's Dear Friends" to come back with a long letter in the *Editor and Chronicle* denying each of Owen's charges in detail and concluding, "What must be thought of a man who so recently aspired to so high a trust as one of the governors of our county, who will thus attempt to blacken the private and professional character of a gentleman, simply because he did not support his claims for a public position for which he was totally unworthy?"

Soon after these exchanges, attorney Wallace told Michael that he had withdrawn as Dr. Owen's attorney after replies to the queries he had sent around the country had convinced him that the Beshoar character and qualifications were all in good order and that he was the victim of a political plot. With Wallace now serving as his attorney, Michael filed a $40,000 slander suit against Owen in Las Animas County District Court.

With the Rocky Mountain Medical Association in disarray as a result of the Trinidad quarrels, Michael resigned and it soon folded up. All eligible Colorado members were taken into the state society while the New Mexico members took steps to form a territorial society of their own.

For a time Michael thought that the slander suit had quieted

Owen, but the cattleman and a colleague, Dr. E. N. Cushing, whom he had enlisted in his campaign against Beshoar, were not through by any means.

When a horseman appeared at his office to summon him to attend an aged recluse who had been mauled by a grizzly near his cabin in the Spanish Peaks country, Michael groaned inwardly. Young Dr. Scott, who was just the man for such an emergency, was off making a call in the east end of the county and there wasn't anyone else to send. He'd have to make a hard, thirty-mile ride across the rugged, piñon-clad hill country between Trinidad and the peaks, and when he got there the man would be dead; or if he wasn't, it would be a messy case to handle under field conditions and when he was all through he wouldn't get a cent for his trouble.

"I'll go," he said. "I'll be ready by the time you get something to eat and a fresh horse."

He had José saddle his best horse, packed his medical saddle-bags, and rolled a heavy wool blanket in a poncho. Annie fixed enough food to carry him two days.

With his guide he rode west up the Purgatoire River road as far as Burro Canyon, struck off in a northwesterly direction to the Apishapa River, and then west again almost to the foot of the peak and to the old man's cabin. His guide knew nothing about the injured man; he had simply found him while looking for some missing horses in the area and had started immediately for help.

"I think he is a prospector," his guide said. "Leastwise he's got the equipment."

The injured man, who looked to be well into his seventies, was indeed in bad shape. The bear had crushed him, breaking several ribs and his left shoulder, and injuring him internally. He had been badly bitten about the shoulder, neck and face, and finally the bear had peeled the man's skin up off his shoulders and neck and halfway across the head leaving a bloody mess hanging from his head. He was conscious when the physician arrived but lapsed into unconsciousness almost immediately.

With the assistance of the horse-wrangler, Michael got the old man cleaned up, filled him full of morphine, and made him as comfortable as possible. He told the wrangler that he didn't think the man had much chance, in view of his age and the extent of his injuries, but that a few hours would tell.

For two nights and a day the physician nursed his patient, doing all he could for him. At times the old man would be rational. During such periods he expressed gratitude to the doctor and said he didn't know how he'd ever pay him. Michael told him he was not to worry about it. The wrangler rustled wood and water, cooked meals, using the doctor's food, the old man's meager grub, and some grouse he found not far from the cabin. He also spelled Michael while the physician slept.

It was the second night, an hour or two before dawn, when the prospector, in a brief period of rationality, told the physician he knew he was going to die and there was a way he could pay him. Holding tightly to Michael's hand while he talked, he told him to get a box from under a pile of old grub sacks in one corner of the little cabin. Summoning more strength than he had yet shown, he managed to root through the contents and pull out a small sheaf of papers. He told the physician that some years before he had prospected in Mexico in the high country between Guadalajara and the west coast, in the Territory of Tepic to be exact, and that he had found a good gold mine about thirty-five or forty miles from Ciudad de Tepic.

Insisting that the physician open up the papers, the old man pointed out the mine on a crude map. The other papers contained notes on the property, the geology of the area, and the like.

"I will never get back there," the old prospector said. "The Temerosa is yours."

The physician told him to rest, drew the blankets up about the scrawny neck as the predawn cold seeped into the cabin. The old man slept for awhile, then awakened and tried to talk again, but he had reached the end. He died just as the sky was beginning to lighten in the east.

Michael sat by the embers of the fire, shivering in his blanket until it became light. When the wrangler got up and brought in more wood for the fire, the physician told him the old man was gone. They cooked their breakfast before they buried him in an aspen grove near the cabin. Then they tidied up the place, saddled their horses, and headed back toward the Apishapa. The wrangler rode with him as far as Burro Canyon and then went off to search for his horses again. As Michael, tired, hungry, and anxious to be home, jogged back to Trinidad, he carried the Mexican mine papers in his pocket. He thought of them only as a curiosity to display to Annie and his cronies.

Most of 1879 was a time of peace for Michael. He was busy, as usual, but things were going pretty well. Mike wrote from Texas that times were hard and the crops poor, but that he was still hanging on to his farm. Annie presented him with a second daughter, whom he named Blanche Bazelia out of *The Book of Names*. His practice, his businesses, and his prospects were all good. He had good coal land claims at the head of Gray Creek six miles southeast of Trinidad on a straight line, or eleven miles by wagon. He had town lots and farm lands, and he was operating three ranches, the one at Stonewall, another on the lower Apishapa, and the third on the plains east of Trinidad. But increasingly his mind was on mining. He leaped at the chance when George Eaton, a former patient who had had some experience in mining, asked him to grubstake him for a prospecting trip into New Mexico. Having worked out one of his "legal agreements," he got so excited about the project that he insisted on buying Eaton's outfit himself: a gun from Frank Jackson, good, strong burros from J. W. Lewellin, stove, tent—all the necessities for $285. Eaton was well equipped. The written contract called for him to be paid three dollars per day in return for which he was to use his "best energies and talents to discover the best mines, and to secure and retain legal claims thereon, and to report to Michael Beshoar promptly every appearance of good discoveries."

In a few weeks the physician discovered that Eaton was a problem. He had lost his burros, his tent, and most of his other equipment, and there were constant demands for money. Finally Hugh McIlvain, a New Mexico mining man who had once lived in Trinidad, wrote the physician that he was wasting his money with George. "He doesn't know any more about mining than his burros," McIlvain wrote. "In fact he can't tell pyrites of iron from crystallized ore." Sadly, the physician called George Eaton back to Colorado.

A short time later his household was augmented by the arrival of Annie's parents from Kentucky. John Maupin's hair and beard were white, but otherwise he looked much the same as he had at the time of their first meeting in Missouri. Michael was genuinely glad to have the old couple come to live with him; they would be company for Annie and the children whenever he was away. Maupin, with a wealth of experience as a farmer, had hoped to make his own living as a nurseryman but there was little demand for his talents. To satisfy his father-in-law's need to be useful, the physician sent east for trees and other plants, and the old man set out an apple orchard and a rose garden between the house and the corral. Rachael, Annie's mother, helped organize the Presbyterian church soon after her arrival.

With the coming of the senior Maupins, the Beshoars had more visitors than ever. Smith Sayre had left Willow Spring and the stage line in 1874 and was ranching in Las Animas County twenty miles down the Purgatoire, not too far from brother-in-law Burns. Their wives and children were frequent overnight visitors to see Grandpa and Grandma Maupin. Sometimes they stayed a week or more, much to Annie's delight and her husband's pleasure. Without the crude adobe rooms Michael had built behind the house, the company could never have been accommodated.

As it was, with Annie, the two little girls, the senior Maupins, José, a hired girl, Lucy the bear, assorted cats, chickens, and rabbits, a cow, a burro, and four horses on a 120-by-500-foot lot, 611 East Main Street was a busy and often noisy place.

Old John Maupin, in addition to tending his orchard and gardens, also drove the physician on long calls and to and from El Moro whenever he was using the Rio Grande. José was not pleased at this usurpation of what had been one of his most pleasant duties, but Michael found other things for the boy to do around his office. He sold his drugstore at this time but enlarged his office, and purchased an amazing new medical device. Henry Sturges, editor of the *Trinidad Daily News*, came around for a demonstration:

We were last evening shown, through the courtesy of Dr. M. Beshoar, a new and wonderful little instrument, just perfected, called the phonographic sphygmograph . . . to give a practical knowledge of the beating of the pulse of the human system and for detecting the true condition of the blood. With delicate needle it traces upon a dark plate the beating of the pulse and in reality writes out in sound waves the murmurs of the heart. Any defaults in the arterial workings of the heart are at a glance detected, and accurately, too. This is the first one ever introduced in this country and is to be used in the doctor's practice. He is taking the little machine to the meeting of the Colorado State Medical Association in Colorado Springs next Tuesday and will there show it to the fraternity. Will wonders never cease!

Another wonder came to Trinidad before the year was out. Delos A. Chappell, a Michigan engineer, constructed a waterworks for the city of Trinidad under a ten-year franchise. A tall, well-proportioned man of thirty-eight with prematurely gray hair and moustache, Chappell was a dynamo of energy. He sank a deep well near the river, built a pumping plant over it, and constructed a reservoir on a hill 312 feet above the south edge of town. Gravity provided the necessary pressure for the system's hydrants.

The physician, busy with problems of his own, had paid little attention to the waterworks project and was not fully apprised of the terms of the franchise and the rates permitted until after Dr. Owen, in his capacity as president of the board of trustees, and the trustees themselves had signed on the dotted line. When he did get a look at the rates, he was extremely unhappy, viewing them as still another example of Dr. Owen's unfitness for public office. He went up and down the streets complaining that a lean man could not take a bath for less than twenty cents and that a fat man could not wash for less than forty cents.

Chappell's rates, which would be effective until October 1, 1889, charged householders five dollars a year for each tub, twelve dollars for a pair of kitchen faucets, two dollars for a wash basin, and five dollars for a water closet. The water cost five cents a gallon for the first 200 gallons, four and a half cents for the first 1,000 gallons, four cents for the first 2,000 gallons. It was not until consumption amounted to 8,000 gallons or more that the rate got down to two cents per gallon.

Scores of citizens, unwilling to pay such exorbitant charges, clung to the water-wagon system, but Michael had made a promise to Annie. He had faucets put in the kitchen and a hydrant in the yard. The upstairs storage closet was converted into a bathroom complete with built-in tin tub, washbasin with faucets, and a water closet. The Mexican workmen who installed the water closet were pretty sure the device was insanitary and perhaps immoral. "Pero, Senór Doctor . . .¿en casa?"

Early in 1880 Dr. Scott decided he would establish a practice of his own, probably in Leadville or one of the other booming gold and silver camps in the northern part of the state. He had been a satisfactory partner in most respects, but Michael agreed to a termination of their agreement without protest or regret as he was aware that of late Scott had become increasingly chummy with Dr. Owen and his sidekick, Dr. Cushing. That he was well advised to be wary of Owen and Cushing was demonstrated in the late spring when the two informed the ethics committee of the State Medical Society that they would bring formal charges against M. Beshoar. They said they would show that he used his picture in advertisements and on labels and prescriptions, and that he had been a member of the faculty of Dr. John Buchanan's American University, which was under heavy attack by the *Philadelphia Record*. The newspaper was charging in editorials and news stories that this medical school was simply a diploma mill.

Michael's old St. Louis friend, Dr. H. A. Lemen, now a trustee and officer of the State Medical Society, wrote that the charges would undoubtedly be filed before the regular summer meeting and asked him to be in Denver June 29. He was on hand when the ethics committee convened at 10:00 A.M. in the supreme court room. The committee had only the letter that had been sent to Lemen; no charges had been filed as promised. After an hour-long wait, the committee reported: "In the case of Dr. M. Beshoar, on whom notice was served that charges would be preferred against him, we beg leave to report that such have not been preferred and your committee would recommend dismissal of the case."

As he left Denver, Michael was an angry man, even angrier after he got to Trinidad and found that Owen and company were continuing their harassment, this time in an anonymous circular they were distributing via the mails. It quoted articles in the *Philadelphia Record* attacking Buchanan and listing M. Beshoar as an 1873 graduate of his "fraud-fostering establishment," as its instructor of medicine in 1875 and 1876, and as emeritus professor of the practice of medicine in 1877–78.

In public Michael ignored the circular, but his outrage knew no bounds when a friend tipped him off that Dr. Scott, now practicing in Alpine, Colorado, had given Owen a statement saying he had found a Buchanan diploma among Dr. Beshoar's traps while serving as his partner, and that it was this statement that led Owen, with Cushing as his front man, to write the state society that charges would be filed against Dr. Beshoar. Later the pair, having had doubts, resolved to confine their attack for the present to the unsigned circular. In his anger Michael wrote Scott a sharp letter, expressing surprise that his onetime partner had joined in the attack on him "at the sounding of the first bugle note of Cushing and Owen's latest onslaught." He asked whether Scott thought himself invulnerable and whether he remembered "the course pursued by me when Cushing filled the town and country with the most damaging reports concerning your past life." He concluded with: "Does your judgment dictate to you that, granting all that is charged against me, it would finally and forever squelch me? Do you presume that I would tamely submit to ruin or even great injury without at least a crude analysis of the characters of the conspirators to that end? Neither boasting nor begging quarter, I candidly declare that all that Cushing & Owen have placed on my back is no load, and I am sure I can carry you, too. Now, Doctor, follow your inclination and, if nothing but causeless enmity will satiate you, wade in, never whine if you find yourself in the dirty water deeper than you expected."

It must have stuck in the throats of Owen and company, but by fall Beshoar was serving as chairman of a committee of ten distinguished Colorado physicians and surgeons appointed by the State Medical Society to draft suitable regulations to govern the practice of medicine in the state and protect its people "from the horde of incompetent and unscrupulous charlatans who, driven from the many states east of us by stringent laws, have settled upon our State, being protected here by the absence of any law against them."

The Atchison, Topeka & Santa Fe had built westward from La Junta, then on up the Purgatoire, and over Raton Pass. February 7, 1878, had been an exciting day for every resident of Trinidad when the first train had gone over the pass into New Mexico, and there had been some attentiveness ever since, with distinguished visitors glimpsed as they passed through or paced up and down in front of the handsome new Santa Fe Depot during stopovers. But there hadn't been anything to equal the occasion of July 22, 1880. Former President Grant, who had been in Europe for the past two years, was a potential candidate for a third term and was making a tour of the United States. He arrived from Santa Fe at 6:30 P.M.

to find most of Trinidad awaiting him at the depot. As the train came to a stop with much choking and snorting, the Trinidad Band struck up "Hail, Columbia." The town's hose companies were drawn up in formation, the team members all standing at attention. Behind them hundreds of citizens set up a cheer as Grant descended from his car, followed by Mrs. Grant, Mrs. Fred Grant and her daughter, the general's aide Captain Loud and his wife, General and Mrs. Ed Hatch, and New Mexico's Governor George T. Anthony. Everyone was surprised to see General Hatch, as he was supposed to be busy in New Mexico chasing the renegade Apache, Victorio, and his ragged little band.

Dr. Cushing, arrayed in his best and proud as the marshal of the occasion had a right to be, led the Grants to the first of two waiting carriages, then put the rest of the general's party in a second carriage. They moved right out, since time was short. With Cushing in charge, the procession crossed the Commercial Street Bridge and started up the curving street with the tooting band in the lead followed by the E. Jay Rice Hose Company, the Grant carriage, the carriage bearing the rest of his party, the W. G. Rifenburg Hose Company, the C. C. Gordon Hose Company, the Ed West Hose Company, citizens on horseback, citizens on foot, and finally citizens in carriages. It was a brave and inspiring sight, and all along Commercial Street there were cheers as the former president, cigar stuck firmly in his mouth, raised his hat to the people.

At the intersection of Commercial with Main, the procession turned left and stopped briefly while Grant alighted and was escorted to the stairs leading up to Mitchell Hall. The procession then went on to the United States Hotel with his family and the rest of the party.

At the head of the stairs leading into the hall, which was packed tightly with an expectant crowd, Grant was met by the committee: Chairman and *Trinidad Daily News* editor Henry Sturges, Dr. M. Beshoar, and General E. P. Sopris. They escorted the former president to the front of the hall where Sturges introduced Judge S. S. Wallace, who bore the distinction of being able to talk longer than any other man in the county. The judge had been warned and double-warned, however, and held his welcoming talk to reasonable length. Grant responded in kind and then took up a position at the door, with Sturges, Beshoar, and General Sopris, as the people filed out, each being introduced by the committee and each

receiving greeting from the man Sturges called "Our Guest" in his
newspaper.

The committee then hurried the general to the United States
Hotel to give him a few minutes to get ready for the grand banquet
scheduled for the hotel's dining room at eight o'clock. Just about
then, a huge bonfire was lighted in the street in front of Mitchell
Hall and a second one, made up of big piles of dry brush, was
lighted on the summit of Simpson's Rest, high above the town on
the north side. The merchants had their stores on Main and Commercial lighted up, and most of them were taking this grand opportunity to do a little business.

Minutes before dinnertime, with barely enough time to get to
the hotel, a special train came in bearing Colorado Governor Frederick Pitkin and former governors Routt and Hunt.

At the head table in the hotel dining room sat the former comman-
der of the Union armies and former president of the United States,
Mrs. Grant, Mrs. Fred Grant, Captain Loud, editor Sturges, Mrs.
Sturges, Governor Pitkin, Governor Anthony, former Governor
Routt, former Governor A. C. Hunt, former oxteam driver Casimiro
Barela, and the former medical director of General Hardee's Com-
mand and former surgeon of Colonel Shaver's Seventh Arkansas
and his wife Annie, sister of former Quantrill guerrillas.

There were several short talks including one by Barela, who
spoke in Spanish despite cries of "Talk English, you can do it!"
Grant made a short but graceful talk, in which he told the group
he hoped to spend as much as three weeks visiting various parts
of Colorado and getting to know its people. When the affair broke
up at midnight, the fire on top of Simpson's Rest had become one
huge, glowing ember.

By six the next morning Grant, cigar in mouth, was sauntering up
and down Commercial and Main streets, greeting the merchants as
they swept out their places of business. Within an hour there was
a circus air along the streets as people crowded into the business
section and gathered in knots near the United States Hotel in hope
of getting another look at the visitors. At noon Grant was to take a
Denver & Rio Grande train from El Moro north to Pueblo and
Colorado Springs. He had said his family would like to make the
four-mile trip to El Moro in a carriage but that he would prefer to
go by horseback if it could be arranged. It could indeed. At ten
o'clock, the hour set for departure from the United States Hotel,

fifty of the leading citizens, dressed in their Sunday finest and mounted on their best horses, or some neighbor's or friend's best horse, were gathered in front of the hotel. They had a good mount for Grant.

Some of the escort had obviously not been on horseback for quite some time, but most of them sat their horses well enough. Barela carried a big American flag, which he managed to drop a time or two, but cattle king George Thompson rode beside him and made a recovery after each mishap. General E. B. Sopris rode beside Grant, with the rest strung out in twos and threes behind them.

During the four-mile ride, several galloped up alongside Grant long enough to tell him some anecdote or other of the war. The diminutive saloonkeeper, Harry Mulnix, told Grant that his big black horse had been used by Lee in his Virginia campaigns. Old Confederate cavalryman and surgeon Michael Beshoar stayed in line, letting the former Union Army boys tell their anecdotes. He could tell a few himself, but this time he was content just to ride along and enjoy the show.

At El Moro a tiny, narrow-gauge engine and cars awaited, as did a large welcoming crowd that raised a cheer as Grant and his escort galloped in. Grant gave his well-wishers a military salute and, after he had dismounted at the train, thanked them cordially for coming to see him off.

It had been a lot of fun, and everyone had behaved; Grant had handled himself well, and the Trinidad citizens had laid their political rivalries and feuds aside for the duration of his visit. Editor Sturges noted in his report of the Grant visit: "The Cavalcade that escorted 'Our Guest' to El Moro are all taking their meals from the mantle pieces in their respective dining rooms." Also, Grant did not say 'I have heard the royal bands of Europe, the bands of China, Siam and Japan, the Marine and Ninth Cavalry Bands, but the Trinidad Band is the cheese of all.' "

The year 1880 was the time for Michael to give up the office of county judge and make a try for the legislature. He had been on the bench nine years, and it was time some of the legal lights of the town had a crack at the post; besides, he wanted to nurture his medical legislation at the state level and he was anxious to keep a close eye on land legislation.

He attended the state Democratic convention and then in October, when the oak brush on Fisher's Peak had turned to red and gold, was nominated at the county convention for one of the three house posts to which Las Animas County was entitled. His running mates: José Benito Martinez and José Ramón Aguilar.

Between the time of his nomination and his election in November, a family tragedy occurred. Smith Sayre had made a deal to sell his herd of 600 head of cattle to Sam Doss (the stockman whom Michael had unsuccessfully nominated for county commissioner) at a price of $15.50 per head. It wasn't a very good deal for Sayre, and before delivery of the cattle was made, a number of his cattlemen friends told him he had sold much too low. A nervous, irritable man, Sayre refused to turn the cattle over to Doss when the latter was ready for them. There were harsh words on both sides. The matter was widely discussed in cattle circles, some believing that Sayre was morally obligated to give Doss the cattle at $15.50 since he had agreed to, even if the agreement was only oral; others thinking that in the absence of any written contract or agreement, Sayre was within his rights in reneging. While the debate was at its height, Doss made a trip to the Sayre ranch on the Purgatoire and, after a bitter argument, got a written agreement. But again Sayre announced Doss could not have the cattle. Doss then said he would allow Sayre to backtrack on 300 head if he would go ahead with the original agreement on the remaining 300 head. Sayre's friends thought this a good idea and that the issue was resolved.

But on October 20, Sayre went to the Doss home in Trinidad and argued with Doss until a late hour. Since it was a long twenty miles back to the ranch, Doss invited him to stay for the night. Sayre tossed in his bed until two o'clock, then put the muzzle of a .38 caliber pistol into his mouth, and pulled the trigger.

When Drs. Beshoar and Gordon got to the Doss home some forty minutes later, Sayre was still alive, but there was no hope for him. The ball had passed through the roof of his mouth, through the brain and out the top of his head. He died shortly before 4 A.M.

Messengers were sent to the Sayre ranch to bring the family in to the Beshoar home, and the Burns family came hurrying in from their ranch. Sayre had left behind him not only his wife, Annie's sister, but twelve children—four girls and eight boys. He had also left a letter addressed to Michael in which he told of his years of poor health, of the many accidents that had plagued him, and his regret.

He directed that Michael sell all of his cattle to Sam Doss at the original price of $15.50 per head, use the money to pay up his debts, and give the balance to his family.

It was a sad waste, and everyone agreed with the verdict of the editor of the *Trinidad Weekly News*: "There seems to be nothing in extenuation of this rash act, either in cause or surroundings. It is one of those lamentable affairs that chills the public pulse and forces from charitable lips the verdict of 'temporary insanity.'"

The family crisis cut into the time Michael could devote to his campaign for the House, but it made no difference as he, Martinez, and Aguilar were elected without any difficulty late in November.

Before he got to the legislature in Denver, he had to attend another shooting case again involving more than just his professional skill. This time the patient was Dr. E. N. Cushing, who had been devoting a disproportionate amount of his time to attacking Michael, writing anonymous circular letters about his medical background and practices, and threatening to prove that he was a bogus medical man.

The chain of events that called Michael to the bedside of his dying enemy began on the morning of December 7 when Ed Powell, a former Trinidad resident, arrived in town from Albuquerque and proceeded to round up some of his old drinking pals, including Cushing, for a celebration. They made the rounds most of the rest of the day and early evening, but at ten o'clock that night settled down quietly enough for a game of cards with some other acquaintances in the liquor house of W. S. Iler. They continued drinking, more or less, but concentrated on the poker game rather than on liquor. At about 4 A.M. a dispute arose between Cushing and Powell whereupon the former put his hand on his pistol pocket and threatened Powell's life. The exchange broke up the game, and they all got up from the table and went into the barroom.

Everyone was drinking amicably and the unpleasantness at the card table was apparently forgotten when suddenly Dr. Cushing threw his coat back, again made a move toward his pistol pocket, and shouted that he could whip any man in the room. With that he rushed at Powell and grabbed him. Powell fired five shots in quick succession. One struck Cushing in the side, another in the groin, and he fell heavily to the floor. He was taken to his home, and

Michael and Dr. Gordon, routed out of bed, hurried to the Cushing home, where after a careful examination they pronounced the wounds mortal.

Powell had walked out of the saloon after the shooting but later surrendered himself to Sheriff Juan Vigil. Cushing, conscious during the medical examination and calm when the doctors told him frankly that he might go at any minute, said he wanted Powell brought to the house. With family, physicians, sheriff's officers, and Powell gathered around the dying man's bed, the lamentable affair was discussed in a most friendly manner. Cushing said he was at fault in the matter and that no blame attached to Powell.

"He must not be charged or prosecuted," the dying doctor said. "The fault was all mine." His deathbed request carried with it the voice of authority as the forty-eight-year-old Cushing was in his fourth term as county coroner when he died at two o'clock the next morning. "He was a good physician and a likable enough fellow when he wasn't drinking," Michael told Annie. "The trouble was that, lately, he never stopped drinking."

Coroner Cushing hadn't been the only one who did too much drinking in Trinidad. Cynical observers said there was more liquor consumed in the saloons and dives of Trinidad in twenty-four hours than there was water in the Purgatoire in a similar period. One of the largest consumers was Mike Beshoar, Jr., who had returned from Texas late in the fall. He said he had lost his ranch because of poor crops, but his father suspected its proceeds probably went to saloonkeepers, gamblers, and fancies. Not knowing what else to do with him, he sent Mike to one of his ranches east of Trinidad and put him to work at ranch hand's wages, building fence and doing other chores. In December, soon after the Cushing shooting, Mike rode into town, put his horse up at the Park stable, and disappeared into the saloons and dives of the west end without so much as reporting in to his father at office or residence. The physician had immediate reports on the whereabouts of his son but decided he would not seek him out; he would show up the moment his money was gone.

But the rest of December passed and the physician had gone to Denver to take his seat in the Third General Assembly, which convened January 5, 1881, when he next heard from Mike, by mail:

Dear Father—

I tried to get a talk with you before you left for Denver, but was unable to—on account of your time being engaged by others.

I have before this made declarations that amounted to a little more than nothing, and I doubt, yes, I have serious doubts, as to your lending an ear to this one. Should you turn a deaf ear to me this time, I shall meet my fate with due resignation. I am fully convinced that I have behaved since my return from Texas in a most unbecoming manner. And today I am more fully convinced of my littleness than ever before, and you cannot imagine how I feel about my situation. It is useless for me to try to pin down my feelings. I am wholly incapable. I leave that for you to judge. I should have approached this subject before, but thought I would wait and give you a chance to see my actions and conduct. What I want is to be obedient in all things and I want regularity in all things. I want to act & conduct myself in such a manner as to cause you to be proud of me. I shall adopt truthfulness as my policy. I want to quit the saloons &c and confine myself to your office in study.

I want to be a pharmacist and if competent more than that *a Dr.*

I pledge myself to do and carry out the above and in failure of which you can discard me. Give me one more chance and you shall never regret it.

I await your answer.

Your Son—

M. Beshoar Jr.

In Care W. H. H. Gage, Trinidad, Col.

The letter excited Michael. Though he had heard such mea culpas and assurances from Mike many times, this one seemed to ring true. He hoped he wasn't guilty of wishful thinking, but Mike was only twenty-six years old, and if there was a chance that he meant what he said, it was still not too late for him to make something out of his life. Since Michael was tied up with the legislature, the best thing he could think of was to get Mike, Jr., out of Trinidad and its saloons as quickly as possible. By wire he contacted an old friend, U.S. Senator Stephen W. Dorsey from Arkansas, who agreed to give Mike a job on his ranch at Chico Springs, New Mexico Territory. The physician told his son that if he proved he could stay sober, hold the job with Dorsey, and make a decent record for himself for a few months, he would see that he had a chance to become a pharmacist, and if that worked out, then medical school would be next.

He had just got that settled when he received a letter from Dr. Gordon saying that daughter Bonnie had broken out with measles. "She also has some tonsillitis with a very minute white spot showing," Dr. Gordon wrote. "She is all right and there is no danger. Your wife's anxiety to send for you, I appeased. In case anything unfavorable should come up will telegraph you at once." Gordon gave him a report on some of his patients, said the weather was stormy, and told him not to worry.

Michael wrote Annie: "I hope Bonnie has fully recovered her health and that the rest of you are well. I am quartered now at 496 Arapahoe St. and have board next door—good board at $4.50 per week. It now costs us $6.25 a week for everything and we are well cared for. Our landlord is professionally a counterfeit detector and teacher and seems a gentleman."

Gordon next wired to say: "Bonnie convalescing nicely. Blanche well. All others okay." Then came a second wire: "Blanche developing measles. Nothing unfavorable. Rest of family well." But two days later another wire came from Gordon: "Blanche symptoms not so favorable. Family anxious. Come tonight."

He took the next Rio Grande train, sitting bundled up in a heavy overcoat all night. He thought the train would never make it over the divide. A snowstorm was sweeping across the state from the west, driven by a strong wind. Once over the divide the little train dawdled through the bitterly cold night; it sat on sidings, backed, went forward, sat on more sidings while he fretted. But it finally found its way south through Pueblo and on down to El Moro, arriving two and a half hours late. When he alighted from his car, tired, stiff, hungry, and worried, he could barely make out the outlines of some of the buildings. John Maupin was there, waiting by the big stove in the depot with a stack of heavy robes for the ride home. He had put the team in a livery barn when he found the train would be late, and together they made their way through the storm to the barn and set out for Trinidad immediately. Michael was sure Dr. Gordon would not have sent him the message if the baby's condition weren't serious. Old John Maupin could only tell him that the baby was very sick. When they got to the house in Trinidad, Annie met them at the door. As the physician kissed her and asked, "How's Blanche?" she buried her head in his shoulder and sobbed—little Blanche had been dead for an hour.

It was an anxious period in the days after the funeral. Mike had not yet left for New Mexico and was a help, as were John and Rachael Maupin. Annie's parents were calm people of great faith who could take the loss of a baby as an act of God, and they could comfort Annie with their steady faith. She was expecting her third child about May 20. During the week he stayed in Trinidad, the physician got Mike, Jr., off to New Mexico, and made arrangements for Annie and Bonnie to make a trip on the Santa Fe to Las Vegas, New Mexico, in February for a visit with some of her close friends—Captain and Mrs. Stark. A change of scene would do his wife good.

Back in Denver he found he had a hard fight on his hands in the form of mounting opposition to the medical control bill. At the start of the session, the Democrats had acknowledged his leadership by putting him up for the post of speaker. Though he was beaten, they had continued to follow him, but he would need strong Republican support if the anti-quackery measure was to make it. A number of doctors around the state—including the very articulate and vocal Dr. Thomas D. Worrall of Leadville—who had nothing to fear from any of the provisions of the proposed bill still opposed it. They contended that, while illegitimate practice was working great injury to the people of Colorado and should be banned, the simple possession of a diploma from an acknowledged medical school was sufficient evidence of the right to practice and that anything more would be restrictive and undesirable class legislation.

When the bill was finally passed by both houses and signed by the governor, the State Board of Medical Examiners sent copies to every physician in the state. A graduate of a medical college not only had to display his diploma but produce a catalogue in which his name appeared and "other information in regard to his Alma Mater. This is intended to give information in regard to colleges little known." The state board said it hoped "there will be no injustice done to anyone." Michael had known exactly what would happen with the passing of the bill, and it did happen promptly: a lot of "doctors" took in their shingles and went into "some other line of business."

Michael very much wanted an appointment to the Board of Medical Examiners, but Republican Governor Pitkin wasn't about to appoint M. Beshoar, a potential Democratic threat, to anything. Dr. F. J. Bancroft, president of the State Medical Society wrote, "I pled your case with the Governor for an appointment to the Ex. Board, but to no avail. The profession are, however, indebted to you for the passage of the bill."

Before their third child arrived Michael and Annie had two or three scares about the pregnancy, for a time both fearing she would not carry the baby to term, but each time he gave her morphine and put her to bed until the immediate danger was past. At other times he forbade any strenuous work and saw to it that she got plenty of light exercise such as walking. The baby was due May 20 and finally arrived on June 8, delivered by the father. Exulting in a fine eight-pound girl, Michael once again hunted up *The Book of Names* and had the new arrival baptized Benedicta Burnett.

During the last half of 1881, he practiced medicine spottily, having two and three physicians at a time working in his offices to care for patients while he spent much of his time on his projected coal development. Coal production in the county had passed 1,500 tons per day and was mounting steadily. More than seventy coke ovens were throwing a lurid light into the night skies, and still the demands for coke were not being met. Michael was sure he had a fortune tucked under the protecting shoulder of Fisher's Peak and that the time to do something about it had arrived. He was confident his Gray Creek property was as rich as, if not richer than, any coal land in the county.

Through his own connections in the East and those of A. J. Shotwell, a mining engineer with broad experience in both mining and mine-financing, he began to send feelers to eastern capitalists. He brought mining experts into Colorado to examine the property and write reports; and during the summer and early fall he made three trips east to talk with investment bankers. In November, after two trips by him to Cincinnati and visits to the Colorado property by prospective investors from the Ohio city, the Cincinnati-Colorado Coal, Coke and Iron Company was incorporated with John R. Davey of Cincinnati as president, S. S. Davis of Cincinnati as treasurer, and M. Beshoar as vice-president. Headquarters were set up at 61 West Third Street in Cincinnati, and a branch office of the 4C & I, as it came to be known, was opened in Trinidad.

Capital was fixed at 150,000 shares of common with a par value of ten dollars per share, of which 70,000 shares went to the company, 2,500 shares to Davey, 2,500 shares to Davis, and 5,000 shares to Davey and Davis for $5,000. Michael retained 70,000 shares.

F. E. Dowd, a director, and Shotwell, in exchange for 7,500 shares each, agreed to sell 50,000 of Michael's shares for not less than three dollars per share, free of all expenses.

Mining engineer Shotwell, named superintendent of the 4C & I, shortly made a written report to the new company in which he said, "Your vein of coal is twelve to fourteen feet thick and is uniform, underlies your entire 5,000 acres. In this one vein you have enough coal to yield a thousand tons of coal per day for a period of 150 years of constant mining. The coal is of superior quality, free from sulphur, solid and compact in structure, rich in carbon, well suited to all domestic and manufacturing purposes, and is readily converted into most excellent coke. There are five to six other veins of coal on your land, overlying the main vein, all of workable thickness and all good coal. There are six or more veins of band-iron ore of commercial value. A number of large springs in the higher part of your land furnish an abundant supply of pure, running water, ample to meet mining and manufacturing demands. They may be used as a source of power to compress air for driving coal-mining machinery. In this way you will easily mine and put coal aboard cars at an expense not to exceed 40 cents per ton."

Shotwell told the directors that in five years the number of industrial furnaces in Colorado and New Mexico had increased from six to more than fifty and that they would double again in three years: "Railroads are pushing into all the mining districts; cities and towns are springing up as if by magic and factories will follow. Coke is in large demand, sells at the place where made for $7 per ton. You can make it on your land for $1.50 per ton."

It was heady and exciting. Michael began to devote practically all of his time "to my business," attending only such patients as would not accept one of his assistants. He saw himself as a rich man within a very short period, maybe two or three years at the most. All over southern Colorado, and up north of the divide this time, they were beginning to boost him for governor.

Chapter 10

The Editor and the Medicine Man

EARLY IN 1882, while a prospectus of the 4C & I Company was being mailed to potential investors throughout the country and Dowd and Shotwell were making the rounds of financial houses in New York, Boston, and other money centers of the East looking for capital, Michael decided to write a book about his town and county. He had two compelling reasons: one was promotion; the other, a desire to preserve the history of the area. Eastern newspaper and magazine writers almost invariably made Denver the headquarters of a Colorado visit and were soon captivated by the glamour of the gold and silver camps, but the physician thought his own area had a story to tell. On the few occasions when Denver newspapermen wandered into the southern tier of counties, their copy was almost always colorful, as when Ben Chase, a *Denver Tribune* writer on a swing through the south, caught some of the flavor of the bustling little city on the Purgatoire:

> You see the old and the new grotesquely commingled. Americans speaking Spanish and Mexicans struggling with Anglo Saxon speech. American and Mexican and African children mastering the English language in the schools common for all. All worshipping at the same altar or no altar at all. You see Mexican women, their heads wrapped in tapadas gliding along modestly, meek and tired looking; Mexican men wrapped in blankets, chill, uncheerful, seeming strangers in their own land; Indians in long hair, in blankets and buckskin, with moccasin feet—most humiliated and despised race— once master of all this broad America. These jostle and are jostled by the newly-come Americans—a strange mixture of incongruities out of which is to come social harmony, not im-

possible if given time.

Michael intended to use some of the same sort of color, but he was more interested in factual information that portrayed the progress of the area. For weeks he gathered data from all available sources, from county and town records and from the files of newspapers, from his own recollections and from those of other pioneers who had settled in the town or the county in the sixties. He wrote the text in such spare hours as he could command, some of them on trains. He made a contract with the Times Steam Printing House and Book Manufactory in Denver to print his *All About Trinidad and Las Animas County, Their History, Industries, Resources, Etc.*

His 118-page book covered the pre-white period, climate, scenery, resources, industry, agriculture, stock-raising, taxes, and new coal-mining camps; tables of statistics, records of county and town officeholders, organizations, and lodges; distances, elevations, and other pertinent data. It was a history, encyclopedia, directory, and almanac, with a salting of his own observations:

> If the air is light, the gold and silver are heavy. If we do pay heavily for a few luxuries, we pay nothing for quinine and calomel. You will miss nothing in the West that you find in the East except idleness, and that you can well afford to live without; you can find just as good society here as anywhere in the East, for society ranges between virtue and vice, between decency and nastiness. Here you are measured by what you are . . . by what you can do . . . by your ability, integrity and brains . . . and thus you will drift into your proper place in society.

He warned his readers they would no doubt find many imperfections and inaccuracies in his book, adding:

> It would not be surprising if such were the fact, but you are asked to bear in mind that the matter was prepared for publication while the author was engaged in a large practice, almost momentarily subjected to interruptions and harassed by all the continual anxieties occurring in one of the most exhausting, as well as thankless professions in this country.
> While the author asks no indulgence from this circumstance,

yet he apprehends that a practice of twenty-nine years, with its too often accompanying annoyances—compelled to view human nature in every possible light, and encounter it in its most humiliating aspects—eminently fits him to bear the murmurs of those who suppose that a volume can be as easily written as read.

In a section about roads in the area, he did a bit about the burro that was widely reproduced in newspapers in the West:

Sometimes only a footpath will lead one to the abode of a rancher, and again the patient burro will be called into requisition in order to traverse the deep, dark cañon; he alone can carry a 400 pound burden and go where other beasts of burden can't; he alone possesses the endurance, gentleness and stomach which are required in such places; he will breakfast on a cactus, dinner on a pine knot and supper on what is left from breakfast and dinner; he never complains, never grumbles, never strikes for better fare; he sometimes brays, but not very frequently. When he gets ready to practice his vocal organs, he simply braces himself, opens his mouth up about as wide as the gap between Genesis and Revelation, and then throws his whole soul into his song; he usually starts off with a coarse heavy bass and then runs up the scale until he strikes a beautiful, sweet straining alto, and then gradually opens up on the chorus, with a heavy bass, opens his mouth still wider and then throws more soul into his song and repeats the chorus with a voice that shakes the earth and sounds like ten thousand locomotives loaded down with freight, and whistling for water. This practice seems to be his only earthly enjoyment, and he goes at it in such a systematic way that it leads his tender hearted owner to forgive him and let him enjoy this simple freak in his own modest way. Such is the burro, such he has been from time immemorial and, in all probability, such he will be to the Day of Resurrection.

Hiring agents in Denver and Trinidad to handle sales, he sent review copies to newspapers and complimentary copies to libraries and followed them up with display advertisements stating that the book was "printed in the very best style" and that it would be "an indispensible reference book." The first edition of 3,000 copies was quickly sold out at seventy-five cents per copy.

The book finished, he launched two new businesses, a steam laundry and the Standard Brick Yard—bringing Mike home from New Mexico to manage the brick business. Mike had done well on the Chico Springs ranch, according to all reports; he had worked hard and had apparently curbed his drinking. Although his letters had said he still thought he might want to be a pharmacist, perhaps he ought to have some business experience first. Mike admitted he still had doubts about his ability to undertake any more schooling but decided that if he could do well in business he would be happy. The physician, in turn, said that more schooling could be held open and that, meanwhile, the brickyard job would be an important and responsible assignment, one that would give Mike a chance to test himself against a possible business career.

In addition to the brickyard, he planned to use Mike, if all went well, as an assistant in the development of the Gray Creek coal lands. He saw the brickyard as a stable business with a future; whereas he viewed the coal lands as an investment, hoping to make a quick killing on them and be out of the coal land business. When a Samuel W. Pease of Chicago asked what he would accept for his Las Animas County coal lands, he replied that they were now in the form of 4C & I Company stock, but that he would sell the stock and all of his other land holdings in the county, with the exception of his home and business properties, as a package for $295,000 cash.

He wrote to Pease that he had not previously offered his non-coal lands for sale, "but the state of mind is always like that of the unnamed girl of history who declared she would never submit to 'such a thing' unless *she was tied*, but at the same time remarked that 'there is a rope behind the door.'"

While the coal land proposals simmered, Mike arrived home and went to work as manager of the brickyard. Some of the first bricks produced under his management were used to veneer Michael's adobe house, thus eliminating the annual maintenance chore of re-plastering the exterior walls.

In June he went east to try to peddle his coal stock and to push for more railroad lines into southern Colorado. Also hoping to drum up some industry for the area, he went first to Cincinnati, where he, Davey, Dowd, and Shotwell held a series of meetings with prospective Colorado investors, after which he went on to New York to talk with Jay Gould, Sidney Dillon, and their consulting engineer. The physician carried with him to Gould's offices engineering reports, maps, reports of the U.S. Geological Survey, 4C & I circulars, and other material—all designed to interest Gould in southern Colorado in general and Las Animas County in particular. En route he stopped in a telegraph office to send Annie a dispatch: "Have your letter. On way to see Gould. Glad cow got through her trouble all right."

Before he checked out of the Windsor in New York to go to Philadelphia, he wrote Annie that he didn't know how long he would stay in the East, that it might be a matter of days or weeks. "But I will stay until my business is concluded. Today I attended Mass in the great New York cathedral. This very remarkable structure occupies an entire square. I saw Cardinal McCloskey—the first American to occupy such a high church post. This evening I propose to go to Cooper Union to hear a Free Thinker's Lecture." Apparently he was impressed less with the freethinkers than with the cardinal as the next day, in his letter to Annie, he dismissed the Cooper Union lecture: "It put me in mind of an old-fashioned, long drawn out Methodist camp meeting in Arkansas."

He wrote Annie daily, sometimes twice a day, from New York, Boston, Philadelphia, Pittsburgh, Baltimore, and Washington, and from the Geneva Hotel in Cincinnati where he made his headquarters. On one trip across Pennsylvania, he alighted from the train at each stop as it traveled up the Susquehanna and Juniata rivers. The fragrant, earthy smells of the Pennsylvania countryside overwhelmed him with nostalgia for his boyhood home near Mifflintown and Lewistown. It had been a long time since he had roamed the woodlands on the hill behind his father's house and played in the haymow of the big barn. With a shock he realized he had not been "home" for almost thirty years; he had been twenty when he left for Arkansas, a slender, smooth-faced young man with a medical diploma. The years had made some changes. He was a good twenty-five pounds heavier, the eyes were hard and sharp, the face had some lines, and he wore a moustache and goatee. He wondered if, at age forty-nine, he would be recognized by anyone, if there was anyone left from his boyhood days, or if any of his family still lived in the area. Impulsively he decided he would visit the old and familiar scenes once more, make his first stop at Mifflintown, and from there go out a mile and a half to Lost Creek where he had been born. Inquiries in Mifflintown would soon tell him who was left in the way of relatives, old neighbors, childhood friends. Then he would go a few miles west to Lewistown, where he had first studied medicine under two preceptors, Drs. Hoover and Moss, and from there to Dry Valley where his father had bought a farm when Michael was still a very small boy.

He stepped off the train at Mifflintown at 5 A.M. June 22. After a hurried breakfast he engaged a buggy and driver, and set off, driving east toward the blue green mass that was Shadow Mountain. A great peace filled him. This was indeed home. As the loquacious liveryman pointed out farms and told him who owned them, he recognized names that he had not heard or thought of for many long years. Here were the same big two-story stone houses that had stood since before the Revolutionary War, the same neatly painted fences, the low stone walls, and the big overshot barns of the Pennsylvania Dutch country. The fat cattle looked just like the fat cattle that were standing in those same meadows and cow pens when he was a boy. And as they drove along, he saw the same stolid farmers along the road, farmers like his father, thrifty, hard-working, God-fearing men. They visited a dozen farms, all owned by relatives most of whom he had never seen. He found himself lapsing once again into the voice inflections and idioms of the area. Uncle Michael Beshoar, just past seventy-nine and a bit tottery, greeted him with tears in his eyes. He met a score of solid, short-statured men whom he recognized as his own blood even before he heard their names— Andrew Beshoar, John Beshoar, John Zook, Joseph Rothrock, Uncle Daniel Seiver, and others. When he would stop at one farm, word was sent out and relatives would hurry from adjoining farms for a look at the Mike Beshoar who had gone west so long ago. In a letter to Annie he wrote:

> On the morning of the 23rd, Uncle Daniel had me delivered at the depot at Mifflintown about five minutes before the train came along. It was on time (5:07 A.M.) and in 20 minutes from that time I stepped on the platform at the depot at Lewistown, Mifflin County, Pa. . . went to the National Hotel . . . thence to the barber shop where I got shaved, shoes blacked, and clothes brushed . . . thence back to the hotel

where I had breakfast and at 7:10 A.M. my buggy was at the door. I started in the right direction for I knew it well . . . but when near the eastern end of town it occurred to me that some of the roads might have been changed since I was last here. Seeing a man working at a sidewalk I stopped and inquired the road, and in order that he might know the better how to direct me I mentioned that I wanted to see old Mr. Jacob Mohler. He said, yes, he could direct me exactly . . . that Mr. Mohler was making his home at his (the sidewalk carpenter's) father's house and so I said 'You are a son of William Howe?' He said yes. I then asked him to whom he was married and he said Sadie Karns. And who was Sadie? She was the eldest daughter of Joseph Karns, the last public school teacher to whom I went when a boy. Joe married after I left, reared a family, and died before I returned, and his eldest daughter was married to a man whose father was first married soon after I left there. What remarkable effects of time! He called his wife to the door and introduced me to her, which resulted in her getting in the buggy and going with me as my guide, saying she wanted to go see Grandma Howe anyway. In order not to detain me she bundled her baby's clothes and took them along so as to dress it after she got there.

First we started to the old homestead. In going there we had to pass within 400 yards of James N. Martin's, whose oldest daughter and I always claimed each other as sweethearts during our school days. It would be unkind to pass so close by and not call upon her as a friend, and Mrs. Howe insisted on my doing so. We went there, but Mary was at school about 500 yards further away where she would close a summer term school, which she had been teaching, that day. Mrs. Howe remained at the house while I went on to the schoolhouse and knocked at the door. She opened it wide, looked me full in the face, and called me by name. She is the first one that I met in all my visit that recognized me so as to call me by name. Cousin Joseph Rothrock, the day before, said he knew I was a Beshoar; that he recognized a face that he knew well, but that time had made some changes and he could not venture to name me. Mary at once gave recess for ten minutes. Before that time was out I bid her goodbye,

(I did not kiss her) and when I got back to the house Mrs. Howe was all ready to go. We went thence to the old homestead upon which now lives an old nearest neighbor, John Mitchell. There is the same big white house with the green window blinds . . . just as it was before . . . there is my bedroom . . . the furniture is changed but the room is the same . . . all the rooms are just as they were. The door handle on the front door which my father made with his own hands of a piece of fine German steel and which I rubbed with leather and chalk until it was perfectly polished is still there. The old pump with the same old iron pump handle which I swang on many a time when I was a boy was still there in the same place. There is the same old wash house, the same old pig pen, the same old wagon shed and corn crib, the old red barn with its white cornice and seventy-two white windows is there just as I left it . . . the mows, the feeding rooms, the stables, the granaries, the beam in the mow where my father carved his initials and the date 1842 . . . all just as I left them. Down the lane in front of the barn is the same pond on which I used to run my tugboats and sailing vessels. Everything was there except my father and mother, and the girls, my crippled sister, Susan, and the babies, and the old mare, Rock, and her oldest son, Bully, and the dog, Lige. They were all missing, and I could no longer restrain my feelings. My visit was more painful than pleasant though it was some of both.

From there we went to Uncle Jacob Beshoar's where we had dinner . . . thence we went to the old cemetery where I viewed the graves of my sainted mother, my angel brother and three sisters, all marked with plain marble head and footstones of the same design. I read the simple inscriptions and remembered—oh, how plainly—when I stood there and saw the bodies lowered and the clay shoveled in over them and how, in the simplicity of my childhood, I felt outraged that clay should be thrown upon them with shovels as they would throw it upon the carcass of a brute. I stood there and remembered that time was doing its work steadily and surely. Time laid them there; time had covered their graves with a tough sod; time had caused the grass to grow and fall and die and grow again till the stones that had been placed there were almost concealed in the growth.

From there we went to Cousin John Hoop's, Cousin Joseph
Mohler's, Uncle William Howe's, with whom Uncle Jacob
Mohler has his home. While there, two men who had worked
for my father in my boyhood time, heard of my being there
and came to greet me. Uncle Jacob Mohler, over eighty
years old, embraced and kissed me and wept for joy as did also
Uncle Jacob Beshoar and Aunt Mary, his wife; and all the
younger Beshoars, Rothrocks, Mohlers, and Hoops, seemed
blithe and gay because Cousin Mike had come home.

From Uncle Howe's we went back to Lewistown and I
mounted the train at 5:20 P.M. and in 22 minutes from then
was in McVeytown. I went to Maelin's store (he has kept store
there 50 years). He was glad to see me and assisted me in
getting a buggy to go to my brother-in-law's, Mr. Musser, about
four miles out. While the driver was getting his supper and the
buggy ready, I called on Dr. Rothrock, a second cousin, who
had practiced there about fifty years. At about 7:30 o'clock we
started out to Mr. Musser's (my sister Sarah) and got there
about 8. Though I had not seen this sister for 31 years,
she suspected it was me, but was by no means certain. She
seemed confounded, and did not get over it fully while I
stayed. Her two daughters, very elegant young ladies, seemed
wonderfully pleased at meeting their Uncle Michael of whom
they had heard, but had never seen. My sister and they all told
me next morning that, so surprised and muddled were they at
my sudden appearance, that they had not slept during the
night. They had breakfast ready for me at 3:30 next morning
and Mr. Musser took me to town in his buggy. He landed me
at the depot about fifteen minutes before train time. Traveling
yesterday and last night brought me to Cincinnati.

And a bit more traveling took him home, bearing white gloves
and a parasol for Annie, kid-body dolls for Bonnie and Burnie, and
a new suit for Grandpa Maupin. Annie was carrying another child,
but she looked well and happy and was glad to see him home again.
He had traveled a lot of miles, enjoyed his Pennsylvania visit, met
a great many important and wealthy men, but none who was ready
to invest in undeveloped coal lands under some remote place called
Fisher's Peak in the wilds of southern Colorado. But he had hopes
and prospects.

While he was in the East in June, the State Medical Society, holding its annual meeting in the Pueblo courthouse, found that the old charges brought by Owen and Cushing were again before the ethics committee, this time at the instigation of his former partner, Dr. W. G. Scott. When the committee couldn't arrive at a conclusion one way or another, Dr. Scott asked the society to go into a committee of the whole to consider the charges, which included advertising, using his picture on prescriptions, having no diploma and no license to practice medicine other than a permit to peddle patient medicines in Arkansas. The society did so, taking less than two minutes to move that the whole matter of the charges against its legislative chairman, the man who had steered the medical control bill through the last legislature, be referred back to the committee on ethics until such time "as proper charges are presented against Dr. Beshoar."

During the remainder of the summer and well into the fall, a number of engineers and financiers journeyed to Colorado to look at the coal property. When parties of two or more arrived, Michael put them up in one of the hotels, but singles were usually "accommodated in our front bedroom." The physician took them to the property himself, with Mike driving the team. He didn't want outsiders listening to conversations, and besides, Mike was helpful in other ways than driving, in that son, like father, was beginning to speak knowingly about the geology of the area and the mountain, depth of coal veins, composition of the coal, mining costs, and such other resources on the property as iron, fire clay, building stone, grit stone, pasturage, timber, and water. The spying threat was very real as other coal companies were watching Gray Creek closely, keeping tab on the physician's out-of-town visitors and even having them followed. When he found they were bribing telegraph operators and getting copies of his dispatches to and from the Cincinnati office, Michael devised a code for use in all telegrams. It was strictly Southwest in flavor: New York became Chilili (a tiny Mexican village just east of Trinidad); an option, a calf; a power of attorney, a chaparral; Philadelphia was Apishapa, and Washington, D.C., was Pueblo; banks were bucks, brokers were hogs, and congressmen were eagles. And a series of handy sentences and phrases were worked out: beef meant "look for particulars by mail"; pasture said "they want more time to investigate"; and hay was the code word for "they will pay for an option."

While Michael was hurrying down Main Street to his office one hot July morning, he got himself into still another project, one that was to take a good deal of his time for the next twenty-three years. He had his head down, deep in thought, when suddenly his way was blocked by A. K. Cutting, owner and editor of the weekly *Trinidad Democrat*. Cutting wasn't the most beloved resident of Trinidad, for he had deeply offended a number of his fellow citizens at one time or another. He was strictly a pistol-packing, frontier type of editor who was continually in hot water. But for all his faults and erratic journalism, Michael much preferred him to Olney Newell, the Episcopal clergyman who was editor of the *Trinidad Daily News*. This time he eyed Cutting suspiciously, knowing the editor was in financial trouble and thinking he was about to be hit for a loan. "Doc, you used to run the *Pueblo Chieftain* and a newspaper in Arkansas, didn't you?," Cutting asked. The physician said he had indeed, hastening to add that he had "taken the gold cure insofar as newspapers are concerned." He just thought he had. When Cutting offered him the *Democrat* at the ridiculously low figure of $1,200, he was back in the newspaper business. He set up the Trinidad Publishing Company with himself as secretary and Casimiro Barela as president. Capitalization was $5,000 divided into 500 non-assessable shares of ten dollars each. Cutting received 120 shares of stock and was made general superintendent and manager of the newspaper at a salary of $100 per month, Barela got ten shares of stock, and the physician kept the remaining 370 shares. In exchange for nothing he had acquired a weekly newspaper that consisted of a name, presses, a few cases of type, a battered desk, a couple of chairs, and some odds and ends worth not more than a few dollars. At the outset Cutting informed him the Trinidad Publishing Company would have to spend $325 immediately for additional type and paper supplies. Michael easily raised the money by selling 130 of his shares at three dollars per share to people he met on Main and Commercial streets. It wasn't a very auspicious start for his third newspaper venture, but he was pretty sure he knew how to make it grow.

He continued the newspaper as a weekly and as the *Trinidad Democrat* until January 4, 1883, when he issued Vol. 1, No. 1, of a handsome new morning daily, the *Trinidad Daily Advertiser*—"Devoted to the Best Interests of Trinidad." His new paper, named after his first newspaper in Pocahontas, was six columns wide, twenty-two deep. The first issue consisted of four pages, containing ten columns of straight matter and fourteen columns of advertising. Unlike the *Chieftain*, which he had published without advertising on its front page, the new *Advertiser* conformed to the custom of the day, carrying two columns of advertisements on the front page. There was no salutatory, but there was an announcement saying there had been a delay in getting telegraphic dispatches but promising that within two or three days they would appear regularly each morning. In addition to a large number of personal items about comings and goings in Trinidad, some livestock news, and one or two short local stories, the new *Advertiser* ran a gossip story saying that Bismarck would quit soon, as chancellor of Germany, that there were some problems about the Gambetta funeral in Paris, and that there was a land boom underway in Springer, New Mexico.

In his third issue he wrote:

The *Advertiser* appears this morning with the Associated Press report as promised our patrons and the public. We intend to give the public all they pay for and maybe a little bit more for the present. We believe, however, that Trinidad's businessmen will appreciate the benefit that a live, first class newspaper such as the *Advertiser* will be to the town and will give us a substantial encouragement in continuing to make our paper a true representative of the town and county. We are doing much for this section, and running business risks in putting the *Advertiser* before the people, but we do it in behalf of the people as well as ourselves and must of necessity rely upon the people for support.

He ran his telegraphic news each morning thereafter, short, pithy news paragraphs, grouped under a heading that he wrote and liked very much: "Telegraphic Hash."

His new paper received good notices from the state press. The *Denver Times*, in its January 8, 1883, issue said, "When Dr. Beshoar took the *Trinidad Democrat* a short time ago he made great improvements in it, but the greatest was made on the 4th inst. when he knocked it in the head and brought the *Daily Advertiser* out of the ruin."

And the proprietor of the *Advertiser* was most pleased when the much-admired Ouray, Colorado, editor, David F. Day wrote in his

Solid Muldoon: "The *Trinidad Advertiser* is the latest. Wish it luck? To Beshoar we do, oodles of it." The physician reprinted it with the comment: "Ah-h-h-h-h!"

The *Advertiser* wasn't his only new baby in January 1883. On the nineteenth Annie presented him with a son. He noted in his date book that he had delivered a seven-pound boy, that Annie was in labor for a total of fourteen hours, and that it was a normal presentation. Then he went back to his name book and decided the boy should be called Benjamin Bernardin. But he had to pull the legs of his friends and the editors downtown. The *Advertiser* noted on January 20, "There was an arrival at the residence of Dr. M. Beshoar yesterday, the visiting angel being a bouncing baby boy. He has come to remain for some time and will be christened Ben Butler Beshoar—if he can survive the allegation implied by the name. He already shows a marked tendency toward spoons and may become governor of Colorado." The *Trinidad Weekly News*, in its January 25 issue, said, "Dr. Beshoar says he would name his boy Ben Butler, but he is afraid he could not find a minister in the city who would christen him with that name." Annie saw both items and was alarmed, but was assured that her husband was not really going to name his new son after the infamous greenbacker and one-time Union General—who was also known as the "silver-spoon thief" of New Orleans. Butler, at the time of the birth of Michael's son, had just been elected governor of Massachusetts and was much in the news.

It was a fine month for him. His practice was doing well, the *Advertiser* was thriving, his book was selling well, the brickyard and the steam laundry were showing a profit, his daughters were well, the baby was happy, Mike, Jr., seemed to be behaving reasonably well, the 4C & I was going to make him wealthy, and the weather was splendid—for oysters, clams, eggnog, Tom and Jerry, and hot scotch, all available in almost every other business establishment on Main and Commercial streets.

In the spring the 4C & I Company enlarged its holdings with five thousand acres of promising land contiguous to the original property in the Gray Creek area, and Michael, burning with mining fever but still without any real capital, took another flyer at New Mexico Territory. This time he sent Alfred Stevens, an experienced

mining man and prospector, and Mike, Jr., off to prospect the Magdalena Mountains. Mike had been drinking again, and his father
thought a prospecting trip, away from the saloons and other diver-
sions of Trinidad, would do him good. Meanwhile he had plenty of
help: two physicians in his medical office; a business manager for
his *Daily Advertiser* plus a staff of reporters, an ad solicitor, a circulation man, and printers; a combination business manager–book-
keeper for his other properties; satisfactory foremen at the laundry
and the brickyard; and good ranch foremen. In all he had a regular
payroll of about thirty-five persons, and things were going pretty
well, at least for the moment. His problem was that, while he had
a lot of irons in the fire, most of them, with the exception of his
practice, were not providing him with much in the way of cash.
Gray Creek was undoubtedly a rich coal property, but it wasn't
producing any coal; he had a lot of stock, but he hadn't realized
more than $25,000 from sales of shares when he was thinking in
terms of $250,000 or more for his 4C & I stock. Aside from two quick
trips to Cincinnati, he spent the summer in Trinidad practicing
medicine and attending to his local businesses and mail. The last
grew in volume with each passing week, keeping one secretary
busy much of the time. There was the regular business mail, correspondence with doctors, letters from soldiers seeking his help in
getting pensions, inquiries from people who were thinking about
moving to Colorado, and a heavy volume of mail from former Trinidadians and from Arkansas residents asking his medical help by
mail. One new arrival in Colorado, who wrote from Denver about
her tubercular husband, received a typical reply:

My advice is short, but I know it is good. Tell him to dismiss
all thoughts of curing his lungs; it can't be done, never could
be, never will be by way of lung remedies. Nature will cure
them if she can. No doctor can. This is the dark side of the
picture. Now for the bright: most consumptives die because
they depend on lung remedies. Many get well, but usually
because they have quit the use of lung remedies. If your
husband has had consumption long he knows that when his
appetite and digestion are good he gets better (his lungs,
too) and that whenever his digestion fails his lungs get worse.
That is the whole secret. Now let him profit by his own
knowledge obtained in his own experience. Let him quit all

cod liver oil, hypophosphites, expectorants, etc. To relieve
distressing cough let him inhale warm vapor or something of
the kind. If must be let him take a little henbane internally
and rather than lose a whole night's sleep he had better take
morphine or if it sets unpleasantly on him chloral. But he ought
to use these things only when he must. For regular treatment
tell him to wear none but woolen underclothing. To go out
every day, never being afraid of too much clothing. He must
wear more here in Colorado than where he came from. He
must double the bed clothing he would use in a lower
altitude at the same temperature. His diet should be the
best—milk, beef, eggs, etc. If milk does not agree with him
he can make it agreeable with salt. Tell him to get an ounce
bottle of Laco Pepin Powder and whenever he is doubtful of
his digestion to take two measurefuls after each meal (there
is a measure with each ounce bottle). When he is pretty sure
his stomach will do its work without it he need not take it. If
he will follow these directions, keep a cheerful disposition,
not get overtired but get plenty of outdoor exercise he is nearly
sure to get well if he stays in Colorado.

In October, Annie packed herself and three children off to Indian
Territory to visit her brother John at Colbert's Station, leaving her
husband in charge of her parents and the household. José, he of
the indenture, had left with his rewards, and the staff now consisted
of Harriet, the hired girl, and a man to replace José. No sooner had
Annie left than the house was practically taken apart for cleaning.

"The house cleaning goes gloriously on," Michael wrote in a
letter to Annie. "It will be finished tomorrow, I hope. The washing is
put off till Wednesday to finish the cleaning. Our room and Bonnie's
are finished. Your mother's room and the "little room" will be
finished today and the sitting room and parlor tomorrow. I had the
floors done over and new carpet laid on the stairs. We will pull
the turnips tomorrow. Will pull enough to do for the winter and
cover the others with straw. We intend to mulch the trees with
straw and cover the blue grass with straw manure this week if we
get time. The cat and the banties and the big chickens and the
cow and Harriett and your father and mother and myself are well
'and feedin' . . . hope these few lines may find you enjoyin the same
God's blessins . . . so naught else remains except I am 'yourn till

deth.' Kiss Bonnie and Burnie and Bennie for me. Stay as long as you wish."

José's replacement, a man of forty-five, bore the impressive name of George Washington Turner and was the proud holder of a written contract that guaranteed him board and the munificent sum of twenty dollars a month. For his part he was required to take care of the horses of Beshoar, Slater, and Edwards, physicians and surgeons, their buggies and harness, and "to perform the duties of janitor in the office every morning before eight o'clock; to pasture the cow on the lawn every day, to water the lawn, cultivate the garden and raise such truck as may be requested by either Mrs. Beshoar or Mrs. Maupin, to take the wash water every Monday afternoon from the kitchen and with it wash the trunks of all the trees on the premises, also the lower branches; to carry away to the canal each morning before nine o'clock all buckets of ashes and unclean water and other refuse which he may find sitting on the back porch and immediately return the buckets; to keep the front porch, sidewalk, alley, drive, yard and corral in a neatly policed condition; to provide kindling wood on the kitchen porch every evening; to close the poultry house door every night after the chickens have gone to roost and open the door early every morning, also to keep the poultry house in good condition; and when supplies for the house or hay and grain which teamsters cannot conveniently handle are delivered, said George Washington Turner is to help unload and properly care for the property."

Annie had thought the Turner contract unnecessary and had told Michael as gently as she could that a written contract was not really needed for every minor employe, but her husband loved law and lawing and was never happier than when he was drafting "a legal document." Besides, he insisted that the contract would be useful when he wanted to discharge George Washington Turner and that, if the man lived up to it, he would never want to lose him.

Soon after Annie got home from Indian Territory, the physician had an opportunity to play the lawyer in a deal that almost made him wish he was big in cattle rather than coal lands; almost, but not quite. His old friend Colonel George W. Thompson solicited his aid in selling his cattle ranch to eastern capitalists "because you know more about this law business than half the lawyers in the country, Doc."

The physician handled the correspondence for Thompson, who

empowered B. G. Jayne of 120 Broadway in New York to make the sale. Thompson's famed Chiquaque Ranch sold quickly, going to the New York and Boston Cattle Company headed by George Mc-Crary, former U. S. Secretary of War and general counsel for the Santa Fe Railroad. The eastern company got 1,000,000 acres of grazing land, 17 miles of water frontage on the Arkansas River, 40 purebred Hereford bulls, 50 purebred shorthorn bulls, 44 saddle horses, wagons, and 15,700 head of cattle listed as "high grades and smooth native brutes." Colonel Thompson wanted to express his appreciation in a material way; but though Michael was dollar hungry, he made a grandstand play, waving Thompson off with notice that as soon as he sold his Gray Creek holdings he would take his friend's $575,000 away from him at the poker table.

The truth of the matter was that the Thompson sale rankled. Michael wrote the other officers of the 4C & I Company in Cincinnati, who were supposed to be pushing sale of his stock, that it seemed odd that big money investors were difficult to interest in a good natural resource such as coal, a product that was "a sure thing," but would jump to invest in cattle and horses "that might be swept away in a matter of hours by a plague, by storms or some other disaster."

The Thompson sale was a humdinger, but it didn't particularly startle Trinidad's business entrepreneurs, all of whom expected to get rich. The town was building up fast with signs of growth on every side. Commercial Street got its first iron bridge across the Purgatoire, and business of all kinds hummed. In the west end of town, a growing red light district testified to the increasing number of cowpunchers and coal miners who came to town to spend their money. Bat Masterson, who had served as city marshal in 1882, came back to do a brief term as a lawman before going to Denver and into the sporting world of boxing, but most of the handling of roughs and the keeping of order was done by Louie Kreeger, who didn't have to take second place to Masterson or anyone else when it came to law enforcement.

By mid-1884 business was good enough to warrant an expansion of Michael's newspaper enterprises. Since the prospecting venture in New Mexico didn't seem to be getting anywhere, he canceled it, brought Mike back to Trinidad, and put him to work soliciting subscriptions and advertising among the cattlemen of southern Colorado. At the same time he launched the *Cattlemen's Adver-*

tiser and *El Anunciador*, the latter being "the only Spanish secular newspaper in the state." The Advertiser building was busy day and night turning out the *Trinidad Advertiser* six mornings each week, the *Weekly Advertiser*, the *Cattlemen's Advertiser*, and the Spanish paper. He pushed the Spanish paper hard with advertisements in his *Advertisers* and with posters tacked to poles and trees, and on the doors of cantinas, grocery stores, and elsewhere:

EL ANUNCIADOR
EDICION SEMANAL

———

LITERARIA Y FAMILIAR
EL ÚNICO PERIÓDICO

———

SUBSCRIBANSE DE UNA VEZ
SOLAMENTE $2.00 AL AÑO

———

COPIAS SUELTAS 10 CENTAVOS

———

DIRIJANSE A MIGUEL BESHOAR, PROP.

The expansion of his newspaper enterprises wasn't accomplished without attacks from competing newspapers, particularly the *Trinidad Daily News*, which devoted considerable news space to commenting on the *Advertiser*, its editor, and the activities of the 4C & I Company. The physician didn't really mind much, as it was customary for editors to fall on each other with knives and hatchets on any pretext. He was of the same school and rather enjoyed the give and take.

Mike stayed with his soliciting job for almost three months. Attending big roundups, visiting ranches, and seeking out cattle kings in their offices and on the range, he kept a stream of advertisements pouring into the *Advertiser*. The proprietor had promised Mike, Jr., a vacation if he procured 250 advertisers, but before the goal was reached, a dispute broke out between father and son, and Mike, Jr., was fired from the *Advertiser*. The father's complaint was that Mike had not signed cattle companies to formal contracts as he was supposed to, and that he had withheld advertising and subscription money. Mike, who had been traveling the counties of southern Colorado and northern New Mexico by horseback, complained in turn that he had not been given enough for living expenses and had been forced to withhold some of his collections to feed himself and his horse. It is not clear from their correspondence who was in the right, but Mike's reputation for drinking and wenching was against him in any such argument. It was an unfortunate and serious break, Mike returned to Trinidad and went to work as a telephone company representative and installer. Michael had reports that the young man was spending everything he made and more on whiskey and girls on "the hill" in the west end of town. After a few weeks the physician heard that his son had gone back to Texas. He regretted the latest break with Mike but was more philosophical than he had been at previous leavings. Mike was no longer a boy; he could come and go as he pleased. Michael wished things were different as far as Mike was concerned, but his responsibility these days was to Annie and their children.

Annie, heavy with another child, had been much disturbed by the row with Mike, Jr., and by his roistering in the west end. She stayed away from social functions and would scarcely leave the house. To make matters worse, her brother John Maupin wrote that his wife Helen had suffered a mental collapse and was in an asylum in St. Louis. This bad news was followed in December by the word that John had died in Colbert's Station in Indian Territory. When Annie's fifth child, a boy, was born just a month later, Michael and Annie agreed to forego the name book and its names beginning with B, to name the new boy after Annie's father and late brother. The physician admired his father-in-law, and he had liked his brother-in-law, a steady, hard-working man whose calm demeanor and gentle manners were difficult to reconcile with his reputation as John Maupin, Quantrill guerrilla, who, after his brother Tom was killed in an ambush in Missouri, ran down the captain commanding the Redlegs, killed him, cut off his head, and stuck it upon a gatepost to shrivel and blacken in the sun. Annie never acknowledged that she knew of such things, but her husband had learned of them from Frank and Jesse James on one of their hideaway visits to Trinidad.

Michael had a theory that anyone who had served in the War Between the States ought to have a pension, and he did his part to see that they got one. He had kept many of his records from the Fort Kearny Post Hospital, but whether he had a record on a soldier or not he would recommend him for a pension, would "testify" to statements that their debilities were the direct result of their service. Sometimes he had to stretch his memory and the cords of veracity a little to make a good case for the man's pension, but he usually managed. And in almost every instance, the man seeking the pension was in dire need. If Michael couldn't remember any details, the supplicant would recall them for him. When John Ladner wrote from Santa Fe in 1885, the physician couldn't place him at all, but when Ladner came back with a second letter and said, "You will remember that I kept the Commercial House on Commercial Street in 1873 and you treated me for the rheumatiz and deafness. I got the deafness from the cannonading below Charleston, S.C. in 1862 when I was on board the U.S.S. Bienville." Michael then remembered perfectly and made out the required forms for Mr. Ladner who said he was "complete broke down."

Sometimes the pension letters involved more than a simple prodding of Michael's memory, as in the case of James H. Kennedy, a former Fort Kearny soldier. Kennedy wrote from Sigourney, Iowa, for assistance: "The surgeon who attended me at the time of my injury was later dishonorably discharged and his evidence will not be accepted by the pension authorities. However, I remember well of your doctoring me and of my discharge being made out though it was later destroyed. I was ruptured on the right side." The physician filled out the papers and had them notarized. In a few days they were back; it seemed the rupture was all a mistake and that the problem was varicocele. Would the doctor refresh his memory and make out the papers again? He would and did.

"I have been living in Mexico," Kennedy wrote, "I am going back there when I get my pension and on my way I'll stop over in Trinidad and give you some idea of the mineral, agricultural and general resources of that country. I have traveled a great deal and have been a tolerable close observer. I have seen the country as it is and I have examined a great many mines in case you have any interest in mines."

The physician was delighted. Any interest in mines? He was practically burning up with interest, but it appeared his Gray Creek coal properties were going to simmer for awhile yet. A suit brought by the federal government against the Rio Grande Railway questioning its title to some of the railroad lands in the area had scared potential investors off, at least for the moment. Michael was certain his titles were good, but he knew he'd probably have to sit tight until the government won or lost the Rio Grande suite. Meanwhile he was ripe for something else. When Kennedy, as good as his word, stopped off in Trinidad, the physician had the old papers and maps on the Temerosa mine ready to show him. Kennedy said he had heard of the Temerosa and that, while it was supposed to be rich, it was very isolated in extremely rugged country. When Kennedy, after two wonderful days of talk about Mexico, went his way, the physician regretfully put the Mexican mine papers away. He just had too much on his hands at the moment to go gadding off to Mexico on a wild mining venture. Old John Maupin had just passed away and he was needed at home by Annie and her mother.

Although he passed up Mexico for the time being, he got himself deeply involved in a zinc property in Arkansas. He took an option on 640 acres near Powhatan in an area where the American Zinc Company had properties. He hired experts to look at the property and was excited by their reports showing zinc, both sulphates and carbonates, in substantial quantity at a depth of fourteen feet in purest "black pack" along with good quality kaolin. He tried to interest a number of his Arkansas friends in the property. One former soldier named W. F. Henderson, a successful Little Rock attorney, wrote effusive letters to "My Dear Old Captain," but it turned out he was more interested in reminiscing about Shaver's Seventh Arkansas and Randolph County than investing in zinc. And so it was with others until the physician had to let his option lapse.

But he was soon deep in mining again. It came about on a cold winter night in January 1887. He was at home, working on his invention, a railroad-crossing guard, and hoping he wouldn't be called out on such a night, when a man arrived at the door, heavily muffled against the blowing snow and cold. The visitor was Delos Chappell, the Kalamazoo engineer who had built the waterworks. Although Michael had criticized the water franchise and branded Chappell's rates as robbery, the two men got along well enough on a personal basis. Chappell said he was sorry to trouble him on such a night but that he had a proposition: he wanted to get into the coal business and hoped to work out some arrangement whereby he could undertake development of the doctor's Gray Creek holdings. They talked for an hour or more. The physician wanted to sell outright, but Chappell said he could not possibly raise $250,000 for undeveloped coal lands. Instead he proposed formation of a new company designed specifically to develop the property. The subscribers of the 4C & I Company would be protected by a new issue of stock.

Michael was wary and said he would have to talk with the Cincinnati people. A day or two later Chappell, having been called to Kalamazoo because one of his sons was ill, sent the physician a handwritten note saying, "The only question is whether we are willing to grant each other reasonable protection so far as may be done without imperiling the other's interest."

When Chappell returned, they resumed discussions. After several days of talks, Michael went to Cincinnati for a special meeting with 4C & I officers and major stockholders. Some favored doing business with Chappell; some were anxious to be rid of their 4C & I stock and out of the whole business. Drawing on Trinidad banks, Michael bought up most of their stock. After the Cincinnati meeting he went on to New York and again made the rounds, for he had a feeling he would rather not be associated with Chappell. On his return to Trinidad, he stalled through the summer though he was fully empowered to act by his remaining associates in the 4C & I Company. He kept hoping something would turn up. Late in August, after a last exchange of letters with his associates in Cincinnati, he decided to do business with Chappell. The eastern groups had dillydallied long enough. A contract was drawn and signed September 2, 1887. It provided for a new corporation to be known as the Gray Creek Coal and Coking Company, with a capitalization of $200,000 divided into 2,000 shares of $100 each. M. Beshoar and associates would hold 1,000 shares, and Chappell would sell 1,000 shares at 60 percent of par value to obtain money needed for delinquent taxes and development, and once he had done that he would receive 100 shares from M. Beshoar for the service. Work on the property would begin within thirty days.

On the day the new company was organized, it developed that the shares Chappell was selling were all going to three of his former associates in Kalamazoo, H. H. Johnstone, J. C. Sherwin, and P. H. Shipley—all of whom were named directors. When Michael insisted he must have representation on the board, Sherwin resigned and was replaced by the physician's choice, Murdo MacKenzie, manager of the Matador Cattle Company. No sooner had MacKenzie been named than Shipley resigned in favor of Chappell, who then became both a director and general manager of the new company.

Within the prescribed time the rough road to Gray Creek was improved and was lined with teams hauling supplies to the mine site, which swarmed with construction workers.

While the hammer and saw were busy at Gray Creek, Trinidad also thrived. A building boom sent prices of land and materials sky-rocketing. Good lots within the city were at a premium, and Michael cashed in heavily on his holdings. Money was free and easy. The payrolls at the surrounding mines enriched the town, which no longer had a rival in El Moro as the principal trading center of a fast-growing coal-mining and stock-raising domain. Every train brought new residents, some to open businesses of their own, some to go to work in the mines or one of the proliferating service industries. Still others came by wagon to settle on the rolling prairies in the eastern part of the county. The businessmen agreed that the time had arrived when Trinidad needed an organization common to eastern cities but hitherto unknown in southern Colorado, to wit: a chamber of commerce. When the first meeting was held February 7, 1888, Thomas B. Collier, who was both county treasurer and mayor of Trinidad, was elected president. Named to the all-important roads and transportation committee were Delos Chappell, capitalist; M. Beshoar, physician-editor; John Conkie, real estate broker; Joseph Hausman, druggist; and John Davis, grocer.

The Advertiser Steam Job Print House printed a comprehensive directory that listed not only the citizens of Trinidad and El Moro but also those of such growing coal camps as Starkville and Engleville, the latter a new camp between Trinidad and Gray Creek. From a mud village with a few hundred Mexicans and a handful of American adventurers, the town had grown into a city of seven thousand with another eight thousand residents in the immediate area. The directory, compiled and edited by W. H. Whitney, listed 19 real estate firms, 7 restaurants, 6 liveries, 3 brickyards, 13 dressmakers, 14 laundries (including 13 strung along "Chinaman's Row" on Main Street), 3 daily newspapers, 4 weeklies, 4 dentists, and 18 physicians. Leading the business procession: 35 saloons, of which 21 were elbow to elbow along Commercial Street. Brick and stone were replacing the native adobe everywhere, and Anglo-Saxon names now predominated on the tax rolls. Michael was proud of the growth; he had played a role in practically every phase of it. He had started hundreds of his fellow citizens out with a slap on their bare bottoms upon their arrival in Trinidad, and he had brought others in from Arkansas, Nebraska, Pennsylvania, and other states. He prided himself on knowing every man and woman in the city and county, despite the rapid influx. When a new family arrived, he was one of the first to call. Sometimes the newcomers were at a loss how to take the portly gentleman in the silk hat and gaudy vest who came to their new home to welcome them and ask them all sorts of questions about their background, likes and dislikes, hopes and aspirations. He used various ruses to meet the new arrivals. When Thomas F. Shanly moved to town from Lake City, the mining town in the San Juan Mountains, and opened an insurance office at 103 East Main Street, the physician went to his office to greet him. Shortly afterward he met old Finch on the street, and in the course of exchanging views about the newcomer, the liveryman said Shanly certainly had a fine-looking wife. When they parted, Michael headed straight for the Shanly home. He must get a look at this handsome wife immediately. Mrs. Shanly eyed him suspiciously and inquired his business. He said he was the physician who had been called to this address. When she said she had not called a doctor and started to close the door, he stuck his foot in it and argued with her. Surely somebody must be sick. He held on until he had satisfied himself that Mrs. Shanly was indeed a good-looking woman, particularly when angry.

When Shanly returned home, his wife was still hopping mad, demanding to know "just who was that robin red breast who came to the door this afternoon?" When she had described the visitor, her husband laughed, told her the visitor was Dr. Beshoar, "a town character who owns half of the place and has to know everyone and everything that is going on. He was in to see me, too. Some of the people call him 'Hippocrates in a Red Vest' behind his back, but they respect him."

Not long after his arrival Shanly became a police judge. He was a horse fancier, and when a small circus slipped out of town leaving a horse as payment for its ground rent, Judge Shanly paid the rent in exchange for the animal. Within a few weeks he had shaped it up into one of the finest horses in town and presented it to his wife. On her first time out she was riding up Commercial Street, a marvelous figure in green corduroy riding habit and plumed hat who sat side saddle as if she were born to it. But not being an expert horsewoman, she was soon in trouble when, near the intersection of Commercial and Main streets, a Salvation Army band rounded the corner, tooting and thumping for all it was worth. The horse began to dance. Mrs. Shanly flicked it on the shoulder with her crop whereupon, to the great delight of beholders, the former circus animal bent its right knee, bowed deeply, and then went into a fancy cakewalk that took it up over the sidewalk and through the window of the telegraph office before the music could be stopped.

Judge Shanly tossed the band in jail for disturbing the peace, whereupon Michael, the managing editor of the *Advertiser*, rushed to the defense of religion in an editorial the next morning: "It is too bad that an organization devoted to a good and noble cause cannot toot a horn on the main streets because a police judge's wife wants to ride a show horse through the business district. The band should be released immediately and the judge should be put in jail."

The band was released, and though the judge didn't go to jail, he and the *Advertiser* editor were on nodding terms only for some weeks after the incident.

Chapter 11
Farewell to a Prodigal Son

IN THE EARLY SPRING of 1887, Michael overruled his hostler by insisting he hitch a couple of young horses that had been taken in on a delinquent bill. The hostler argued that the animals were only "rough broke" and dangerous, but the physician said he had handled hundreds of horses in his day and that this pair didn't look any different to him. He had scarcely gone two blocks before the team bolted and smashed up the buggy and its occupant. Michael had a fractured skull, a broken left arm, and several broken ribs. He was nursed by Annie at home for more than a month and by April was fit enough to get back to work.

Aside from the accident and tedious convalescence, things were going very well for him. While he was out of the drugstore business, the physician still dispensed sizable quantities of drugs, many of which he compounded, at substantial profits. He sold the laundry and concentrated on his other interests. The Gray Creek property hadn't produced much for him in the way of money, but the development work was going ahead and he believed it would eventually pay off. Meanwhile, he had sold some undeveloped coal lands north and west of Trinidad for $150,000, and this windfall—along with sales of lots in Trinidad and farm and ranch lands in Las Animas, Huerfano, and Pueblo counties, plus a portion of some lands he had picked up in Iowa and Illinois on a speculative basis—put him in a comfortable position financially.

The *Advertiser* wasn't making a lot of money, but the printed reports that business manager Frank D. Goodale filled out for him at the close of each month were consistently gratifying. The report for May 1887 was typical. Under "Business Done" Goodale reported: job work $620; display advertising $505.25; locals $100; daily subscriptions $235; weekly subscriptions $100; and miscellaneous $145—for a total income of $1,705.25. Under "Expenses" he listed labor $675; rent $25; telegraph $78; paper stock $250; oil $12; fuel $14; freight and express $18; and incidentals including printing plates $50—for a total of $1,122.00, which left a profit of $573.75. Michael was an aggressive publisher. He watched expenses closely, and he watched the opposition newspapers; if a merchant placed an ad in one of the other newspapers and didn't show up at the *Advertiser* promptly with the same or more advertising and some job printing, he was sure to get a dressing down.

In addition to the income from the newspapers, money was coming in from his practice, the brickyard, farms and ranches, and occasional speculations in cattle and sheep, making it possible for him to clear an average of $1,700 a month, which was very good indeed for the time and place. He signed a contract with the Santa Fe Railroad for his street-crossing guard and felt reasonably sure he would realize a few thousand from it. He was a medical examiner for a half-dozen insurance companies and had surgeon's contracts with both the Santa Fe and Rio Grande railroads, which kept him supplied with both money and passes, the latter being by far the major consideration for a man addicted to travel.

Although he was affluent, with money for clothes, new carriages, things for the house, and stocks and propositions that appealed to him, he found himself unable to relax and take things a bit easier as Annie thought he should. He ran for county superintendent of schools and, as soon as the office was his, began to work on an ambitious program to improve the quality of teaching for Mexican children in the rural areas.

By late May he had a busy month planned: he would deliver a paper on "The Medical and Surgical Practices of the New Mexico Indians" at the regular June meeting of the Colorado State Medical Society, and he had reservations to attend a semicentennial celebration of the University of Michigan in Ann Arbor. It was at this moment that the blow fell in the form of a letter from a fellow Mason and physician in Clarendon, Texas:

June 2, 1887

Dr. M. Beshoar
Trinidad, Colorado
Dear Doctor:
    Having known you by reputation for some time and being

advised by those who know you better I write to say that I have
been victimized by your son, M. Beshoar Jr., who is known
here by the alias of R. E. Murray. On May 26th he passed a
check to me for seventy-three dollars which I cashed and I
find the check worthless and that your son forged the check
and signature. I cannot well afford to lose this amount of
money. Can you afford to make up my loss when you are fully
assured this is a correct statement? Mr. John Farrington, who is
in the employ of Mr. Charles Goodnight, whom you may
remember, suggested that I communicate with you at once.

Fraternally & resp. yours
J. D. Stocking, M.D.

Had it been a matter of just the one forged check passed on Dr.
Stocking, Michael might have been able to stave off disaster, but it
quickly developed that Mike had strewn forged checks throughout
several Texas counties. The father, after much agonized debate with
himself and consultations with close friends and attorneys, decided
he would do nothing more than provide Mike with a Texas attorney. He thought there was a remote possibility that the punishment
that seemed inevitable might bring Mike to his senses where nothing else had. In July, when he came to trial, Mike pleaded not guilty
to one indictment but was found guilty and sentenced to three years
in the Texas State Penitentiary; he pleaded guilty to a second indictment of forgery and was given an additional two years. Still
other charges involving more checks were dropped.

The Texas lawyer and friends who sat in on the trial as observers for Michael reported that Mike had "shown little evidence of
sorrow or determination to reform."

The physician had canceled his trip to Ann Arbor and sent his
family off to Kentucky for a protracted visit. He stayed in Trinidad
and conducted himself as though nothing had happened. Except for
his lawyers and a few intimates, no one knew anything about Mike's
problems and Michael let it stay that way. To the rest of Trinidad,
that likable, lovable, goodhearted, two-fisted drinker of a Mike
Beshoar, Jr., was off in Texas punching cows again.

Trinidad's new Chamber of Commerce and its transportation committee had little to say when the Denver & Rio Grande Railway,

convinced at last that its plan to make El Moro the business center of the area had failed, built the remaining five miles into Trinidad in 1888. It was a victory for Trinidad, but the town's citizens could not easily forget that the Rio Grande management had kept its terminus in El Moro twelve long years, and while it hadn't been able to destroy Trinidad as it intended, it had unquestionably retarded the city's growth.

With the advent of the Rio Grande, Trinidad had four railroads, three of them equipped with tracks, locomotives, coaches, freight cars, and other equipment. The fourth had no such encumbrances and paid neither salaries nor dividends. However, it was cherished because it gave many of the prominent men of the city the right to the title of railroad president; once each year the Trinidad and El Moro Railway changed presidents, and sometimes its name. Thus it was sometimes known as the Trinidad, El Moro & Eastern and sometimes as the Trinidad, El Moro & Pacific, depending upon which direction Trinidadians were looking at the time. Occasionally the name was changed to compliment the current president. When businessman Salazar was serving as president it was called the El Moro, Chilili, Trinidad and Chihuahua Railroad Company, and when dry goods merchant Sol Jaffa was president it was the Trinidad, El Moro & Jerusalem Line.

On the serious side, the three railroads with trains and tracks, the burgeoning coal industry, and the general growth in population raised the question of a hospital for Trinidad. Father Pinto, the parish priest, announced that the Sisters of Charity of Cincinnati, who conducted the parochial school, would operate a hospital in Trinidad if land and building were provided by the community. Within a matter of hours, Michael drove up to the rectory, invited Father Pinto for a buggy ride, and took him to the top of a flat-topped piñon-clad elevation at the east edge of town. He told the good padre he owned the hill and all the land around it, that he had been saving the hill site for a new home for his family, but that if the priest thought it suitable he could have thirty-five lots as a gift for the sisters. Father Pinto accepted with one word: "Done."

A fund-raising committee headed by the energetic Casimiro Barela went to work with such enthusiasm and the response was so good from all groups—Catholics, Lutherans, Presbyterians, Methodists, and others—that money was soon in hand for a building. The sisters came in almost immediately and opened a temporary hospital, Trinidad's first, on Gordon Street "just across the arroyo" at the east edge of town near the hospital site. At the outset the sisters intended to name their new hospital St. Michael's in honor of the archangel and the physician who had been named its first chief of staff. However, there was a last-minute change after the good nuns discovered that Michael Beshoar would be away on the first extended vacation of his life when the bandy-legged little Bishop Machebeuf came down from Denver to preside at the ground-breaking ceremonies, August 29, 1888. And anyway the highly esteemed Don Rafael Chacón, stockman, owner of Chacon's Addition, and sometimes newspaper publisher, had been an even more generous benefactor; hence St. Michael became San Rafael.

The hospital was not only a major community asset, but it was also a source of pride to all who had lent support, including the members of the sporting fraternity; these had been among the more liberal contributors, as was only fitting since a substantial percentage of the town's money went into their pockets. In Ben F. Springer's gambling room under his saloon in the Grand Union Hotel, as well as in other gambling places, ten- and twenty-dollar gold pieces stood in foot-high stacks on the roulette and faro tables. And in the west end, which had come to be known to many as "Chancre Hill," there were literally dozens of places run by madams with such names as Big Dutch and Little Dutch. Miss May Phelps kept one of the better places, "a nice, quiet, orderly establishment with about fifteen girls." The cheap house was run by Cunny Cunningham. Not all of them were in the west end; Madam Wilson's place in an adobe house at the intersection of Maple and Elm streets was convenient to the roaring saloons and game rooms of the central business district.

The sporting life put money into the pockets of the physicians of the town, and most of them gave some of it back. For his part, Michael was cutting down his liquor intake and had even shocked some of his best friends by speaking well of the temperance movements that were popping up around the country. This lapse on the part of the physician was thought by some to be a temporary aberration resulting from the wild excesses of Mike, Jr., while others thought it more serious, ascribing it to his age and growing responsibilities as a man of affairs. However, he still patronized the gambling rooms regularly, would win a thousand or lose a thousand in an all-night poker session, and never mention it later.

Michael had gone off on expeditions with whole armies, regiments, troops of cavalry, both Confederate and Federal, and had organized and conducted a wagon train across the plains in the dead of winter, but never had he experienced anything approaching the excitement and sheer chaos of getting a wife, a mother-in-law, and four small children organized for the vacation that was to keep him out of Trinidad for three months, the longest period he had spent out of southern Colorado. Nearing his 55th birthday, he felt the need for a good rest, though he was somewhat dubious of what lay ahead by the time the bags and trunks had piled up into what looked like a small mountain. Somehow it worked out, and they managed to get off, traveling first to Galveston where they had reserved three staterooms on the top deck of the Mallory steamship, "Lampasas." They had a day to look around Galveston before they sailed, and while the family enjoyed the sightseeing, the physician wasn't impressed with the port city. In a letter to the *Advertiser*, titled "Notes of Our Journey," he wrote in part:

> During the day we were in Galveston, we took our meals
> at the Tremont House which advertises its rates at $2 per day
> or fifty cents per meal, but charged us five dollars and
> seventy-five cents a meal for a party consisting of three adults
> and four children. Trapping weasles is an old game, but
> weasles are still caught by the same traps as of old. . . .
> Galvestonians claim their city is very healthy and I presume
> it has had no yellow fever for years past, yet the number of
> bean-pole formed children and delicate looking women and
> men will incline the stranger to suspect there is something
> seriously wrong with the climate or the habits of the people.
> The suspicion is that their knowledge of climatology is
> confined to the marshy regions of southern Texas.

In most of the letters he sent to the *Advertiser* as the "Lampasas" made its way to Key West and then on up the East Coast, it was the physician-vacationer speaking, but by the time he got to New York, he was suffering from the hunger that all newspapermen experience when on a holiday: he wanted to see his hometown papers. After enduring "Bartholdi's statue island by electric light, Castle Garden, Grant's Tomb, Cardinal McCloskey's church. . . ," he went to the offices of Thomas T. Woodruff, who had large real estate holdings around Trinidad, and asked to see his Trinidad newspapers. Subsequently he wrote the *Advertiser*: "He informed me he had a high opinion of the Trinidad press, but doesn't take any of the papers because he 'really hasn't time to read them.' How is that for a stand-off for the people who don't take them because they 'haven't hardly anything in them'?"

And after they had done all the usual things in Boston, he commented for the *Advertiser* about the beauty of Boston women, saying that he was most "impressed with the happy result of having burned all the ugly ones for witches years ago, thus improving the beauty of average New England stock for generations to come."

From Boston they worked their way north, spending some time in Montreal, where he carried off an awkward situation with considerable aplomb. Attired in dark suit, flowing black cape, and high silk hat, he was walking with the family when a woman, spotting his ornate signet ring and mistaking it for a bishop's, kneeled, grabbed his hand, and kissed it. While his family stared in astonishment, he gravely blessed her in Latin and sent her on her way happy. His only comment was a whispered aside to Annie, "I wonder where she thinks this particular bishop is going with all these women and children?"

They did Niagara Falls, posed for the customary family picture with the falls in the background, and then went to Chicago. Here they separated, Annie and her mother taking the children to Kentucky for a quick visit before school opened, while he made a short run south of Chicago to White County, Indiana, to visit his stepmother and half brothers and sisters. During his visit old Daniel Beshoar's body was moved from Monticello to Burnettsville, and the physician signed a contract for a suitable monument to be placed over the new gravesite. Then he hurried back to rejoin his family in Trinidad, refreshed in mind and body and eager to get back to work.

Through the fall, winter, and spring, he kept a close eye on the hospital construction. The original plan called for a one-story stone structure, but the sisters decided, and wisely, that a larger, two-story building of fifty-six rooms would be more in line with the community's needs. In January 1889 work was held up briefly by severe weather and a shortage of skilled workmen, but by April the new building was under roof. The temporary hospital and the prospect of a modern, efficient one in the near future elated Michael, who had not had hospital facilities of any kind available to him in the more than two decades since he had left Fort Kearny.

In May, while plasterers were at work on the new building's interior, Michael had the war on his mind for the first time in some years. The old ball in his leg was giving him some pain whenever he walked any distance, and also the E. R. S. Canby and Abernathy posts of the Grand Army of the Republic had by unanimous vote called on old Confederate Michael Beshoar to deliver the annual Memorial Day Address. He found humor in the situation, telling Annie that some of his comrades in the Seventh Arkansas might be puzzled at his accepting the invitation, but after all, he had served in a Union Army uniform in St. Louis and at Fort Kearny. On Memorial Day when they went to the Masonic cemetery, hundreds of tiny American flags fluttered over graves. He called Annie's attention to them and to the undeniable fact that many of the assembled G. A. R. members were beginning to look quite old. When it came time for him to speak, he gave a straight Union speech:

The men of the Grand Army of the Republic gave their services and their all for a great moral principle to benefit and ennoble mankind for all time to come. In this respect they waged a holy warfare, in this they performed a duty to God. One side was prompted by sentiments and principles of justice and liberty, the other by property interest and the supposed rights of states. The one was moved by heavenly inspiration, the other by worldly motives. . . .

The war is over. The cause no longer exists. The fact is established that the states have no right to secede; that we owe allegiance primarily to the general government and that the Union can't be destroyed or even divided on any pretext whatever. These facts were established by the war. There are now none to gainsay them. There are not now any Americans who would for a moment entertain the thought of raising their hands against the flag of our country or the integrity of the nation. More than this there are not any who would consent to return to the institution which caused that dreadful war. There are not any who will deny that the war in which the Union soldiers served was a holy war which preserved the union of the states, abolished human slavery and accomplished more for private morals than any other war in history.

That night, while Annie was sewing, he sat with her and talked about the crowd and his address. In a reminiscent mood, he spoke for some time about the G.A.R. and about what some of its members had done in the war. Since Annie seldom did any sewing, he asked her what she was making. She replied primly: "A silk flag for papa's grave." When she held up the stars and bars, he roared with laughter: "Annie, I'm afraid you will always be a Reb."

In July, Annie gave birth to her third son. The attending accoucheur had his name book ready once more and selected Bertram Bruno for the new arrival. Fourteen days later Annie was able to accompany her husband to the formal opening of the new hospital. A contemporary account of the first weeks of operation noted, "At present one ward is devoted to the sick and wounded [sic] of The Denver, Texas and Fort Worth Railroad under Dr. Olmstead and one ward of the county sick under Dr. Palmer. Dr. Beshoar is the physician in charge of the staff . . . the rates charged to private paying patients are very moderate, being only one dollar per day in neat wards. Elegant private rooms are furnished at fifteen dollars per week, including board, attendance, etc."

When the Democrats held their convention in the fall, the old guard—sometimes referred to as the Machine to the amusement of old guarders Michael Beshoar and Jesus Maria Garcia—found it was facing challengers again. It was accustomed to them and expected them, but it never underestimated them. Michael considered that he and Garcia were the Democratic party. If any of the faithful deviated, they could expect private admonishments from Garcia and Beshoar, and public ones in the editorial columns of the *Advertiser*. Its proprietor listed the newspaper as "Democratic-independent," but the "independent" bit was designed to give him leeway when he found a Democrat intolerable. Mostly the *Advertiser* was as consistently Democratic as its rivals were Republican.

The challenge this time was short and intense. With the advent of big coal companies in the area and their importation of Europeans to work as miners, politics was becoming a little more difficult all the time, but the old warriors thought they knew how to handle it. In the current squabble, which came to a climax on the convention floor in Lynch Hall, Michael, rather than the gentler and more persuasive Garcia, played the leading role. The fight was over the nomination for a commissioner, and John A. Gordon, a Trinidad attorney who was to become clerk of the State Court of Appeals, was serving as chairman. Gordon made a brief talk at the opening of the session in which he informed the packed hall, "The Democratic party is in the ascendancy." A ponderous man who liked to roll his words in the oratorical style of the day, he was usually regular, but it soon became apparent he was on the insurgents' side in this convention. Time after time he ignored the old guard when they sought the floor, recognizing the opposition instead. At a critical moment up rose M. Beshoar, all five feet six of him, to address the chair:

"Mr. Chairmannnnnnn!"

Gordon ignored him and started to recognize another delegate.

The physician's voice rose: "Mr. Chairmannnnnnn!" All eyes were on him except those of John Gordon, who again motioned to delegate Ransom to proceed, and again delegate Beshoar's voice boomed out:

"Mr. Chairmannnnnnn—you son of a bitch!"

His face flushed, Gordon pounded with his gavel and said in his slow-speaking way: "Dr. Beshoar, you cannot address the chair in any such fashion."

The physician's voice boomed out again:

"Mr. Chairmannnnnnn. . . . When this convention convened you made the statement that the Democratic party is in the ascendancy and you were right, Mr. Chairman. It is ass-ended, what with a son of a bitch for chairman, a horse thief for vice chairman and the rapist of a fifteen-year-old girl for secretary."

It was a study in red: Gordon's red face, the red faces of the convention officers sitting on the platform with him, the red face of delegate Beshoar standing in the middle of the floor, and the red vest showing beneath his unbuttoned coat. One or two timid delegates slipped out the back door. Said chairman Gordon; "There will be a thirty-minute recess."

During the half-hour period the old guard forgathered in nearby Ben Springer's to fortify themselves. Delegate Beshoar kept winking at delegate Garcia, who winked back. They were still in charge, and so it proved when the convention reconvened.

Shortly after Thanksgiving he told Annie that he would like to do something about Mike, Jr., that his eldest son ought to have learned his lesson by now, and that perhaps he should take steps to get him released on parole or perhaps even a pardon. Mike had been much on the physician's mind ever since the trip on the "Lampasas." He had watched his younger children romp happily on the deck and in the parks of the cities they visited, and it had hit him hard: between the war and his years in the Christian Brothers' Academy, Mike had had a poor sort of boyhood. He had been no better off than an orphan. Annie agreed Mike ought to have another chance and encouraged her husband to do whatever was necessary.

The campaign to free Mike was carefully mapped, but it turned out to be long, difficult, and expensive. He used lawyers, Democratic party and Masonic affiliations, Confederate and Union veterans, friends and acquaintances, and a judicious placement of money. In the spring of 1890, when the Purgatoire was singing its annual requiem to winter and now and then flexing its muscles as a score of canyons sent their muddy contributions to the river's annual floods, a pale, wan Mike, Jr., stepped off the train in Trinidad. He had a pardon, requiring him to make regular reports to Texas by mail, as would his father.

The next problem was rehabilitation, if that was possible. In their first long talk, Mike was quiet and rather reserved, saying the words he had said so often before: he was sorry, he realized he had behaved badly, he wanted above all "to be a dutiful son." The physician told Mike that at age thirty-five the question was less one of his being a dutiful son than a man who could stand on his own feet and make a decent life for himself. They agreed Mike would go to one of the ranches for a month or so to give him time to shake the prison smell and reorient himself, after which he would come back into Trinidad and become manager of the Standard Brick Company.

After his son took over the brickyard, everything seemed to be going so well that Michael was elated, but by fall there were incidents that filled him with foreboding. He kept getting tips that Mike was gambling and that he was drinking heavily and throwing money around on west end women. After the inevitable blowup and Mike's departure from Trinidad some weeks later, Michael wrote a most difficult letter to Major H. M. Holmes, the executive assistant to Governor Ross in Austin:

> I promised Governor Ross I would let him know at the end of the year how my son, Michael Beshoar Jr., alias Robert E. Murray has behaved since his pardon. Soon after he came

home I wanted to encourage him by showing confidence in him. I placed him in charge of a brickyard. For three months he did remarkably well, but I discovered at the end of the fourth month that he had okayed bills for more than the true amount and had the recipient refund the surplus to him. I immediately discharged him and refused to help him find another position. He was not long, however, in securing the appointment of deputy county clerk and recorder and was much liked by his superior and the board of county commissioners. About a month ago he began to drink again and nightly association with tin-horn gamblers and loose women soon followed. About a week ago he found his income short of the demands of his associates so he filched out of the county office more than three hundred dollars in county warrants which had been made payable to the bearer. His crime was suspected and the next I knew of him he had skipped, going northward on the Denver & Rio Grande train. I think I will pay his defalcations in the hope he will not be brought back here and will not come here again.

I now know that Governor Ross was eminently correct in his suspicion that reform was next to hopeless, but I, as his father, could not help hoping—even against reasonable hope—that three years punishment would awaken in his mind the enormity of crime and three years total abstinence would demonstrate to him the possibility as well as the desirability of a drunkard remaining sober all the days of his life.

I shall be ever grateful to you for your courteous treatment and to Governor Ross for his magnanimity in behalf of my erring son and regret that his clemency has been abused. I need not tell you that I most acutely regret the fact that the bright, intelligent boy who for many years was the greatest hope of my life, has proven over and over that his destiny is sin and shame. If I even suspected that my five little children had a destiny similar to that of my first-born their deaths in childhood and innocence would be my greatest pleasure.

In January he leased the brickyard and promised himself to be rid of it as quickly as he could find a buyer. As was his habit after an emotional crisis, he looked for a campaign, a battle of some kind to forget his troubles. This time it was a fight over water rates, which he and a great many other Trinidad citizens thought much too high. They gathered in Lynch Hall to get their sights lined up on Delos Chappell and launch a campaign for a municipal water system. It was just the sort of fighting campaign the editor of the *Advertiser* liked best, and, besides, he thought the people ought to own their own water system and not pay tribute to a private corporation. When Chappell reproached him angrily, saying he thought he was entitled to better treatment from a man with whom he was associated in a coal-mining venture, Michael made a gesture of friendliness, by having the *Advertiser* design and print a thousand fancy business cards and send them to Chappell as a gift.

The *Advertiser* staff was accustomed to such orders as the physician had a penchant for different kinds of calling cards, carrying as many as a half-dozen different ones at a time. Some of them were simple; for example, he had three different *Advertiser* cards—one listed him as "owner," another as "proprietor," and the third as "managing editor." Another card carried his name, the letters "M.D.," and a red seal bearing the words "University of Michigan, 1853." Still another carried the emblem of the Knights of Pythias, his name, and the designation "Past Grand Commander." There were a number of others, but the one that really got the printers into a tizzy, and caused even manager Goodale to grumble, was his masterpiece, which he insisted be printed in pyramid form:

M. BESHOAR, M. D.

UNIVERSITY OF MICHIGAN, 1853

PHYSICIAN AND SURGEON   TRINIDAD, COLORADO

Ex-City Physician.
Ex-County Physician.
Formerly Surgeon C. S. A.
Formerly A. A. Surgeon, U. S. A.
Formerly Surgeon Arkansas State Militia.
Member of the Colorado State Board of Health.
Member of the Pan-American Medical Congress.
Member of the American Public Health Association.
Member of the Association of A. A. Surgeons, U. S. A.
Permanent Member of the American Medical Association.
Member of the American Association of Examining Surgeons.
Member and ex-Vice-President of the Colorado State Medical Society.
Member and ex-President of the Las Animas County Medical Society.
Present Examiner of the Leading Life Insurance Companies—Too numerous to name.
Member of the Association of Medical Officers of the Army and Navy of the Confederacy.
Delegate from American Public Health Association to the American Congress of Tuberculosis.

Handing out some of the cards for the first time at a medical meeting in Amarillo, Texas, he enjoyed watching the faces of recipients as they studied the pyramid and then gave him startled looks. The new possessor of the card invariably pocketed it carefully while Michael chuckled to himself and speculated about what that person would say when he next displayed it: "joker," "crackpot," or what? A blizzard detained him in the Texas city after the meeting. "I am not certain whether I can reach home Tuesday," he wrote Annie. "A fearful blizzard causes me to lose two days here and as you know I have stops to make before I get home. I might have hired a rig and driven to Panhandle City, but the wind has been blowing so strong and the snow flying so thick I am afraid I might get lost on the prairie. I'd rather lose another day than be lost on the prairie in a storm."

Soon after he got home, he had an office visitor who said he had been reluctant to speak before, fearing the doctor might not want to hear anything against Chappell since they were associates, but after reading what the *Advertiser* had said about Chappell in connection with the waterworks, he was now ready to speak. The physician urged him to do so and was told there was gossip in local coal circles indicating that M. Beshoar might not really own the Gray Creek property. Pressed for more, the man said he had heard there was a secret agreement between Chappell and the Colorado Coal & Iron Company allowing this company to do the development work at Gray Creek, and not the Gray Creek Company.

Early the next morning Michael went to Chappell's office and said he wanted a look at the books of the Gray Creek Company. Chappell said they were being posted but that he would send them to the doctor's office in the opera house "within a day or two."

That night the physician saw patients in his office until ten o'clock. When the last one had gone, he locked the door and got out his own Gray Creek files, including his agreement with Chappell. He studied them until almost midnight and then started home. As he passed in front of Chappell's new house at 321 East Main, he wondered whether Chappell would keep a copy of a secret agreement in his office or at home. He stopped and stared at the big stone mansion. There were no lights. The street, too, was dark and deserted. On a sudden impulse he went up the front steps and around the west side of the house to the rear. Chappell's study was dark. Eying the porch outside the study speculatively, he decided it would be difficult to climb. He went back to the front of the house and tried a window. It opened easily. He stood listening for a minute or so, but the only sounds he heard were the barking of a dog off in the distance and the creaking sound of a wagon somewhere on Main Street up toward the center of town. He climbed quickly over the sill.

He was in Chappell's study with the gaslights lit and was going through Chappell's desk when the door opened suddenly and capitalist Chappell, in nightclothes and holding a kerosene lamp, stood staring at him. Michael felt like a fool. In as calm a voice as he could muster, he said he had been informed there was a secret agreement with the Colorado Coal & Iron Company. Chappell readily admitted he had such an agreement, adding that he didn't see that it was any concern of Michael Beshoar's. When the physician accused him of not using the proceeds from the sale of the 1,000 shares he had been given for development work at Gray Creek, Chappell said that was true but that the wording of their agreement only provided that $60,000 be spent on the work and didn't specify the source from which the money should come. He said $60,000 had been spent and that it was his business where he got the money. With that Michael walked out into the night. He was mad, mad at Chappell but madder at himself. He could have hired any one of a hundred men to go to the Chappell home and get his papers, his desk or the capitalist himself, nightshirt and all. Still, he had verified the report that Chappell had some sort of secret deal with the CC & I Co. It was time for a showdown on Gray Creek.

The battle over Gray Creek was fought in the courts of three judicial districts over a period of years. There were suits and countersuits, secret sales of stock, charges of fraud, and countercharges of more fraud. Michael had a dozen attorneys working for him in Trinidad, Pueblo, and Denver, and Chappell had as many or more. There were as many as five separate cases in the courts at one time.

In an effort to protect himself, Michael incorporated the Rocky Mountain Medical Institute Association with his wife and mother-in-law the principal officers, and then assigned to the association ownership, with all rights and income, of his practice, the Standard Brick Company, the Beshoar Realty Company, the *Advertiser*, *El Anunciador*, stock in two ditch companies, the Yellow Rose of Texas and Green Chloride mines in the Magdalena mountains of New Mexico, lands in Colorado, Iowa, and Illinois, city lots in Trinidad, his home, and everything else in the way of real property. As an additional safeguard he converted some other assets into gold, $50,000 worth, and then worried about what to do with it. Afraid to trust it to a bank and afraid to keep it in his office or home, he finally solved the problem by moving a tenant out of a two-room adobe house at First and Convent streets that he had once used as an office. He put the gold in some old glass battery jars and buried them under the flooring of the tiny building. He did the job himself; carrying a shotgun under his lap robe, he transported the gold to the adobe in his buggy, and kept the gun handy while he was hiding the gold away. But no one disturbed him.

Later, on the chance that something might happen to him, he confided the whereabouts of the cache to Annie, Mrs. Maupin, and his secretary but told no one else. The first intimation he had that his secret was out came within a few days after Judge David C. Beaman, chief counsel for the Colorado Coal & Iron Company and one of the many litigants in the Gray Creek cases, had obtained a judgment against him for $16,000. Judge Beaman's problem was how to collect since Michael no longer owned anything except the clothes on his back. Everything else was in the new institute. The physician was sitting at his desk in his business and editorial office above the *Advertiser* when the postman came in and dumped the morning mail on his desk. He got up to take it to his secretary, who was sitting at his own desk across the room busily writing. But as he picked up the pile, an envelope on top caught his attention. It was addressed to "Hon. M. Beshoar, Trinidad, Colorado" in the neat handwriting of Judge Beaman. Slitting the envelope open with his shears, he saw with surprise that it contained a letter on *Advertiser* stationery. As he read it, an angry flush spread over his face. Signed by the secretary sitting a few feet away, it offered to disclose "where Dr. Beshoar has hidden his cash assets for $1,000." Across the bottom Judge Beaman had written: "Dear Doctor: You have a traitor on your payroll," and signed his name.

Michael stood for a minute or two and studied the back of the man who had been his trusted employe, secretary, and confidant for four years. Then he picked up a heavy seal and walked slowly across the room. With the seal in his right hand, he passed the letter in front of the man's eyes with his left. The man's back stiffened, but before he could say anything or turn, Michael brought the heavy seal crashing down on his head. He slumped and slid out of the chair, blood gushing from a deep cut. The physician stood over him for a minute or so, then threw the seal on the floor, walked across the office, and raised a window opening onto Commercial Street a floor below. He caught the unconscious man up under his armpits and dragged him to the window. Business manager Frank Goodale had heard the heavy thud when the seal hit the floor. Rushing upstairs, he burst into the office just as the doctor was stuffing his secretary out the window.

"For God's sake, stop!" Goodale cried. "You'll kill him."

"Stay back, Frank," the physician yelled. "That's just what I intend to do to this son of a bitch."

With that he gave a final shove, and his secretary slipped from sight over the window ledge. Goodale ran downstairs and out on to the sidewalk, where he found three very puzzled cattlemen whose conversation had just been interrupted by a body falling on top of them. The secretary, inexplicably alive, was rushed to the office of Dr. Palmer, and was sufficiently recovered by late afternoon to announce that he would leave Trinidad just as soon as Dr. Palmer gave him permission to travel. That night, after supper at home, Michael had his carriage hitched, loaded it with various mysterious articles, and asked young sons Ben and John if they would like to take a ride with him. They were delighted.

He drove them west along Main to Commercial Streets, down Commercial to the bridge, then back up Commercial to Main again and thence to the house at First and Convent. He had the boys help him carry a tool box and pick and shovel into the adobe, and told John he wanted him to stand outside the door while he and Ben did some work inside. John's face fell, but all was well again when his father told him he was a guard and was to warn them with three knocks on the door if anyone approached. By the light of a lantern, the physician and Ben took up the flooring, dug up the battery jars, and put them in the buggy. Michael threw a robe over them, clucked to the horse, drove slowly down Convent to Main, and turned right to Ben Springer's. He sent his son Ben inside to ask Springer to come out. When the saloonkeeper came to the buggy, Michael told him he had "a little money for your *caja fuerte*." Springer pulled out a little notebook and asked how much. When told the sum, he made a brief notation that completed the formalities, as no one ever asked for a receipt or expected one when they had Ben Springer put their valuables in his big safe. "Okay,

Doc," Springer said matter-of-factly, putting his notebook away.
"I'll help you carry it inside."

As a result of his failure with Mike, Michael kept a protective eye
on his young family. He spent more time with them than he had
ever been able to spend with Mike and he kept himself advised
of what they were doing and whom they were seeing. When his two
daughters began to bloom and he saw young men turning to look
at them, he told Annie it was time to send them off to another en-
vironment for awhile. Soon he had them packed off to the Frederick
Female Seminary in Maryland. Ben and John were getting along
fine in Trinidad schools; Ben, the studious one, had already announced his intention of studying medicine. John had thought
about his career too and decided he would be either a baseball
player or a prizefighter. The husky lad hadn't decided which he
liked best, but judging from the number of black eyes around the
neighborhood, his father believed the prize ring would get the nod.
However, he assured Annie he would see to it that John went into
some other profession when the time came. Meanwhile he let the
boys choose their own companions, white, brown, black, or red.
He knew all the fathers, knew what was going on, and had a good
idea of what to expect in all instances. He intended, through close
surveillance, to do a better job than he had with Mike. Not only
would his younger children have his attention and help in every
way; best of all, they had a good mother in Annie.

During this period he continued to travel a good deal. He made
trips in connection with mining properties and land speculations,
Masonic work, and the Independent Champions of the Red Cross,
of which he was supreme commander. He continued to serve as
superintendent of schools but would not consider any other offices
because he had too many interests and too many demands on his
time. He even restricted his civic work, although he did join with
other citizens in an abortive effort to build a railroad to Creede
when a boom hit that camp after a silver strike in 1892. Silver was
causing a lot of excitement throughout Colorado and a strong swing
to the National Peoples party, which had been organized a year
earlier in Cincinnati. Democrats were deserting their party in large
numbers for the Populists. For his part, Michael refused to take any
part in the new movement; a Democrat through and through, he

turned down urgent requests to attend the State Silver League's convention in Denver in July. Tom Patterson, now owner of the *Rocky Mountain News*, was going, as were a number of other prominent Democratic leaders. As it turned out, Patterson walked out of the meeting, but the Democratic party was badly disrupted.

The Republicans were having their troubles too but managed to avert a split at their state convention in Pueblo, September 8. When the Democrats met four days later, everyone knew the party was in serious trouble. A great many party stalwarts were missing. Patterson and Charles S. Thomas insisted the convention support J. B. Weaver of Iowa, the Populist candidate for president. The Cleveland Democrats refused and bolted the convention to back Grover Cleveland and designate a state ticket headed by Joseph Maupin of Fremont County. While the Cleveland people were picking their ticket, the Patterson and Thomas factions split over the manner of the Weaver indorsement. When the smoke cleared away, the Democratic party was in shambles. Michael went back to Trinidad in a huff. In the political storm that followed, he was the only Democratic editor in the state to stand by Cleveland. Patterson's *Rocky Mountain News* supported Weaver, who carried the state by 14,694 votes.

Soon after Cleveland took office, Michael was offered the post of minister to Argentina. He and Annie talked about it for days. He wanted to accept and he could afford it, but there were a lot of other things to consider: young children, aging mother-in-law, continuing coal litigation, newspapers, brickyard, large real estate holdings that needed constant attention. He regretfully declined.

The hard fight over Grover Cleveland marked a turning point in the physician's political philosophy. He had always been a Democrat—but a southern Democrat, an establishment and property rights man—but more and more he found himself in alignment with those elements in the Democratic party that were moving, slowly and agonizingly, to the left. A stand must be made against the arrogance and power of the coal barons who operated the Colorado Republican property with all the assurance and control they exercised in the management of their properties, but he didn't believe for a minute that the old-line Democratic leaders were capable of providing effective leadership any longer. Too many of them differed from their Republican counterparts only in their political label. However, he thought there was a possibility the labor movement might provide the needed counterforce.

His first opportunity to demonstrate his changing philosophy publicly came in the spring of 1893. On April 20 a national convention of the United Mine Workers, meeting in Columbus, Ohio, issued a call for a general strike. The managing editor of the *Advertiser*, who had been watching events closely, wrote several editorials saying a strike was needed to force the coal operators into better labor practices. Before the national board canceled the strike call on June 1, miners in Fremont County, north of Trinidad, walked out. Headed by a band and American flags, they marched south, five hundred strong. Although spring rains had made the roads almost impassable, they moved through the coal districts of Huerfano and Las Animas counties holding rallies. At each mine they picked up recruits, despite threats and intimidation by heavily armed coal company police. They finally went into camp at Sopris, just west of Trinidad, to await aid from the national union.

For all their enthusiasm, the miners were in bad shape; they had no money, few had tents or bedding, and there was little to eat. Michael tied his cow to the back of his buggy, drove slowly out to the miners' dreary encampment, and gave her to them for their empty cooking pots. They cheered him and demanded a speech. As it just happened he had made some rough notes on the way out with the cow, he stood in the buggy and gave a short talk:

"I have lived sixty years in this world and it seems to me that it is not the same world that I lived in in the past. When I was young, there were no difficulties between labor and capital; there were very few rich men and no very poor men. When a man and his employer could not get along, they separated and the man went to the next place to work.

"Conditions are now changed. Capital is organized to protect itself against the rest of the world and especially against its employes. The employes must organize. The laws of our day are made for corporations: they do not recognize the rights of the working man. They must be changed to suit the changing times. What surprises me most, however, is to see two thousand men asking for their just rights in a peaceable manner. You have been met with hired deputies and rifles. I am afraid that if I were a miner I could not behave myself as well as you have done. If the coal deputies shoot down a few of you, you will still triumph, for that is the way all great causes are won. Persecution and tyranny have ever been overcome by peaceful methods."

He paused and looked into the upturned faces—dark Mexican faces, Italian and Slav faces, Greek faces: "I read in the *Chieftain* this morning that the miners have been intimidated at Rouse and will not lay down their picks." A dozen voices shouted in reply: "No, no, they are here with us." The old doctor beamed. "Good, good. The newspapers and everything are against you, but you will overcome all opposition. Labor is bound to win."

In his capacity as editor of the *Advertiser*, he took on not only the coal barons but anyone else he thought was out of line. At times he combined the functions of editor and senior medical man of the town, as in an editorial scrawled hastily in pencil a few days after his visit with the miners:

> The *Advertiser* calls on the city authorities to appoint a competent food inspector. Some of our leading butchers have during the past two months sold more meat that was not fit for for food than meat that was wholesome. Next month native mutton will begin to form a large part of the meat sold during the summer and as in the past tape worm animals will be offered at 10 to 15 cents a pound. Besides paying an exorbitant price for the meat, the consumers will be subjected to a protracted ailment and the expense and time required to get rid of the parasites, sold them knowingly and criminally by the meat dealers.

And there were times during this period when his dual roles of doctor and newspaper editor became entangled with his duties and responsibilities as a father. When his young children became involved in a neighborhood rock-throwing incident and the editor of one of the evening newspapers gleefully printed a story about it with some gratuitous advice to Dr. Beshoar about rearing children, editor Beshoar responded with a resentful note in the *Advertiser*: "A man who cannot have children as a result of the sins of his youth should not presume to tell better men how to handle their children."

And when ten-year-old Ben was seriously injured while running an errand, Michael the physician and Michael the father found themselves in conflict. The lad, becoming impatient when a freight train blocked Commercial Street, had crawled up between two cars to cross. As the switch engine jerked the train, his foot was smashed in a coupling and Ben fell screaming to the street.

At the hospital the physician and several of his colleagues hastily summoned for consultation examined the boy's crushed and mangled foot. The consulting doctors were unanimous: the foot had to come off. Michael put his boy under sedation and brooded overnight, and then announced his decision to a tearful Annie: "They are right, of course. If it were anyone else, I would amputate immediately—but not Squire Ben."

During the months that followed, he carefully rebuilt Ben's foot in a series of operations. When he was done, his son walked and ran again with other boys, suffering not so much as a limp.

As he worked to save Ben's foot, his thoughts were often on Mike, Jr. He hadn't had any direct word from his eldest since he had skipped out of Trinidad, leaving his father to make good on the county warrants. The physician knew Senator Barela had given Mike a short-term job as clerk of a senate committee during the 1892 legislative session, and he knew that Mike had since been in a number of northern Colorado mining camps, a fact attested to by the steady stream of letters reaching his office from merchants, owners of cafés and saloons, grocers and keepers of boardinghouses—all complaining they had extended credit to Mike and had not been paid. He did not answer them, nor did he respond to a letter from Mike written June 5, 1893, from Gold Hill, a mining camp in the mountains west of Denver: "Dear Father: Can I go to your Chicosa Ranch as hired man? Will never go to town. I am crippled, left arm broken and rupture worse than ever before. I am growing old fast. I must settle down. Answer at once. Your son, Mike."

On June 10, five days later, there was a telegram from Mike, sent from Littleton, a small town just south of Denver: "I am broke and crippled. Can I come home? Mike." It sounded much like dozens of other pleas he had had over the years and his first inclination was to ignore it as he had the letter, but after a night of mental torment, Michael went to the telegraph office and wired Mike the amount of a ticket from Littleton to Trinidad plus two dollars. His telegram simply said. "Come home. But it will be absolutely your last chance."

When Mike failed to put in an appearance within the next two days, his father was angry and bitter. "It is the same old story," he told Annie. "I should have ignored him. All I did was provide him money for another drunken spree."

But on June 16 there was another wire from Littleton, this one from Arapahoe County coroner John Chivington, saying that the badly decomposed body of a man tentatively identified as Michael Beshoar, Jr., had been found in a clump of willows on the east bank of the South Platte River, one fourth mile north of Littleton. The coroner said the man had been dead since June 11, the day Michael had telegraphed the money.

Chivington's wire was handed to Michael at his home at 8 A.M., just as he was leaving for his office. It was the first time Annie had ever seen her husband weep. She comforted him as best she could and helped him pack, and an hour and a half later he was on a train headed north. He was met at the Littleton station at 6 P.M. by Colonel Chivington, who drove him directly to the Walley and Rollins Undertaking Rooms where he went through the nightmarish experience of identifying his boy. Chivington said burial could be made immediately if that was all right with the doctor. The father agreed, and he, Colonel Chivington, and the undertakers took Mike's remains to Denver's Fairmount Cemetery that night.

Before they left the undertaking establishment, however, he went to the telegraph office and found that his wire and money had not been picked up; they still awaited Mike Beshoar, Jr.

The next morning the *Daily News* said Mike's "ability was of a high order and as a young man he gave bright promise. But the habit of drinking fastened on him too firmly." None of the Denver newspapers ran more than a few paragraphs on Mike's death as their columns were crowded that weekend with another story: Lizzie Borden had just been acquitted of the axe slaying of her father and stepmother.

Before leaving Trinidad the physician had told the *Advertiser* staff to treat the story as they would any other. Upon his return home he found they had followed his instructions with one exception—one staffer had added a sidebar to the straight news report:

> Mike, as he was familiarly known, has not left an enemy in the world. The writer, like many others in Trinidad, knew him well, and knew him only to love him for his great big heart and his generous impulsive nature. Improvidence was his only fault and like countless others gifted with a rare intellect he fell its prey. He carried his heart on his sleeve and it bled in

sympathy with human suffering. He was a friend to all and in the final balance his good deeds will surely outweigh the errors 'tis human to make. . . . Dear Mike, if there is a better world than this it may be yours to see. May a just judge pardon you if you have erred, and would that my tears bedew the cold sod of your untimely grave.

Dr. Michael Beshoar in 1882, at age forty-nine a busy man of affairs.

The Las Animas County Courthouse with stone jail in rear.

Looking south on Commercial Street, Trinidad, in the early 1900s.

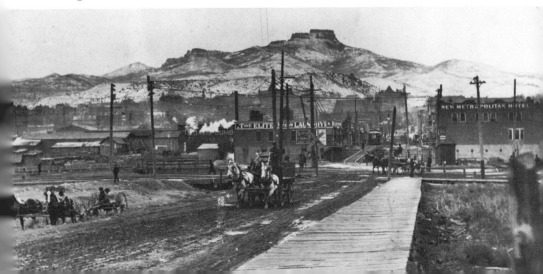

The Beshoar family in 1896: Seated, Michael and Annie with Bertram; standing, John, Bonaventura, Benedicta, and Ben.

After the tragic death of his first son, Mike, Dr. Beshoar distributed this card to his friends; it shows Mike at ages 3, 13, and 33.

Michael Beshoar in the costume he wore among the Indians in Mexico, where he had a promising gold property.

One of several large liveries that served Trinidad in the nineties.

Horse-drawn street cars on the bridge over the Purgatoire River. Driving horses across faster than a walk was forbidden by city ordinance.

Trinidad's Grand Union Hotel, built in 1880 at Main and Commercial streets, was later renamed the Columbian.

Trinidad in the 1800s, as seen from Simpson's Rest, looking south across the Purgatoire River toward Fishers Peak.

The founder, owner, and editor of the Morning Advertiser—*Michael Beshoar (in silk hat)—with some of his staff and friends.*

The intersection of Main and Commercial streets in Trinidad, 1915.

During the eighties and nineties, when Trinidad was booming, wealthy citizens built mansions along East Main Street.

One of the last family pictures: standing, Benedicta (Gulley), Annie, Bertram, John, and Ben; seated, Dr. Beshoar, Bonaventura (Fox), and grandchildren John Gulley, Benedicta Gulley, Michael Gulley, and Francis Fox.

The original San Rafael Hospital in 1889, on the hilltop where Dr. Beshoar had planned to build his home.

Typical of the day, Dr. Beshoar's office was packed with x-ray machines, pill bottles, books, and diplomas. Dr. Ben is at left.

Commercial Street looking south in 1909. At the extreme left is the Daily Advertiser, *with the Beshoar medical offices on second floor.*

Chapter 12
New Times, New Century

MICHAEL STARED OUT the Pullman's dirt-streaked window at the countryside as it flashed by, a magic-lantern show of green fields, green trees, weathered cabins on stilts, with mule-drawn wagons and black-faced drivers waiting patiently at each country road crossing. It all looked about as it had thirty-one years earlier when he had ridden and walked out of northeast Arkansas a prisoner of the Federals. In a few minutes he and Miss Bonnie would alight and take a stage for Pocahontas. Although he sat quietly, hands folded in his lap, he was filled with anticipation at the prospect of seeing once again the little county seat town where he had begun his adult life. Pocahontas, good old Poca, would be as quiet and serene as before the war, and there would be the familiar names: the Martins, Blacks, Waddells, Daltons, Symingtons, Hills, and many others, including Maggie James. She had been sixteen when the Federals came raiding; if they hadn't taken him off to Missouri, he would probably have married Maggie and spent his life in Randolph County. Jim Martin was dead, but there would be a few old buckskins around who would remember Michael Beshoar, physician, druggist, legislator, county judge, and cavalry captain, though he knew from correspondence through the years that most of the faces he would see would be strange ones.

The idea of a trip to Poca had come to him when it had become necessary for him to escort Bonnie to Parkville, Missouri to matriculate in Park College for the fall term. He had asked her whether she'd like to see his old stamping grounds, and when she showed the proper amount of enthusiasm, he had quickly made all the necessary arrangements.

In Poca they went first to the St. Charles Hotel, which he found pretty much the same as on the afternoon he and Jeff Thompson and other members of the general's staff were held prisoner within its walls. After looking it over and showing his old room to his daughter, he hired a rig and drove to the Hill home where they were to be houseguests. The next three days were busy and happy ones for the physician. He had long visits with Maggie James, the Martins, the Jarretts, the Hamils, and other old friends. The highlight was the second day when they all gathered in the public square and escorted him into the courthouse and sat him in the county judge's chair. It was a new courthouse, but the chair was the same one he had used during his term as judge. Lawyer Rufe Black, empty sleeve neatly pinned up, read an indictment, charging one Michael Beshoar with staying away from Poca too long, and a jury of oldtimers, including two who had been in his garrison company and had taken part in the attack on Leeper at Greenville, heard the "case" and then acquitted him because he had returned of his own free will. Dr. Green, who had served under him as a lieutenant of the garrison company, made a speech:

"This old fellow was a clever young man. When he came to Randolph County he had some fancy clothes, an education and a gift of gab, but not a lot of this world's goods. He made money, though, and I'm going to tell you how he did it. He was idling on the bank of the river one day when he conceived his great money-making scheme. In those days most of the hogs ran wild. He hired some laborers to build rafts and tie them in close to the bank. Then he sent the men off with sacks of corn on their shoulders. They sprinkled it along the hog paths and down to the river. As fast as the hogs showed up on the river bank he had the men tie them up and load them on the rafts. Ladies and gentlemen: he loaded all of our hogs on his rafts and pushed off down the river. This man stole practically every razor back in northeast Arkansas!"

"We'd better try him for that, too!" someone called out, but Michael pounded his gavel and said sternly: "Enough of that. As long as I am on the bench in Randolph County there will be order in this court. If I hear any more such fantastic charges I'll fine everyone of you for contempt. Besides, it was barrel staves, not hogs, that I shipped down the river."

The next morning he and Bonnie drove north on the old military road to visit the graves of his two wives on the Spike farm and arrange for their perpetual care. Afterward he drove Bonnie about the Fourche area, showing her his old farm and other sights.

On his return to Trinidad, after dropping Bonnie off in Parkville, Missouri, he found his current partner, Dr. Albert W. White, not only swamped with work but extremely unhappy about his income. They had a contract, negotiated by mail and signed by Dr. White before he ever left Auburn, New York, for Trinidad, which provided him with board and room, and horse and buggy, and fifty dollars a month in cash. It also contained an interesting clause specifying that whichever party broke the contract within one year would "emigrate hence."

Michael reminded White of the clause and told him, "Now, Doctor, you know what the word emigrate means. It means get out of town."

Dr. White said he was positive that the contract was invalid, that Michael Beshoar might be the senior medical man of southern Colorado, senior newspaper editor, and senior politician, but he couldn't run people out of town, and finally that he intended to open an office of his own on Main Street and practice medicine.

In the subsequent litigation, in which Michael claimed breach of contract, the district court held that, while Dr. Beshoar could not compel Dr. White to leave Trinidad nor prevent him from practicing his profession in the city, he was entitled to damages, and awarded him $5,000.

When White's attorney, James M. John, brought a certified check to the physician's office, Michael pushed it back across his desk, saying he would not accept "a piece of paper." Lawyer John went away and returned with $5,000 in bills. Again the physician refused to accept the payment, saying he wanted "money."

"If this isn't money, what in heaven's name is it?" the exasperated attorney demanded.

"It's paper, just paper," the physician replied. "Money is gold, and I want gold."

When John finally brought gold, Michael was delighted, as much with John's discomfiture as with the settlement. Actually he had hated to lose as competent a man as Dr. White; it put him to the necessity of finding another physician for his office. He couldn't keep up with the *Advertiser*, his practice, and other businesses without help. The heavy burden he was forced to carry after Dr. White left made him irritable. He was sitting at breakfast, worrying about a baby case at Trinchera, twenty-five miles to the east, and the heavy schedule ahead in his offices when Annie scolded him about his personal appearance. He bristled and wanted to know what was wrong with it.

"You need a haircut badly," she said.

The blowup that followed left the family staring in surprise. Michael was always serene, always polite to Annie and her mother, and polite to the children, whom he treated with the same courtesy he accorded adults. But this morning he was in a bad mood. He didn't see why he had to have a haircut unless he wanted one and he didn't see why he had to run to a barbershop on schedule like every other fool in town, "and besides I'll grow my hair down over my shoulders if I feel like it. It wouldn't be anyone's business but mine."

When everyone laughed, the physician glowered. Annie, alarmed, attempted to save the situation by saying of course he could do whatever he wanted with his hair and that if he wanted to wear it long she was sure it would look very nice. He bristled again, snapping: "That does it. From now on I will wear it long." When he saw the look on her face, he added: "I get a cold every time it's cut." With that he got up from the table and stalked out of the house.

His hair was coarse, straight, and black. As it grew down over his neck he tucked it into his collar, but by the time it reached his shoulders he wore it loose in the plains fashion except when he was on the street. Then he tucked it up into his high hat. He ignored hints from family and intimates that he might be mistaken for a patent medicine man or a quack, meeting all references to his hair with "only the weak are slaves of convention. A man can wear his hair long, clipped, shaved or however else he pleases."

The *Advertiser* was again engaged in a campaign that delighted Michael in every way. And the target was again Delos Chappell and his waterworks franchise. Both were denounced every morning in editorials, front-page stories, and peppery little paragraphs salted throughout the newspaper: "The meanest man in Trinidad has been found. He opened a water hydrant on the north side yesterday and the stuff that emitted therefrom forced the residents in the neighborhood to buy large quantities of iodoform to improve the odor in the vicinity."

After a barrage of several weeks, Chappell sent his good friend Dr. W. L. South to see his tormenter. A tall, immaculate figure with a drooping moustache and courtly manners, South was a retired physician who devoted his time to banking and stock-raising. The moment he walked in, Michael knew instinctively what he was after. With much blowing of his nose into a linen handkerchief, interspersed with apologies for taking up Dr. Beshoar's time, Dr. South said he'd like to buy the *Advertiser*. Michael knew, of course, that South had no use whatsoever for a newspaper and was actually representing Chappell. All smiles, the proprietor of the *Advertiser* said he would be glad to sell "the plant" for $15,000, cash in hand. Although he thought the price was high, in the end Dr. South met it and left the office as the owner of the newspaper's press and mechanical equipment. When he and Chappell realized they had been tricked into buying some machinery and not the *Daily Advertiser* and not the Advertiser Publishing Company, they were a sad pair. But there was nothing they could do about it; there had been no misrepresentation, and the transaction had been legal in every respect. After another nose-blowing session, Dr. South transferred the equipment back to the Advertiser Publishing Company, M. Beshoar president, for half what they had paid for it. Bigger sums were being won and lost on the turn of a card in the town's gambling establishments night after night.

With a neat profit of $7,500 and, more importantly, a coup counted against Chappell, Michael tucked his long hair into his silk hat and headed for the Second Pan American Medical Congress in Mexico City. Before he left, he had thriftily arranged to swap the Gulf Railroad advertising space for his train tickets and had gotten a letter of introduction to President Porfirio Díaz from the Mexican consul in Denver, who was kind enough to say in his letter, "Como médico y periodista El Doctor Beshoar no tiene rival en el estado de Colorado (As a medical man and journalist, Doctor Beshoar is without rival in the State of Colorado)." He took with him the Temerosa papers he had inherited years before from the dying prospector. He was going to a medical congress, but he had mining on his mind. He wanted to talk with Mexican mining people on their home ground and scout the Territory of Tepic.

He arrived in Mexico City November 14, checked into the Iturbide Hotel as Miguel Beshoar, and spent the next two days sightseeing and shopping. Mexico was as he had pictured it. Enchanted with the city and its people, he wrote Annie, "The climate is much like Trinidad's in early June and you can get a big saucerful of full-flavored strawberries for only 12½ cents American." He was not quite so enchanted after he bought a fine gold watch for $100 American and had it snatched from his vest pocket by a woman as he knelt piously for the consecration at a pontifical Mass in the Cathedral of Mexico. She passed it to the man on her right who passed it to the next man. Dr. Beshoar sorrowfully watched his new timepiece travel from hand to hand until it disappeared from sight.

In articles to the *Advertiser* he made no mention of the loss, contenting himself with describing the city and its people and some of their customs: "At entertainments full dress is usually required along with the admission ticket. A claw hammer coat, stove pipe hat, starched white shirt, low cut vest and high-heeled boots are prerequisites for social gatherings of a formal nature or even an evening call."

He attended sessions of the four-day medical congress faithfully, mingled with the medical men of twenty-five countries, but found himself most interested in the Mexican physicians and surgeons, whom he sized up as "urbane, but slothful in their profession." After the congress he stayed on in the city for several days and made calls on President Díaz and other government officials, not as *el doctor*, but as a mining and business entrepreneur interested in possible investments in Mexico. With his obvious prosperity, long flowing hair, and command of Spanish, the "médico y periodista sin rival" was respectfully received wherever he went.

From Ciudad de Mexico he went to the old colonial city of Guadalajara where he called on government officials, mining engineers, and bankers to seek information about the Territory of Tepic and the Santiago Mountains, where he was going to find the Temerosa and make a fortune bigger than that of any Colorado gold or silver king. It was all business in Guadalajara except for some shopping and trips four miles south to the village of Tlaquepaque to sit for an Indian sculptor, Panteleon Panduro, whose lifelike *bultos* were all the rage in Mexico. His next stop was Tepic for more talks with mining engineers and government officials, including Governor Pablo Rocha. He signed a contract with Julian Rocha, the governor's mining-engineer son, to act as his engineer and representative in the territory. A visit to the site of the Temerosa would have to await his next visit. He arrived home late in December with presents for everyone, including a jug of tequila for intimates who could not find any such exotic drink in the saloons of Trinidad. Full of enthusiasm for Mexico, he told Annie they might want to make their home there if his plans progressed well in 1897. The post-Mexican glow extended to all of Trinidad as evidenced by a signed New Year's Day editorial in the *Advertiser*:

With the first day of 1897 begins the sixteenth year of the *Advertiser's* existence—having remained during the entire time under the management of its founder and present managing editor.

In the first issue it was promised that all profits of the business should be invested to improve the plant and the paper as a disseminator of news among our own people and advertiser of the material resources of Trinidad and its environs. That promise has been redeemed literally; personal likes and dislikes of the editor, whether the affairs of life ran smoothly or otherwise, have never been ventilated through the columns of this newspaper. I have on many occasions advocated the just claims of my bitterest enemies and opposed that which I deemed wrong among my warmest personal friends. Upon all questions which have arisen in our community I have only asked myself the single question, 'Is it right?' and have left the consequences to take care of themselves.

The result of this course has been that I have succeeded in building up a newspaper in whose utterances the common people have confidence—one that has wronged none through malice while it has not hesitated to censure wrong without regard to the standing of the wrong-doers in the community. From the start it has been the leading newspaper of the city with more bonafide readers than all other newspapers circulating in the city and county—a position which it continues to maintain and may reasonably be expected to continue for an indefinite time.

With malice toward none and wishing all a happy new year I remain as ever,

M. Beshoar
Managing Editor of the *Advertiser*

His appraisal of the *Advertiser* as one of the leading newspapers of southern Colorado and foremost among the five daily newspapers printed in Trinidad was shared by many journalists who wrote about job openings. The managing editor handled all of the hiring, answering all mail queries about positions, often somewhat flippantly. When the publisher of the *Savona Weekly Review* in Savona, New York wrote for a job, editor Beshoar replied that he would consider him for the first opening, concluding his letter with: "I will suggest, however, that I have undertaken to do all the drinking of intoxicants, the eating of all the opium and cocaine (and their products), and the chewing and smoking of all tobacco that is consumed by attachés of the office and anyone encroaching upon my exclusive rights in this respect will be treated as a mortal offender against me personally. No excuses."

He received almost as many letters from doctors wanting to move to Colorado and Trinidad as from newspapermen and printers, and answered many of them in much the same tone. When a physician wrote that he intended to move to Colorado from Chicago and needed advice about setting up a practice, he got a quick answer:

Dear Doctor:

I received your letter several days ago. I do not see how I can answer it definitely. 'A graduate of Rush . . .' that's all right— 'high morals and studious habits . . .' that's all right. Now if in addition to these commendable qualities you are entirely innocent of physical languor (commonly called laziness)—if you have a cheerful disposition, bodily vigor and fair social magnetism you are sure to succeed anywhere, unless you should, as unfortunately many bright young men do, entomb yourself from the wide world by becoming the camp doctor of some mine or the station doctor of some railroad.

If you should decide to come to Trinidad I will insure your life against starvation for a few months. If, after becoming acquainted with you, I should conclude that I could make you useful to me I would be willing in return to make myself, in a certain degree, useful to you.

Trinidad is the best opening in Colorado for the right men.

Very truly &tc.
M. Beshoar

He continued to fire away at Delos Chappell and his waterworks, but by late fall of 1897 was confronted with a situation that was to put him out of the newspaper business for the next four years. Chappell had bought up enough scattered shares of *Advertiser* stock to gain control. Michael kept his own stock but bowed out as managing editor when the new management took over. His long time business manager, F. D. Goodale, had a few shares of stock, but he had gone into business for himself with the *Sentinel*, an evening newspaper, which was soon consolidated with the *Advertiser*. The physician thought he was just as well out of the newspaper business, that he was getting a little old to handle so many enterprises, and in any event he intended to devote more time to the Mexican prospects. A short time later he sent Dick Kaapcke, a Trinidad mining man, to Tepic with letters to the Rochas and full authority to act as superintendent of the Temerosa, hire miners, buy equipment, and do whatever else was needed to get the isolated property on a development basis. He had intended to follow Kaapcke within the month, but an important family occasion, his silver wedding anniversary, intervened.

The anniversary celebration, Saturday evening, November 13, 1897, took place in the Columbian Hotel—formerly the Grand Union and on the exact site of Mrs. Bransford's jacal and gentlemen's mess where he had boarded when he first came to Trinidad—and was the social affair of the season. At 8:30 P.M. more than three hundred guests were gathered in the reception room, almost directly above Ben Springer's gambling rooms, when Michael and Annie, with daughters Bonnie and Burnie and sons Ben and John as their attendants, entered to the strains of a march, to be met by the Rev. Father Salvatore Persone. They renewed the wedding vows that had united them in the United States Hotel before Father Munnecom in 1872. A substantial number of the guests who had been present at their wedding wore badges with the numerals 1872. The renewal of the vows was followed by speeches by Judge S. S. Wallace, who spoke feelingly of his twenty-two years of friendship with "the good doctor who was one of two things I found when I came to Trinidad. The other was Fisher's Peak," and by attorneys J. M. John and A. W. Archibald. After the speeches there was a dinner and dancing, including a special quadrille by the oldest settlers present. Each guest received an inscribed silver spoon from the Beshoars. Later, when the doctor and Annie had toted up their gifts in preparation for sending out thank-you notes,

he observed that they had "traded commemorative spoons for bon-
bon and berry spoons."

He was home with his family for Christmas and New Year's, but
by late January 1898 he was off to Mexico again. He took the Santa
Fe to El Paso, the Mexican Central to Guadalajara and Grendain,
and then traveled by stage to Tequila and on to Tepic where he
called on Governor Rocha, the revenue collector, and the mineral
claims agent. Although Kaapcke and a crew had been at work on
the Temerosa for some time, the Mexican officials advised that new
claims to the property be filed. That done he went to the mine on
muleback with a small escort of soldiers commanded by Lieutenant
Miguel Rocha, another son of the governor. He found Kaapcke
optimistic about the richness of the gold ore but decidedly pessi-
mistic about the area and the chances of getting the ore out. The
Indians in the neighborhood were unfriendly; there were no roads;
the mine could be reached only by a tramway down the steep side
of a mountain; it would be costly to build and operate a mill in
such an isolated spot, and expensive to try to take ore out by mule
trains. Under the existing conditions, Kaapcke thought they would
be hard put to meet even the limited production quotas and time
limits imposed by Mexican mining laws.

The physician asked Kaapcke to stay on another three months
at the end of which time they would see where they stood and make
a final decision on whether to go into a large-scale operation or
give it up entirely. A really big operation would depend on his
raising additional capital.

When Michael climbed onto his mule for the long ride back to
Tepic, he was feeling his sixty-five years. He had been bone tired
from the train, stage, and mule trip, and the few days he had spent
in Kaapcke's rough camp had only increased his weariness. When
he finally got to El Paso, he stopped over for a day and slept around
the clock. When he reached home, he told an anxious Annie that
he didn't know whether he'd win a Mexican fortune or not, that he
no longer had the strength and zest needed for such ventures.

A few weeks of his regular routine restored him somewhat, and in
May he went to Greeley, fifty miles north of Denver, to the annual
convention of County Superintendents of Schools to oppose a
proposal that teachers in public schools be required to conduct all

classes in English. The war with Spain was responsible for the proposal, which was aimed primarily at the Spanish-speaking teachers
in the schools of southern Colorado. When the convention opened
May 3, two days after Dewey had moved on Manila, Las Animas
County Superintendent Beshoar was one of the first to speak.

In his address, titled "Teaching in the Rural Districts of Southern
Colorado," he told the superintendents the average American
studied German, French, or Spanish in school but never learned to
speak the language nor gained any understanding of the thought
processes, traditions, and customs of the people who spoke the
particular language as their native tongue.

"There is more to speaking a language than knowing the words
and the grammatical constructions," he told the convention. "You
must be familiar with the manner in which thoughts are communicated, with the home life and with the prejudices of the people.
We find Mexican teachers more successful with Mexican pupils because they understand them better. An American, knowing nothing
of Mexican home life, labors under an almost insurmountable
handicap.

"One of the most competent teachers in the Trinidad public
schools began her professional career as teacher of a country school
in a Mexican community during one of my former terms in office.
There was one pupil, and one only, who knew a little English and
upon him she was obliged to depend as interpreter. About the third
day of the term she desired to take the sense of the pupils on a
certain question, and directed that all who were for the affirma-
tive should rise to their feet. The boy communicated his interpre-
tation and immediately, with countenances expressive of un-
questioning obedience, all feet were raised as high as the length
of the lower extremities would permit. There was a great variety of
feet. There were long feet and short; broad feet and narrow; feet
encased in black leather and russet, and brown moccasins, and
gray gunny bags; with toe ventilation and without; whole soles and
no soles—just twice as many feet as legal voters in that election.

"I happened to visit the school just as the pupils were voting.
The teacher saw me come in the door, but she was much too surprised by the many feet in the air to even speak. She turned ex-
citedly to the interpreter and asked him what he had said to the
school. He replied 'just what you told me—to rise their feet.' The
lady was convinced she was incapable of teaching such a school and

a short time later I transferred her to another school where the pupils were Americans. There she made an excellent record. I have had frequent occasions to hear with admiration the recitations of Mexican pupils under Mexican teachers. Our state law requires the use of English textbooks. The Mexican teacher requires his pupils to translate sentence by sentence to show that they understand what they have read in English. In this manner he teaches them the English language in a most efficacious way—in a manner that would be impossible with an American teacher. I am convinced that with a sufficient supply of Mexican teachers, the Mexican people will learn English much more rapidly than through any other agency; and after learning English will associate more closely with Americans, and will, in two or three generations, become thoroughly Americanized in language as well as in methods of reasoning."

That done, the Las Animas County superintendent invited the superintendents to hold their next convention in Trinidad, "a city nestled at the foot of one of the most famous Rocky Mountain passes, with a broad prairie like a vast ocean stretching off to the East." The educators would, he knew, endorse the proposal that classes be conducted only in English. Not only was English their stock in trade, but the usual amount of prejudice against Mexicans and the Spanish tongue was being enhanced by the nationwide war fever.

He had thought himself immune to the war excitement, particularly since he felt it was an artificial war inspired by jingoists and empire builders anxious to grab territory from a weak Spain, but by midsummer he was caught up in it too. In July, when the fighting began in Cuba, he offered Washington, through the good offices of U.S. Senator Edward O. Wolcott, a regiment of Mexican soldiers with himself as colonel and commanding officer, and Major Rafael Chacón of Trinidad, a Civil War veteran, and Captain Felix Martinez, El Paso newspaper editor, as the second- and third-ranking officers. Governor Rocha had agreed to provide the rank and file from the Territory of Tepic and the state of Jalisco, all "trained fighting men." They would be shipped to El Paso by railroad at the personal expense of el Coronel Miguel Beshoar and would there be entered into the service of the United States Army destined for Cuba. *El coronel* had everything planned, had worked out an agreement with the Mexican Central Railroad to transport the men to the border at a rate of one cent per mile per recruit. It was a fascinating project, and for a time there was interest in Washington; but the final decision was negative on the grounds that use of Mexican nationals would inevitably involve Mexico, a neutral country. During all the excitement the physician felt like a new man. He galloped a horse every morning to toughen his aged legs and did some shooting with his .41 Colt in the piñon-clad hills back of the hospital.

By fall he was in pretty good shape for a man his age, but to Denver attorney Caldwell Yeaman he professed to be on his last legs after Yeaman wrote, "Mr. Chappell tells me he thinks he has an opportunity of selling the stock in the Advertiser Company controlled by the Water Works, 60 shares, and it has occurred to me that perhaps you might desire to re-establish yourself in newspaper work." Yeaman said he thought the stock might be secured in lieu of possible cash M. Beshoar might obtain from a pending coal land suit against Chappell, and he "would thus secure a certainty for an uncertainty." The physician recognized the offer for what it was: an attempt to buy him off and one that would get Chappell out of the newspaper business, which was costing him money every month. He was pretty sure that the longer Chappell had to suffer along with a business he didn't understand, the more cheaply Michael could get his *Advertiser* back. In his reply to Yeaman, however, he said, "I must say that I do not entertain the slightest thought of ever again embarking on a daily newspaper enterprise. Were I twenty years younger it is very likely that I would give the offer favorable thought, but I realize, painfully, that I am aging rapidly and that my appearance of vigor is artificially maintained and cannot long bear the strain of heavy work and depressing care."

His reference to artificial maintenance of his vigor was a bit of poking fun at himself as he had taken to carrying a flask of peach brandy, nipping at it frequently throughout his working day. He kept himself perfectly sober as he had become a temperance advocate, but he also believed strongly in the efficacy of alcohol in maintaining the bodily functions of men and women past their prime. In a paper titled "Cure of Intemperance," he wrote that "the effect of a moderate amount of ordinary distilled liquor is to accelerate the circulation, quicken the mental perceptions, promote nutrition and invigorate the system." He complained that such temperance movements as "Sons of Temperance," the "Good Templars," the "Temples of Honor," and the "Murphy Movement" expected drunkards simply to stop drinking without any regard whatsoever for the pathological and psychological effects of long-time abuse of alcohol or any effort to find remedies for the illness that caused overindulgence in the first place.

Despite his professed worries about advancing age and the dangers of overdoing, he continued to keep a close eye on all of his business affairs. No detail was too small for his attention. When his feed bills seemed high, he checked out sales slips against days of feeding and then wrote a memorandum to his hostler, even though he talked to the man several times each day:

> David Mauk:
>
> A horse cannot retain good health very long if he eats more than 14# of hay or fodder per day and 12# of oats or 8# of corn and drinks more than four gallons of water. This is for a horse 15 or 16 hands high, weighing 900 to 1100#. Old Joe ought not to eat exceeding 420# of alfalfa a month, each of the cows the same and the burro 140, or all together 1400# per month. If they have eaten 5500# in six weeks they have eaten a little over 3700# a month, which is 2300# more than 1400# or at least 2½ times as much as is good for them.
>
> Mr. Miller may have been mistaken as to the amt. of hay he brought for it seems incredible that they would eat 2½ times as much as the most liberal allowance of the civilized nations of the world for the feeding of their large cavalry, artillery and draft horses. But the mistake in weight cannot be so great but that the amount you feed ought not to exceed one half as much as you have been feeding.

Hostler Mauk and Mr. Miller apparently hadn't realized they were dealing not only with a Pennsylvania Dutchman and onetime cavalryman, but also with an employer who carried with him at all times, and had for years, the proper daily ration for a horse and for a hundred men.

At the end of the three-month period, he went back to Mexico and spent two days in Tepic with Kaapcke and engineer Rocha. They had rich ores without a doubt, but mining costs would be exceedingly high. Regretfully, he told the two men that if he had plenty of risk capital he would go ahead, but since he had not been able to interest any American capital in such a remote venture and since he was not at a time of life when it would be prudent for him to risk his own money in the amounts that would be required, he would drop it. Before he left Mexico, a Mexican mining man named John R. Barton tried to interest him in a placer operation near Colima known as El Placero de los Naranjos. Barton said there was $3,000,000 in sight in six-hundred-thousand tons of auriferous gravel of a minimum value of fifty cents per ton with plenty of water and timber available, but the physician, having backed out of one Mexican venture, was not going to get involved in another.

"If I were twenty years younger, I would join you within two weeks," he wrote Barton, "but as it is, I no longer have the strength and energy nor do I wish to risk what I have gathered through the years, because if I lost it there is not time enough left for me to make it back again."

He got home in time for a series of family emergencies: Grandma Maupin had fallen and broken her hip, and a new physician in his office had put her in a body cast. Michael removed the cast, saying it would mean her death in short order and got her up and into a wheelchair. The second emergency involved son John whose proclivity for fist-fighting was causing the family trouble. Michael solved that one by enlisting John in the navy, "where you will get good training for awhile and perhaps even some boxing." The third emergency came up suddenly like a June wind and hailstorm on the prairies. A teacher from El Moro, in the office for medical advice, gave the physician a rude shock when he remarked that he supposed Miss Bonnie would be getting married pretty soon. When the physician seemed surprised, the teacher blurted, "Didn't you know she was engaged?" Michael hastily assured the man he knew all about it and got him out of his office. Bonnie getting married? She had been his deputy superintendent of schools since she finished college in Missouri, and somehow he had thought she would be quite permanent. But she was 22 and, of course, she might be thinking of getting married. He put on his hat and hurried to his county superintendent's office. When he bustled in and asked, without preliminaries, whether she was getting married, Bonnie simply laughed and patted him on the cheek. By the time he left he was somewhat reassured, but not completely.

A few days later Michael decided he had spotted the man, a some-time patient and oftentime patron of the town's sporting houses. The physician knew what he would do if he could not stop Bonnie from marrying such a man: he would shoot him. But before he could tax her with the man's name or take any action, Bonnie had disappeared. Her father found the superintendent's office locked. He drove to the homes of several of her friends; no one had seen her. Filled with foreboding, he decided to try the railroad depots, going first to the Santa Fe, where agent Hartwell said, "Yes, Doctor, Miss Bonnie bought a ticket for Kansas City and took the late train east."

"You fix me up a ticket on the next train and send this wire to Kansas City," the physician directed, scratching hastily on a pad: "Chief of Police, Kansas City, Mo. Hold Miss Bonnie Beshoar on arrival there for her father." He told the agent to put in the train number and time of arrival in Kansas City and "get it right off."

By the time he mounted the steps of the next train to Kansas City, the whole town knew that Miss Bonnie had eloped. The *Advertiser* asked him to please send a story back on the wire as soon as he got to Kansas City. The physician promised and was as good as his word, wiring back the story carried by the *Kansas City Times*, March 27, 1899. It said in part:

> Miss Beshoar has not been in charge of the police. She was detained several hours Friday and was then allowed to go to the home of G. W. Gulley in Argentine, Kansas.
>
> She was at the depot when her father arrived yesterday and when asked by him to explain why she had left home without telling where she was going, she said she came to the city for the purpose of visiting friends, and that she did not tell him because she wanted to see what he would do. She told him she was ready to return home whenever he was ready. She was very anxious to do nothing displeasing to her father.
>
> Dr. Beshoar claimed he would not have come to Kansas City to see his daughter only he suspected she was engaged to a young man of Trinidad and that they were to meet here and be married. The father objected to this wedding and said he came here determined to prevent it at any cost. As soon as he met his daughter he asked her about this young man and if

she was engaged to him. She told him she was not, but she was engaged to Roy Gulley of Argentine with whom she had attended Park College at Parkville.

Dr. Beshoar went with her to the Savoy Hotel and during the afternoon Roy Gulley and his father called to see them. Dr. Beshoar was pleased with the appearance of young Gulley and told both his daughter and Gulley that if they intended to marry he was willing. The young couple then decided to be married immediately.

Bonnie had gone to Kansas City with another Park College friend, Miss Pearl Keys, daughter of Dr. Keys of Colorado Springs, so all ended happily. The physician wired Annie, "It is all right. It isn't the man I thought."

He and Annie were going to find their house rather empty with Bonnie gone. Burnie was in medical school, and Ben would be off to medical school in the fall; John was in the navy, and Bert was planning on going into the priesthood.

Soon after the turn of the century, Michael got the *Advertiser* back, partly in settlement of judgments, partly in exchange for cash, and was once again happily engaged as its proprietor and managing editor. He enjoyed the give and take with the editors of rival newspapers, priding himself on being able to take their best and deliver telling blows in return. But sometimes his dual rolls as physician and newspaper writer–proprietor got him into trouble. Such was the case when the *Chronicle* asked him to write an article for it during an epidemic in January 1901, featuring it on the front page under the head "Dr. Beshoar on La Grippe." The article was in the nature of a warning to the public. One paragraph in particular caught the eye of editor E. O. Blair:

"There is no known specific for the cure of the grippe. The nostrums placed upon the market are a delusion and a snare. They are worthless. To relieve the suffering and depressing effects, there is probably nothing equal to a combination of Dover's Powder, quinine, and strychnine, or Dover's Powder, quinine, and camphor. Great care should be taken against exposure to cold during and after an attack."

Editor Blair put the article aside, picked up a copy of the *Adver-*

tiser for that same day, and scanned it carefully. A day or two later the *Chronicle-News* carried a short editorial:

> The *Advertiser* makes a great boast over the fact that it gave five columns of real live reading matter one day last week, but the long-haired modesty of its editor prevented him from making mention of some five or six columns of testimonials recommending the following remedies:
>
> Kodol Dyspepsia Cure, Bucklen's Arnica Salve, Chamberlain's Cough Cure, Chamberlain's Pain Balm, Foley's Honey and Tar, Foley's Kidney Cure, Chamberlain's Stomach and Liver Tablets, Dr. Bo-san-ka's Piles Remedy, Dr. Gunn's Nerve Tonic, Dr. King's New Discovery, Perry Davis' Pain Killer, Confidential Cure, Dr. Gunn's Improved Hammerless Pills. And there are others.
>
> The *Advertiser* is to be congratulated for its enterprise.

The editorial pricked the physician and surgeon but not the hard-boiled editor of the *Advertiser*. The nostrum advertising helped meet the payroll. Something would come up that would call for bouncing one on the head of editor Blair.

Sometimes the supposed conflicts between medicine and journalism took odd turns as when he rejected an applicant for insurance and the man protested to the Penn Mutual Life Insurance Company. The company, in turn, wrote Dr. Beshoar, that it had been informed he ran a newspaper and did he really have time to be their medical examiner in Trinidad? He gave the company a detailed answer:

> I have to admit that I am managing editor of a newspaper which occupies about 30 minutes of my time each day, consulting with the business manager and local reporters and perhaps writing an editorial. I also own some real estate and spend an average of about 15 minutes each day with real estate brokers and attorneys. I also have a wife, a mother-in-law and family with whom I spend about two hours every day during which time I partake of three frugal meals. I sleep seven hours out of each 24 and since my wife is over 45 and I am over 65 our repose has the advantage of one angelic quality which insures a more reliable result than was uniformly attained 25 years

ago. I read periodical literature and at chance times a medical work for about 45 minutes a day. I meet old time acquaintances and friends on the street and it takes about 30 minutes each day to exchange salutations with them and make sure of the well being of their dear ones at home. At more or less regular intervals I take a bath and have my hair trimmed and get shaved which take up an average of about seven and a half minutes a day (my wife blacks my shoes before I get up each morning if in her judgment they need it). The remaining thirteen hours and twenty-two and a half minutes are devoted strictly to the practice of medicine and examining applicants for life insurance. During those hours and minutes and fractions of minutes in the seclusion of my office I not only examine your applicants, but I treat patients. I try to convince them that I have arrived at a correct diagnosis or I wisely instruct them on matters of hygienic and moral conduct. My local or private practice is usually cared for in three hours and twenty two and a half minutes which leaves me ten hours each day or ample time to examine ten applicants for life insurance each day.

Dr. D. G. Thompson, your other examiner at this place, is a single man who sleeps in his office and needs about an hour and a half a day to go out to his meals and another hour to visit patients. I estimate that he takes in the neighborhood of 7½ minutes each day for toilet purposes. He never shaves, bathes only with the seasons, and is not known to have used a tooth brush or toilet syringe during the last two years. So for twenty-one and a half hours of every twenty-four he may be found in his office waiting for your business. If your agents should call upon him during sleeping hours all they would have to do would be ring his bell and he would be up and ready for action.

Since your query resulted from my refusal to examine Mr. Goldstein I must say that if your company wants to insure invalids and chronic uncurables as is the case of Mr. Goldstein you will need another examiner for that kind of applicants.

There is nothing in the doctor's papers to indicate the insurance company's reaction, but he did continue as its examiner.

The style of his letters at this time was matched in the speeches he gave with increasing frequency. Some of his talks before groups were serious in tone, as in the case of one delivered at the San Jacinto Battleground in Texas where he spoke for the Arkansas Valley Editorial Association at a newspaper gathering: "Shortly after I settled in Arkansas in 1853, I made a trip to Texas. I saw your great state at an early date and I met many of the men who fashioned the Lone Star State and helped win independence from Mexico. They were strong men, vigorous men, and I know that the present-day citizens of Texas are fully as strong and fully as able to carry on along the road marked for them to a glorious future." But mostly his speeches were reminiscences of pioneer days, treated with good-natured humor. At the silver anniversary meeting and banquet of A.F. & A.M. Lodge No. 28, he reviewed its history and told the members something about each of the charter members including himself, whom he described as "just a hanger on around Trinidad."

"At the time the lodge was organized," he said, "our water came from the river. Most of those assembled for the first meeting wore freshly laundered clothes, but the garments looked as though they had been washed in a buffalo wallow and ironed with an adobe brick. We had no gas works and no electric lights. The more prosperous of our brethren used kerosene at fifty cents a gallon, but candles were the staple lighting material. When we held our first ball, cross sticks supporting numerous candles were suspended from the ceiling. You could tell a Mason for days afterward by the candle drippings on his shoulders and back.

"There wasn't much in Trinidad at the time. The county treasurer kept his office in the store where he was a salaried clerk, but the time for keeping the accounts with different colored beans had passed. The treasurer had a pencil. The county superintendent of schools preserved the files and records of his office in a match caddy. Newspapers sprang up occasionally and sprang down as frequently."

His status as "the pioneer" grew with each passing month and year as the oldtimers began to drop off. He attended every funeral, delivered eulogies, and with Uncle Dick Wootton organized the Old Settlers Association, which he headed as president with Wootton as secretary. Each fall, when the old settlers gathered, looking grayer and knobbier and frailer each time, at Wootton's lake or Kit Carson Park or on the courthouse lawn, he gave them his "annual farewell address."

But though he was fast becoming a pioneer and the nestor of Colorado medicine and journalism, and reveled in such comments as one by a northern Colorado columnist who described him as "an original and cunning old gentleman," Michael had more zip than most men his age. He practiced medicine vigorously, edited the *Advertiser*, stayed active in politics and education, continued to buy and sell land, and even launched a number of new enterprises, including the Trinidad Oil Company. He was reappointed to the State Board of Health by Governor Charles Thomas and took special interest in water supplies and school hygiene. Also, at this time, he started a monthly magazine, *The Medical Educator*. His prospectus for the new publication trumpeted that it was "for the common people. Laymen Need It. Doctors Can't Get Along Without It." The general ignorance of the public about new discoveries in medicine together with their lack of knowledge of the simplest health rules inspired him to start the magazine, he informed prospective readers, promising that in addition to medicine he would do one article each month on the medical customs and history of the Indian and Mexican peoples.

In the first issue he roasted the medical profession and attacked quackery and Christian Science as dangerous menaces to health. The *Educator* surprised him by being a success from the start; subscriptions poured in from every part of the country; newspapers hailed it as "the first medical journal to handle the medical profession and its absurd code of ethics without gloves." He got praise from the profession, but he also got some scorching letters, particularly after he ran an article on "Puncturing the Bladders of the Medical Profession." It remarked, among other things, that:

> The doctor's profession is the funniest on earth. They live by guessing. In everything else the practitioner is required to know something positive about his business, and to occasionally accomplish positive results. In every other line, the adept has some principles which, if applied, are absolutely certain to produce a stated condition. But the physician looks at his patient, uses every device, centuries of study, roomsful of mechanical appliances, and all his skill and learning, and then is not certain he has the right diagnosis. This will make the doctors very mad as they are not in the habit of having bladders

punctured unless they do the puncturing. But this is the un-happy truth, and I know whereof I speak.

And then comes the treatment. Doctors have been guilty of great pretensions; they have assumed a monopoly on nobility and dignity; they have arrogated so lofty a tone for their pro-fession that a good deal has been conceded them except that they, like Samson after the shaving, are as other men.

Along with the new *Medical Educator* he had a couple of new de-vices to add to his own "roomful of equipment" in the form of the first X-ray and first Finsen or violet ray brought into southern Colo-rado. He had seen the machines demonstrated at a medical meeting in the East and had bought the biggest and most expensive he could find. The machines gave him pleasure, and his patients many anxious moments, as they crackled and a blue line of electricity danced between big metal balls behind the glass of the heavy oak cabinets. His first X-ray picture was of the old Federal ball in his leg. When it showed up beautifully and he had determined that it had moved downward slightly, he amused himself with keeping tab on it until the novelty of having an X-ray had worn off. He used the violet ray to treat patients suffering from arthritis and tuberculosis.

When Ben went off to medical school in Kansas City, the old physician told John it was about time he got out of the navy and went to school. After some writing back and forth, John agreed and said he thought he would like dentistry. This pleased the father no end. Annie shushed him up when he told visitors that he was think-ing of adopting a son to become an undertaker since he already had a daughter, Burnie, and a son studying medicine, would soon have a dentist and a priest, and all he needed was an undertaker "to sew things up pretty tight around here." He made a trip to the West Coast to the naval station at Goat Island to make certain John was serious, then bought him out of the navy, and sent him off to West-ern Dental College in Kansas City.

At this juncture he lost another and highly valued member of his family when his mother-in-law, Rachael Maupin, died. A pious old lady, deeply devoted to family and Bible, she knew nothing of the rough and tumble business world, but her name was widely known to Colorado businessmen and to bankers and businessmen elsewhere in the United States. She had, over the years, been a director and officer of numerous corporations, had bought and sold huge acreages of land, coal mines, gold mines, and businesses of one kind or another, and been involved in numerous lawsuits. At the time of her death, she was an officer of the Rocky Mountain Medical Institute Association and a director of the Advertiser Publishing Company. Mrs. Maupin had signed anything her son-in-law handed her without ever reading it or knowing what it was all about. She trusted "the doctor" implicitly and he, in turn, thought highly of her even while using her time after time through the years as a legal stooge in his many schemes.

Grandma Maupin was buried in the Masonic cemetery alongside her husband and little Blanche. After the rites at the graveside, the physician decided he would build a mausoleum for his family, that he would not "again go through the horror of burying a loved one in the ground like a brute." He bought the crown of a small piñon-covered hill at the edge of the Masonic cemetery, worked out a design, and engaged stonemasons. He drove out every few days in his buggy to see how they were getting along. Constructed of native stone, the building would have nine crypts. As it neared completion, he took off for Denver, simply telling his family and staff that he had "business in the capital." He returned with a sealed copper box, 24 by 24 inches in size, which he put under a table in his library without revealing what it contained. When the mausoleum was finished, he had the bodies of the Maupins and Blanche moved into it. At the same time, the copper box disappeared from his library, and on one of the crypts appeared the inscription: "Michael Beshoar Jr. Born Pocahontas, Ark., June 21, 1854. Died Denver, Colorado, June 12, 1893." The physician's firstborn had come home, this time to stay.

Not long after completion of the mausoleum, which caused a good deal of talk in Trinidad, Michael did something that caused even more talk: he got a haircut. When he marched into Raimondi's and told the barber to give him a traditional, short trim, a crowd gathered. After all, Dr. Beshoar hadn't had a haircut in seven years; he was one of the few oldtimers left in the area and the only professional man who wore shoulder-length hair. It was an event of the first magnitude. Most watched in respectful silence, but one brash cattleman from the eastern end of the county, who hadn't been long out of Texas, asked whether he could have the hair.

When the old doctor replied politely that he might have it, the cattleman winked at the crowd and drawled, "I'm fixing to make me a hair rope." There was a moment's silence. The crowd didn't know what to expect. But the doctor smiled benignly. "A good idea," he said. "And when you get it made you might throw it over enough of your stuff to pay that bill you owe me." The onlookers roared with laughter.

The haircut was not a spur-of-the-moment thing. He had been tired of the long hair for some time; it was no longer a novelty in Las Animas County, and it had lost its value elsewhere as times were changing rapidly. The only medical men still wearing long hair were notorious quacks and medical fakers. He was about to do a lot of traveling, and the haircut was indicated.

He attended a reunion of Confederate officers in Dallas, an American Public Health Association meeting in Washington, D.C., State Board of Health, Colorado State Medical Society, and University of Michigan Alumni Association meetings in Denver and Colorado Springs.

Also at this time he got the last money he could expect out of Gray Creek through settlement of a judgment. Most of the many suits had been compromised or had frittered themselves away in legal complexities. The fortune Michael had expected to make out of Gray Creek had dwindled to not more than seventy thousand dollars or so by the time he paid attorneys' fees. Delos Chappell had done much better. The mine had passed over to the Victor Fuel Company along with Chappell, who now headed Victor as its president. He had long since shaken the dust of Trinidad from his polished shoes in favor of a brownstone mansion on millionaire's row along Logan Street in Denver.

But though his financial return from Gray Creek had been a disappointment, the physician had the satisfaction of knowing that the property was as good as he had always said it was. Gray Creek, with a payroll of 225 miners, was producing coal at the rate of 174,000 tons per year and coke at the rate of 35,363 tons per year. The Victor Company had another 675 miners at work in Hastings, north of Trinidad. Elsewhere in the kingdom of Las Animas, 6,000 miners were digging more than a half million tons of coal per year, and it was only the beginning. King Coal ruled the county.

Chapter 13

Conspiracy and the Coal Barons

THE OLD-TIMERS OF TRINIDAD might have their differences and they might, on occasion and with very little provocation, beat, shoot, and abuse one another, but they closed ranks when one of their number was threatened or injured in anyway by an outsider. And so it was when George Hammond, the veteran stove and hardware dealer, was brushed off by his wealthy sister and her family during his last illness and death in February 1904.

George Hammond, his sister Mrs. George Tritch, and her husband had trekked west from Council Groves, Kansas, where the men had worked as tinners, to open a hardware store in Denver. The partnership had lasted about a year after which Hammond moved to Trinidad and opened a hardware store at Commercial and Elm streets in partnership with with E. J. Post.

In the years that followed, Hammond's store prospered in a modest sort of way, and though he wasn't Trinidad's outstanding success in business, he was a popular and respected citizen; good-hearted and charitable, he would have shared his last crust with a beggar. Then, in his old age, all kinds of trouble came his way: his business declined, his wife left him, his only son spurned him. And George, old and confused, turned increasingly to the bottle.

George Tritch's hardware business in Denver had done much better. In the years before his death, he had become a wealthy man and had entered the ranks of the Denver Establishment, hob-nobbing with such men as Bela Hughes and John Evans. He had been an officer of the Denver, South Park and Pacific Construction Company and a member of the first board of regents of the University of Colorado.

Michael had no doubt in his mind that the family would help when he called at the big Tritch store in Denver to report that

George Hammond was dying. The Tritch boys listened, had the old doctor repeat Hammond's name a time or two, and then said they had never heard of him. When Michael insisted Hammond was their mother's brother, they decided they had heard Hammond's name as that of a friend of their father's with whom he had crossed the plains.

"He came with George Hammond—your mother's brother," the physician replied somewhat testily.

"I guess you've heard that from that fellow Hammond," one of the nephews replied.

Michael retorted that he had met them all on the plains in the sixties and that he heard of the relationship from George Tritch. Then he turned on his heel and walked out.

A short time later Mayor Brown of Trinidad made an appeal to the Tritch boys and was given ten dollars to help old George through his troubles. When George succumbed, the Tritch family was immediately notified by Mayor Brown. The venerable Mrs. Tritch sent twenty-five dollars with a note that the sum was the absolute limit.

The twenty-five dollars hit Trinidad like a bombshell. The members of the Early Settlers Association insisted that the money be returned to Mrs. Tritch and promptly raised a purse to put old George Hammond away in proper style.

The funeral service in the R. G. Sipe & Sons' Undertaking Parlor was conducted by M. Beshoar, president of the Early Settlers Association. A wreath of white marguerites rested on the simple casket as he stood in front of it to address a big turnout of leathery-faced pioneers and their wives who had come to say goodbye to George Hammond.

He told them of his first meetings with the Tritch family and George Hammond in Nebraska Territory, of his visit to the Tritch nephews in Denver, of Mayor Brown's efforts including the final telegram to Mrs. Tritch and the receipt of the twenty-five dollars.

"The good people of Trinidad then took the matter into their own hands and in a few hours raised the sum of $102 to give George a decent burial and ordered the Tritches' twenty-five dollars to be sent back to them as too mean a sum from a millionaire to bury a blood relative—a sum not more than enough to drag out and bury a horse or an ox in frozen ground.

"I am glad to see so many of the better people of Trinidad here today to pay the last tribute of respect to the memory of one of the best-hearted men that ever lived in this community—Early Settlers who one by one are falling away till in a few years all will be gone the way of George Hammond. We may sometimes see faults, but let us bear with one another and remain friends till the end comes—it will not be long."

The Hammond funeral was just one instance when he paid honor to old friends and associates. At picnics of pioneer settlers, at lodge meetings, and on other occasions, he had warm and friendly anecdotes to tell, and they in turn paid honor to him, at functions in Trinidad and elsewhere in the state. In the spring of 1903, he was invited to attend the June commencement exercises of the University of Michigan. As he was one of the oldest living graduates—the Class of 1853—it was suggested that he should be "re-graduated" with the Class of 1903.

After talking it over with Annie, he decided he would accept.

As the four o'clock Michigan Central whistled into Ann Arbor, the knot of people on the station platform pressed forward, crowding tightly around President James Angell and the faculty committee on hand to welcome the old doctor from southern Colorado. There had been some speculation among both faculty and members of the Class of 1903 as to what the Class of 1853 specimen would be like. Some had expressed belief that the old gentleman from Colorado, who was to be the feted alumnus at the forthcoming commencement exercises and who was the subject of much advance attention in the Detroit, Chicago, Ypsilanti, and Ann Arbor newspapers, would arrive in a baggage car as that was where the railroad usually carried fossils, while still others envisioned a bent old codger, complete with wheelchair, ear trumpet, and attendant.

Young Earl Cooley of Trinidad, who was getting his law degree at Michigan had perhaps unwittingly added to the speculation, and even caused some apprehension in the administration, with his descriptions of Dr. Michael Beshoar's red vests and long hair "which falls down over his shoulders whenever he removes his high silk hat." The young senior, anxious that his family's physician make a good impression now that the great moment had arrived, was up front when a well-groomed, well-dressed man stepped jauntily down from the Pullman and shook hands with President

Angell. Smoothly shaven and well trimmed, the oldest living graduate looked much younger than Earl Cooley had remembered him.

"Where is the long hair?" another senior whispered accusingly. The gentleman from Colorado, far from looking like a member of Buffalo Bill's Wild West Troupe, had short hair, neatly parted on the side, and looked like any other prosperous business or professional man.

President Angell and his committee escorted the doctor off to the Cook House where a short welcoming program was held. There were brief talks by the president and Dean Harry Hutchins, after which a number of faculty, newly arrived alumni, and students crowded around to be introduced. Cooley, by now proud of the impression his family doctor was making, was even prouder when the physician recognized him and called him to come and stand beside him. Michael prided himself on knowing the young people of Trinidad and being able to call a surprising number of them by name; and he always treated them with the same dignity and respect he accorded men and women of his own age.

During the week that followed, the physician from some obscure place called Trinidad in distant Colorado was a stellar attraction. There were several affairs in his honor, including a dinner at the home of President Angell. In between times there were newspaper interviews and talks before various groups. But Michael, bent on enjoying himself to the utmost, had a little joke going, and by the end of the second day everyone on campus knew about it and helped him repeat it time after time. As alumni arrived from every part of the United States, he would seek out the more elderly and ask, "And what was your class, sir?" When they would proudly say they had been graduated in 1859, or 1866, or 1878, and then ask him politely about his year, he would wave his hand airily: "Oh, I'm just a freshman myself. I was graduated with the Class of 1853."

Michael didn't spend any more time with the oldsters than he could help, devoting most of his free hours to drinking beer with the students in the Oriental Bar three blocks from the campus. The Oriental had a long table where the students regularly gathered. It was their custom to carve their initials in its top, and when one top was completely carved, it would be removed from the table, hung on the wall, and a new one put in its place. Michael gleefully carved his initials deep in the wood and sat with the students each night telling stories and laughing until the 11 P.M. closing hour. Although he never seemed to notice, the students marveled at his capacity for Müncher beer, which he drank, quart after quart, without any discernible effect.

"Some of these pompous old roosters make me ill," he told the students one night. "Personally I don't intent to hobble around like everybody's great grandfather. There is good leather in me yet."

When he was alone, the physician was not so debonair. Ann Arbor bore no resemblance to the town he had left a half-century before. And the day when he had stood with Orrin Arnold, Hoyt Smith, Frank Barross, William Fitch Hovey, and twenty-nine other young men, many of whose names he could no longer remember, seemed dim and far away. He could still see some of his professors as clearly as if he had attended their classes only yesterday—men such as Moses Gunn, his professor of surgery, J. Adams Allen, physiology and pathology, and Samuel Denton, theory and practice of medicine—but most of the men he knew in his university days were becoming vague shadows.

Graduation day, Sunday, June 21, 1903, was clear and warm. Michael had turned his old diploma over to the university several days earlier. Although worn by years of packing about the South and West, the signatures of Dr. Tappan, president in 1853, and the eight regents of that distant day still were legible. He sat at the exercises with 816 young men and women who were about to become the newest alumni of the university. When their names were called, his was among them. President Angell handed the veteran back his old diploma, bearing a new seal, affixed by the official sealer of the university, and the yellow and blue ribbon that adorned the diplomas of 1903. Michael was as proud of his battered old diploma as any young physician who received a treasured sheepskin that day.

He had been just as proud two months earlier when son Ben was graduated from Kansas City Medical College. He had always looked forward to having a son in practice with him, but on the eve of Ben's graduation, his Pennsylvania Dutch closeness with money came to the fore when Ben wrote for money to buy things he needed for the graduation exercises. The father replied that since Ben would graduate only once he could easily rent whatever he needed. After Annie tactfully intervened, he relented, sent his son a check for sixty-five dollars "to pay for a new suit, French gloss or patent leather shoes, a silk hat, a white shirt, a fine necktie, class pictures, etc."

Upon his arrival home, diploma in hand, Ben was admitted to the practice on a salary of fifty dollars a month plus one-fifth of the earnings of the Rocky Mountain Medical Institute Association and the title of vice-president of the association. It was a little better than the "insurance against starvation" he normally gave to doctors starting out in his office, but not much.

The "good leather" he exhibited at the Ann Arbor homecoming was creaking loudly two months later when he placed advertisements in national farm publications to unload the last of his Iowa and Illinois land. After a detailed description of the properties he was offering for sale, he wrote: "Fortune knocks at every man's door once in a lifetime. If the call is not answered it may never come again. I am neither a real estate broker nor a promoter, but just a weary old man who wants to unload worldly cares before the end comes."

Even Michael Beshoar was surprised at the number of persons who were more than willing to aid a weary old man, particularly if there was a chance that he was so weary he didn't know or care about equitable prices. But he did sell the properties and decided he would also sell off more of his holdings in southern Colorado. The less property he had, the freer he would be to travel, make speeches, and do lodge work and other such activities that were dear to his heart. At a thirty-fifth anniversary party given by the *Pueblo Chieftain*, in conjunction with the annual Colorado State Fair, he and Captain Lambert were the guests of honor at a banquet in Pueblo's Imperial Hotel. Called on for a speech, he gave them a bit of history:

"When Colonel Chivington's regiment was on the march to New Mexico to check the advance of Sibley's command, he followed alone on horseback a day or two in the rear. Reaching Zan Hicklin's ranch about thirty miles south of Pueblo, he asked if he could remain overnight. Zan said no. 'But,' said the colonel, 'it is now late and twenty miles to the next house.'

"Zan replied, 'It being twenty miles to the next house is no fault of mine, and as for you being late, that is your fault.' The colonel straightened up in his saddle and said, 'Do you know who I am?' 'No, and I don't give a damn who you are.' The colonel then said with some asperity, 'I am Colonel Chivington.'

"'Now, by God, that is getting old,' Zan shouted irately. 'You are the third man that's come along here today and claimed to be Colonel Chivington.'

"The application of this story is that I was in Pueblo a few weeks ago, and besides visiting popular resorts, I called at the *Chieftain* office and stood around till a feeling came over me of being a stranger among strangers in my old home. The young men I encountered struck me as pretty good-looking and well-groomed tenderfeet.

"I introduced myself as Doctor Beshoar. They had me repeat the name two or three times and then gave up in evident despair. I then told them I was the founder of the *Chieftain*. That settled it. They did not say so, but their manner indicated that I might be the fifth or sixth man that had come around and claimed to be the founder or the foundered of the *Chieftain*."

He told them of the early days of the paper, "My feeling toward the *Chieftain* can be no other than that of a loving parent towards a promising child, and I'm glad that it is in the care and keeping of such excellent ownership and management as Ikie Stevens, J. A. Barclay, and their associates.

"The changes since my day are wonderful. We did well to turn out 200 copies a day on our Washington hand press. Today the *Chieftain* prints 30,000 an hour. Instead of one-man power, the *Chieftain* is now run by powerful steam engines. All is changed. The old *Chieftain* is a story of the past, but not entirely without interest. The new is the story of the present with every prospect that the next thirty-five years will bring as great changes as the last. God grant that it may continue to grow in power for good."

He sat down rather heavily.

The editors, gathered from every city, and professors from the various colleges, who were in Pueblo for the fair, arose.

"A toast," Dr. Aylesworth, president of the agricultural college, called. "A toast to the founder of the *Chieftain*."

A month later he was in Washington attending a medical meeting and shaking Teddy Roosevelt's hand at a White House reception, but by the end of October he was sticking to his desk in the *Advertiser* as a long-smouldering dispute between the big coal operators and thousands of miners broke into the open in the southern Colorado coal fields. On October 26, 1903, John Mitchell, national president of the United Mine Workers, issued a strike call and on November 9 more than 6,500 coal diggers in Las Animas County and thousands more in neighboring counties quit the mines. Violence broke out almost immediately as the corporations sent in armed guards and strikebreakers.

The editor of the *Advertiser* aligned his newspaper on the side of the miners while the rival *Chronicle* and most other newspapers in the area, and in the state for that matter, lined up with the coal barons. By the end of the year, it was evident the strike would have important political repercussions. Governor James H. Peabody, a Republican lackey of the coal corporations, was the *Advertiser*'s principal target. Day after day it fired its editorial guns at him. Editor Beshoar practiced medicine, but he practiced journalism more during this period; he wrote most of the editorials and saw everything that went into the newspaper. He directed that every piece of copy relating to the strike, the coal companies, or politics be submitted to him before it went into the paper. The editor made few public appearances aside from Pythian and Masonic gatherings. Late in March 1904, Major Zeph T. Hill arrived in Trinidad with 400 militia troops, slapped on a press censorship, and established his signal corps in the telephone and telegraph offices to see that it was enforced. Three nights after his arrival, Major Hill, with Trinidad under rigid martial law, started wholesale deportation of strikers. Union miners and those suspected of union affiliation were rounded up and sent "down the river" with orders not to come back to the coal fields.

When the tension eased a bit, the editor of the *Advertiser* and Annie ducked out of town to attend the Louisiana Purchase Exposition in St. Louis and pay a quick call on daughter Bonnie in Kansas City, but he was soon back at his desk. Not long after his return, the troops were withdrawn. Officially the strike was still on, but it was lost and would soon be ended. Before the troops left, editor Beshoar showed up at the military headquarters, receipt in hand, and demanded and received the big, muzzle-loading shotgun and the .41 caliber Colt he had turned in when martial law was first declared. He felt better when his favorite Colt was again tucked in his waistband—the .44-40 Peacemaker he had held out in case he needed to shoot a militiaman was a good gun but a little big for his hand.

During the relatively quiet period that followed the departure of the troops, Michael was able to turn his attention to a number of other things. His bonus from the coal strike was a bright young addition to the *Advertiser* staff named Alfred Damon Runyon, who had come into Las Animas County as a militia cavalryman. He had spent much of his time riding payroll escort at Tabasco, one of the nearby camps; he had also spent some time under military arrest for roistering. He was sharp, obviously a comer, and a strong addition to the staff. But the old doctor had to give up his self-proclamed monopoly on liquor, tobacco, and "opium eating," once he had Runyon on the staff, as the newcomer was the archetype of all of the drunken and whoring newspaper reporters of all times. He had a room in the Corinado Hotel, a city block from the office, but no one ever looked for him there. When he wasn't at the *Advertiser*, he was roaring from saloon to saloon or was on a major binge in Big Dutch's or Little Dutch's in the red light district in the west end, or in the hospital recovering from one. For awhile Michael thought he couldn't keep Runyon, but the young man soon had a happy arrangement with his counterpart at the *Chronicle* whereby the sober one would do double duty, working both the morning *Advertiser*'s news desk and the evening *Chronicle*'s desk while the other one was dead drunk in some dive.

In addition to getting Runyon started, Michael's summer was marked by a venture and an adventure. The first took the form of a well-equipped party of four men that he sent into the Bitter Root country of Idaho in search of placers on the Salmon River. Unfortunately, the expedition ended prematurely when its leader and only experienced prospector suffered a heart attack and died soon after beginning work in the field. The adventure, a physical encounter with a non-advertising Trinidad businessman, ended on a better note, enabling the physician to boast that he could still take care of himself despite his seventy-one years.

The merchant, a big, bulky man of forty who stood head and shoulders above Michael, was incensed by an item in the *Advertiser* criticizing him for allowing trash to accumulate in the rear of his establishment in violation of city ordinances. He rushed into the editor's sanctum and, without so much as a word, let go a haymaker that landed the surprised old medico on the flat of his back. His attacker then jumped on him, straddling his chest as he flailed away with both hands. The doctor wasn't carrying his gun and couldn't have reached it if he had been, but he had spent too many years on the frontier to be caught completely unprepared. He grappled with the man, pulling him as close to him as possible to reduce the force of his blows. Holding as tightly to him as he could with his left arm, he reached into his hip pocket with his right hand, pulled out a long, slender, single-blade knife, and opened and locked it with a flip of his wrist. Then he reached up and neatly severed an artery in the man's temple. Blood spurted while the physician held tightly until he felt the merchant relax in a faint. He pushed him off, and then took care of him as though he were a prized patient. When he had his assailant patched and restored, he led the still woozy man down the stairs and solicitously held the door for him.

"You will get a statement for an office call," he said as he bowed the man out. "And the next time you come calling bring an advertisement for the *Advertiser*."

Editor Beshoar's judgment that the coal strike had been merely one battle in what promised to be a long war with the big coal companies seemed confirmed as coal company officials and Republican party leaders from Denver, including his old antagonist Delos Chappell, buzzed in and out of Trinidad, talking with the Republicans they owned and Democrats they would like to own. Michael's worst fears were realized July 11, 1904, when Senator Casimiro Barela, a Democratic office holder since the sixties and the party's best vote getter in southern Colorado, announced he was withdrawing from the party to become a Republican. Some of the lesser Democrats also were leaving the Democratic ship as the coal corporations shared their wealth in the right places.

Michael upbraided his old friend Barela for his defection, first in a personal encounter and thereafter in the *Advertiser* where El Senador Perpetuado, as Barela was known to many, became as prime a target as Governor Peabody. Barela had come into Las Animas County from Mora, New Mexico, driving a team of oxen. Unlike many of his compatriots, he had had some formal education, in a Jesuit college in Mora, and he proved to be an apt pupil when two astute professors, Jesus Maria Garcia and Miguel Beshoar, inducted him into politics. For twenty-four years his heavily accented voice had been the voice of the people in the state capital. Now it would be the voice of the coal barons; that is, it would be unless he could be defeated. The Democratic party had only one place to turn, but when a committee called on Michael in advance of the nominating convention and told him he would have to oppose Barela, he turned it down, claiming he was much too old. "My days in active politics are passed," he told the committee. "I simply don't feel equal to making such a race."

But in the end he gave in. Once decided, he entered into the campaign with something of his old vigor. He was formally nominated September 29 at a party convention in the Jaffa Opera House. A steady, all-day rain would have kept a lot of party members away most years, but not this time. There was a great deal of ill feeling about defections to the coal companies and a determination to do something about them. The convention, which got underway at 10:15 A.M. and lasted until midnight, heard the old doctor promise he would "punish the man who has proved a traitor to the party that honored him for so long." He said that the party must fight not only the Republicans and such turncoats as Barela but also the great coal corporations, and that it must stand with the coal miners in their fight for justice.

Within a week the campaign was in full swing. The first move of the coal companies was to march aliens into Trinidad from the coal camps under the watchful eyes of their bosses and register them. The *Advertiser* ran a lead story every morning under banner headlines: "The Fraudulent Registration—The Desperate Straights to Which the Republican Gang Is Put!" Friends of many years quit speaking to each other, and households were divided. The *Advertiser* editor, veteran that he was, managed to keep his balance and even his sense of humor through it all, as per the day he was leaving the office when a fire broke out in the basement of the *Advertiser*. Dense clouds of smoke rolled out of the building. He stood with the rest of the *Advertiser* force in the street and watched the firemen, their faces covered with handkerchiefs and sponges, plunge into the building; he laughed with the others when the office boy ran up to business manager Stevens and shouted "The office safe is open," and Stevens replied, "That's all right, boy, you're new in this business. There is never anything in a newspaper safe."

The damage was small, about three hundred dollars' worth, and as soon as the mess could be cleaned up, the editorial guns continued to blaze away: "If the corporations are successful in the coming election Las Animas County will become the Kingdom of Chappell. There will be stretched across her hills this sign 'Private—Keep Out!' The Chappell-Barela gang, backed by the money and influence of the corporations, will endeavor to poll so large a fraudulent vote in the coal camps that it cannot be overcome."

Through each morning issue he salted such paragraphs as "A paper-covered five-cent novel telling how our former highly esteemed citizen, D. A. Chappell, obtained his riches would be more exciting than any novel about Diamond Dick, the boy bandit."

Chappell had both office and residence in Denver, but he was spending much of his time in Las Animas County, working day and night for Barela.

"The coal camps are under armed guard and everybody who is not openly in sympathy with gang methods is made to stand aside," the *Advertiser* said. "Trinidad merchants are prevented from delivering goods they have sold in the camps; law and order are set aside and everything that the devilish ingenuity of corrupt gang politicians can devise is being done to override the liberties of the people to the end that James H. Peabody shall again be elected governor of Colorado and Casimiro Barela returned to the senate where he can work for his employers' interests."

The Democratic state organization sent its biggest guns into Las Animas County, men such as John Shafroth, the party's candidate for Congress in 1904, and Alva Adams, the candidate for governor, who told a major rally in Trinidad: "Doctor Beshoar has taken many scalps during his long residence in Las Animas County and he will take many more. He will hang to his belt the scalp of that old man of the sea, Señor Don Casimiro. Foreigners have appeared in the courts, wearing the same jackets they wore when they left the old country, to become citizens for the purposes of this election. When 1,700 names are presented for registration from one camp where there are only 100 legal voters, it is more than decent citizens will stand. Who is doing this work? Chappell and Barela. If elected governor I will have the contents of every ballot box examined and the perpetrators of frauds punished."

The day after the rally the *Advertiser* charged, under the heading "Desperate Methods of a Desperate Gang," that the registration lists in the Victor Fuel Company camp of Hastings, had been packed, just as Adams had contended in his speech, and that the packing had been done by Chappell and Barela, who had elected themselves election judges in Hastings: "As Mr. Chappell is a voter in Denver and Barela a resident of El Moro the actions of these two are simply ridiculous. Oh, yes, these statesmen want a fair election."

Candidate Beshoar campaigned assiduously, traveling the big county from one end to the other. He was well received everywhere except at the coal camps, most of which barred him from entering. The guards on the gate, armed with Winchester carbines, would tell him he could not enter without a pass. To get a pass he would have to see the superintendent; the superintendent was inside; to get in to see him to ask for a pass, he would have to have a pass from him to get through the gate. *El doctor* was particularly well received in Mexican villages though Barela had raised the race issue in an effort not to lose the normally Democratic Mexican vote. Editor Felix Martinez of *La Voz Del Pueblo* in El Paso, Texas, campaigned through the county calling on Mexican voters to support "that great, Democratic, nonassuming, plain, genuinely American figure, Doctor Beshoar, the man who is the father of Las Animas County." Chappell and Barela sought to counter Martinez by bringing in another "father," a Catholic priest. The *Advertiser* said Father Malone had "a big corporosity, a big voice and a big opinion of himself. Imagine the representative of the meek and lowly Jesus Christ coming to our city between two such fellows as he was finally crucified with and by his powerful gift of gab trying to make his hearers believe that vicious and unlawful government is good government—that Peabody and Barela are greater saints than Peter and Paul, and you have a mind picture in which Judas Iscariot isn't in it."

When the *Chronicle-News* accused the sheriff of placing deputies at polling places during registration of voters, the *Advertiser* admitted the truth of the statement, begged leave to paint a picture of the registration in Primero, one of the largest coal camps:

Registration began at nine o'clock in the morning. When the sheriff's deputies reached the polling place at 8 o'clock on the first registration morning they found Rube Baldock, who acts as Primero town marshal, there before them. Mr. Baldock was wearing a great belt filled with cartridges. A heavy gun hung from the belt. In a few minutes Andy Johnson, manager of the company store, drove up with a double-barreled shotgun protruding from his buggy. Then came the mine superintendent, then the stable boss with his belt and gun. Then followed others. Finally the pit boss arrived with a wagon literally filled with Winchesters. On Tuesday of this week conditions were the same only more so. There were more corporation men and more guns. Yes, the sheriff had a few deputies at some of the polling places. Is it any wonder that he did?

Throughout the campaign of 1904, the big corporations—for example, the Denver & Rio Grande and the Colorado & Southern railroads, the Victor Fuel Company, the Rockefellers' Colorado Fuel & Iron Company, the Rocky Mountain Coal and Iron Company, the Guggenheim American Smelting and Refining Company, and the Mine Owners' Association—used their influence and their money to win the election. Terror tactics, using armed deputies and thugs, were the order of the day. The prime objectives of the corporations were to reelect Governor Peabody, preserve the Republican majority in the state senate, and insure a sympathetic supreme court that would use its powers to manage elections and maintain established policies.

Intimidation of voters, primarily miners, was brazen and bold in the last two months of the campaign. Miners in the metal districts, such as Cripple Creek, were told there would be no work if the Democrats won; and Delos Chappell, who had registered voters by the carload in Hastings, had the gall to deny later in an election-contest hearing that he had intimidated men who worked for him. "I think perhaps I could be construed as advising them," he said coldly. "I think my remarks were along the line that our interests were mutual in the election."

By election day, November 8, 1904, Michael was worn out, mentally and physically, but he was confident of success. He went to his ward polling place shortly before noon. Voting was heavy for so early in the day. Some of his friends were on hand, as were corporation men who eyed him sullenly. After he had voted, he went home and slept until dark. He had been too tired to hang around headquarters, too tired to do anything at the *Advertiser* or in his medical office; the campaign had taken a lot out of him. His years were telling on him heavily. After a light supper he was driven to the *Advertiser* office. Hundreds of persons were gathered in the street in front of the office to watch the bulletins. Wild rumors were everywhere: ballot boxes had been stolen, gunmen had marched illiterate foreigners to the polls and voted them straight for Peabody and

Barela, using a sample ballot with cutouts which could be placed over the regular ballot. There were cries of fraud on every side. The *Chronicle-News* charged the Democrats had imported hired guns from Denver to intimidate miners into voting the Democratic ticket.

The *Chronicle* boasted that the Republicans were sweeping the nation, state, and county. Early tabulations, however, showed Beshoar leading El Senador Perpetuado everywhere except in the coal camps. The *Chronicle*, while claiming a victory for Barela, printed a tabulation of thirty of the forty-two precincts that showed Barela with 3,704 votes to 3,932 for the physician. Alva Adams was trailing Peabody by just fourteen votes in the thirty precincts. Although the small outlying precincts, some of them as far as eighty miles or more from the county seat by wagon road, were slow coming in, the Democrats had obviously won. Alva Adams had carried the state by more than 11,000 votes, and the key Democratic candidates for the state senate, including Ward in Boulder County and Beshoar in Las Animas County, had won. The old doctor had a majority of 900 in Trinidad and, though the Republicans had succeeded in getting several Democratic precints thrown out, had carried the county with the result the county clerk finally certified to the secretary of state: a vote of 5,143 for Beshoar, 4,585 for Barela.

The Republicans announced they would contest the results in the gubernatorial election and the Democratic victories in Boulder and Las Animas counties. Under the heading "Peabody's Supreme Gall," the *Advertiser* contended "the fraud committed by the Peabody forces in Colorado never has been equaled in a civilized nation. It staggers one's faith in our institutions when we realize the depths of infamy to which these men went in their attempt to carry this county for their ticket. At Hastings, Delos Chappell, the president of the Victor Fuel Company, remained outside the polling place all day with a view to intimidating the miners. He unfolded several of the ballots so as to fully impress his employes with the fact that he would be permitted to know how they cast their votes. At Primero an armed mob of over 100 men took possession of the ballot boxes and election supplies, moving them three miles from the place selected by the county commissioners for holding the election. In face of all this, these men now are trying to burglarize the people of the state by shouting that fraud has been committed against Peabody."

In the midst of the political warfare, the Masons of southern Colorado managed to carry off a pleasant interlude when they held their annual election of officers and a celebration of Michael's fiftieth anniversary as a Mason. Men who had not spoken for weeks sat down together to eat salmi of duck chasseur and extol each other's virtues for an hour or two. In his short speech, attorney A. F. Hollenbeck said:

"I was going through my old geography book the other day looking for the location of Liao Yang. While I was busy at the task I came across a town in Europe named Beshoar. That intrigued me and I looked up its history only to find that it was founded hundreds of years ago by Dr. Beshoar. It thus became evident that while Ponce de Leon searched for the fountain of eternal youth our physician has found it. It is thought by some to be located in the Southwest and I have become convinced that the annual trips the doctor makes each year are for the purpose of visiting the springs and renewing himself. I think he is acting in a most un-Masonly manner in not communicating the secret to his brothers."

The Masons had a lot of fun, but by morning they were back at one another's political throats.

The elective officers of the state, sitting as the official canvassing board, met December 28 in the State Capitol Building in Denver to canvass the 1904 returns. It turned out to be a hectic day. Denver District Judge Samuel Carpenter, acting on a petition submitted by attorneys John A. Rush and Everett Bell of Trinidad, issued a writ of mandamus to prevent the board from "going behind the election returns" until the various charges of fraud could be aired in the courts. Chief Justice Gabbert of the State Supreme Court countered by calling the high court into special session to issue an order denying the writ and ordering Judge Carpenter to appear before it the next day and show cause why the writ should not be dissolved.

As Justice Gabbert finished reading the order, Senator Barela rushed from the courtroom to Governor Peabody's office where he conferred with the executive for several minutes behind closed doors. When he came out, he literally ran to the secretary of state's office, his face beaming, and within five minutes the canvassing board was assembled in the secretary's office. When reporters attempted to attend, Governor Peabody blocked their way, shouting, "You'll not be allowed in here."

The only outsider in the star-chamber session was an attorney, James H. Brown. The door was locked and bolted; members of Secretary of State Cowie's staff stood in front of it, warning away all who approached.

Meanwhile, at the behest of attorneys Rush and Bell, who had not been officially notified of the supreme court order, Deputy Sheriff John Bramer attempted to serve the Carpenter writ on the canvassing board. Deputy Bramer was not familiar with the many rooms and corridors in the rambling capitol building, but he made a valiant try. He went through the executive department until he reached the bolted door behind which the canvassing board was sitting. He went back into the corridor and to the basement to try to gain entrance that way. Bell and Rush directed him back to the first floor and the bolted door, where a clerk seized him by the arm and tried to pull him away. Barela appeared as Bramer cried, "I am an officer of the court and will not be interfered with." El Senador Perpetuado grabbed the deputy sheriff around the neck, but the deputy shook him off, yelling, "You get out of here. Let go of me or I'll throw you in jail. I'm a deputy sheriff. Now get out, you have no business here."

Barela backed off, but Deputy Secretary of State Timothy O'Connor planted himself in front of the door. "I have orders to let no one in here," he said defiantly.

"I demand of you as an official to tell me if the canvassing board is in there," attorney Bell said.

"I don't know."

"I'll call for more help," attorney Rush said, grabbing up a telephone, but Deputy Sheriff Bramer was a determined man and didn't think he needed help. Shoving O'Connor aside, he said, "I'm going to begin reading, and you had better get back, O'Connor. I'll read through the keyhole."

At that moment, attorney Brown, who had left the canvassing board room by another door, appeared and, in commanding tones, began: "I have come from the supreme court and in the name of the court I demand that this business stop. I am directed to tell you that if you have any business on matters that are before the canvassing board you are to come before the bar of the supreme court. I command you to appear before them."

"Bosh," shouted attorney Rush, his face flushed with anger. "By what authority do you command in the name of the supreme court?"

"By the authority of interested parties."

"More bosh. I will obey any order of the court when the proper writ is made." Rush screamed the words. "No private party can tell me what to do . . ." And to Bramer: "Now read!"

Just as Bramer stooped to read into the keyhole, three sharp raps came from inside. This was the board's prearranged signal to Deputy Secretary of State O'Connor. That worthy stepped aside and the deputy sheriff began to read. Before he had finished more than two or three lines of his writ, the door flew open and all except the governor filed out. Peabody, still sitting in his chair, was roaring with laughter.

The first official out was Secretary Cowie, and he had Barela's certificate of election in his hand. He thrust it at El Senador Perpetuado and went on into his private office. Barela gleefully held it up for all to see, and then turned and ran out of the office.

The board would not disclose how each member voted, but said that by a vote of four to one it had thrown out the returns in Precinct 31 in Las Animas County, thus changing Barela's total from a deficit of 124 votes to a majority of 296 votes, making the final count Barela 4,816 to Beshoar's 4,609, and it had tossed out the Lafayette precinct in Boulder County to unseat Democrat Ward in favor of Republican Millard.

Said the *Rocky Mountain News*:

"Secretary of State Cowie will learn from the people the degradation to which his vote has sunk him. Benedict Arnold was a brave and honorable man compared to Cowie, Miller and Auditor John A. Holmberg. Governor Peabody—was ever a state disgraced with such a chief executive?—voted with Cowie, Miller and Holmberg. Think of the spectacle. Peabody, repudiated by the voters of Colorado by 11,000 majority, casting his vote for two men, who like himself, had been repudiated at the polls, that they, in turn, might remove additional Democratic senators, that a sufficient number of corporation tools may in the joint assembly declare him—Peabody— governor for the coming term. Thus the conspiracy moves along. Truly, has Colorado ceased to be regulated by law.

Michael Beshoar was probably the most disgusted man in Colorado, but the end was not yet. He resolved to carry his fight on to the assembly even though there seemed little hope of victory. Mass meetings were held in Trinidad and other cities. The *Advertiser* warned that two sets of election returns would go to the legislature to be canvassed and that a certificate of election would be awarded to Peabody over Adams.

The legislature completed its canvass of the vote, January 8, 1905, and, surprisingly enough, gave Adams 123,078 to 113,304 for Peabody. The Democrats apparently had the governorship, but the unseating of Dr. Beshoar and Ward had given the Republicans a majority in the senate. It was freely predicted that the majority would be increased by senate action to unseat two more of its members, Senator R. M. Born of Alamosa and Senator Daniel Healy of Leadville.

While the incoming general assembly was organizing in January 1905, a Denver grand jury probed the election frauds, bringing in a report that charged, among other things, that the unseating of senators Charles Ward and M. Beshoar "was a corrupt and deep-seated conspiracy." As predicted the legislature dumped two more Democratic senators, Born and Healy, their seats going to Dick of Huerfano County and Jesse F. McDonald of Leadville. The latter would sit in the senate for a week, and then be sworn in as lieutenant governor. Democrat Alva Adams was inaugurated January 10, 1905, in a colorful but tense ceremony. Peabody filed a contest immediately after Adams took office, and the unhorsed Democratic senators and senators-elect did the same. Michael subsequently showed up at Room 20 in the state capitol building with his lawyers and twenty witnesses for the trial of his contest by a senate committee consisting of eight Republicans and one Democrat. The eight Republicans made short work of his contest. They voted not to hear Michael Beshoar, his witnesses or his lawyers, and with that the eight voted to sustain the action of the canvassing board. The lone Democrat, Webster Ballinger, wrote a minority report, but the senate quickly approved the majority report. Had the committee done anything different it wouldn't have changed the outcome, since the Republicans and coal barons controlled the legislature.

The morning after the committee's action, Michael's newspaper told its readers: "Barela Gets Seat. One More Step in Foul Conspiracy for Criminal's Friend." It also said, "The Peabody senators didn't waste any time disposing of the contests of Messrs. Ward and Beshoar. They simply told the contestors they didn't have any rights the corporations were bound to respect and that they could take their evidence and go back home and sit down."

Michael did just that, but he seated himself in his editorial chair rather than at home and banged away at Barela, Peabody, and the corporations in general.

"Little Jack Williams, a former tinhorn gambler in Trinidad, used to say that $20 stolen was just as good as $20 earned if used with the same frugality," he wrote. "Casimiro Barela no doubt reasons a seat in the Senate, stolen, is just as good as a seat elected to, if used to the same advantage. Jack and Casimiro reason alike."

Appeals were carried to the supreme court, but that body speedily found for the Republicans. In the Adams-Peabody contest, the assembly named a committee of fifteen members to investigate charges of fraud in the gubernatorial race. El Senador Perpetuado and other Peabody men were named to the committee, while Democratic newspapers ranted about such "horrible depravity" and even the *Pueblo Chieftain*, which had supported Peabody, complained the move was "a defiant violation of constitutional rights."

The gubernatorial contest dragged through February and into March. On March 15, the fifty-ninth day of the session, the investigating committee found the "legal disability of Alva Adams, governor de facto." An interrogatory was sent to the supreme court, which promptly answered in behalf of the Republicans. The majority party was having its troubles, though, as the whole bit was too raw for many Republican senators, some of whom were threatening revolt. A meeting of top Republican and corporation leadership was called to consider the crisis, and after hours of quarreling it was agreed that Peabody would be seated as governor for one day, but only one day, after which he would resign and Jesse McDonald would become the state's chief executive.

The conferees shook hands all around and sent for Peabody. He came and quickly, for these were the men who owned him: William G. Evans, representing the powerful Denver Tramway Company and the Denver Water Company; Frank J. Hearne and Cass Herrington, representing the Rockefeller-owned Colorado Fuel & Iron Company; Frank Guiterman, Guggenheim's American Smelting & Refining Company; J. M. Herbert, Colorado & Southern Railway, and Delos Chappell, Victor Fuel Company.

Governor Peabody was ordered to sign a previously dictated resignation, which the conferees then turned over to W.C. Boynton of Colorado Springs on his solemn promise to file it with the secretary of state within twenty-four hours after Governor Adams was out of office and Peabody was seated.

The stage was set. All that remained was to get Adams to agree to step out.

Adams had the fort but little hope of holding it against the forces arrayed by the opposition. Both the legislature and the state supreme court were stacked against him. Many of his advisors urged him to stay put, but the *Rocky Mountain News* editor Thomas Patterson told him to quit, saying he would be vindicated at the proper time. At the last moment, Adams yielded and resigned. Peabody was immediately given the oath of office and within twenty-four hours, as the timetable prescribed, Boynton dutifully trotted up to the secretary of state's office and filed the Peabody resignation. McDonald, another flunky of the interests, then became governor, the state's third in just a fraction more than twenty-four hours.

The Democrats had made a fight of it, but they had lost. Their candidate for the senate in Las Animas County was tired, disgusted, and mad. With each passing year the coal corporations and their railroad allies grew more powerful.

Chapter 14
A Final Toast to the Red Vest

THE HEATED POLITICAL BATTLE had an unexpected aftermath and one that was to prove a great embarrassment to the power structure. Senator Barela, contending his life was in danger, insisted on putting one of his more dangerous hirelings on the state payroll as his personal bodyguard. The senators and representatives had done a lot of odd things and put out a lot of patronage over the years, but none had had a personal bodyguard. However, with some corporation nudging, they obligingly agreed to give Joe Johnson a state salary as a "night watchman." The *Rocky Mountain News* taking note, said Johnson "is a stalwart Mexican, tall and swarthy, steely nerved and quick with a gun of such proportions as would chill the blood of the most courageous person. Senator Barela is occupying a seat to which another was justly elected."

Michael chuckled, but at the same time he hoped the "night watchman" and the *News* comment wouldn't give the public any idea that Colorado's oldest general practitioner and newspaper editor was about to invade the state capitol building with a view to assassinating El Senador Perpetuado. Instead he assassinated him in the columns of the *Advertiser:*

"Casimiro, who occupies a stolen seat, imagines that someone is thirsting after his heart's blood and has secured the services of his campaign bodyguard, Joe Johnson, to protect him until after the Legislature adjourns. Like all criminals, Barela is afraid that justice will be handed out to him and Joe's special duties are to see that Casimiro does not get what he deserves. The corporation managers of the Legislature regard Casimiro as too valuable a man to lose and assigned Johnson to look after him at state expense."

The physician looked over the piece when the first papers came off the press, and then added a little touch for the next edition:

"Verily, Casimiro must be nutty."

The crack, as was so often the case when Michael seemed to be joking or making light of something, was more than just an editorial jibe. He knew that Joe Johnson was dynamite and thought that Casimiro, who was no fool whatever else he might be, must know it, too.

As a physician and county judge, Michael had had a long and intimate association with the Johnson family. He had treated Joe Johnson the small boy for childhood diseases and Joe Johnson the hulking man for a variety of ailments including syphilis. He had cared for Joe's epileptic brother for many years and had been at Frank's bedside when he died of an embolism in the brain; and he had treated their mother for mental disturbances. As county judge he had presided from time to time over sanity hearings for members of the family. The idea of Joe Johnson's being a sometime deputy sheriff and a professional gunman didn't disturb the physician particularly, as most of the gunmen he had met on the frontier were about as bright and stable as Joe, but he was disturbed that a state senator could employ such a man as a bodyguard at state expense and flaunt him in the state capitol.

To the layman Joe Johnson was a big, 200-pounder with long black hair that hung down over his collar, and a huge black moustache. He had small, beady eyes that shifted constantly, the same beady eyes that Michael had noted in gunmen in the Ozarks, Dobytown, Pueblo, and Trinidad. Joe Johnson never looked at another man's face, only at the other man's hands. Some said this was a sure sign of "the steely-nerved gunman," but Michael didn't believe gunmen were steely nerved. His own theory was that most of the Johnson ilk were cowards who seldom shot anyone except in the back. He pointed, as proof that Johnson fitted this concept, to the manner in which he had killed William Wootton, one of Uncle Dick's sons, in a saloon in Hastings, Delos Chappell's coal camp. It had happened six years earlier when Johnson, working as the Hastings marshal, accosted Wootton in the saloon and told him to take off the gun he was wearing. Wootton agreed but said he would give the gun to the bartender, not to the likes of Joe Johnson. As Wootton turned to hand his gun to the bartender, Johnson drew his and shot Wootton to death. He was subsequently acquitted, but most people considered it a black mark on Johnson's shady record. He was also reputed to have killed a man in Walsenburg years ago.

During the Beshoar-Barela election fight, Johnson hadn't beaten or shot anyone, but voters were not unmindful that the glowering man who always stood at Barela's elbow was capable of it if his master gave so much as a nod.

When the legislature convened in January 1905 and Johnson went to Denver with El Senador with his title of "night watchman" in the capitol building, everything went smoothly for a time. But Joe, big, moody, and menacing, was omnipresent, and after awhile Barela's fellow senators became uneasy. Every time they turned around in senate chamber, cloakroom, or corridor there was the big, dark man with the tiny eyes and the bulge under his coat.

Finally it became too much, and Barela's colleagues, after holding a closed caucus, told him that Joe Johnson would have to go. The ensuing argument was long and bitter, but the senators were adamant. Johnson had to go.

Joe left for Trinidad almost immediately, but not without a protest to his patrón. He liked the big city and he liked the state capitol; the antics of the general assembly had amused him, and he found pleasure and a strange sense of power in standing around with the men who supposedly ran the state. Barela had blamed his fellow senators for Johnson's banishment, but Joe was positive that he had in some way offended his patrón. El Senador Perpetuado was a big man and didn't have to give in to anybody else, but *el senador*'s word was law, and Joe realized he had no other recourse than to go home, at least for the moment. He would be back on Barela's personal payroll, but he was resentful, nonetheless, feeling that he had been unfairly treated. Back in Trinidad he loafed about the streets and in the saloons, brooding over his exile and telling his friends there must be some way to get back in *el senador*'s good graces once more.

El Senador Perpetuado's bodyguard had a headache when he dragged himself out of bed shortly before noon Saturday, April 8, 1905. Telling his wife he didn't want any dinner, he put on his hat and walked downtown. He stopped in Aiello's Saloon, had a stiff drink, and then exchanged a word or two with attorney E. S. Bell in front of the Columbian Hotel before starting across the street toward the drugstore to get some headache tablets. At that moment, 1:42 P.M. by the best reckoning, he caught sight of John H. Fox walking toward the post office, which was on the ground floor in the rear of the First National Bank Building.

Johnny Fox was probably the most popular man in Trinidad and Las Animas County. It was true he had been defeated for the office of county treasurer at the last fall election, after serving three terms, but that was just a cyclic changing of the courthouse guard and in no way reflected on Johnny, who was liked and respected by everyone. A forty-two-year-old native of Paris, Kentucky, Johnny lived with his aged mother and two sisters, and was pointed out as the ideal son. When his mother's second husband, Dr. E. N. Cushing, was mortally wounded in a saloon brawl in 1880, the then seventeen-year-old Johnny was reported in the Trinidad newspapers to have taken his mother in his arms and said, in the words of a Victorian novel, "Fear not the future, Mother, for I will care for you, love you, cherish you as long as we both live."

On this particular morning, when the beady eyes of Joe Johnson fastened on his back, Johnny Fox had three minutes more to live.

After Johnny had completed his last term as treasurer, it had been found that his deputy, Vidal Shoblo, had stolen more than a thousand dollars in tax money. When Shoblo was arrested in Oakland, California, Sheriff R. W. Davis, a loyal servant of El Senador Perpetuado, decided to send Joe Johnson to return the erring Shoblo. Johnny Fox, who knew that Shoblo and Johnson were cousins and close friends, went to the commissioners and objected, arguing that Joe Johnson was not a proper person for the assignment. Late Friday afternoon, when Joe Johnson had his bag packed for a Saturday morning departure on the Santa Fe, the commissioners decided to send Lige Duling, one of their own number, after Shoblo. The turndown hit Joe Johnson like a physical blow; he sat numbly in a chair at home most of Friday night, holding his head in his hands. First El Senador Perpetuado had sent him home and now John Fox, a Democrat, had done him out of a trip he had very much wanted.

Joe Johnson walked rapidly toward the post office. He stopped in front of the door, taking no notice of the woman sitting in a buggy at the curb, pulled his .44-40 caliber revolver from its holster, and walked into the post office. If he even saw the young woman or the little girl getting mail at the bank of boxes, he paid no attention to them. His little eyes were fastened on Fox, who had just taken mail out of his box and was standing at a desk against the wall reading a copy of the *Pueblo Chieftain*. Joe walked up behind Johnny, put the heavy gun against his head just below the left ear, and fired.

While the young woman stood frozen and the little girl screamed and screamed, Joe Johnson walked calmly out of the post office, nodded to merchant F. E. Griswold, who was going in for his mail, turned south on Commercial Street to First Street where he met Squick Kreeger, son of Deputy Sheriff Louis Kreeger, and told him he had just killed a man. Kreeger told him he was under arrest and to go to the jail, a little more than a block east. Kreeger followed a short distance behind him. From that moment on events moved swiftly. In a matter of minutes, word of the murder was all over town; people said no, it couldn't be, but on the floor of the post office lay popular Johnny Fox, empty eyes staring at the ceiling and a pool of blood under his head.

Quickly, a crowd gathered a few yards away in the intersection of Main and Commercial. It swelled to two, three, and five hundred, then more than a thousand. Michael came hurry up Commercial Street from his office. There were cries of "Let's get him. Let's lynch him." Young attorney Earl Cooley, who had a new law office but few clients and had recently been defeated in a bid for election to the office of city attorney, emerged from a hardware store with a rope and led the shouting mob off toward the courthouse where Sheriff Davis had drawn up a line of deputies armed with Winchesters and revolvers. In the next few minutes, the crowd surged forward and then back, forward and back, but was finally convinced Davis meant business and his deputies would shoot.

Once it appeared the mob was not going to rush the jail, Sheriff Davis made a bold move. He had the Colorado & Southern Railroad move an engine and caboose to the point where the tracks crossed Chestnut Street two and a half blocks below the jail, then smuggled Johnson out a side door surrounded by deputies. They made a run for it down the street. When the crowd saw what was happening, it howled in pursuit. As the deputies and their prisoner, who stumbled and almost fell several times, reached the caboose, Johnson was shoved aboard, and the little train took off. A few hundred yards distant, after crossing the bridge over the river, the caboose came uncoupled. Once again the mob took up the chase, but the engineer backed up, coupled again, and managed to get off, delivering Johnson ninety miles north to Pueblo for safekeeping.

The excitement in Trinidad was intense. The *Advertiser* led its full front page coverage with the statement: "In the criminal annals of Las Animas County there has never been a crime that so completely stunned and horrified the community." Michael wrote two editorials. In one he said that "the brutal assassination of John Fox yesterday by the man who has heretofore acted as Barela's bodyguard is only the natural outgrowth of a continuous and open violation of the law that has been countenanced and winked at by the legal authorities in this county for the past two years." He cited assaults on UMWA organizers during the 1903 coal strike, said "every citizen who dares to criticize the men who steal elections, manipulate courts, employ thugs to wield the bludgeon or even commit murder, takes his own life in his hand. He does not know how soon he may be called on to meet the fate they have handed to others." In the second editorial he described the murder as one of "the saddest blows ever to fall on Trinidad . . . strong men sobbed in the streets yesterday when they fully grasped that their friend was dead. Grown to manhood in the community, his course in life, undeviating and straightforward through all the years, watched by all around him, John H. Fox was loved by his fellow man with a love that falls to few mortals in this age."

Emotions were still running high Wednesday as more than five thousand persons gathered to hear former Governor Alva Adams deliver the eulogy at the funeral. His moving message was a simple one: "Here is where reason ends and faith begins." Meanwhile Delos Chappell had arrived from Denver in his private railroad car, and he and El Senador Perpetuado had had several conferences.

When Joe was arraigned May 8, two surprising things happened. First it became obvious that the corporations and El Senador Perpetuado were going to abandon Johnson, at least publicly. Secondly, since Johnson didn't have any money for a lawyer, District Judge Jesse G. Northcutt appointed Earl Cooley to defend him. With the same enthusiasm he had shown in leading the mob, Cooley went about preparing the defense. In a conference with his family physician and fellow University of Michigan alumnus, the young attorney quizzed the old doctor closely about the Johnsons. It was true, the physician said, that Johnson was insane and that there was a great deal of insanity in his family. "You shall be my principal witness," Cooley said enthusiastically. "I will plead Johnson not guilty by reason of hereditary insanity." If Cooley gave so much as a thought to the fact that Michael had been a close friend of Johnny Fox and had only recently been the victim of Barela perfidy, he never mentioned it.

At the trial everything moved with smoothness and dispatch. A jury, composed primarily of cattlemen, was quickly selected from a venire of fifty-four men. District Attorney A. Watt McHendrie used only nine challenges. Cooley used his full quota of fourteen, and nineteen other prospective jurors were excused by Judge Northcutt for cause. The courtroom was packed, but every person had been searched for weapons at the doors. A deputy sheriff sat directly in front of Johnson, another at his right, a third at his immediate left, and a fourth directly behind him. The gunman sat stolidly, a contradiction to newspaper reports that he was so nervous he paced his cell and was living on strong black coffee and black cigars.

The district attorney had twenty-two witnesses, but his case rested primarily on the testimony of the young woman in the post office, Miss Blanche Albert of Paris, Texas, who had been visiting in Trinidad with a sister; her brother-in-law's mother, who had been waiting for her outside of the post office in a buggy; Marion Ingall, the twelve-year-old girl; and a man who had heard Johnson growl the day before the killing that "Fox ought to have his head shot off." Miss Albert testified she had not seen the shot fired, but when she heard it, she turned and saw Johnson with the smoking gun in his hand. Little Marion gave similar testimony.

When Earl Cooley put on his defense, he had several members of the Johnson family, including Joe's wife, all of whom were ready to testify to insanity in Joe and the family. And he had Dr. Michael Beshoar whom he carefully qualified as a medical expert.

Q. Have you become acquainted with Joseph Johnson and his family during your residence here?

A. Yes.

Q. Do you know Joseph Johnson's mother?

A. I do.

Q. Did you ever as county judge pass upon her mental condition?

A. I don't remember.

If that startled Cooley, he didn't show it. He continued the questioning blithely, bringing out that the physician had cared for the family for more than twenty years and had treated Joe for syphilis. Then he got to the big question: "Is Joe Johnson insane?" The answer: "I have known Johnson since he was a boy and have been his physician. I have never noticed any indication or symptom of insanity about him." Startled, Cooley stood in front of his star witness, hand upraised and eyes popping: "What about his mother?" he boomed. The old physician favored Cooley and then the jury with a benign smile before he replied in an even voice: "A little nervous perhaps."

Cooley tried to pull it out with other witnesses, but it was hopeless. The case went to the jury at 5:20 P.M. the second day of the trial. Thirty-eight minutes and one ballot later, Joe Johnson was found guilty of murder in the first degree. The penalty was fixed at death by hanging.

That evening Earl Cooley stormed into the physician's office. The young man who had been almost afraid to speak to such an imposing figure as M. Beshoar on the station platform in Ann Arbor two years earlier, now shook his big fist under the old doctor's nose and yelled, "You dirty crook. You scoundrel . . . you liar . . . you no good liar . . . you murderer."

The physician listened quietly and then said, "Now, Earl, sit down over there. I want to talk to you a bit. You are a fine young man and you are going to make a fine lawyer. And I must say I admire you for the way you have done everything you could for your client. You have conducted yourself well and are a credit to your profession."

"And what about you and your profession?" Cooley asked hotly.

"Now, Earl, calm down. I was only doing what I could to make certain that son of a bitch hangs."

All summer the word was around that Joe Johnson was threatening to tell tales but that El Senador Perpetuado was keeping him quiet by assuring him that he had secured pardons and commutations for nineteen convicted murders during his tenure in the senate and that he would save Joe's neck too. Emphasis was given the story in September when Johnson gave a confident interview in his cell on death row in which he was quoted as saying: "When I get out of this trouble I shall go far away and start life over again. I have had all the excitement I want, but I was not really in my right mind when I shot Fox. I was crazy then, but the jury refused to believe it."

The Denver Post also reported that none of the attorneys connected with the case, the judge, or the jurors would enter into a plan of Senator Barela to seek clemency from the State Board of Pardons, and that Johnson would be hanged the night of Friday, September 15. Warden John Cleghorn announced he had tested a hempen rope and determined it would sustain 450 pounds dropped six feet; but that, instead of dropping Joe Johnson through a trap, a new device, triggered by a heavy weight, would jerk him into the air and break his neck.

On Wednesday, September 13, lawyer Cooley, belatedly deciding to ask the State Supreme Court for a temporary stay pending an appeal, boarded the night train for Denver. His train got in at 8 A.M. and he went directly to the statehouse. As it was still locked, he sat down on the steps on the East Colfax Avenue side to wait for the doors to open. Seeing a newsboy go by, he hailed him and bought a paper to while away the time. As he started to read, the first head that caught his eye was:

JOE JOHNSON HANGED

For a week the physician regaled Trinidad with the story of the advance in the execution date without public announcement and the story of Joe's last hours: "Barela kept sending him word: 'Don't worry, don't talk. When they come for you, don't talk; when they stand you on the trap, don't talk, because at the last second we will rush in and save you.'"

Not only did El Senador Perpetuado not rush in at the last moment, he abandoned his henchman completely three days before the hanging when, in an interview, he said that he had not made any effort to save Johnson, that he had no thought of doing so, and that Johnson should hang.

With son Ben doing more and more of the medical work, Michael got additional recruits in the early summer of 1905: daughter Burnie had earned her medical degree and had married an eye specialist, who joined the staff, and son John, his big, popping brown eyes still filled with visions of baseball rather than crowns and plates, had his degree in dentistry and a spanking new office with the Drs. Beshoar. John had given up any thought of being a professional fighter or champion bicycle racer but remained passionately devoted to baseball. While in the navy he had played first base for the "U.S.S. Wheeling" team and later had played the same position for Western State Dental College in Kansas City. He had been first baseman for the nearby Engleville team and had had his own team, the Beshoar Athletic Club, in 1904. The B.A.C., with the old physician footing the bills, had won the championship of southern Colorado in its first year of competition. In this summer of 1905, the B.A.C. again looked like a hot outfit, much hotter in fact than its aging sponsor, who was perfectly happy when Steve Patrick, proprietor of the Big 6 Saloon, wanted to take it over. The Big 6 had a fine pitcher, easily won the Colorado championship and was scheduled to go to the Southwestern Baseball tournament in Albuquerque, New Mexico, when a crisis developed. Pitcher Tommy Lochard was ill. First baseman John Beshoar rushed to his father for assistance.

The doctor had hoped he had heard the last of baseball, but a crisis was a crisis and he thought he might help. Without any fuss or feathers he arranged for Ralph Glaze, a Dartmouth College pitcher who was rated as one of the top amateurs in the United States, to put on a Trinidad uniform for the tournament. It was agreed all around that the name of Ralph Pierce would do for the purposes of the tournament and preservation of Glaze's amateur standing.

The team made a creditable showing in Albuquerque, and the physician was quite proud of it, feeling a keen sense of involvement with John at first base and his pitching ringer on the mound, but the team failed to win the tourney. However, Glaze, alias Pierce, thought he had made a discovery in the person of a big Indian boy named John Tortes, the catcher for the Clifton, Arizona, team. Glaze and John lured Tortes to an Albuquerque restaurant and asked him how he'd like to play football at Dartmouth and catch for the college baseball team.

Tortes said he wasn't much interested in football and had never played any, but later in the day Glaze got the tournament's chief umpire, former heavyweight champion of the world, James J. Jeffries, to talk to Tortes about the glories of Dartmouth and the opportunities it would afford. The husky Indian lad admired Jeffries and said if Jeffries thought Dartmouth was a good idea he would go. However, there was a problem. Although Dartmouth's charter made special provisions for admission of Indians and payment of their tuition, Tortes never had gotten beyond the third grade in a reservation school. John said his father could fix anything and the problem should be taken to him. At a subsequent conference in the physician's office in Trinidad, Michael listened thoughtfully before coming up with a solution: Son Ben's name was removed from his Trinidad High School diploma with a chemical, and the Indian's name was put in its place. The superintendent of schools and the principal of the high school were instructed to refer any inquiries from Dartmouth to M. Beshoar, president of the Trinidad Board of Education.

When Glaze and his prize caught a train east for Hanover and the opening of the fall term, the senior Dr. Beshoar solemnly adjured the young Indian always to uphold the honor and traditions of Trinidad High School. Alas, though Tortes was vigorously tutored by relays of enthusiastic young volunteers at Dartmouth, he didn't survive beyond the second semester when some sharp-eyed spoilsport discovered his high school diploma had been issued to a reddish-haired lad, five feet six inches tall. But Tortes, as Big Chief Meyers, made out all right, going on to a notable career under John McGraw as the great catcher for the New York Giants. Thousands would thrill to the announcement: "Today's battery: Mathewson and Meyers."

Family opposition was something new to Michael, long the ruler absolute of his household, but he sensed that the family was against him the morning he casually remarked at breakfast that he was planning to buy an automobile. The response was raised eyebrows and stares. The day before he had had trouble with a new horse while making house calls; it had balked and tried to kick its way out of the shafts. Unhitching it, he had tied up the harness straps and mounted the beast, but after it had pitched two or three times, he slid off, tied it to a nearby pole, and made the rest of his calls on foot, no mean accomplishment in hilly Trinidad for a man of seventy-two, burdened with a heavy bag. When he got home, weary from the unaccustomed exercise, he sent a liveryman to get the animal, announcing, "We are retiring that horse because he hasn't treated us right. He will be replaced by a Christian horse." By morning he had decided the replacement would be an automobile. He had been longing for one since the day W. E. Pierce had chugged down Commercial Street in his one-cylinder Oldsmobile and had stopped to show it off to the physician, just as Michael had shown off the town's first buggy at almost the same spot on the same street thirty-seven years earlier. Now there were three more

cars in town, all Oldsmobiles. The physician had had several rides
in them and had made up his mind to have one of his own.

In the days that followed, he talked about an automobile several times. Annie thought he ought to wait awhile; perhaps automobiles would be nothing more than a fad. Ben joined his mother in
urging delay, saying undoubtedly they would work but that they
were still in an experimental stage. The old physician thought the
two had a very mossback attitude. "Everyone will be riding in one
of them before long," he snorted.

Without saying anything more to the family, he entered into correspondence with the Daimler company, looking toward purchase
of either an automobile or a good engine suitable for mounting on
one of his carriages. While the correspondence was still in progress, he made a trip to Louisville, Kentucky, to attend the eighth
annual reunion of the Association of Medical Officers of the Army
and Navy of the Confederacy. On the way home he stopped off in
Kansas City to see Bonnie and her family and to visit an automobile dealer. After an enthusiastic sales talk and a ride, he was allowed to handle the car himself. He found that he couldn't crank
it and that, once it was cranked, it was difficult for him to operate;
and when the car broke down twice during the demonstration,
he decided it was not for him. When he got home, he told the family
he had decided to pass up automobiles until they were more ad-
vanced. "I can sometimes repair a human being and in an emergency I can do the same for a horse, but I couldn't keep one of
those things running, at least at their present stage," he said.

He was weary from the trip and very much feeling his age when
the State Board of Health announced a few days later that a survey
had disclosed that Dr. M. Beshoar of Trinidad had been in practice longer than any other physician in Colorado. The announcement inspired the Trinidad doctors to give a dinner for their distinguished colleague. The toastmaster, Dr. T. J. Forhan, opened the
dinner by saying: "There is no clergyman present so we will ask
our oldest and most pious member, Dr. M. Beshoar, to say grace."
The old doctor complied:

"Bless us, Dear Father, and bless these five dollar plates."

When he was called upon to make his talk, being introduced as
the Nestor of Colorado Medicine, he told his colleagues: "There
are some who think I have practiced too long and have forgotten
what I learned in my youth. If so, it is to my discredit. A physician

must be a student all of his life if he wishes to be competent to winnow the grain from the chaff. I have been on the frontier fifty-three years. I went west with the frontier, but when I got to Trinidad I met another stream of civilization coming in from the West and I could find no further place to go."

He gave the doctors a good deal of history and then retired early, weary from his exertions.

He discontinued the *Medical Educator* some weeks later, telling his associates that, while the Nestor of Colorado Medicine might have some obligation to continue the magazine, the Nestor of Medicine felt an increasing urge to conserve his energies as much as possible. He would continue to edit the *Advertiser*, but he was frankly in the market for a suitable buyer. He also insisted he was through with politics and that he had shot his last round as a candidate and active participant in the campaign of 1904. When he was approached as a possible candidate for mayor he turned the committee down with scarcely more than a wave of his hand. But he was still good for an editorial round or two when the need arose. An example occurred during the summer of 1905 when he tried to provoke the Colorado Supreme Court into jailing him for contempt. The court, in a far-reaching decision, had ousted several Democratic officeholders in Denver County and given their posts to Republicans.

The *Rocky Mountain News* had responded to the court's decision with a dramatic cartoon that filled most of the upper half of the front page. It depicted the justices leaning over the bench with their right hands extended, thumbs turned down. Chief Justice Gabbert stood in front of the bench, holding an executioner's bloody axe. Prostrate in front of him lay the headless body of Denver's Sheriff Armstrong while Judge Johnson, treasurer Elder, and other officials stood waiting their turn to be beheaded. On a shelf to Chief Justice Gabbert's left rested eight funeral urns bearing the labels Alva Adams, senators Ward, Beshoar, Born, Healy, McGuire, Belford, and Delaney. The caption read: "The Lord High Executioner— NEXT."

The supreme court cited editor Tom Patterson for contempt. The physician wrote a scathing denunciation of the court, which he printed on the front page of the *Advertiser* and which was reprinted on the front page of the *Rocky Mountain News* the same morning:

When the people are led to believe that the decisions of the highest tribunal of the state are not based upon right and justice, but are dictated by corrupt wire-pullers and unscrupulous corporations preying on the rights of the people, it may be truthfully said a sad state of affairs exists. The court may arraign persons who express their contempt for a court believed to be subservient to corrupt influences, but the severest penalty will not purge the soiled judicial ermine. . . . Colorado is a pitiful sight at this time and if all who feel contempt for the highest tribunal were to be imprisoned, and those who do not made jailers, it would convert the state into a prison where one guard would have to do duty for ten, twenty or more prisoners.

He signed the editorial and had messengers deliver marked copies to each of the justices in the state capitol. The supreme court quickly decided it would drop its action against Tom Patterson. The blast at the court led to a series of editorials over the next few weeks attacking the corporations and their political dupes. Senator Barela answered in a speech or two and immediately drew fire in the *Advertiser*:

Senator Don Casimiro Barela, lord of the southern end of Colorado, was in town yesterday looking as prosperous, if not a little more so, than ever. He waxes sleeker in appearance, and waxes his moustache blacker as the years roll onward, and he looks just the same now as he looked twenty or more years ago. Dr. M. Beshoar, who defeated Senator Barela at the last election and was then deprived of his right to sit in the Senate through fraud, has a story on the don which may explain the prosperous appearance. The doctor said, "When I first knew Senator Barela his worldly possessions amounted to a team of steers. He used them for freighting for a time and then, tiring of that, turned the steers out to pasture. In a few years those steers had multiplied into a large herd of cattle."

Late in the year he sold the *Advertiser* but continued as its editor, with the masthead reading "M. Beshoar, Editor and Sole Owner" through the issue of January 7, 1906. He bowed out of the *Advertiser* after twenty-three years as its founder, editor, and publisher without a valedictory or word of any kind to the subscribers. He ran mostly foreign news on the front page in his last newspaper: revolution raging in Russia, and the United States attempting to mediate a dispute between Germany and France over Morocco, but he also gave a good page-one play to a scarlet fever epidemic in the county.

On February 4, 1906, a month after the *Advertiser* passed to other hands, he announced his retirement, telling Annie, "If I am to live much longer in this altitude I will have to take it easier. It is a hard thing to do, but I have no other course." He was fairly vigorous, walked with a springy step, and his mind was clear and alert, but he tired easily. In a statement to the Las Animas County Medical Society at a regular meeting, he said:

"I will retire on my birthday, February 25. I want to thank all of you for your many courtesies and kindnesses in the past and I hope I have conducted myself in the same way toward each of you.

"I will not discontinue my office practice, but I will leave the running around that a doctor must do to my son and to all of you. I'll continue to be a hanger-on around the office and around Trinidad, that is for sure."

The first thing he did was to take a trip. He went to Indiana to visit his father's grave and his half brothers and sisters. While there he gave several newspaper interviews and was so tickled when they referred to him as "a millionaire from the West" that he carried the clippings around in his wallet until they were frayed. A quick run on to Pennsylvania and then to Arkansas proved disasters. He knew almost no one in Pennsylvania and found that attempting to establish conversational bridges with the sons and grandsons, and even great-grandchildren, of friends long dead was a painful experience. In Pocahontas he found exactly eleven persons who had been living there when he was captured by the Federals. To make matters worse, it rained steadily, all day and all night, for the four days he was there. When he left Poca, he realized that the places of his youth were part of a very distant past and that he had only one home: Trinidad.

Before returning to Colorado he made a semiprofessional visit to Chicago at the request of his daughter Bonnie, who had moved there with her family from Kansas City. Her eldest son, Michael, needed a tonsillectomy and she wanted Papa there even if he didn't do the surgery. It was done at Rush Medical College. Grandfather Michael stood at the surgeon's elbow until it was finished, although he confessed later to Ben that he would rather have been almost any place else but that he was glad to make Bonnie feel more at ease about such a minor operation.

He wrote Ben:

> I'm disgusted with the miserableness of the miserable climate of Chicago and feel like changing it for a better one. The day I arrived it was as dark and cloudy as midnight and the sun has not shed its rays on this beclouded place exceeding five minutes since my arrival. I hope my presence is not to blame for this condition, but on the chance it is I think I had better go away and let the people have the benefit of the lifegiving rays of the sun before it is too late.
>
> Verily,
> M. Beshoar.

While many of his older patients would not let any other doctor touch them, there were fewer of them with each passing month. Michael mostly puttered around his office. The X-ray, the Finsen ray, and anything else electrical fascinated him. Occasionally he and Ben would have words, usually about the older man's increasing tendency to be careless about asepsis. At times the son was not sure that his father really understood the need for it. And sometimes Michael would pull some stunt that would have Ben in a high state of nerves. There was the day they were climbing the office stairs together after a beer and a quick lunch in a nearby saloon. Ben had been greatly embarrassed at lunch to hear the latest story on his father and have the old doctor confess that it was true. It seemed that two days earlier Michael had been in Richter's saloon at noon with a huge schooner of beer and a sandwich on which he was gnawing with the side of his mouth. When District Attorney A. Watt McHendrie came and stood by him, the old doctor acknowledged his greeting and then said, "You know, young man, I've practiced medicine for fifty-three years, but there is one thing I'll never understand about the human body."

Attorney McHendrie asked politely: "And what is that Doctor?"

The physician gnawed a few seconds more, then grumbled, "Well, sir, I can't understand why a man in his seventies loses his teeth and not his testes."

As they got to the top of the stairs, Michael, stopping to catch his breath, glanced out the window. He grabbed Ben's arm. "Look at that," he said. The window looked out on the tar and gravel roof of an adjoining building. On it was a wire fly trap, filled with dead flies and buzzing flies. Ben said, "What a disgusting thing. We'd better ask the people next door to get that thing out of sight."

"You know something, Ben," the old physician said, "If a man swallows a fly and knows it, he will vomit. I swallowed one once unknowingly and promptly vomited. There was the fly. They must have an emetic property."

Agreeing that it might be so, Ben thought no more about it until four days later when he saw his father placing a bottle on the medicine shelves in the office. The Drs. Beshoar wrote prescriptions, but they also dispensed, as many patients wanted their medicine from their doctor and not from some store.

"What is that, Papa?" Ben asked.

Michael beamed at him.

"It is my newest concoction," he said. "I have labeled it 'Tincture of Moscas Domesticas.'"

Ben didn't have to ask anything more; with a sinking feeling he realized what was in the brown bottle.

"The next time that old chronic of a Jerome comes in I want to try it on him," the old man said, rubbing his hands together. "I am sure it is an emetic and a good one. Jerome has been getting medicine from us for years and selling it. He's never paid us a dime, not a dime."

Ben thought his father was joking, but a day or two later when Jerome showed up complaining of many and sundry pains, the senior Dr. Beshoar listened with a sympathy and interest he had not shown in Jerome for several years. His face was filled with concern.

"We have a new preparation that is just the thing for you," he said finally. "Ben, Jerome's symptoms are serious. Bring me the new tincture and a spoon."

The young physician shook his head and made frantic signs behind Jerome's back.

"Be quick about it, Ben," the father snapped. "There is no time to lose."

Jerome decided he really must be sick. He slumped in his chair.

With a shrug, Ben finally brought the bottle and spoon to his father. The old man filled the big spoon.

"Now open wide, Jerome."

Ben had never seen such a diabolical grin on his father's face or anyone else's for that matter.

"Get a basin, quickly," his father told him. "It will work. I'll wager a new hat on it."

Ben put the basin beside Jerome. The wall clock ticked. The Drs. Beshoar waited, staring at Jerome in fascination. Suddenly Jerome squirmed a little, turned deathly pale, and rumbled. He missed the basin by a matter of inches.

"A discovery, Ben, a discovery," the old physician said when he could compose himself enough to talk about it. "We must put it on the market. I can see the label: 'M. Beshoar's Famous Tincture of Moscas Domesticas.'"

But such episodes were infrequent, fortunately for Ben. More often the father's long experience was of value. He might not be up on the latest in medicine, but he knew a great deal about human beings and their ailments, and he had practiced medicine a long time, often under adverse conditions when his only guides were his own judgment and ingenuity. There was the day Mrs. Nuavez was brought in from Aguilar, a town twenty miles north of Trinidad. She was paralyzed from the neck down as a result of being thrown from a buggy in a runaway.

The older man took immediate charge of the case. While Ben watched with misgivings, his father summoned a harnessmaker to the office, sketched out for him on paper what he wanted made. He had the janitor rig a pulley on the wall close to the high ceiling in the office waiting room. When the harnessmaker returned with a strong leather head harness for Mrs. Nuavez, the old physician fitted it on her very carefully. Then, passing a light but strong rope through the pulley, he hung Mrs. Nuavez by her head in the presence of Ben, John, his son-in-law, and various other people who rushed in to see what was going on.

Later, to Ben's "My God, think what a smart lawyer could have done to us in court," his father said, "Now, Ben, we're not in court and it worked." Indeed it had. The woman made a nice recovery.

In addition to puttering around the office, Michael played a satisfying role as the town patriarch. He walked between his home and office each day, sometimes with a cane, but more often without. It was a slow walk, not because he was infirm, but because he stopped to talk to every child and adult he met. He asked the children about their schoolwork, their teachers, their games, and their parents; the adults about themselves, their work, and their families. He almost always had an anecdote or two for them. On Saturdays, when the weather was warm, he would gather neighborhood children under the willow tree at the back of his house and cut their hair with clippers; and he began to take a personal interest in the flower garden. When he found that Ben's wife Fay, was carrying his first Beshoar grandchild, he cut several baskets of his ever-blooming tea roses and completely filled her back screen door with the fragrant blooms. He was repeatedly sought out by young reporters who interviewed him on a wide range of subjects varying from the proper name for Fisher's Peak, which he contended should be called Raton Peak, to how to keep young. His recipe: be moderate in everything and don't worry about anything.

One of his major interests in 1907, as it had been for several years past, was the Old Settlers Association of Las Animas County, which he had headed continuously as president. At each annual meeting he read the names of those who had "passed on" during the preceding twelve months and then delivered his "farewell address." In the fall of 1907, when eighty old men and women gathered on the courthouse lawn for their picnic, their president was all smiles and good cheer, but he was sick at heart. In past years the list of those who had died usually contained no more than ten or twelve names. The list in his pocket this time contained forty-nine names.

This year he had furnished most of the food, including a large number of cantaloupes from the Arkansas Valley. The pioneers ate and told stories and had a fine time. Michael ate sparingly. Heavy eating, like so many other pleasures, was something for the young and not for men of his age. When it came time to make his address, he passed up the list of those who had died. No one asked for it; everyone seemed to understand that it should not be read. In his talk he told them, "I do not expect to be with you again, but I want you to know that each and every one of you is forever in my heart." When he had finished, A. W. Archibald, who was eighty, but still firm of step and mind, and S. W. DeBusk gave short anecdotal talks.

When it was all over, someone gathered up the leftover cantaloupes and sent them to the Beshoar residence. It was two days later that he ate one and became ill. Ben was called to see him at the house.

"I'm all right," the old doctor said. "Weak, but nothing to worry about. I believe I'll stay around the house as I have some paper work I can do here."

He spent the rest of the day at home, leaving only once to go next door for a short visit with Fay and a peek at her six-months-old boy.

The short walk and visit tired him, and when he got back to his own house, he went to bed. Annie was solicitous, but he assured her that he was better, just a little tired.

"Annie, I'm a little chilly. I wonder if you would bring me my mother's blanket?" he asked. "I think I'll sleep awhile." She got him the cherished blanket, which had been woven in the 1840s in Pennsylvania by his mother, Susannah. Annie spread it over him.

She was scheduled to attend the meeting of the Eastern Star, of which she was Worthy Matron, that night but had decided not to go. When she peeked in to see whether he wanted any supper, he was awake and asked if she was going to the meeting. "I can't go with you feeling this way," she replied.

"You go right ahead, Annie. They will be expecting you and I am perfectly all right."

Annie left the house at seven-thirty. When she returned at ten, he was sitting up in bed reading.

"How do you feel, Doctor?"

"Fine, but still a little weak, probably because I haven't eaten anything all day. Would you make me an eggnog, Annie?"

She was back upstairs in a few minutes.

"Here you are, Doctor. This will help you get to sleep."

He put aside his book and took the glass.

"Ben was here shortly after nine. Annie, if anything should happen to me . . . "

She shushed him as she turned to her bureau to take down her hair: "Nothing is going to happen to you."

"Did the Eastern Star sisters have a big time?" he asked.

While she gave him the details of the meeting, he sipped his drink.

"Here is the glass, Annie."

As she reached to take it, it slipped from his hand and fell to the floor. His head rolled gently on his pillow, but he made no sound. Annie cried, "Doctor, doctor . . . !" and then ran down the stairs to call Ben from his house next door.

The news passed swiftly around town by word of mouth. Dan

Stone, editor of the *Chronicle-News* and an antagonist of long standing, hurried to his office after midnight and set to work with pencil and paper. His product, which appeared the next day along with a detailed story of Michael Beshoar's life, read:

> Dr. Beshoar is dead.
>
> Last night, while the city lay in deep midnight silence, Death claimed him for his own, and the great-hearted physician, who had fought off the Grim Reaper thousands of times for others—whose whole life had been devoted to keeping the Shadow at bay—answered the call.
>
> The end was as he would have wished, suddenly, yet peacefully. And throughout the length and breadth of these United States, wherever he has been during his long and eventful life there will be men and women who will shed a tear in his memory. In the halls of learning, in the dwellings of the rich and in the humble homes of the poor he was loved, and justly so.
>
> And here, in Southern Colorado, where he has spent a half century doing good among the people, in the cities, and over the broad mesas where the long grass waves, and deep in remote cañons where the feet of white men seldom tread, his multitude of dark skinned friends will hear of his passing; in the pueblos and among the scattered huts of the sheepherders, the Answering of the Call will be told, and their heads will be bowed in sorrow, for he was ever and always their true, staunch friend in their greatest hours of need.
>
> Such was the man who has gone.
>
> Eloquent words of tribute will be paid over his clay, but these, however true, will someday be forgotten.
>
> But in thousands of hearts a silent tribute will always be given him; and this is the greatest homage of all and the one which will abide unto eternity.

During Michael Beshoar's lifetime he took care of literally thousands without compensation or any hope of financial reward. He practiced medicine because he loved it and because he had that all-important qualification, the healing instinct. As with other ambitious men on the western frontier, he hoped to make a fortune, but he hoped to make it out of the natural resources of the area, not out of the pockets of the poor.

He fought the rapacious coal barons of the time in his newspaper and in the political arena; sometimes he won, but more often he lost as his opponents were the financial titans of the day—the Rockefellers, the Osgoods, the Guggenheims—and their vast fortunes were used freely to buy governors and legislators and to employ private armies to enforce their will.

Although he left a good deal of property, his chief legacies to his children, particularly his sons, physician Ben, dentist John, and lawyer-judge Bertram, were compassion for the poor and the minorities, a special feeling for the Spanish-speaking peoples of the Southwest, and a willingness to carry the battle to the forces of special privilege. Dr. Ben, often at the risk of his life, was to fight the coal barons in the political field and, as a doctor for the United Mine Workers of America, during the long and bloody coal strike of 1913–14, which saw women and children massacred at Ludlow, a few short miles north of Trinidad, by Rockefeller gunmen.

Michael Beshoar lost his first son in a tragic tangle of war and frontier circumstances, but the children Annie bore him, without exception, loved and honored him, almost to the point of veneration. Decades after he was gone, "Papa" remained their inspiration and a strong influence in their lives. Whatever they were doing and whatever the problem confronting them, their conversations were sprinkled with "well, Papa always said. . . ."

Annie, devoted to "the doctor" during the thirty-five years of their marriage, remained devoted to him during the twenty-seven years of her widowhood, keeping his books, papers, and traps intact as long as she had the physical strength to do so. Annie, her parents, and five of her children, all rest with him—and with Mike—in the stone mausoleum overlooking his town and the Valley of the Purgatoire.

Author Notes

CHAPTER I

Michael Beshoar was surgeon of the Sixteenth Arkansas Militia under Major (later Colonel) James T. Martin from 1858 to 1861. When the militia was reorganized in 1861, he was elected chief surgeon of Colonel Shaver's Regiment. He accompanied Colonel Shaver to Little Rock where, on June 20, he was examined by a board of examiners and was commissioned as a surgeon. In September, 1861, when the Arkansas troops were transferred to the Confederate service, he was commissioned as a regular surgeon and was appointed chief medical officer of General Hardee's Division, a position he held until relieved by Montrose Pullen who received the appointment from General Cooper over General Hardee's objections. Beshoar then became surgeon of the Seventh Arkansas.

The surgical technique used by Michael Beshoar at Shiloh was somewhat similar to the so-called "guillotine" technique used by other southern surgeons under field conditions. The description used in this chapter is Michael Beshoar's own description as related to his son, Dr. Ben B. Beshoar, many years after the historic battle. As in the account of the action in the hospital tent, Surgeon Beshoar gave attention to arms and legs, but men with abdominal wounds were put aside as such wounds were almost invariably fatal. Men with chest wounds fared better, the mortality being only 60 percent!

CHAPTER II

Most southern doctors relied on copaiba, an oleoresin derived from several species of South American trees, to allay inflammations of mucous membranes, especially those of the genito-urinary tract. Dr. Beshoar's prescription for gonorrhea: gum acacia and white sugar, of each 7 oz.; compound spirits of lavender, one fluid dram; balsam copaiba, 7 fluid oz.; camphor water, 7 fluid oz.; spirits of nitri dulcis and tincture of cubebs, each one fluid ounce. The dose: a tablespoonful three times per day.

Surgeon Latham was a colorful adventurer. After his service at Fort Sedgwick he intended to follow Michael Beshoar south into central and southern Colorado, but he never made it. He became a Union Pacific Railroad surgeon, then a Wyoming stockman and booster. He had a fine ranch near Laramie and was one of the organizers of the Wyoming Stock Graziers Association. He went bankrupt in 1873; next turned up in Japan as the superintendent of a railway system and an official of the Imperial College. Still later he sold real estate in northern California, died in Alameda, California in 1902.

Dr. Gehrung practiced medicine in Denver before going to the medical college in St. Louis. He got his degree in 1870 from the College of Physicians and Surgeons in St. Louis, again practiced in Denver for a time before moving to St. Louis, where he earned a reputation as a specialist in obstetrics and gynecology.

Dr. Harrison A. Lemen received his M.D. from St. Louis Medical College in 1864, and subsequently practiced in Denver. He was a member of the University of Denver School of Medicine faculty and president of the Colorado State Medical Society, 1881–82.

CHAPTER III

It is likely Surgeon Beshoar read John Erichsen's *The Science and Art of Surgery* (Philadelphia, 1860) as he was using this reference at Fort Kearny. Erichsen took a grave view of scalp wounds, held that they were not only serious in themselves but were more likely "to be followed by erysipelas than those of other parts of the body." He recommended stitching, application of water dressings, and purgation. Under Surgeon Beshoar's treatment, Private Twyman made a good recovery and was mustered out of his regiment Nov. 29, 1865. He returned to Hodgenville, Kentucky, where he ran a store, became town marshal, and fathered a large family. He wrote periodic letters to Dr. Beshoar for thirty years, describing the state of his health in minute detail.

The Dobytown property was purchased from Major John Talbot of the First Regiment Nebraska Volunteers for $650 cash "in hand paid." The physical description, contained in the bill of sale signed by Talbot, was typical of the day: "Three lots and houses situated on the south side of Main Street in Kearney City, Nebraska Territory and described thus—The lot lying between Deuel and Compton's residences and Charles Diefendorf's Saloon and bounded on the east and west by Main Street—and bounded on the south by a line running parallel from the north line and one hundred and twenty feet therefrom—also all that piece or parcel of ground described as follows: Beginning from the northwest corner of Charles Diefendorf's Saloon—running west to the northeast corner of the sod house directly west of Diefendorf's Saloon—thence south to a point directly west of the southwest corner of Leighton's Corral—thence east to a point directly south of the beginning thence north to the starting point. Also a piece of ground described as follows: Beginning at the northwest corner of Leighton's Corral and running west twenty feet—thence east twenty feet—thence north to the starting point."

Michael Beshoar would have been able to purchase oxen for his wagons for less money, but having become accustomed to mules in Arkansas and in the army, he understood them better. Besides, mules were capable of covering as many as twenty-four miles a day without being pushed as compared to the ten or twelve miles that could be expected of oxen and at the end of a trip would bring higher prices on resale. Also mules were not susceptible to anthrax, hoof and mouth disease, and the so-called Texas fevers that plagued oxen. While a heavy mule brought $125 in most markets during this period, Beshoar was able to buy his mules at $75 per head from Fort Kearny's surplus stock.

CHAPTER IV

The small stream that passes through Trinidad arises in the Culebra Range forty miles to the west. It was first named El Rio de Las Animas Perdidas in Purgatorio (the River of Lost Souls in Purgatory) by the early Spanish, who heard sounds resembling moans and groans while they were camped along its banks. The French shortened the Spanish name to Purgatoire and the Anglo-Americans distorted Purgatoire to Picketwire. The Purgatoire drains into the Arkansas River.

In its January 16, 1868, issue the *Rocky Mountain News* told its readers that the Pueblo correspondent responsible for its reports of the Trinidad affair "was either non compos mentis or under the influence of sod corn."

Deputy Sheriff Juan Cristobal Tafoya won respect on all sides for his conduct, particularly from M. Beshoar, who praised him for saying no to the Ute offer of help. Gutierriez seems to have played a somewhat different role. He was slow to move, so much so that he was later accused by the Americans of procrastinating in the hope that the irate Mexicans would get to Blue and kill him. There may have been truth in the charge as Gutierriez felt strongly about the killing of Pablo, who had been one of his most trusted sheepherders.

CHAPTER V

Practicing medicine among the Spanish-speaking residents of southern Colorado and northern New Mexico was similar in many ways to practicing among Indians. Both were suspicious of American doctors, both had their own native "doctors" and healers, their own *curanderos* and *parteras* (midwives), their own pharmacology and their own home remedies, some brought from Spain by their ancestors, some borrowed from the Indians and used either as the Indians used them or modified to suit their special needs, and some developed out of necessities arising from isolated living on ranches or in tiny villages.

M. Beshoar, as a result of years of practice in the back country of northeast Arkansas, service in the Confederate Army when he had to make do with limited facilities and supplies, and contact with Indian medical practices and herbs on the plains, was well prepared. Had he stepped from some big eastern center or hospital into Trinidad, it would have taken him years to make any headway among the Spanish-speaking. As it was, he was accepted from the beginning. And he in turn was sympathetic to their past medical practices, not hesitating to use them when he thought them of value.

He made careful notes on their drugs, herbs, and remedies. He listed ailments and their specifics, e.g. "Purges: *sobandos*, quick silver, wild pumpkin, barbasco, and sabadilla (drastic and quick); cholera: maliola and red pepper; postpartum hemorrhage: a flat boulder from the bed of a river laid on the abdomen with one edge resting on the pubis; pleurisy, thunderbolts heated and applied hot over the seat of pain—also scarifications with a flint and cuppings with a horn; wounds and ulcers: no woman admitted to the room unless very sure she has not her menses nor leucorrhoea, gonorrhea, nor any other vaginal flux."

Splints for fractures were made of the green inner bark of sappy trees, kept green by constant applications of water. If the fracture was of the compound variety, willow sprigs were woven together with willow bark and fitted to the arm or leg with the appliance kept in place by strips of cloth or buckskin tied around it. The natives were less expert, he noted, in handling dislocations. A *sobando*, or masseur, was called in to knead and rub the disconnected joint, "but the dislocation was seldom reduced."

At Fort Kearny he discovered osha root and continued to use it thereafter in his practice as he found it not only efficacious but familiar to the Mexicans. In Colorado he discovered a new remedy that interested him: Herba del Buey (ox weed), which grows in abundance in southern Colorado, New Mexico, and the northern states of Mexico. He found Mexicans using it widely to treat gonorrhea, and since this was one of the most common complaints among his clientele, both Mexican and American, he did some experimenting with it, writing in his notes:

"Herba del Buey is made into a decoction in the proportion of about one ounce of the herb to one pint of water of which about an ounce is administered from three to six times a day. It is used in all stages of the disease. During the active, inflammatory symptoms one, two or three saline purgatives are usually given — Sal Catharticus (Epsom salts which is magnesium sulphate) being usually preferred. In case of much 'ardor urine' amole or soap root is added to the Herba del Buey and in case of chordee 'liquor de cebollas' or onion juice is also added. When no active inflammatory symptoms are present the herba alone is used. It is used in all stages of the disease.

"I procured ten pounds of the herb and placed five patients upon it alone, three of which cases were in the second and two in the third stage of the disease. I dispensed the decoction in half-gallon canteens and directed from one to two ounces be taken every three hours till six doses had been taken daily. Two of them recovered in ten days from commencement of the treatment, one in three and the other two in four weeks — the gleet cases having consumed about twenty pints of the decoction.

"My plan of treatment is as follows: Decoction of Herba del Buey six times a day in doses of half to one ounce at a dose. If there is much fever, saline purgatives, diuretics and demulcents. If much *ardor urine* alkalies. If chordee, camphor and opium and cold applied to the perineum. After the inflammatory symptoms have subsided I add cubebs to the herb making a decoction representing two ounces of the herb and one-fourth ounce of cubebs to the pink of decoction, and give laxative doses of Compound Colocynth or Compound Cathartic pills U.S.P. every second or third night. If the disease has not entirely disappeared in ten or fourteen days I give the following injections to be used seriatim and repeated six times a day.:

No. 1
  Pulv. Alumen   dr. I
  Aqua Pura   oz. IV

No. 3
  Plumbi acetas   dr. I
  Aqua Pura   fl. oz. IV

No. 2
  Sodii Biboras   dr. I (sodium borate)
  Aqua Pura   fl. oz. IV

He noted that, after trying Herba del Buey in 200 cases, he much preferred it to the copaiba he had used for years as a specific for gonorrhea.

In his analysis of Herba del Buey, he found the buds, flowers, and stems rich in resin and at first believed the medicinal value of the plant resided chiefly in the resin, but decoctions of the whole herb carried a pleasant aroma with no hint of resin. He made an alcoholic tincture of the buds and flowers, found it superior to pichi and saw palmetto, but not apparently to the decoction of the herb in therapeutic effect.

In still other investigations of native medicine, he found both Mexicans and Indians using uterine pastils, tampons, and rectal suppositories. The pastils were usually made of gum turpentine or balsam of fir into which was incorporated astringent and aromatic herbs, while the tampons were made of leaves or barks thoroughly softened by boiling water or maceration for insertion as a tampon. He wrote: "Sometimes the herbs used in pastils and tampons are used while green and soft, but sometimes are applied in dry powder form and are permitted to remain in place some days before the application is renewed. The rectal suppositories are sometimes not very soluble and when passed off are reapplied time after time until the patient deems himself cured or the suppositories have disappeared. That they are often effective is proven by the fact that the Mexicans still use them, but many Mexicans are beginning to use American-made pastils furnished to the retailer at the rate of a dollar a dozen—and they can't use them more than once."

In cases of pleuropneumonia, known to the Mexicans as either *pulmonia* or *dolor de costilla* (pain in the ribs), most preferred the Indian treatment to that provided by American doctors. From the outset of the disease, aromatic herbs were boiled with prickly pears to a pulp and applied over the entire chest. At the same time the patient was given demulcent teas and "caused to inhale vapor by placing cedar twigs on hot stones upon which water was poured while a blanket or skin was formed into a small cone or tepee with the base encompassing the hot stones and herbs."

If that didn't clear up the lungs, a more drastic treatment was begun. Wrote M. Beshoar:

"A hole something like a shallow grave is dug into the earth and fire is made in it till the hole is quite hot. The patient is wrapped in a dry blanket and then a wet blanket is wrapped around the dry one. Outside of all this another wet blanket or a tanned deerskin. The coals are raked out of the hole and the patient is laid in it and covered with dry earth, leaving only his head sticking out. He is kept in this position for hours, then taken out, wiped off and re-wrapped in a dressed deerskin or buffalo robe.

"I treated a number of Americans, Mexicans and Indians in the Rocky Mountain area for pneumonia 'secundem artem' and they all died. I took the hint from the Indians and loaded the atmosphere with hot moist air and soon had much less mortality than I had when practicing in the Mississippi River swamps which was about three per cent. Lately I have used creosote for its antiseptic qualities in lieu of the Indians' spruce branch and with good results."

He found the Mexican method of delivering a baby much the same as that used by the Indians in Nebraska Territory with the exception that most Mexican women, being extremely modest, remain fully clothed from the first pain to the first wail. Neither the Mexicans nor the Indians pretended to have any understanding of or treatment for smallpox. The Indians regarded it as a curse, the Mexicans as "the will of God" and not to be interfered with by vaccination or other means.

When a Mexican baby was constipated for several days, the average Mexican mother or father diagnosed the ailment as *empaqueda* or an impaction and treated it with quicksilver, which they bought, not by weight, but by ten, fifteen, twenty-five or fifty cents' worth. They gave whatever they purchased to the baby in one dose. Dr. Beshoar found babies passing the metal for several days and, worse yet, encountered a number of cases of salivation. He never was able to find where the Mexicans got the remedy. He finally concluded that both the Mexicans and the Pueblo Indians, who also used the quicksilver remedy, got it from the Franciscans.

Early in his practice among the Mexicans, he encountered two ailments that were completely new to him: *empapelada* (papering) and *oxalote* (salamander).

His first cases of empapelada baffled him, but once he knew what it was he was able to treat it successfully. Regarded as a slow, but fatal ailment, empapelada was the punishment inflicted by a jealous husband or *casero* (keeper) for the supposed unfaithfulness or other transgression of a wife or *casera* (kept woman). Dr. Beshoar's description:

"The man places pieces of wetted, porous paper on the end of his penis which, in a malicious act of coitus, becomes disengaged and is deposited in the vagina. I have found all of the cases to be acute superative vaginitis; in three of them I discovered several particles of the paper and in one woman, the casera of an American, I found an article known among the "bloods" of the sporting fraternity as a 'yarnell' (condom). The removal of these foreign bodies and the syringing out of the parts with warm water followed by an application of cotton saturated with an astringent glycerine quickly effected cures. Some of the cases were complicated by unusually virulent gonorrhea which recovered under ordinary treatment."

Where the Mexicans attemped to treat the difficulty themselves, whether it was gonorrheal or not, they used an infusion of onion juice with Herba del Buey decoction, then stuffed the vagina with tampons of astringent herbs.

Although empapelada gave him trouble at first, the cases of oxalote (salamander) were even more difficult, forcing him to resort to psychology to save his patients from death.

His Mexican patients believed that the oxalote is, as Dr. Beshoar wrote in his notes, "a lecherous reptile with an unconquerable propensity to enter a woman's vagina. He can run up a woman's leg as fast as lightning would travel, and he halts not at the Port of Felicity, but enters without ceremony and without regard to the conventionalities of polite society. As in the fable of the boy and the frogs, what is fun to the reptile is sure death to the woman. On any evening after a rain should you see Mexican women walking forth or in a ballroom if you will fain great surprise and fear and call out "oxalote!" you can have no doubt of the disposition they will make of their hands to guard their persons against the improper advances of the dreaded reptile. It is their belief that once inside the reptile luxuriates on the flesh of the woman until she dies."

In his first case of oxalote, his explorations failed to find any trace of the reptile. What he did find was a bleeding excrescence on the os with chronic metritis in a very anemic young woman. She insisted she had an oxalote and he insisted she did not, but before the patient could be convinced she succumbed to anemia, leaving her family and neighbors convinced that she was killed by the reptile and that while the American doctor was a nice fellow he didn't know very much.

"As drowning men will clutch at straws, so the families of four more women called upon me in the hope that I might extract the rapacious reptile or kill it before the woman should die," Dr. Beshoar wrote. "Two of the patients were dismenorrhagic and two were menorrhagic females. They knew the reptiles had entered and were luxuriating on their 'innards.' At the supplication of the distressed women I explored for the rapers. In two instances I succeeded in convincing the women that the fiends in reptile form, having satisfied their low desire, had voluntarily retired from the scene. The other two insisted the reptile was still there. I persuaded one of them that though I had everything in my hand which a moment before had been in her vagina (my index finger) it looked so nasty that the sight of it might have a bad effect on her mind and possibly cause deformity of her unborn (and unconceived) offspring.

"The other woman would not be satisfied without seeing the reptile 'with my own eyes.' I searched her vagina for it, told her I had found it and that I would have to go home to get instruments with which to seize it. I searched the prairie for half a mile around. The ground was pretty dry and consequently water dogs were scarce, but I finally succeeded in capturing a lizard. I took it back to the house, 'extracted' it, showed it to her and she was soon well."

CHAPTER VI

In 1865, Uncle Dick Wootton received authority from the Colorado and New Mexico territorial legislatures for his Trinidad & Raton Mountain Toll Road to build a twenty-seven-mile long road over the pass. He and a partner operated it for thirteen years or until the arrival of the Santa Fe Railroad.

The *Colorado Pioneer* of October 6, 1877, listed Uncle Dick's toll rates as follows: For three span of horses, mares or mules, $4; for one or two spans of same, $1.50; for horsemen, each 20 cents; pack animals, each 10 cents; loose horses, mares or mules, each 5 cents; sheep or goats, each one-fourth cent. He and his toll-keepers waved all Indians through without charge.

Michael Beshoar related both the United States Hotel and the flour incidents to family and friends many times over the years, sometimes in the presence of a sheepish Uncle Dick. Wootton and his family were Dr. Beshoar's patients throughout their lives in the area.

CHAPTER VII

A total of 326 vigilante movements in thirty-two states are listed in *The History of Violence in America* by Hugh Davis Graham and Ted Robert Gurr (New York, Frederick A. Praeger, Publishers, 1969) pp. 218-226. Trinidad's is not listed though it preceded in point of time twelve of the fifteen listed for Colorado. Most vigilante groups used the term vigilante or regulator in their name. Only one Committee of Safety is listed for Colorado. It was organized in Durango in 1881, nine years after Trinidad's Committee of Safety came into being.

CHAPTER VIII

Although Beshoar and Sam McBride were friends, the physician and Pat McBride never were close. Pat was his patient for many years, but they were business and political rivals and mutually antagonistic. Some of Pat's hostility in 1875 may well have stemmed from the fact that in June of that year the physician sued to collect a long delinquent account, won a judgment, and was awarded a piece of McBride's property, Lot No. 2, Block 10, Town of Trinidad, in payment of the $176 judgment.

Pat McBride was found dead in the American House in Denver, July 23, 1877, after a three-week bender. A coroner's jury ruled that his death resulted from "too much indulgence in intoxicating drink." He was buried in Denver, courtesy of the Irish-American Progressive Society.

CHAPTER X

Dr. Scott renewed the charges in 1883 and again in 1884. In 1885 the committee on ethics held that the charges were false and recommended that the State Medical Society censure Dr. Scott. The committee report was adopted by the society without a dissenting vote.

After leaving Trinidad, Cutting edited a newspaper in El Paso, soon became embroiled in a running feud with the postmaster of Juarez, Mexico.

On one occasion, when he crossed the Rio Grande to the Mexican city, he was tossed into the Juárez jail. The State of Texas, which had become unhappy as a result of several such arrests, threatened to send an armed force into Juárez to release Cutting whereupon, in September 1886, the Mexican authorities turned him loose. In a subsequent suit against the Mexican government, Cutting won a judgment of $250,000. He went to Mexico City, collected the award in cash, and disappeared. His family spent many years trying to find out what happened to him.

CHAPTER XI

By 1890 the annual production of coal in mines of the Trinidad field was 1,134,845 tons and that of the field's 635 coke ovens was 149,503 tons of coke. Engleville, two miles from Trinidad and between the city and the Gray Creek Mine, was producing 1,500 tons per day while Gray Creek's daily production was 1,000 tons. Trinidad and Las Animas County in this year had a population of 17,208, a gain of 8,305 in a decade.

The Chappell mansion in Trinidad, built in 1881–82, was one of the most pretentious in the city; it was reputed to have cost $50,000 and to have been a gift from a contracting firm grateful to Chappell for favors. In addition to its stone, hand-carved tiles on the walls, ornate fireplaces, and stained-glass windows, it had (and has) a unique feature. The citizens of Trinidad drank whatever water Chappell's waterworks provided, but not Chappell and family. In the attic of the house is a huge water tank complete with pump and pumper. Chappell had it installed because he feared someone might poison him.

Chappell's activities were not limited to the waterworks and Gray Creek. He had an interest in the First National Bank of Trinidad and eventually headed up the Victor Fuel Company which had more than thirty thousand acres of selected coal lands, including Gray Creek. He sold the company to coal baron J. C. Osgood in 1905 and spent the next two years with his family in Europe in "rest and relaxation," after which he became president of the Nevada-California Power Company, which played a major role in the development of the Los Angeles area.

In the Battle of Glorieta Mountain in New Mexico in April 1862, Colorado troops led by Colonel Chivington helped turn back Confederate troops which had launched an invasion from El Paso with the objective of capturing the gold mines of the mountain West and cutting the Union off from California. Subsequently, Colonel Chivington's reputation was blackened when he led Colorado troops in the infamous Sand Creek Massacre in southeastern Colorado November 28, 1864, a bloody horror in which Chivington's men killed and mutilated men, women, and children who were presumably under the protection of the United States government.

CHAPTER XII

One of the treasured stories still told in Pocahontas in 1973 about Uncle Bob Hamil: three decades after the war he was approached by a candidate for prosecuting attorney who wanted to know how to find Randolph County's remote Union Township. Said Hamil: "Young man, I can't tell you how to get there, but I can tell you how to recognize it when you do get there: you'll find the women folk still knitting socks for Confederate soldiers."

Bibliography

Books

Bancroft, Hubert H. *History of Neveda, Colorado and Wyoming*, Vol. XXV. San Francisco, 1890.

Beshoar, Barron B. *Out of the Depths, The Story of John R. Lawson, a Labor Leader*. Denver, 1942.

Beshoar, Michael. *All About Trinidad And Las Animas County, Colorado*. Denver, 1882.

Conrad, H. L. *Uncle Dick Wootton*. Chicago, 1890.

Dalton, Lawrence. *History of Randolph County*. Little Rock, 1946.

Dispensatory of the United States. Philadelphia, 1918.

Gressley, Gene M. *Bankers and Cattlemen*. New York, 1966.

Hall, Frank. *History of Colorado*. 4 vols. Chicago, 1889.

Herringshaw, Thomas William. *Herringshaw's Encyclopedia of American Biography of the Nineteenth Century*. Chicago, 1898.

Hildebrand, Samuel S. *Autobiography*. Ed. James W. Evans and A. Wendell Keith. Jefferson City, Mo. 1870.

Martin, Lantie. *Martin Family History*. Pocahontas, Ark., 1965.

McMurtrie, Donald, and Allen, Albert H. *Early Printing in Colorado*. Denver, 1936.

Perkin, Robert L. *The First Hundred Years: An Informal History of Denver and The Rocky Mountain News*. New York, 1959.

Stone, R. French, M.D. (ed.) *Biography of Eminent American Physicians and Surgeons*. M. Beshoar, pp. 43–44. Indianapolis, 1894.

Stone, Wilbur Fisk. *History of Colorado*. 4 vols. Chicago, 1918.

Taylor, Morris E. *Trinidad, Colorado Territory*. Pueblo, Colo., 1966.

Taylor, Ralph C. *Colorado, South of the Border*. Denver, 1963.

War of the Rebellion: A Compilation of the Official Records of the Union and Confederate Armies. War Department, Washington, 1902.

Articles and Papers

Baca, Luis. "The Guadalupita Colony of Trinidad," *The Colorado Magazine*, XXI (January 1944).

Beshoar, Barron B. "No Windy Promises," The 1961 Brand Book, The Denver Westerners, ed. Don L. Griswold, 1962.

————. "One of Randolph County's First Physicians," *Randolph County Historical Review* (Pocahontas, Ark., June 1966).

Beshoar, Michael. "Medical Customs of The Rocky Mountain Indians and Mexicans," a series, *The Medical Educator* (Trinidad, Colo., May 1902–September 1904).

————. "Oration." Reprint, Trinidad, Colo., May 30, 1889.

————. "Slight Ailments and How To Cure Them," *Denver Medical Times* (August 1901).

————. "Teaching in the Rural Districts Among the Spanish-Americans." Greeley, Colo., May 3, 1898.

Christy, Charles. "The Personal Memoirs of Captain Charles Christy," *The Trail* (Denver), I (January 1909).

Clark, O. S. "Clay Allison of the Wichita," *Frontier Press of Texas* (Houston, 1954).

Davis, Joseph. "Some Recollections of Trinidad," *The Chronicle-News* (Trinidad, Colo., September 29, 1952).

Day, Daniel S. "Fort Sedgwick," *The Colorado Magazine*, XLII (Winter 1965).

DeBusk, S. W. "Some Recollections of Early History: Reminicences of the Early Days of Trinidad, With Some Interesting State History in Connection." Paper before Early Settlers Association, Trinidad, Colo., August 27, 1901.

Field and Farm (Denver) IX (June 7, 1890). Unsigned article on "Dr. Beshoar Saves Companion From Rattlesnake."

————— (December 1907). "Frontier Sketches, Dr. Beshoar Wrestles Cowboy in Bunkhouse Encounter."

Hastings, James. "Boyhood in the Trinidad Region," *The Colorado Magazine*, XXX (April 1953).

Hornbein, Marjorie. "Three Governors in a Day," *The Colorado Magazine*, XLV, No. 3 (Summer 1968), 243–260.

Humphries, Rolfe. "How the Chief Made the Big Leagues," Empire, *The Denver Post* (August 20, 1967).

"Joseph Davis — Pioneer," (unsigned) *The Trail* (Denver, Colo.), XIX (January 1927).

Publications of the Nebraska State Historical Society, XXI. (Lincoln, Nebr., 1930).

Rice, Elial Jan. "Pioneering in Southern Colorado," *The Colorado Magazine*, XIV (May 1937).

Snyder, J. Richard. "The Election of 1904: An Attempt at Reform," *The Colorado Magazine*, XLV, No. 1 (Winter, 1968), 16–26.

Sons of Colorado (Denver), I, No. 10 (March 1907). Two unsigned articles, one dealing with Michael Beshoar's encounter with Indian John Smith on plains in 1865, the other relating his escape from Indian war party in 1865.

Sopris, W. R. "My Grandmother, Mrs. Marcellin St. Vrain," *The Colorado Magazine*, XXII (March 1945), 63–68.

Taylor, Morris F. "Early Days of Trinidad," *The Colorado Magazine*, XL (October 1963).

Documents and Reports

Advertiser Printing Co., articles of incorporation, filed in office of Las Animas County, Colorado, Clerk, February 20, 1884, and in office of the Secretary of State, Denver, Colorado, February 21, 1884. Advertiser Printing Co., Record Book, containing articles of incorporation, records of stockholders' meetings, 1885–92; Beshoar Family Papers. Annual Reports of the Board of Regents of the Smithsonian Institution for 1875 and 1876, Government Printing Office, Washington, 1875 and 1876. Beshoar Realty Company, 1906 articles of incorporation, minutes of meetings; Beshoar Family Papers. Circular No. 4, War Department, Surgeon General's Office, "A Report on Barracks and Hospitals with Descriptions of Military Posts," Government Printing Office, Washington, D.C., 1870. Colorado House Journal, 1881. Colorado Supreme Court, Case No. 3454: M. Beshoar, plaintiff in error, *vs.* Delos A. Chappell, A. H. Danforth, Charles P. Treat, Tabor S. Skinner, Ed. S. Jenison, J. B. Wycoff and the Gray Creek Coal & Coking Company. District Court of Las Animas County,

Colorado, Case No. 4287: The People *vs.* Joe Johnson. National Archives and Record Service of the United States, Washington, D.C.: Confederate Military Record of Michael Beshoar, oath of allegiance and correspondence relating thereto. Ordinances of the City of Trinidad, compiled by S. S. Wallace, City Solicitor, Trinidad, Colo., 1880. Rocky Mountain Medical Association, articles of incorporation, bylaws, records, and correspondence, 1874-75; Beshoar Family Papers. Rocky Mountain Medical Institute Association, articles of incorporation 1899, minutes of directors meetings, daily medical journal, etc.; Beshoar Family Papers. St. Louis Medical College, Catalogue of Students, Session 1863-64. Senate Journal, Fifteenth Legislative Session, State of Colorado, 1905. Superintendent of Public Instruction, State of Colorado, Sixth Annual Report for biennial term ending June 30, 1888. Transactions of the Colorado State Medical Society, 1880 through 1887. Transactions and reports, Nebraska State Historical Society, Lincoln, 1893. Trinidad Publishing Company, bylaws, September, 1882; Beshoar Family Papers.

Manuscripts and Unpublished Material

Beshoar, Michael; Letter books for years 1881 through 1890; Beshoar Family Papers. Beshoar, Michael; Medical Daybooks, 1863 through 1907; Beshoar Family Papers. Carnegie Public Library, Trinidad, Colo.; Local History Collection. CWA Interviews, Las Animas County, Colo.; Vols. I and II, State Historical Society of Colorado. Las Animas County, DeBusk Memorial, State Historical Society of Colorado Library. M. J. Solomon Papers, Manuscript Division, Duke University Library, Durham N. C. M. Jeff Thompson Reminiscences, Vol. 3 MS, Folder 4 (1863), Southern Historical Collection, University of North Carolina Library, Chapel Hill. Smith, Honora DeBusk, "Early Days in Trinidad and the Purgatory Valley," Unpublished Master's thesis, University of Colorado, Boulder, 1930. University of California, Bancroft Library, MMS P-L 354; 3-1 Michael Beshoar 1883; P-17 Trinidad in 1866. Willman, Lillian M., "The History of Fort Kearny;" Master's thesis, University of Nebraska, July 1928; Publications of The Nebraska State Historical Society, Vol. XXI, Lincoln, 1930.

Newspapers

TRINIDAD, COLORADO: *Advertiser-Sentinel,* 1898–1901; *Cattlemen's Advertiser,* 1885–87; *Chronicle-News,* 1903–69; *Citizen,* 1888; *Colorado Chronicle,* 1875; *Colorado Democrat,* 1878; *Corriere di Trinidad,* 1907; *Daily Advertiser,* 1883–98; *Daily Enterprise,* 1879; *Daily News,* 1878–99; *Daily Sentinel,* 1898; *Daily Times,* 1882, 1889–90; *El Anunciador,* 1883–87; *Enterprise and Chronicle,* 1875–79; *Monitor,* 1897, 1904; *Pioneer,* 1875–76; *Republican,* 1880–82; *Trinidad Advertiser,* 1901–07; *Trinidad Chronicle,* 1889–99; *Trinidad Enterprise,* 1872; *Trinidadian,* 1875; *Tri-Weekly Lyre,* December 2, 1889; *Weekly Advertiser,* 1888–98; *Weekly News,* 1878–99; *Weekly Times,* 1889–90. DENVER, COLORADO: *Colorado Pioneer,* 1877; *Daily Democrat,* 1877; *Daily Times,* 1876, 1877; *Denver Mirror,* 1876; *Denver Post,* 1905; *Evening Independent,* 1876; *Republican,* 1893, 1903; *Rocky Mountain News* (daily and weekly), 1865–1969; *Tribune* (daily and weekly), 1875–78. PUEBLO, COLORADO:

Colorado Chieftain, 1868–75; *Daily Chieftain*, 1872–76; *Democrat*, 1876; *Courier*, 1900; *Catholic Register*, February, 1907; *Pueblo Chieftain*, 1876–1969; *Pueblo Star-Journal*, 1952–69. OTHERS: *Avalanche*, Canon City, Colo., 1876; *Colorado Transcript*, Golden, Colo., 1876; *Cripple Creek Forum*, Cripple Creek, Colo., April 15, 1905; *Detroit Free Press*, Detroit, Mich., June 22, 1903; *Gazette*, Raton, N. M., 1907; *Huerfano Independent*, Walsenberg, Colo., September 9, 1876; *Index*, Rosita, Colo., September 23, 1886; *Kansas City Times*, Kansas City Mo., September 21–28, 1876; King Features Syndicate, Damon Runyon's "The Brighter Side," columns re M. Beshoar, April 22, 1937, and February 23, 1938; *Odessa Herald*, Odessa, Mo., 1886; *Prospector*, Del Norte, Colo., September 16, 1876; *Revista Catolica*, Las Vegas, N.M., November 21, 1897; *Star-Herald*, Pocahontas, Ark., August 2, 1934; *Stockman*, Springer, N.M., June 15,1889.

Index

The body text for *Hippocrates in a Red Vest* is set in Caledonia
by CBM Type of Mountain View, California. The chapter heads are
Craw Clarendon Condensed set by Hazeltine of Oakland, California.
The book was printed and bound by Kingsport Press, Kingsport, Tennessee.

Design by Dannelle Lazarus.

Hippocrates in a Red Vest is a warm, human biography of a frontier doctor who not only brought his compassion and healing talents to the rugged country of southern Colorado, but who envisioned the land as one of myriad opportunities and numerous challenges. By the time he reached his mid-thirties (circa 1866) Michael Beshoar had participated on both sides in the Civil War as a surgeon, had established a private medical practice, had become an editor, legislator, judge, farmer, cotton speculator, businessman, and mayor of Dobytown, the toughest town on the Oregon Trail.

Although written with personal insight and understanding, *Hippocrates in a Red Vest* is at the same time an objective, well-researched work, with the succinct and lucid style of a professional journalist. Michael Beshoar was ambitious, hot-headed, courageous, a complex personality capable of handling his Colt .41 as skillfully as he did his scalpel. He entered politics, not for glory, but to campaign for the causes he felt were just and necessary in a newborn state; he started the *Colorado Chieftain* (which later became the *Pueblo Chieftain* and remains, even today, a leading newspaper in southern Colorado) to wage war against rapacious coal corporations, unjust water works, and other causes he considered unfair, illicit, or aggravating.

This is more than the story of a man . . . it is the story of a new horizon, the forging of a western frontier. The book tells of the growth of cities and